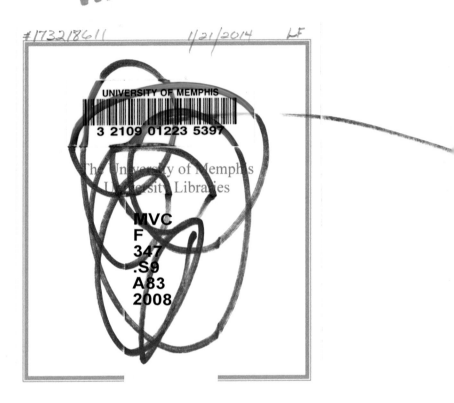

The Senator and the Sharecropper

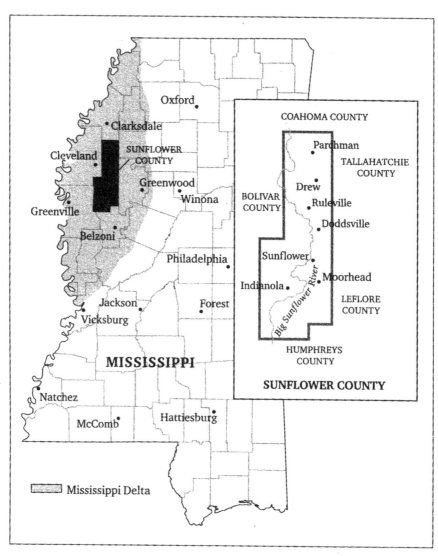

Sunflower County, Mississippi

The Senator and the Sharecropper

The Freedom Struggles of
James O. Eastland and
Fannie Lou Hamer

CHRIS MYERS ASCH

THE NEW PRESS

NEW YORK
LONDON

Requests for permission to reproduce selections from this book
should be mailed to: Permissions Department, The New Press,
38 Greene Street, New York, NY 10013.

Published in the United States by The New Press, New York, 2008
Distributed by W. W. Norton & Company, Inc., New York

LIBRARY OF CONGRESS CATALOGING-IN-PUBLICATION DATA
Asch, Christopher Myers.
The senator and the sharecropper : the freedom struggles of James O.
Eastland and Fannie Lou Hamer / Chris Myers Asch.
p.   cm.
Includes bibliographical references and index.
ISBN 978-1-59558-332-1 (hc.)
1. Sunflower County (Miss.)—Race relations—History—20th century.
2. Racism—Mississippi—Sunflower County—History—20th century.
3. African Americans—Civil rights—Mississippi—Sunflower County—
History—20th century.   4. Civil rights movements—Mississippi—Sunflower
County—History—20th century.   5. Hamer, Fannie Lou.   6. African
American civil rights workers—Mississippi—Biography.   7. Children of
sharecroppers—Mississippi—Biography.   8. Eastland, James O. (James
Oliver), 1904–1986.   9. Legislators—United States—Biography.
10. United States. Congress. Senate—Biography.   I. Title.
F347.S9A83 2008
305.8009762'4709045—dc22   2007037378

The New Press was established in 1990 as a not-for-profit alternative to the large,
commercial publishing houses currently dominating the book publishing industry.
The New Press operates in the public interest rather than for private gain, and
is committed to publishing, in innovative ways, works of educational, cultural,
and community value that are often deemed insufficiently profitable.

www.thenewpress.com

Composition by NK Graphics
This book was set in Minister

Printed in the United States of America

2   4   6   8   10   9   7   5   3   1

For my family and the students
of the Sunflower County Freedom Project

It is a peculiar plant.

Stiff and strong stems
rise from labored earth,
arms reaching hopeful toward God
sinewy fibers wrapped like muscle
around big bones.

These dirty limbs end in silky chocolate
hands that present the pure white
puff to the heavens,
palms open in sacrifice.

The fate of the unblemished fluff undecided,
to be worn, slept or wept on but
always cleaned, cared for
and protected.

The fate of the stem decided.
To be chopped, crushed, and buried
in unhealthy soil,
fed false nutrients yet,
somehow able
to try again
next fall.

—Alex Quigley, "Cotton"

Contents

Preface
xi

Prologue
Sunflower County, 1994
1

1. Sunflower County, 1904
6

2. Planter's Son, Sharecroppers' Daughter
33

3. "Cotton Is Dynamite":
New Deals in Sunflower County
65

4. "An Enormous Tragedy in the Making":
Revolutions in Sunflower County and Abroad
99

5. "From Cotton—to Communism—to Segregation!":
The Senator's Rise to Power
132

6. "No One Can Honestly Say Negroes Are Satisfied":
The Sharecropper Embraces the Movement
167

7. 1964: Confrontations
198

8. "This Is America's Sickness"
221

9. "The Pendulum Is Swinging Back"
253

10. "Right on Back to the Plantation"
279

Notes
299

Index
355

Preface

I love Sunflower County, Mississippi.

Writing that may undermine my objectivity as a historian, but I don't care. I love Sunflower and its people, I enjoy its food and its music, I revel in its fields and the vast expanse of sky above them. I met and married my wife in Sunflower County, and I made lasting friendships there. It is where I spent most of my early adulthood, first as an elementary school teacher and later as the co-founder of an educational nonprofit organization called the Sunflower County Freedom Project. The area is and always will be part of who I am and who I aspire to be.

But as much as I love Sunflower County, I recognize that it is a deeply troubled place. Economic divisions and racial mistrust remain profound, and no amount of surface civility can mask the terrible toll that the culture of segregation continues to take on the community, particularly the children. There is ingrained poverty that still can shock the uninitiated—large families living in run-down trailers or decaying shotgun houses, idle men whiling away countless hours on the street, single mothers raising a fourth generation on welfare. Stagnation is the reigning motif of the economy, the education system, the social structure. Even in the age of the Internet, many people seem blissfully unconcerned with the world beyond Sunflower County. This book aims to explain how and why Sunflower County is the way it is.

The title notwithstanding, what you will read is not a biography of either Fannie Lou Hamer or James Eastland—I will leave that to other scholars with more talent and patience than I. As a civil rights heroine, Hamer has been the subject of numerous articles and biographies by scholars, journalists, and children's authors, and their effusive praise has been almost universally shared. "Initiative, courage, and selflessness best describe Fannie Lou Hamer's life," writes one admiring historian. She was a "heroic and unlettered black leader whose personal courage and vision of the future had so changed Mississippi," observed another. She "would stand out as extraordinary in any demographic category," notes a third. I am indebted to Kay Mills and Chana Kai Lee in particular for their excellent and pioneering work on Hamer and her contribution to civil rights.[1]

Ironically, perhaps, the sharecropper has basked in the historical limelight while the senator has eluded the historian's eye. Partially this neglect is a matter of sources—Eastland's personal papers were sealed until 2001 and only now are available to researchers—and a general preference for studying history's heroes rather than its villains. The neglect of Eastland's story also is a function of shifts in the profession of history during the past two generations that have sought to balance a traditional focus on "great men" with a sustained search for voices of the powerless that are not heard in standard sources such as newspapers, letters, and other written documents. This "history from the bottom up" has reshaped and enriched how we understand American history, and it has complicated our sense of who we are as a nation. But focusing solely on the powerless can be as distorting as concentrating only on the powerful. We can miss the essential dynamic between the two, the ways in which the actions of the former constrain and influence the latter, and vice versa. To understand Hamer and her world, we must look honestly at Eastland and his world as well. Only by studying Hamer and Eastland simultaneously can we fully understand the story of Sunflower County. That is the story I will tell in this book.

I will be honest. When I first started this project, I wanted to "get" James Eastland, to give him his due by shining the harsh light of history on him. Anyone who had studied the civil rights movement, as I had, knew the thumbnail sketch of Eastland. *Time* magazine had labeled him the "spiritual leader of the segregationists," and historians called him a "virulent racist," a "ranting demagogue who . . . [was] as rabid as his unbalanced colleague, Senator Theodore Bilbo," and a "narrow-minded, arbitrary, arrogant, bigoted, and vindictive" man who was "simply unpleasant to be around, unless you drive a pickup truck and burn crosses on Saturday night." He jumped out of the pages of history with eye-popping comments that marked him as the very embodiment of evil, the ruthless villain against whom civil rights activists had to battle. Every time I drove by his family's plantation in Doddsville on my way between Ruleville and Sunflower, I would get duly outraged. Shaking my head, muttering, cursing (if none of my students were in the car), I would condemn him and his legacy. So I thought I would write a scathing history that would expose him in all his racist hypocrisy and vilify him for his assaults on the civil rights movement. But a funny thing happened along the way: I became a historian. I came to see that writing a self-righteous book that simply denounced Eastland for his racism was not only an exercise in moral grandstanding but also intellectually lazy and historically superficial. As my undergraduate mentor Peter Wood once told me, my responsibility as a historian was to "fight like hell for the dead"—which meant I could not take cheap shots, even (or perhaps especially) at people I detested. The dead can't defend themselves; they need historians to work responsibly to get their stories right, even if it is not the story the historians had hoped to tell.[2]

The idea that a historian would "fight like hell" for both Hamer *and* Eastland runs counter to how we tend to approach the history of race in this country. We like our history to resemble a fairy tale, with the heroes clear and noble and the villains unambiguously evil. When I told people about my topic, many of them assumed that my project would be an enlarged version of the two-dimensional caricature of him they already knew. "So," they would ask excitedly, "was Eastland *really* racist?"—thinking that my work would definitively answer that question. To me, the question was rather elementary. *Of course* he was racist! Proudly so! Racism was central to his worldview, and he could not imagine life without white supremacy. And . . . ? Was that it? If so, this book would be pretty boring—ranting about the obvious is rarely very interesting. White racism was and is a sad and debilitating part of

Sunflower County life, but it alone cannot explain why inequality has remained so ingrained in the area more than a generation after the civil rights movement. Racism was a starting point, not a finish line. There was more to the story than that. History is not a fairy tale, and rarely do we encounter the simple villains we might like to fight. Instead, we find that the villains can be complicated, that they are driven by a variety of sincere and base motives, that they sometimes even can be thoughtful and prescient. And so it is with the notorious James O. Eastland.

Giving Eastland and Hamer their historical due meant more than just condemning him for not being as morally enlightened as we are today or exalting her for being more courageous and noble than our current leaders. I began to see that focusing on Eastland's overt racism was a cheap way for us—enlightened, educated Americans of the twenty-first century—to distance ourselves from him, while fawning over Hamer was an easy way to show our own goodness and morality. Either way, we avoid dealing with the more ambiguous, complicated nature of the world they shared and our own world. Living in Sunflower County for the better part of a decade helped knock me off the outsider's pedestal and forced me to confront certain uncomfortable truths about the world we inherited from their generation. Try as we might, we simply cannot pin the blame for Sunflower's (and America's) persistent inequality solely on unreconstructed racists such as James Eastland. We must recognize that other powerful factors, particularly global economic forces that have only grown stronger in recent decades, created conditions that circumscribed both the senator and the sharecropper, just as they continue to constrain us today. Though we may prefer not to acknowledge them, we also must confront the unintended consequences of the civil rights movement, particularly its effect on poor black communities in places such as Sunflower County. Finally, as much as we may not want to admit it, we must see that Sunflower is not so different from Washington, D.C., (where I grew up) and countless other places across America that continue to struggle with how to reconcile our professed values with the reality of poverty and unequal opportunity.

In the end, I hope that *The Senator and the Sharecropper* shows the messy reality of life in Sunflower County in the twentieth century.

I hope readers will come to understand that the problems we face to-day, in Sunflower County and elsewhere in America, are products of a complicated history that implicates all of us. I hope people will confront this history not with denial or despair but with a renewed sense of mission to, in Abraham Lincoln's words, "strive on to finish the work we are in," the work of making America live up to the full meaning of its founding ambitions.

In the years that I have worked on this book, I have benefited tremendously from the help, advice, and especially criticism of many people all along the way. A special thank-you must go out to Peter Wood, who embodies what it means to be a scholar and a mentor. Since the day during my junior year when I talked my way into his class, Peter has been a thoughtful advisor, a tough critic, and a loyal friend. There are few like him.

This project started out as a dissertation under the guidance of Jacquelyn Hall at the University of North Carolina. Her keen insights and gentle critiques helped keep me on track as I wandered away from campus and into the working world of Sunflower County. I appreciated the willingness of various scholars and nonscholars alike to read and comment upon drafts of my manuscript, including Charles Payne, Harry Watson, Jerma Jackson, Rachel Reinhard, Todd Moye, Joe Crespino, Jason Deparle, Steve Estes, and Jason Ward. I also owe a great deal to the countless Sunflower Countians who shared their insights with me, both in formal interviews and in informal conversations over the years—especially Mildred and Les Downey, Charles McLaurin, Jim Abbott, Jeannie Russell, Billie Dove Parker, Bessie Gardner, Steve Rosenthal, and Minola Fields.

I first came to Sunflower County, Mississippi, with Teach For America, and I cannot overstate the impact that TFA and my fellow corps members have had on my life—Gregg Costa, Shawn Raymond, Kevin Schaaf, Alex Quigley, and the rest of my TFA "family" have been extraordinary sources of support and insight. Two particularly wonderful TFA alumni, Mark Pett and Tiffany Tidwell, returned to Indianola to live, work, and enjoy the Delta with me—I have mooched many a meal at their Moody Street home, and I am indebted to them for their generosity of spirit and their consistent support.

Most of the book was written from a table in my country home between Indianola and Sunflower. I could not have had a better place to work—I could look out the window at the cotton fields across the way and remind myself of the underlying economic theme of the book. After working on the book in the morning, I spent my afternoons and evenings with the staff and students of the Sunflower County Freedom Project: Michelle Johansen, Ashley Slate Quigley, Greg McCoy, Kristen Hendrix, Chris Perkins, Jasmine Harvey, Lukendric Washington, Arquavious and Tambranikia Gordon, Cornesha Ward, Rokeshia and Johnetta Ross, Candace and Yolanda Durn, Raveen Lemon, Bryan Tucker, Laquita Minton, Michael Burse, and, of course, Clifton Carter. I could go on and on—there are so many great kids in the Freedom Project. They kept me grounded in the real world and helped me remember that my academic work was trivial compared to the challenges they face every day. I hope that readers will learn more about the Freedom Project (www.sunflowerfreedom.org) and the wonderful things the kids there do.

This book is dedicated to my family. My father passed away shortly after I earned my PhD, and one of the happiest moments of my life was seeing his face when I got my diploma. He and my mother always challenged me to live up to my potential as a human being, and they encouraged my adventures even when my plans seemed quixotic. I hope to make them both proud.

Finally, give me a good, old-fashioned Delta whuppin' if I let a day pass without feeling undeservedly fortunate for having found the best thing Sunflower County and San Diego had to offer: my wife, Erica.

PROLOGUE

Sunflower County, 1994

August 26, 1994. It had been a long day for me, a newly minted Teach For America teacher fresh out of college. I had just spent more than eight hours on my feet in an un-air-conditioned classroom with my fifth graders in Sunflower, Mississippi, a pinprick town of eight hundred folks set amidst the cotton fields and catfish farms of Sunflower County. I got home, exhausted, only to hear a knock on the door—a few of the boys in my class wanted to play some baseball. Clifton, Fred, and Kathan were among the most athletic kids in my class, and they came to me, their first male teacher, for all things outdoor and aerobic. Not wanting to disappoint, I grabbed my glove, and out we went.

Even in the heat of late summer, Sunflower can be a beautiful place, and I was thoroughly enjoying my first couple of weeks in the area. As a native of Washington, D.C., I had never experienced rural life, and I found myself loving it—vast fields that stretched to the horizon, unhindered by buildings, trees, or elevation changes; the massive sky filled at night with stars I never knew existed; brilliant sunsets that set clouds aflame. I had left behind a world of frenetic busyness, mind-numbing traffic, and relentless hurry for a town without a stoplight or twenty-four-hour convenience store. I could walk to work in six minutes, and everyone who passed by in a car or pickup waved or called hello. Running errands became a leisurely opportunity to talk with my students' parents and other folks at the post office or Mrs. Russell's grocery store.

But I quickly learned that Sunflower could be an ugly place as well. Soon after my students and I began playing catch out in the front yard, the town mayor, a petite, silver-haired white woman with a syrupy drawl, stopped by in her Mercedes. "You know they're not supposed to be here," she sweetly informed me, pointing to my black students. "You're going to catch a lot of flak." I thanked her kindly, but we kept playing and she drove away, shaking her head. My house, apparently, was on the "white folks' part" of town, and blacks simply were not allowed unless they worked for a white family. No signs warned the uninitiated, but a strict line paralleled the grassy strip of land that once was the railroad track, effectively separating black from white, poor from rich. Within minutes of the mayor's ominous words, a burly, six-foot-two white man flanked by two shorter but equally menacing friends rushed from a nearby house, screaming racial epithets as they charged at my students. I intervened, invoking principles both biblical and constitutional, but to no avail—the children already had taken off toward the safety of the "black folks' part," and the white men were not interested in discussing the issue with a "Yankee" teacher. As I protested that my students were good kids who would do no harm, one of the men locked me in a steely gaze and growled, "I don't care if they're good kids. I send my kids to Indianola Academy [an all-white private school nearby] to get away from those sons of bitches!" We stared at each other in silence for a few tense moments before the omnipresent mayor returned to calm the men down and defuse the situation.

The man's words rang in my ears. "It was so bold in its hatred, so honest in its racism, that it almost struck me as concocted," I wrote in my journal that night. "It was as if some radical liberal writer had created this character as the embodiment of the evil racist. If I had read that somewhere and not heard it myself, I might not have believed it. But this man meant every word of it." The man, it turned out, was none other than the mayor's husband, John Sydney Parker, a notorious racist who had been deputy sheriff of the county during the civil rights era.

News of the incident seemed to spread almost instantaneously after it happened, and the next few weeks brought continued threats, an effort to get my roommates and me tossed out of our rented house, and even a petition to run us out of town because we "showed favoritism to the blacks." I still have no idea to whom the petition was intended to be sent. A few well-intentioned white women sat me down to explain the "rules" of Sunflower—rules that rationalized and ensured the continued racial separation and economic inequality of the area. If I insisted on breaking the rules by having interracial gatherings at my house, that was fine; I simply would have to move out to the country, where no one would see. One of the white fellows who had verbally assaulted my students came by the house to tell me why it was so important to keep blacks, especially young blacks, away from the white side. "If those kids see what we have," he explained, "then they will realize what they don't have and they will want it too." This sort of ambition, which seemed to me an essential part of the American dream, struck him as a dangerous emotion for black kids to have. My black students already knew all too well what they did not have, however. They responded angrily to the incident, which was simply the latest reminder that they were not welcome or wanted. Black adults who talked to me about what happened simply shook their heads, resigned to the fact that even a generation after the civil rights movement little seemed to have changed in their white neighbors' attitudes.

I began to see my new home in a different light. The warm friendliness that accompanied interracial interactions in town now seemed to be simply a cordial veneer covering latent animosity. The slow pace of life struck me as a sign of apathy and resignation, rather than a healthy approach to living. Even the natural beauty only seemed to mock the depressing reality of social, residential, and educational separation between the races, as well as the vast disparities of economic wealth that followed racial lines. How could life in Sunflower be this way? Hadn't the civil rights movement shattered the system of white supremacy and segregation that had marked the South? Had the movement simply passed this isolated rural county by? Was I still in America?

"I'm living in a completely different world now," I wrote to a friend. The rest of America "seems like it's on another planet." Although I was only dimly aware of it at the time, my frustration echoed the sentiments expressed almost exactly thirty years earlier by Sunflower County native Fannie Lou Hamer during the 1964 Democratic National Convention in Atlantic City, New Jersey. Testifying on behalf of the Mississippi Freedom Democratic Party (MFDP), the forty-six-year-old black sharecropper recounted in anguishing detail how she had been forced to leave her plantation following her unsuccessful attempt to register to vote and how she had been beaten severely for her civil rights work. She hoped her testimony would persuade party leaders to refuse to seat the Mississippi Democratic Party's official, all-white delegation. Wringing her hands, on the verge of tears, Hamer concluded her presentation with the question: "Is this America, the land of the free and the home of the brave, where we have to sleep with our telephones off of the hooks because our lives be threatened daily because we want to live as decent human beings, in America?"

As I came to understand during nearly a decade of teaching and living in the area, Sunflower County was indeed part of America, in all its beauty and complexity. I grew to love the area and its people deeply, and I became part of a community that I'd once scorned. I came to see how Sunflower crystallizes issues of race, class, and history that can be obscured elsewhere in the country. From the era of Jim Crow and the New Deal through the civil rights movement and its aftermath, Sunflower sat at the epicenter of the twentieth-century struggle for and against black freedom. The infamous Citizens' Council had been founded in Indianola, the county seat, and Sunflower also had been home not only to Hamer but also to her nemesis, the segregationist senator James O. Eastland. The struggles in Sunflower County had been intense, sustained, and often violent, and they had transformed the area in ways I could not grasp when I first arrived. And yet the culture of segregation, among both blacks and whites, and the economic advantages that white supremacy had bestowed upon Sunflower County whites remained firmly entrenched even in the late twentieth century. To understand how a place could endure such dramatic upheaval and yet resiliently retain its old patterns of segregation, inequality, and deference, I turned to the lives of its two most prominent citizens of the mid-twentieth century: Hamer and Eastland.

An editor might chide a novelist who created two main characters as transparently opposite as Eastland and Hamer. Each was the antithesis of the other in profound ways. Eastland grew up as the only child of Woods Eastland, a wealthy planter/lawyer who had led a lynch mob that murdered six blacks to avenge the killing of his brother in 1904. Named for his fallen uncle, James Eastland inherited not only the family's massive Sunflower County plantation but also a culture of white supremacy and economic paternalism that became his hallmark as a U.S. senator. Hamer, meanwhile, was the granddaughter of a slave, the last of twenty children born of a sharecropping family. Growing up in a world of limitations, she inherited the lack of educational, economic, or political opportunity that crippled all black Mississippians, but her parents instilled within her a resilient religious faith that became her defining characteristic as a civil rights activist.

The lives of James Eastland and Fannie Lou Hamer offer more than a simple morality play about a racist senator and a heroic sharecropper; they tell a story of place and how this isolated county weathered revolutionary changes in seemingly distant realms—the global economy, the Cold War, national politics. The arc of their lives paralleled the national interest in issues of race and economics that always had dominated life in Sunflower County. The two came of age during a segregated era of handpicked cotton and brutal white supremacy, when Sunflower County was a black-majority backwater isolated from the rest of America yet connected intimately to the global cotton economy. They grew into internationally known figures at the height of the civil rights movement, when their home became the center of a national struggle over race, economics, and the meaning of freedom. They grew old in a new world of mechanized agriculture and black political empowerment, when their home once again returned to the shadows of American life. Through the lives of these two consistent yet conflicted public figures, we see how the worlds of Sunflower County, like much of the South, were transformed during the mid-twentieth century yet remained at century's end resiliently separate and unequal.

1

Sunflower County, 1904

Sunflower County awoke cold and wet on the misty morning of Wednesday, February 3, 1904. Winter in the frontier wilderness of the Mississippi Delta could be bitingly cold, as the swampy soil stayed sodden for months on end. "The frogs and mosquitoes had a chill every morning before breakfast," a Sunflower County pioneer joked, and this particular morning had the critters and their human neighbors shivering. As the fog lifted off countless bayous that wound their way through the maze of forest and canebrakes, the residents of Doddsville began their regular winter routine of fence mending, field clearing, and tree burning.[1]

By the standards of Sunflower County and the Mississippi Delta at the turn of the century, Doddsville was a bustling hamlet. Several dozen inhabitants supported a cluster of small businesses nestled just east of a bend in the Sunflower River. More than a decade earlier, two brothers, Jim and Sid Dodd, had slashed their way south from Kentucky to the banks of the Sunflower, establishing a sawmill and commissary in the hopes of making a fortune in timber. They joined another enterprising pioneer, Oliver Eastland, who had purchased hundreds of acres west of the river. Using the profits of a prosperous drugstore in the piney woods of central Mississippi, Eastland quickly expanded his holdings, ultimately bequeathing nearly 2,400 acres to his family when he died in 1899. The Dodds and the Eastlands were among the earliest white settlers of what became known as Doddsville, and the village grew steadily during the 1890s. By February 1904, it boasted a railroad depot, general store, and lumber company. The hamlet remained geographically isolated, particularly for women living on surrounding plantations—one white woman later recalled that she went more than eight months without seeing another white person. It would be another decade before a telephone line reached Doddsville, but residents kept abreast of news from the outside world through regular mail service and local newspapers that covered state, national, and even international events.[2]

What began as a typically dreary February day in Doddsville soon gave way to violence. Though the circumstances are unclear, it all began, apparently, with an argument over a woman. Luther Holbert, a black laborer on the Eastland plantation, had been living with a woman who may have been the wife or ex-wife of another field hand, perhaps Albert Carr. Both Carr and Holbert were longtime employees of the Eastland family and they had followed their boss, twenty-one-year-old James Eastland, when the young planter graduated from Mississippi College and moved north from Forest to help run the Doddsville farm. Little is known of Carr, but contemporary accounts describe Holbert as a "trusted servant of the family," a "harmless and fairly well disposed negro" who had faithfully worked for the Eastlands for years. The dispute between Carr and Holbert festered for some time, and it became serious enough that Eastland intervened, perhaps out of fear that the tension could disrupt the labor on the plantation. Although Holbert seems to have been a faithful servant, his loyalty went unrewarded: Eastland ordered him to leave the plantation.[3]

But by the morning of February 3, Holbert had yet to move and remained with his lover in a cabin on the plantation, a clear challenge both to Eastland's authority and to his romantic rival. Eastland and Carr had been fixing fences that morning, and at about nine o'clock the two men decided to confront Holbert. Riding by horseback the two miles from Eastland's house to Holbert's cabin, the armed men must have recognized the potentially violent nature of their visit. Violence, after all, was woven into nearly all facets of Sunflower County life at the turn of the twentieth century. In a frontier wilderness where a trip to the commissary could involve an encounter with a panther or a bear, men kept themselves armed at all times. Their guns were often trained, however, not at the vicious animals in their midst but at their human neighbors. A pervasive "culture of honor" imbued men with a hypersensitivity to perceived insult, and throughout Sunflower County's frontier era men, black and white, often turned to weapons rather than the law to settle their differences. For Eastland, the prospect of economic disruption on the plantation was reason enough to threaten physical harm; for Carr, the dishonor of the cuckold was a widely recognized justification for violence. As the two men approached Holbert's cabin, they no doubt understood the stakes of this dangerous confrontation.

Holbert, too, must have seen trouble brewing as his rival and his boss dismounted outside his cabin. What could he do? There were no police to call (or telephones to call on), and even if legal authorities had been present, as a black man, he could not count on their support—justice in Sunflower County, as in the rest of Mississippi, was for whites only. Though the state constitution offered the promise of racial equality before the law, "nothing could be further from the truth," as Sunflower County attorney Sidney Fant Davis readily acknowledged. In reality, as Holbert and other Mississippi blacks well knew, courts practiced "Negro law," by which laws were selectively enforced depending upon the race of the accused. "When a white man kills a Negro, it is hardly considered murder," anthropologist Hortense Powdermaker explained in her study of Sunflower County. "When a Negro kills a white man, conviction is assured, provided the case is not settled immediately by lynch law." In a dispute with a white person, the word of a black person carried no weight whatsoever. With the law on Eastland's side, Holbert had to rely on his own resources and cunning.[4]

Holbert may have considered apologizing or asking for forgiveness, but that route would lead to a double humiliation. He would not only lose face with his rival and his lover but would have to debase himself before his boss. Worse, perhaps, going to the door without a gun in hand could be suicidal—Holbert knew that Carr and Eastland would have their weapons at the ready. Making the decision quickly as the men approached his door, Holbert grabbed a Colt six-shooter and a Winchester rifle and prepared to meet his accusers.

No witnesses survived to tell exactly what happened when the door to Holbert's cabin opened, but we know the scene was grisly. When the shooting stopped, Albert Carr lay dead on the veranda,

James Eastland was sprawled across Holbert's bed with a bullet in his forehead, and Luther Holbert had vanished along with the woman who apparently had been at the center of the conflict.

"THE FAMOUS COTTON DELTA OF MISSISSIPPI"

Before we follow Holbert as he and his lover escape into the woods of Sunflower County, let us pause here a bit to figure out how Holbert and Eastland found their way to that fatal confrontation on a cold February morning. To understand the forces that drove them on their collision course, we must dig deep into the soil of Sunflower County's history, a history rich with contrasts—opportunity and oppression, cooperation and competition, civilization and savagery, black and white. What we find is that the prime mover in the county's early history was nature itself, an ever-present force that shaped every aspect of Sunflower County's development and created the context for the striking contrasts of human life in the area.

A narrow county wedged between its neighbors Washington to the west and Leflore to the east, Sunflower stands approximately forty miles east of the Mississippi River in the heart of what the region's early boosters called "the famous cotton delta of Mississippi." To an outsider who might imagine the Mississippi Delta to be near the river's mouth in the Gulf of Mexico, the Delta's name is confusing. The term does not refer to the true delta of the Mississippi River, which forms south of New Orleans. Rather, it marks the Yazoo-Mississippi Delta, the oval floodplain between the Yazoo and Mississippi Rivers that extends, in planter David Cohn's immortal line, from "the lobby of the Peabody Hotel in Memphis" to "Catfish Row in Vicksburg." Thousands of years of unrestrained spring flooding had smoothed the rough edges of the land, leveling the landscape and topping it with up to fifty feet of what one observer called "pure soil endlessly deep, dark, and sweet." Combined with the area's warm, humid weather, the flooding created one of the continent's most fertile soils, a land teeming with life. "Nature knows not how to compound a richer mixture," an amazed geologist commented. "Every square foot of it riots in vegetable life." Only small patches of this riotous wilderness remain in the Delta today, so we must imagine "the thickest timber I have ever seen," as one early Sunflower County resident put it. "Oak, gum, ash, hackberry, and poplar stood so thick, with no underbrush, only big blue cane growing rank and tall, almost to the limbs of the trees." The reigning king of the forest was the cypress, sometimes eight feet in diameter, its soaring trunks shading the knobby-kneed roots that pockmarked the swamp below. Though Mississippi and magnolias are inextricably intertwined in the public mind, Sunflower County's hardwood jungles were cypress country. There was not a magnolia in sight.[5]

In this "chaos of vines and canes and brush," as planter William Alexander Percy described his native region, lived panthers and bears and malaria-bearing mosquitoes, but few people. In the centuries before 1541, when Hernando de Soto became the first European to set foot in the Delta, the region had been relatively densely populated by Indians who farmed, hunted, and built ceremonial mounds that still dot the land. De Soto's arrival triggered a population crash, as the tribes literally were decimated by European diseases such as smallpox, measles, and whooping cough, to which they had no immunity; within a century, much of the Delta essentially was deserted. The few tribes that endured, including the Choctaw, Chickasaw, Chackhuima, and Tiou, tended to live on the fringes of the Delta, along the Mississippi River to the west and in the bluffs to the east. The Choctaw had the strongest presence in the area that became Sunflower County. One of the "Five Civilized Tribes," the Choctaw sought to assimilate with white American culture and often adopted white customs, such as wearing European dress, building colonial-style homes, and owning slaves. Under Chief Pushmataha, a troop of Mississippi Choctaws fought alongside General Andrew Jackson to help crush their rivals, the Creeks, during the Battle of Horseshoe Bend in 1814. Like Luther Holbert, however, the Choctaws found their loyalty unrewarded. First in the Treaty of Doaks' Stand in 1820 and again fifteen years later at the Treaty of Dancing Rabbit Creek, Choctaw chiefs, pressured by white settlement and U.S. military force, ceded the lands that became Sunflower County. The Choctaws' erstwhile ally, now President Jackson, supervised the Choctaws' removal after the latter treaty, which was signed by a slaveholding chief named Greenwood Leflore (today,

Greenwood is the seat of Leflore County, Sunflower's eastern neighbor). Less than a decade later, in 1844, Sunflower was carved from the expropriated lands and became an official county in the state of Mississippi, taking its name from the river that snaked through it.[6]

Earning official county status did not suddenly bring settlers and slaves to Sunflower. Up through the Civil War, Sunflower County, like the rest of the Delta, remained largely unsettled and undeveloped—ironically, this area that so often is considered to be the embodiment of the "Old South" had little antebellum tradition. By war's end, more than 90 percent of the region remained forested terrain; even thirty years later, only 20 percent of Sunflower County had been cleared. The problem was that the area remained "a land of unlevied small rivers, bayous, lakes, pools, ponds, and swamps," Ruby Sheppard Hicks recalled, where thick canebrakes and dense forest growth made travel next to impossible. The only breaks in the brush were the "roads" created by teams of oxen pulling mud boats full of timber on their way to the hastily constructed sawmills.[7] Clearing the land to prepare it for settlement or agriculture could be tricky and time-consuming, to say the least. Thick mats of vines forced early residents to crawl on their hands and knees simply to get in a position to chop trees down. With one eye out for panthers, wolves, bears, and snakes, they also had to brave swarms of mosquitoes so dense, it was said, that they could run through a cloud of the bugs, turn around, and see the silhouette of their body. And yet, despite the nine-foot panthers, despite the millions of blackflies, despite the dreadful diseases that made calomel, quinine, and chill tonic a regular part of the diet, settlers trickled into the area in the years before the war. They came for one reason, the same reason that would spur Sunflower County's development for the next century and a half: cotton.[8]

Upland cotton, *Gossypium hirsutum*, had been domesticated by Aztecs and Mayans in Central America more than five thousand years before Luther Holbert and James Eastland found their way to Sunflower County. Originally a brown fiber also grown in yellow or auburn colors, cotton became a staple in Indian culture, providing clothing, blankets, and other necessities. The first European settlers in what became Mississippi cultivated the plant for nearly a century before the territory became a state. French farmers in Natchez grew cotton as early as 1721, but the crop remained a relatively unprofitable luxury item until the introduction of the cotton gin, which first came to Mississippi in 1795 after a black slave built one from descriptions supplied by a traveler. The impact of the gin on America history cannot be overstated—it transformed slavery from an anachronistic institution on the brink of extinction into a vibrant engine of economic growth driving westward expansion. Slavery blossomed in the decades following the invention of the gin as slave-owning planters moved from the depleted tobacco fields of Virginia and North Carolina into the rich, forested lands of the "southwest"—Alabama and Mississippi.[9]

Well suited to the warm, humid climate of the Delta, cotton flourished in Sunflower County's fertile soil once the timber was cut and the brush burned. "The same amount of labor expended here gives from three to four times the result obtained anywhere else in the Union," one county booster gushed. "There is no richer soil in the world," agreed a scholar surveying the area. Along the banks of the countless streams, farmers rejoiced in the sandy loam soils, the lightly colored, lightly packed dirt with good drainage that proved to be ideal for cotton growing. Further inland, the soil became heavier, more like clay. This "gumbo" or "buckshot" soil—what one observer labeled the "black sheep of the Delta's soil family"—was less favorable for cotton because it drained poorly, but it still was remarkably rich compared to the hilly lands in the eastern part of the state, let alone the depleted lands back in the East.[10]

The soil's potential to grow fortunes was the magnet that drew settlers to the region. Getting access to that soil, however, required a great deal of time, money, and labor. Hence, from the beginning of non-Indian settlement, most whites who could afford to live in Sunflower County and the rest of the Delta were what planter David Cohn called "pioneers with means"—people with enough capital to buy slaves, clear the land, and make cotton profitable. Throughout the antebellum period, the region was little more than a "plantation frontier" where small numbers of white planters used slave labor to hack a fortune out of the disease-infested wilderness. This early pattern of settlement created a population dynamic that fundamentally shaped the course of Sunflower County life. Because the area was the domain of the large planter, Sunflower quickly filled with slaves. The 1850 census, the first in which Sunflower County appeared, showed a population of 1,102, including 754 slaves representing 68 percent of the population; ten years later, the overall population had swelled beyond 5,000, about 78 percent of whom were slaves.[11]

With such a large black majority, white residents lived in fear of being overwhelmed or overthrown from their precarious position of privilege by discontented slaves. This fear of black rebellion, combined with the unhealthy and dangerous living conditions, led many of the largest slaveholders to become absentee landlords. With permanent homes in Jackson, Memphis, or elsewhere, these planters bought tracts of land for speculative rather than residential purposes. They made periodic trips to visit their Sunflower County farms but left day-to-day operations in the hands of managers and overseers. Hence, they did not build the regal, *Gone with the Wind*-style mansions often associated with the antebellum South. The Eastland home, like other planters' homes in Sunflower County, was spacious but not palatial.

When the Civil War destroyed slavery, it eliminated the legal basis of planters' wealth and ushered in an era of upheaval across the South, particularly in black-majority counties such as Sunflower. Slavery had been abolished, but no one knew what labor system would replace it. Blacks no longer were in bondage, but no one knew exactly what freedom would mean economically, politically, or socially. Would blacks be allowed to vote? Would there be land redistribution? Who would run politics? Within the uncertainty of Reconstruction lay unprecedented opportunity. Largely protected by its dense forests and swamps, Sunflower County had escaped the ravages of the war itself and had little to "reconstruct." The land was almost a blank slate, offering the county's majority—its black residents and the black immigrants who came to the area in droves following the war—an unparalleled chance to enjoy life, liberty, and the pursuit of happiness.

The postwar period was an exciting time to be young, Mississippian, and black. For two decades following the war, newly freed blacks such as Fannie Lou Hamer's grandparents in Montgomery County, Mississippi, pushed to give meaning to their freedom by voting, building schools, and advocating land reform. Backed by the federal government, black voters across the state flocked to the polls, electing black men to serve as lieutenant governor, secretary of state, and

Speaker of the state house of representatives; one U.S. congressman and two U.S. senators from Mississippi in the 1870s were black. In Sunflower County, blacks held all sorts of political positions, including superintendent of education, sheriff, and county supervisor, and they served on juries for the first time. Many of these accomplishments would not be repeated for more than a century; some have yet to be achieved again.[12]

Perhaps most impressively, black farmers in Sunflower County and throughout the Delta scooped up land in the undeveloped backwoods of the region. Fearing a labor shortage and hoping to establish a secure labor force, white planters offered increasingly attractive arrangements to lure workers to their farms. Many former slaves were able to parlay their improved economic leverage into land ownership. By the end of the century, roughly two-thirds of the landowners in the Delta were black. In Sunflower County, blacks established small but vibrant communities such as Stephensville far away from white settlements, pioneering a path of self-sufficiency and independence. Next door in Bolivar County, industrious blacks established Mound Bayou, an incorporated, all-black town that drew national attention. Far from being the locus of black oppression, postwar Sunflower County and the Delta were the promised lands of opportunity, and Reconstruction was a golden age of black freedom.[13]

Sunflower County whites saw things differently. The experience of black political empowerment and economic advancement seared itself into their minds as a "tragic era," a time of inverted hierarchies when their social inferiors were placed in unwarranted positions of power. Where blacks saw political opportunity, whites perceived corruption; when blacks bought up land, white feared economic domination; while blacks looked to the federal government for protection, whites seethed at the blue-uniformed troops in their midst. For much of the next century, the specter of "Negro rule" animated white fears of racial equality and created a deep distrust of federal authority and white outsiders bent on upsetting the status quo. Sunflower County whites generally blamed meddling whites, not local blacks, for the difficulties of Reconstruction. Because blacks had "no preparation" for voting, a white congressman from Sunflower County argued in 1900, it was understandable that they used it poorly. But "the crimes that were committed in the southern states in that dread period," he emphasized, "were the work of bad white men who preyed upon the superstitions and ignorance of that [black] race and made it a scapegoat for their own wicked performance."[14] Six decades later, a senator from Sunflower County named James Eastland would use precisely the same logic to denounce the "outside agitators" of the civil rights movement.

Worried white planters desperately sought to reestablish control over the labor force and violently resisted attempts to rebuild southern society on a biracial basis. White resistance to Reconstruction was region-wide, but it had particular salience in areas such as Sunflower County where whites were heavily outnumbered. Many whites believed their very survival was at stake, and they resorted to violence and fraud as a means of reasserting their supremacy. They joined paramilitary terrorist groups such as the Ku Klux Klan, which had been founded shortly after the war by a group of former Confederate generals, including its first Imperial Wizard, Nathan Bedford Forrest, who was a planter in Coahoma County, just north of Sunflower. Often cloaked in noble or benign guise, the Klan and its ideological brethren sought to intimidate black voters, discourage black economic efforts, and assert white supremacy. Gruesome violence teamed with blatant electoral fraud to overthrow ("redeem," in the eyes of whites) biracial Reconstruction governments in 1875 and usher in a return to politics for whites only.[15]

Despite the terrorist coup, Mississippi's black men continued to enjoy voting rights and integrated public facilities into the 1880s. Part of what protected them was the law. To be admitted back into the Union following the war, Mississippi not only had to write a new constitution, it also had to ratify the Fourteenth Amendment, which formally made blacks citizens of both the United States and Mississippi and applied the Bill of Rights to the states. The Fourteenth Amendment, combined with the Fifteenth Amendment, which expressly prohibited voter discrimination on the basis of race, gave blacks a solid legal footing on which to fight white attempts to usurp power. Many white politicians, furthermore, hoped to win power through their adept manipulation of the black electorate, giving them an incentive to defend the black right to vote. To rectify this "problem," white leaders called a constitutional convention in 1890 at which they drew up a new document that would make politics a white man's game. The state constitution of 1890 included a grandfather clause, literacy test, and poll tax to filter out black voters from the voting rolls. Race-neutral on the surface, the new constitution made black voting a thing of the past. It would be three-quarters of a century before black Mississippians regained the political rights they had enjoyed during Reconstruction.

Sunflower County's black farmers may have been removed from the political arena, but they were central to the institution that drove everyday life in the area: cotton. As the county's political situation regressed toward blatant white supremacy, the area boomed economically, primarily benefiting white planters and pioneers. America's King Cotton had been crowned during the era of slavery, but he reached the height of his power as world trade blossomed in the half century after the end of the Civil War. A global population explosion and technological advances in the late nineteenth century, particularly in the textile industry, spurred a tremendous increase in the demand for raw cotton. All across the South, as devastated planters, struggling white tenant farmers, and cash-poor freed slaves sought to rebuild their lives, cotton became the coin of the realm. U.S. exports of cotton increased ninefold between 1865 and 1900, constituting a majority of the nation's export revenue, and by the 1890s the United States was producing three times more cotton than the rest of the world combined.[16]

Much of the increase in American production sprouted from the newly cleared fields of the Mississippi Delta, where the crop became the region's white gold and attracted a rush of would-be plantation owners. The cotton rush was driven by and fed a railroad boom that opened up Sunflower County to land speculators, cotton farmers, and merchants from all over the country. For the first forty years of the county's life, essentially all trade went in and out of the county via steamboat on the Sunflower River, which was navigable for only about half the year even after it was dredged in 1878. The steamboat era began to fade with the coming of the railroad in the 1880s. First, a short line dribbled out from Greenville to Johnsonville, located in central Sunflower County just south of present-day Indianola. By the end of the decade, the Georgia Pacific Railroad Company had incorporated the line into its longer route from the Mississippi River to Atlanta. In 1893, developers added a fifty-mile north-south route from Belzoni to

Ruleville. With railroad access in all four directions, Sunflower County became a hub for the cotton trade. Its population, which had declined for twenty years after the start of the Civil War, more than doubled in the 1880s.[17]

One planter who set his sights on Sunflower County was Oliver Eastland, a successful druggist from Scott County, Mississippi, whose father, Hiriam, was among the most prosperous merchants in the county. A descendant of English Quakers, Hiriam Eastland had moved to Hillsboro, Mississippi, in the 1830s. The Civil War ravaged Eastland's family and home—two of his brothers were killed in the fighting and Union general William T. Sherman burned Hillsboro. After the war, the family moved eight miles south to Forest, where Oliver Eastland grew up. By the early 1880s, Eastland began speculating on property in the Delta. With land selling for but $1 an acre, Eastland bought hundreds of acres along the Sunflower River in 1882. His son, Woods, took charge of clearing the land and turning it into farmland. The family farm proved a windfall, and Oliver Eastland expanded continuously; when he died in 1899, he left roughly 2,400 acres to his second wife and his oldest son, Hiram. Later, Woods and another brother, Oliver Jr., bought out the other family members' interests and became sole owners.[18]

The Eastlands benefited greatly from the global cotton boom in the late nineteenth century that transformed the Delta from a swampy, sparsely inhabited antebellum backwater into a thriving cotton kingdom. The kingdom's realm extended far beyond the borders of the region or even the nation. Cotton was primarily an export crop, and planters depended for their wealth as much on world markets as they did on docile black labor. As far back as the early 1800s, Mississippi's territorial governor, William C.C. Claiborne, deemed it the "duty of government" to prevent "the loss of character which the cotton of this territory might sustain in foreign markets" if planters' interests were not protected from fraud. Cotton planters such as the Eastlands participated in and profited from an economic system that relied upon the labor and resources of poor, nonwhite peoples across the globe, not just in Sunflower County. As the United States and western European nations industrialized in the late nineteenth century, their economies grew at unprecedented rates and helped fuel expansion into foreign markets. "American factories are making more than the American people can use; American soil is producing more than they can consume," expansionist U.S. senator Albert Beveridge declared in 1898. "Fate has written our policy for us; the trade of the world must and shall be ours." The industrializing nations lacked two key factors—producers to supply raw materials and consumers to buy finished goods—and they searched the globe to find potential sources of both. Many of the most important raw materials, including cotton, rubber, and sugar, grew only in the tropical and subtropical climates of Asia, Africa, and the Americas. The United States and western European nations (and, later, Japan) exploited the militarily weak and politically vulnerable nations in these areas to create spheres of influence and exploitative economic arrangements that fueled their own economic growth. By the time James Eastland and Luther Holbert came to Sunflower County at the turn of the century, nearly one hundred years before "globalization" became a buzzword, the Western powers had tied the world together in a web of trade, and cotton was one of its major strands.[19]

Global trade grew in tandem with scientific and cultural developments in the late nineteenth century that strengthened the grip of white supremacy. In the United States, economic and military ventures abroad helped forge racial unity among whites still divided by region and class. The experience of fighting against and subjugating non-white peoples in Cuba, Hawaii, and the Philippines encouraged many northern whites to sympathize with southern racial attitudes and practices. This shared racism was even bolstered by science. Charles Darwin's work on the biological evolution of species triggered scientific inquiries into human evolution, and white scientists turned to eugenics and phrenology (the study of human head size and shape) in an effort to create a hierarchy of races and "prove" the inferiority of non-white races. This "scientific racism" lent an air of objective legitimacy to racial prejudice, and it helped spawn a pervasive ideology of "social Darwinism" in Western culture. Social Darwinists argued that the world's races were engaged in a competitive struggle and only the fittest would survive. Measured by their wealth and industrial progress, white people, particularly Anglo-Saxons, had proven that they were the "fittest" race. As such, they bore the "white man's burden" to lift up the inferior, heathen races. The dominance of the white race thus was the law of nature. Within the context of the late nineteenth century, the racial hierarchy in the Mississippi Delta was not "backward" or anachronistic at all—it was on the cutting edge of Western culture.[20]

Sunflower County planters embraced social Darwinism, along with the "New South" ideology of economic modernization that pushed for federal levee construction to control flooding and private railroad construction to encourage commerce. Segregation became an essential part of the New South's modernization, providing order to the chaos of urbanization and industrialization that marked the period. In rural areas such as Sunflower County, segregation helped codify the increasingly rigid separation between black and white. The region boomed in the 1880s, but Sunflower County's blacks shared less and less in the new wealth; they became mired in a system of sharecropping that led to seemingly inescapable debt.

Sharecropping, or "halvin'," as cotton pickers such as Fannie Lou Hamer often called it, had developed across the South after the Civil War as a compromise of sorts between planters and the newly freed black workers. Planters, desperate to regain control over labor, sought to establish a system that would be reliable and profitable; laborers, eager to shed the constraints of slavery, wanted freedom from white supervision and control. Sharecropping seemed to fit the bill—planters would get their crop and have some control over labor, while workers would be able to set their own pace without the humiliation and harassment of constant supervision. But in Sunflower County, sharecropping did not become the customary means of organizing labor until well after Reconstruction. As we have seen, the Delta was a promised land for black workers after the war, and they managed to carve out pockets of land ownership that they tenaciously protected. But that era slipped slowly into oblivion as the global cotton trade expanded, particularly in the late 1890s. The increase in global cotton demand drove prices up, fueling railroad construction in the area and making previously undeveloped hinterland potentially more profitable. Planters who willingly had allowed blacks to gobble up previously unprofitable land in the interior of the county now found reason to invest in the land themselves. Land values soared. Oliver Eastland had been able to buy prime riverside land for barely $1 an acre in the early

1880s; twenty years later, the average land price throughout the Delta reached $25 an acre. Poor farmers were priced out of the market, and wealthy white planters extended their reach farther and farther into the interior. By the time Luther Holbert opened his door to find James Eastland and Albert Carr, the days of black economic opportunity had passed. The promised land of Sunflower County had become a nightmare of sharecropping, violence, and political repression.[21]

The depths to which black workers had sunk were abundantly clear to Chester Pond, a portly New York businessman with a streak of Christian idealism. In the early 1890s, Pond sought to create a "prohibition industrial colony" in Sunflower County. Located fewer than fifteen miles from the Eastland plantation, the new town of Moorhead aimed to avoid the excesses he saw in surrounding plantations by promoting Christian virtue and giving black workers a fair shot at enjoying the fruits of their labor. Given the time and place of his development plan, Pond was remarkably honest in his assessment of the area, and his insights give us a lens into life for Sunflower Countians in the decade before the confrontation between James Eastland and Luther Holbert.

When Pond surveyed the area, he saw an exploitative economic system of sharecropping that degraded planter and picker alike. "Little land in the Delta is cultivated by the landowner," Pond noted, observing that sharecroppers rented it out for $5 to $10 an acre. Because the law gave planters a lien on the crop, tenants were compelled to sell to them and could not borrow on the crop, thus making it hard "for a poor man to get a start in the world." The lien law created "great hardship" on sharecroppers, Pond argued, because they are forced to buy supplies from their landlords "whether prices charged be reasonable or excessive." Planters thus had little check on their authority and often could not resist the temptation to bilk their workers. If a tenant tried to acquire his own home or land, he had to buy on credit and be "carried" for the first year. "In a great majority of cases he will be obliged to forfeit his land and all improvements made thereon by him before it becomes sufficiently productive to maintain him and enable him to meet his obligations." Hence, Pond emphasized, tenants had little incentive to be productive and seek to move up in the world. This demoralizing state of affairs "naturally tends to thriftlessness and discontent, which are at once a menace to good order and society." Black workers with legitimate grievances found themselves powerless to change their lives, so they gave up and developed "shiftless and improvident, if not intemperate, habits" that made economic advancement impossible. The end result, Pond lamented, was that although the land "returns ample compensation for labor expended upon it, it is a deplorable fact that those who produce such wealth, as a class, live in the most squalid manner, without a reasonable hope of ever bettering their future conditions."[22]

Pond hit the nail on the head. By the end of the century, the white planter elite had regained its nearly complete control of the region's politics, economy, and society, and the black majority suffered accordingly. But asserting the natural order of racial hierarchy and maintaining it were two very different things. The process of reconstructing white supremacy out of the ashes of the Civil War was an arduous one for white southerners, particularly in black-majority areas such as Sunflower County. Mississippi had successfully disenfranchised black voters and crushed black political efforts, but many whites still feared black empowerment and felt threatened by black crime. One result was the rise of lynching as a means of social control. Mob killings became commonplace across the South during and after the Civil War, and by the 1880s the Delta ranked as the worst region in Mississippi for lynching. But the victims were not always black. After a Sunflower County black man was brutally murdered in 1876 by a white man who later boasted about the killing, an interracial lynch mob snatched the murderer from his cell and hanged him, earning the praise of one newspaper: "Public sentiment excuses the lynching." Black mobs roamed the backwoods, and until the turn of the twentieth century, *whites* in the Delta were statistically more likely to be lynched than blacks. But as the area became less and less amenable to black political and economic advancement in the 1890s, lynchings in the Delta changed, becoming more numerous, more brutal, and more racially exclusive. Between 1889 and 1899, there were an average of barely two officially recorded lynchings a year in the region; between 1901 and 1908, the average more than doubled. After 1901, no whites were lynched—mob violence had become an affair for whites to enjoy at the expense of blacks. Furthermore, the excuse whites often used to justify lynching—that it was necessary to protect "white womanhood"—became less and less common as the stated cause of lynching. Murder was nearly four times more likely the reason for the mob violence.[23]

White leaders often preyed upon white fears and gained political advantage from cultivating a sense of white power in peril. In the state's 1903 gubernatorial campaign, James K. Vardaman, a flamboyant newspaper editor from Greenwood, forty miles from the Eastland plantation, swept into office on a viciously anti-black platform. A champion of the state's poor whites, the shaggy-maned "White Chief" harangued his audiences with tales of black crime and white race betrayal. The black man "is a lazy, lying, lustful animal" whose behavior "resembles the hog's," he claimed, and he attacked any white who appeared to aid the black cause, including President Theodore Roosevelt, who invited a "nigger bastard," Booker T. Washington, to the White House for dinner. Vardaman's race-baiting, along with his genuine desire to improve the lot of poor white farmers, helped catapult him to victory, inaugurating a generation of poor whites' control of state government.[24]

Sunflower County became the focus of state and national uproar during Vardaman's gubernatorial campaign because Roosevelt had reappointed a black woman, Minnie Cox, to the prestigious office of postmistress. An unassuming member of the county's tiny black middle class, Cox had served without incident in the job for more than a decade and lived with her husband in a spacious house on the white side of Indianola. She became a target when Vardaman saw political opportunity in making an issue of her post. Addressing a crowd in Indianola, Vardaman mocked his white listeners for "receiving mail from the hands of a coon" and vowed, "We are not going to let niggers hold office in Mississippi!" Fired up by Vardaman's rhetoric, the white citizens of Indianola demanded Cox's resignation. Cox herself offered to quit, but Roosevelt refused to accept her resignation. Instead, he closed down the post office, infuriating Vardaman supporters such as *Sunflower Tocsin* editor J.A. Richardson, who growled that the order "was intended to punish white men for Teddy's love for the negro." The ensuing brouhaha reached the floor of the U.S. Senate and created a mini-furor before Cox resigned her post over the president's objections. (Nearly a century later, the majority-black Indianola Board of Aldermen named a city park and the local post office in Cox's honor; a portrait of her hangs prominently behind the main counter.)[25]

The Cox incident showed that white supremacy, even in Sunflower County, was never total and all-consuming. By the early twentieth century, however, it was hardening into a tougher system to crack. Politically, economically, and socially, Sunflower County was becoming less hospitable to black aspirations, and whites were becoming more aggressive about establishing their supremacy. Black workers had flocked to Sunflower County in search of a better life shortly after the Civil War, but that window of opportunity slammed shut in the late 1890s and early twentieth century. Despite significant success in buying homes, establishing themselves politically, and building community institutions, they could not wrench themselves free from the tightening grip of white supremacy. By the time James Eastland went to Luther Holbert's cabin that morning in February 1904, he did so in the context of a racially tense, economically explosive state of affairs in Sunflower County. Holbert's crime, coming on the heels of Vardaman's election and just a week after Minnie Cox's replacement was nominated for her post, was seen not simply as a murder but as part of a widespread challenge to white supremacy. Whites in Sunflower County felt that blacks such as Holbert increasingly were stepping out of their place and had to be stopped.

"MURDER MOST FOUL"

And so we return to Luther Holbert's bloody cabin. The gunfire that erupted from that cabin had broken the morning stillness. Black workers nearby hurried to the scene and discovered the prone bodies of Eastland and Carr. As the workers tended to Carr, word was sent for James Eastland's older brother, Woods Caperton Eastland. The second of six children in the Eastland clan, Woods was twenty-five years old and managing the plantation when his brother was killed. As the eldest male on the scene, he bore the responsibility of retribution. Like Luther Holbert, he could have chosen the path of nonviolence. Perhaps he could have contacted the local sheriff, informed him of the circumstances, and waited patiently for the law to run its course.

Perhaps he could have spent the next several days making funeral arrangements, contacting family members, and settling his brother's legal affairs. But to choose not to avenge his brother's death with force would have been unthinkable to a white man steeped in a culture of violence. Woods himself had been named for a murder victim—his uncle Woods Caperton had been killed at "Hard Times Landing," Louisiana, a month before Woods Eastland was born—and he understood the necessity of vengeance.[26] A young man with a budding reputation, Eastland was not about to disgrace himself by allowing his brother's black murderer to escape into the hands of the law.

Eastland made an immediate decision to pursue Holbert and cut down anyone who might have been implicated in the murder. News of James Eastland's death "spread like wildfire" through Sunflower County's white community—the death of the black man, Carr, merited little attention from local whites or newspaper reporters. Within an hour of the murder a mob had coalesced around Woods, who quickly set about organizing the manhunt to track down Holbert and his female companion, a woman sometimes reported to be his wife, Mary. He ordered bloodhounds from local planters and the newly established penal farm at Parchman in northern Sunflower County, and he issued a $1,200 reward for the couple's capture. As the mob waited for the dogs to arrive, a restless Eastland murdered another black worker, a man named Winters, who was accused of being an accomplice. When the dogs finally arrived, after dark, the Holberts already had a ten-hour head start. Woods Eastland, joined by at least fifty armed men, including what one newspaper deemed "many prominent citizens of Sunflower County," began the hunt.[27]

Local newspapermen fervently followed the chase, whipping their readers into a frenzy with dramatic stories laced with gory details from Sunflower County. "Murder most foul," cried the Memphis *Commercial Appeal*; "one of the most revolting chapters in the criminal history of Mississippi," lamented Greenwood's *Commonwealth*. But of course foul and revolting stories sold newspapers. This was page-one news, alongside reports of Japanese assaults on Russian ports in the Far East. J.A. Richardson, editor of the *Sunflower Tocsin*, declared the Holbert hunt "one of the most thrilling and persevering human chases" in state history. The *Greenville Daily Democrat* dutifully informed readers to be on the lookout for the Holberts, using a style and language similar to runaway-slave advertisements: "Holbert is a ginger cake colored negro, has sideburns, light mustache, 5 feet 10 inches high, weight 170 pounds. Speaks well and has a good education." The newspapers implicitly lauded the efforts of Woods Eastland, who, in the words of one reporter, would forgo sleep and "all else save the spirit of the lamented dead which cried for vengeance."

Fully aware that a posse would be on their trail, Luther and Mary Holbert had hurriedly fled into the swamps. Luther shaved his mustache with razors Mary had pocketed before they fled, and she cut her hair and dressed as a man to confuse the hunters. The Holberts took advantage of the riotous wilderness to elude their would-be captors, stealthily traveling at night through the dense forests as they made their way southeast from Doddsville. Hoping to reach the Yazoo River and catch a boat to safety, the Holberts may have been helped by their contacts in local Negro lodges. Across the South in the late nineteenth century, black communities formed benevolent associations, fraternal organizations, and other groups that provided social networks and an economic safety net. Luther Holbert was known to be a lodge member, and his fellow lodge members may have provided shelter, food, and horses to help the Holberts avoid capture.

As Wednesday turned to Thursday and Thursday to Friday, the Holberts remained at large. The white pursuers and their allies in the media grew frustrated, and they vented their anger on the lodges. "The white sentiment against negro lodges in this country is at fever heat," one reporter observed. "This will be the beginning of the end of negro lodges in this section." That white rage toward the Holberts would so quickly be transferred to black lodges is telling, and it gives us a clue as to why Luther Holbert's crime necessitated, in the minds of Sunflower County's whites, violent retribution. Like Holbert, the lodge defied white power. It stood as perhaps the only black-run institution that remained off-limits to whites; even black churches were financially dependent on white largesse. Just as Holbert had to be caught and punished, so too the black lodges—and by extension any black ambitions of independence and self-governance—had to be taught a lesson about white supremacy. It was a problem, one observer wrote, "requiring earnest consideration and drastic action."

White rage also turned on blacks who ran afoul of the mob. Though the Memphis newspaper insisted that the mob went about its business without "offering the slightest molestation to innocent negroes in the area," three more black people had been murdered by nightfall on Friday, the third day of the hunt. One party of the hunting posse happened upon two men in a cotton field who seemed to fit the Holberts' description. When the men fled as the posse approached, the whites opened fire, killing them both before determining that they were not the wanted couple. Another black woman was killed when a gun discharged accidentally.

For more than three days across three counties through pouring rain, the posse, which had swelled to several hundred men, pursued the couple; a local sheriff provided fresh horses and reinforcements. Conducted primarily on foot and on horseback with bloodhounds leading the way, the chase bore remarkable similarities to a hunt for fugitive slaves during the antebellum era. But Eastland and his crew also manipulated modernity to their advantage. Passing word by telephone and telegraph, whites were able to relay information quickly to and from the various hunting parties, law enforcement officials, and media. Once it was discovered that the Holberts were heading toward the Yazoo River near Itta Bena, mob members who had remained in northern Sunflower County hopped on a train and headed south to cut off the escape route.

In the end, however, it was dumb luck that spelled doom for the Holberts. A teenage boy happened to see the armed couple by a swamp near Sheppardtown, a dozen miles southwest of Greenwood. He ran to a local general store, where he told two men, V.H. Lavender and E.L. O'Neal. Well aware of the reward offered, Lavender and O'Neal kept the news to themselves. They gathered their weapons and went off to the swamp, where they found the Holberts sleeping peacefully. Awakened, Luther Holbert thought the men were bird hunters and made no effort to escape until he heard one of them say, "Doddsville." In the ensuing scuffle, Holbert was shot twice in the leg before he and Mary were subdued. They were turned over to Sunflower County's deputy sheriff and eventually to the Eastland family, which brought them back to Doddsville. It was Saturday, February 6, three full days since the murder of James Eastland and Albert Carr.

As the newspapers had been reporting all along, Woods Eastland planned to burn the Holberts at the stake, a public burning or "Negro barbecue," as the practice sometimes was called at the time. Eastland's decision to execute the pair in such a public, ritualistic fashion reveals a great deal about the symbolic importance of the affair in Sunflower County history. This was not a "heat of the moment" killing to be explained by mere bloodlust or rage at the enormity of the crime, as contemporary newspapers portrayed it; it was a calculated effort to intimidate the local black community. Like other lynchings across the South, it was more than a reaction to a crime or a ritual of revenge; it also served to reinforce the racial and economic codes of Sunflower County. By enforcing "justice" in such a brutal and public way, Eastland and his fellow Sunflower County whites sent a clear warning to blacks in the region: white dominance must never be challenged again.[28]

Though the Holberts had been captured early Saturday morning some twenty-five miles away, their execution did not take place immediately. Instead, Eastland chose a time and place that would have maximum effect: Sunday afternoon, on the grounds of Doddsville's black church, which also served as a lodge meeting hall. By holding the burning on Sunday afternoon, right after church, he ensured a large crowd of both blacks and whites. By putting the pyre "in the shadow of a church," as one reporter observed, Eastland sent a double-barreled message to local blacks: nothing, not even God or your hallowed lodge, can protect you if you step out of your place in this society.

If the lynching was publicized so well and the entire community knew about it in advance, one might reasonably wonder: where were the police and other authorities? Governor Vardaman, as we have seen, was no friend of black people, but he did have the constitutional obligation to prevent vigilante violence. Fulfilling his duty, he made a pro forma effort to stop the killings by sending state troops by train from Jackson to Sunflower County. What happened to these troops is not known; they were nowhere to be found in Doddsville that day. Sunflower County's deputy sheriff had tried to retain possession of the Holberts after they had been captured but, according to *Sunflower Tocsin* editor J.A. Richardson, he was unable. "The deputy made a stout effort to hold the murderers but the pressure was too great and he being overpowered yielded to superior numbers and the prisoners were taken in charge by this mob."

With no legal or moral authority weighing in against him, Woods Eastland could seek vengeance as he saw fit. Yet even residents accustomed to the brutality of life in Sunflower County must have been shocked by what transpired on that Sunday afternoon. With the ample advance media attention, crowds of people, white and black, flocked to Doddsville—more than one thousand people in a county of barely sixteen thousand. The mob, according to one reporter, "went about its work in an orderly manner" and prepared the pyres even as several white citizens, including the deputy sheriff, sought to prevent the lynching by speaking out. The dissenters were drowned out by shouts of "Kill them!" from the crowd. But killing alone was not enough for this mob. Before starting the fires, the mob tied the two victims to separate trees and forced them to endure what one white newspaperman called "the most fiendish tortures." One by one, the Holberts' fingers and then their ears were cut off and given out as souvenirs—some reached as far away as Illinois. Next came a beating that left Luther Holbert with a fractured skull and one eye hanging "by a shred" from its socket. The worst was yet to come. As the Vicksburg *Evening Post* reported, "The most excruciating form of punishment consisted in the use of a large corkscrew in the hands of some of the mob. This instrument was bored into the flesh of the man and woman, in the arms, legs, and body, and then pulled out, the spirals tearing out big pieces of raw, quivering flesh every time it was withdrawn." Only then were the two, still breathing, dragged to the pyre by two black men "who knew that a failure to obey the instructions of the mob meant death." As Luther Holbert watched, his steadfast companion, Mary, was burned alive first and then he, too, faced the same fate. "It was a scene," one observer commented, "such as a man wants to witness only once in a lifetime."[29]

By nightfall, the fire had been reduced to ashes and the crowds had drifted away, leaving Doddsville to return to the quiet business of winter. But the spasm of violence had left seven blacks and one white man dead, and it would not soon be forgotten. Condemnation of the "Doddsville savagery" was swift. Booker T. Washington, the nation's leading black spokesman, expressed his outrage in a letter to the editor of the *Birmingham Age Herald*, later reprinted in the *New York Tribune*. The accommodationist Washington, who was widely applauded by white segregationists for promoting black vocational education, feared the negative effect that the Holbert killings would have on "the friendly relations which should exist between the races." How could whites and blacks in the South collaborate to uplift their region when mobs could so brazenly defy the rule of law? "These barbarous scenes are more disgraceful and degrading to the people who inflict the punishment than to those who receive it," Washington lamented. Black leaders were not the only ones to denounce the Holberts' lynching. White newspaper editors across the South also condemned mob leaders for undermining the rule of law. "Savagery does not justify savagery," wrote the editors of the *Memphis News*. Given the legal strength of white supremacy, white editors argued, there was no need to resort to undignified, uncivilized mob violence. "The only plea that could be entered in palliation of this savagery is that it was necessary to strike terror to the negroes who might be tempted to murder other white men, but it is doubtful whether such horrible torture has as much effect in this respect as a legal execution."[30]

While race inevitably became the focus of concern, critics also pointed to the economic dimensions of the lynching. *The Voice of the Negro*, an Atlanta-based publication with a wide readership among the black middle class, charged that "nothing is too low and barbarous" for the state of Mississippi and offered a different spin on the events leading up to the original killing that sparked the manhunt. According to the *Voice*'s source, "a prominent and reliable white man," the dispute between Holbert and Eastland had nothing to do with a woman at all. Rather, it was an economic matter of "involuntary servitude." Eastland had been holding a black worker on the plantation, claiming the man could not leave until he worked off his debt. Holbert convinced the man to flee and offered him shelter. Eastland came to Holbert's cabin to retrieve the man and force him back to work, but Holbert intervened. Eastland "started to give Holbert a lesson about how to keep quiet and allow white men to do what they pleased," and the confrontation grew physical. We know the result. In its aftermath, the *Voice*'s editors warned, "There is a growing feeling among Negroes that something must be done. Almost anything is preferable to the shameless, bare-faced humiliations that are heaped upon the race. Whether there is to be a general higira of black men from that sin-stricken section, a determined stand for right, or a surrender to serf-dom, we cannot tell."[31]

The *Voice's* account conflicts with all other sources and may not be reliable given its reliance on a single, unattributed source well after the incident. Yet it sheds light on the economic implications of the conflict between James Eastland and Luther Holbert. Whether East-land went to Holbert's cabin to address a dispute between workers over a woman or whether he sought to force a laborer back to work, the fundamental conflict remained the same: who would control labor on the plantation—the white planters or the black workers? The an-swer was crucial to the course of Sunflower County history during the next century, and middle-class black journalists were not the only ones who expressed their concerns. Like the *Voice*, the white editors of the *Birmingham News* raised the specter of black migration as they con-demned the mob violence. Farmers in Sunflower County and else-where in the Delta had been complaining of a labor shortage, the editors noted, but part of the blame rested with the "lawlessness of the whitecaps" and other white terrorists who took the law into their own hands. "The brutal demonstration of lawlessness at Dossville [*sic*]," the editors warned, "will have its effect in checking the flow of foreign capital into Mississippi."[32] Without outside capital, the rural South would wither away. Restore peace in the countryside and the precious capital would flow freely, allowing the area to grow economically.

The editors of the *Birmingham News* saw lynching as an economic liability, but for Woods Eastland and other white planters who lived in rural, black-majority areas such as Sunflower County the periodic use of lethal violence had a valuable economic function—it helped control the labor force upon which the cotton economy depended. Lynchings created within blacks a profound sense of fear and insecurity that dis-couraged efforts to challenge the status quo. Throughout the South, lynching victims were almost twice as likely to live in cotton-rich areas such as Sunflower County as in non-cotton-producing areas. The Hol-berts' deaths were among at least six official lynchings in the county in the first three decades of the twentieth century; Delta-wide, dozens of black men and women lost their lives at the hands of lynch mobs. Of course, these numbers can be misleadingly low. The deaths of Luther and Mary Holbert count as two lynchings; yet, as we have seen, four other blacks were murdered by white vigilantes during the course of the hunt for the Holberts. Not counted officially as "lynchings," these race-based killings nonetheless contributed to the culture of lawlessness and danger that kept blacks in Sunflower County in their place. Whether official lynchings or race murders, these killings helped planters maintain their grip on cotton production, and thus their economic wealth and political power. As gruesome as lynching was, moreover, it was not unique; from Mississippi to the Congo to the Philippines, white people with the sanction and willful ignorance of their governments tortured, maimed, and murdered nonwhites who challenged their authority or threatened their economic ventures. The willingness and ability to use lethal force gave white supremacy its power. At its base, Sunflower County's cotton plantation economy rested on violence.[33]

Lynching's critics, white and black, hoped at least that the perpetrators of such brazen brutality would face legal retribution. Shortly after the burning, Sunflower County prosecutors dutifully brought charges against Woods Eastland, and a grand jury composed of local whites indicted him for murder. In September 1904, the sheriff of Indianola took Eastland into custody and preparations were made for a trial. Perhaps, critics hoped, the rule of law would indeed triumph. Cynics were less sure. Eastland's arrest and indictment were a "judicial farce," argued the *Greenwood Commonwealth*. "A white man will never be convicted for lynching a negro in Mississippi."[34]

Cynics notwithstanding, New Orleans' *Daily Picayune* hyped the trial as "undoubtedly one of the most hotly-contested in the history of Sunflower County," featuring a prosecutor backed by Governor Vardaman battling an array of prominent lawyers who had risen to Eastland's defense, including one of the state's U.S. senators, Anselm J. McLaurin. A Confederate veteran who served as a delegate to the 1890 constitutional convention, McLaurin had volunteered to serve as Eastland's leading attorney. McLaurin helped ensure that Eastland was indeed tried by his peers by using his peremptory challenges to craft a jury of ten farmers, one merchant, and one laborer—all white, of course. At trial, McLaurin argued that there was no evidence that Eastland himself had lit the fire that burned the Holberts to death, and even if he had, such action was justified given the nature of Holbert's crime. He then asked the judge to throw out the case and the judge agreed, a speedy end that elicited wild clapping in the courtroom—"Mr. Eastland was almost carried bodily from the Courthouse" by the exuberant crowd, reporters observed. Exonerated and elated, Eastland returned to Doddsville and promptly threw a public party to celebrate with his supporters. Whites throughout the county could rest assured that terrorism in the defense of white supremacy retained the state's official blessing.[35]

2

Planter's Son,
Sharecroppers' Daughter

A century after hundreds of people descended upon Doddsville to witness the climax of nearly a week of horrific violence, the town itself is dying. The bustling, up-and-coming plantation town of the early twentieth century has deteriorated into abandoned buildings, deserted streets, and ancient machinery. Passing traffic on Highway 49 barely slows to acknowledge the town's tiny brick post office or the unemployed loiterers who watch the cars pass. A fading Coca-Cola advertisement painted on a side wall is all that is left of the last general store, which closed its doors in the 1980s and collapsed shortly after the turn of the twenty-first century. The only business that remains for the town's hundred or so residents is a gas station with a reputation for illicit slot machines. As time passes, fewer and fewer residents can remember the days when Doddsville boasted a vibrant downtown, when Main Street's vine-covered brick buildings were alive with commerce.

Fewer still know about or discuss what happened in February 1904, even after several academic works in the 1990s unearthed the details. The spasm of violence that left eight people dead shook Sunflower County and sent a shudder of fear through both the white and black communities, but the memory of the event faded over time. The Eastland family did not discuss the events of 1904—Woods Eastland's grandchildren heard nothing about the violence until well into adulthood, and they kept it within the family. In the black community, the names and details faded, blurring into the larger dark landscape of lynching and racist violence. But the death of James Eastland and the subsequent revenge killings orchestrated by his brother had a profound effect on Sunflower County. They shaped the world in which the senator and the sharecropper grew up.

"MY FATHER COMPLETELY CONTROLLED ME"

Woods Eastland emerged from the courthouse in September 1904 a free man. He returned home to his new bride, Alma Austin Eastland, whom he had married at the beginning of the year. The twenty-three-year-old Alma was pregnant with what would be the couple's only child, and with the trial finished they could look forward to the baby's arrival. Just two months later, on November 28, Alma gave birth to a son, James Oliver Eastland. Named in honor of Woods's slain brother, baby James Eastland was born "into a household that was still in mourning," one family member recalled. His name not only paid homage to the dead but also symbolized a new beginning for the Eastland family.[1]

In a larger sense, James Eastland was a symbol of white supremacy challenged and violently maintained. Born on the farm in Doddsville, not far from the site of the Holbert lynching and barely more than nine months after that orgy of violence, young James was raised to assume his rightful "place" atop Mississippi's racial, sexual, and economic hierarchy. Maintaining this hierarchy depended upon preserving white political power. Woods Eastland channeled his political ambitions and influence into his son, helping to propel James first to the state house of representatives and later to the U.S. Senate. Embittered by the death of his brother, Woods Eastland wielded a dominating influence on the boy, controlling young James's education and professional development much the way he ruled the lives of sharecroppers on the family plantation. The Eastland family exemplified what Woods, and later James himself, believed to be the ideal society, one in which older white males wielded unquestioned dominance over their inferiors—young people, workers, women, nonwhites. In a society that valued fixed social roles above all else, James knew his "place," and he played the role of the dutiful, deferent child well into adulthood. Under Woods's watchful eye, he learned not only how to wield power economically on the plantation and politically through elected office but also the importance of protecting white dominance in a black-majority world.

James was born in Sunflower County, but at the age of one he moved with his family to Forest, the timber town in Scott County that his parents had left shortly before. The reasons for the move are not clear, but we must recall that the Delta remained a swampy, unhealthy frontier area with a reputation for floods, disease, and violence—not the best place for a child and a young mother. The advent of artesian wells in Sunflower County provided clean drinking water, but yellow fever and malaria remained common, and doctors were few and far between. Electricity remained more than two decades away. Forest, by contrast, offered schools, churches, and commerce, as well as grandparents and other relatives nearby. From a family perspective, Forest seems to have made sense for the newlywed couple.[2]

As a senator, James Eastland came to epitomize the southern white planter, a man who embodied the values and vigorously defended the interests of the wealthy plantation farmers who were his strongest supporters. Ironically, however, he grew up on the opposite side of Mississippi's Great Divide—he started out as a boy of the Hills, not the Delta. Geography, economics, and history conspired to split Mississippi into these two major regions that fought a perpetual battle for control of the all-white Democratic Party. With its rich soils and flat land, the Delta always had been the province of the plantation owner, where wealthy families amassed huge fortunes by exploiting legions of black laborers; to the east and south lay much poorer counties, areas where white small farmers struggled to make ends meet. These hardscrabble hill farmers resented the lifestyle and power of the Delta's plantation owners—the "Delta aristocracy"—and tensions flared in the legislature over issues ranging from taxes to prohibition. The divisions hardened into cultural stereotypes, and both "Hill people" and "Delta people" often assumed that differences in attitude, personality, or character could be attributed to region. As Eastland's son later recalled about the regional divisions, "Everybody in the Delta thought the Hill people were really different" and vice versa. Even after Eastland had become a nationally recognized defender of cotton planters, some of the more blue-blooded Delta aristocrats sniffed that he was not really a Deltan because of his upbringing in the Hills.[3]

Just forty miles east of Jackson in the piney woods of central Mississippi, Scott County had been the Eastlands' home since the early 1800s. James's paternal great-grandfather, Hiriam, had moved southwest from MacMendel, Tennessee, to pursue his fortune in the burgeoning young state of Mississippi. Scott County, with its bustling timber industry and growing small towns, offered a range of opportunities for a merchant on the make, and Hiriam Eastland made plenty. By age forty, the father of nine had amassed one of the largest fortunes in the area. Hiriam Eastland's son Oliver, James's grandfather, built upon his father's mercantile success by becoming a successful druggist and entrepreneur who established a mini-chain of drugstores across the state. He even marketed a medicine, Eastland's Antiseptic, that was later picked up and patented by the famed Dr. Tischner of New Orleans. Oliver married Betty Caperton in 1876, the year of the compromise that ended Reconstruction, and within a decade the couple had borne six children, four boys and two girls. Born in 1879, Woods Eastland, James's father, was the second oldest.[4]

If young Jim inherited ties to the entrepreneurial New South from his father's side of the family, he had links to the mythological Old South from his mother's family. His maternal grandfather, Richmond Austin, graduated from Tulane University Medical School on the eve of the Civil War and promptly joined the Confederate Army to serve as a captain in the cavalry of General Nathan Bedford Forrest, the widely worshipped and reviled general who later helped found the Ku Klux Klan. A century later, Forrest's portrait would hang prominently in Jim Eastland's senatorial office in Washington. Throughout the South, the war had devastated southern families, and the Austins' relative prosperity did not spare them from tragedy. Five of Jim's great-uncles died in the conflict.[5]

Even more painful to white southern pride than the war, however, was Reconstruction. Jim's mother, Alma, was born in 1881, shortly after the official end of Reconstruction but during a time of political flux when Mississippi still had a black man, Blanche K. Bruce, representing the state in the U.S. Senate. She grew up hearing stories of Yankee brutality and came of age during the height of Confederate nostalgia. Diligent efforts of organizations such as the United Daughters of the Confederacy (UDC) helped forge a shared white southern identity by perpetuating the "Lost Cause" through reunions, monuments, and historical preservation efforts. Raw memories remained for generations. Studying Sunflower County in the 1930s, anthropologist Hortense Powdermaker found that "mere mention of Reconstruction days to the average middle-aged man, whether his family was rich or poor, is enough to release in him a flood of resentment." As an adult, Alma Eastland threw herself into the UDC, serving as president of Scott County's local chapter and helping raise money for a monument to the women of the Confederacy on the grounds of the state capitol in Jackson. She never forgave the Yankees for their "invasion" of the South, and she instilled within her children and grandchildren an abiding distrust of northerners and the federal government. As a child growing up in the 1950s, her grandson Woods remembered how Alma Eastland "used to preach to me about being very circumspect and careful with Yankees." James, too, imbibed his mother's devotion to the Confederacy. "Our people were treated worse than any conquered people in modern history," he wrote. "The courage and patriotic devotion of the sons of the South who overthrew this regime and restored the white race to control is unparalleled in history."[6]

While Jim Eastland's mother cultivated the past, his father focused on building a family empire for the future. Opportunistic and ambitious, Woods Eastland was an affable man with a penchant for politics. As a student at Harperville College in Scott County, he roomed with Paul B. Johnson, a rising political star who later became governor and would have a life-changing impact on Woods's son Jim. Following college, Woods taught himself law, passed the bar, and established a flourishing personal injury law practice that catered to workers hurt in local sawmills. Throughout Jim's childhood, his father was an eminently successful man who did not suffer from his widely publicized involvement in the Holbert killings. He was active in state and local politics, serving for eight years as district attorney, and became a powerful behind-the-scenes political operator in a county that was home to four families that would have a profound impact on Mississippi politics. In addition to the Eastlands and Johnsons, Scott County boasted the Hederman family, which would control the state's largest newspaper, the *Clarion-Ledger*, and the McMullans, who would run one of Mississippi's most important banks, Deposit Guaranty.[7]

Though the family had deep roots in Scott County, Woods Eastland set his sights on the Delta, where true fortunes could be amassed. Profits from practicing law helped the family expand its holdings in Sunflower County, where Woods spent about half the year. Growing up, Jim accompanied his father to the farm when he was not in school. Some of his earliest memories were of taking the day-long train trip from Forest to Doddsville each summer—only a hundred miles northwest as the crow flies, but the iron horse first trekked west all the way to Vicksburg before picking up the Illinois Central line that headed north through the Delta. On the farm, Jim lived in a black-majority world, and he learned firsthand how a planter wielded authority over his black workers. Woods schooled him in the ways of black folks, and Jim embraced the prevailing sentiment of white supremacy. "He felt that blacks were inferior, mentally inferior," one of his daughters remembered. "They were the type of people who would always need strict control." Blacks were like children, Eastland came to believe. They should defer to their white superiors the way children obeyed their elders; whites in turn provided firm guidance and control, much the way Woods Eastland dictated his son's life.[8]

Young Jim grew up in his father's shadow. Woods cultivated his only child for politics, though the youngster did not inherit his father's geniality. Remembered by one clerk in the Forest general store as "an uppity kid," Jim was more introverted like his mother, without his father's warmth. He attended Forest's segregated public schools, making a few friends but remaining a homebody whose most important relationships were within the family. Like many only children, he grew quite close to his parents, particularly his father. The Eastlands, Jim's cousin Chester recalled, were "so close that in the event that a member of the family was to be gone for any length of time, there were always the affectionate good-byes—not merely handshakes, but hugs and kisses on the cheek." Physical affection notwithstanding, Woods made very clear who was the head of the household. As Jim recalled years later, "My father completely controlled me."[9]

By high school, Jim had become more outspoken and popular. Being the only kid in the class with a car certainly helped boost his standing among his classmates. He stood five feet eleven inches, significantly taller than most of his peers, and joined the basketball team as well as the debate club. He graduated in 1922, one of four boys in a class of twelve seniors at the all-white Forest High School. A senior class photograph shows an almond-eyed James Eastland, front and center, staring into the camera with an impish smirk on his lips. Hair cropped close on the sides with a thick mop on top, Jim fingers a ball cap as he sits, wide-legged, cramming Vida Burns, the redhead to his right. Decades later, witnesses before the Senate Judiciary Committee would sit, tense and uncomfortable like Vida, as chairman Eastland, wearing a knowing smirk and fiddling with his trademark cigar, grilled them, often for hours on end. The sense of confidence and entitlement that came with being a rich man's son was instilled early on.[10]

A few months after that picture was taken, Jim was off to college. His father originally selected the Virginia Military Institute for his son, but he changed his mind the night Jim was supposed to board the train. Instead, Woods thought Jim's political ambitions might be better served by the University of Mississippi, the flagship of the state's small but growing network of colleges. "Ole Miss," like many other southern colleges, drew heavily upon classical influences. In the words of a University of Wisconsin professor who studied Mississippi colleges in the 1920s, a "genteel tradition [that] was in vogue throughout our country fifty years ago" still prevailed at the school long after northern colleges had abandoned it. Ole Miss sought to cultivate good southern gentlemen not only through social organizations such as fraternities but also throughout academic life, from the curriculum to academic clubs. As a freshman, Jim joined the Greek Club and the Phi Sigma Literary Society; he later became active in the Hermaean Society, a debating and oratorical club.[11]

Jim attended college during a period of intense racial anxiety in American politics and intellectual life. The end of the Great War, what we now call World War I, had triggered a resurgence of nativism in American culture. Many white Americans sought to protect the nation from the perceived threats of Bolsheviks, immigrants, and other undesirables. A reinvigorated Ku Klux Klan attracted millions of members nationwide, and widespread discontent with immigration from southern and eastern Europe led Congress to pass the National

Origins Act of 1924, severely restricting the number of people allowed into the country. Among intellectuals, the war's impact on Europe raised fears that white civilization worldwide was in peril. Bestselling scholarly books such as Madison Grant's *The Passing of the Great Race* (1916) and Lothrop Stoddard's *The Rising Tide of Color Against World White Supremacy* (1920) gave academic weight to the idea that white people, outnumbered on the world stage, could lose their place of dominance if they did not take active steps to protect white supremacy. These ideas had a profound influence on young Jim. Much of the apocalyptic racial rhetoric he used throughout his career echoed the words of Stoddard, Grant, and other 1920s intellectuals.[12]

He also became involved in politics. His political forays at Ole Miss ranged from the mischievous to the Machiavellian. He once broke open a ballot box to help elect a friend as "prettiest girl" and to steal ballots designating him the "biggest liar" in the class. He also ensured his appointment as business manager of the student newspaper by rigging the selection of the entire appointment board. He spent three years at Ole Miss before transferring to Vanderbilt in the hope of getting better legal training; within a semester he had moved again, this time to the University of Alabama. He never did graduate from college. During his senior year at Alabama, Jim passed the bar and subsequently dropped out, at his father's urging, to run for the state house of representatives. It was 1927. Jim was not yet twenty-three years old.[13]

It would be his toughest election, Jim later recalled. But his father's local political influence helped him win, and he went to Jackson to serve as Scott County's representative. Like his father, he was a strong supporter of newly elected governor Theodore Bilbo, who had campaigned on a "books and bricks" platform that promised to uplift the state's poor white farmers through an expansion of government services in education and transportation. His election was a triumph of the Hills over the Delta, and young Eastland was on the Hill side. A champion of poor Hill whites, the irascible Bilbo antagonized "respectable" Delta planters with his uncouth style of campaigning and his merciless attacks on economic privilege. He was an ardent advocate of activist government and later became an outspoken defender of the New Deal. Back in Sunflower County, the editor of the *Indi-*

anola Enterprise called Bilbo "the mad Mussolini, the 'would be' terror of the piney woods."[14]

As a Bilbo man, Eastland began his career as an economic liberal. Representing the farmers and sawmill workers of Scott County, he shared some of the populist economic impulses not only of Mississippi's "redneck liberal" governor but also of Bilbo's flamboyant Louisiana counterpart, Huey Long. In 1931, Long offered a radical plan to end the Depression by placing a moratorium on cotton growing for an entire year. Long's "No Cotton Plan" sent a horrified shudder up the spines of wealthy cotton planters, but it won the support of small farmers and their representatives, including Jim Eastland. Eastland supported the entire Bilbo platform: building paved roads, setting up a public printing plant for schoolbooks, and making the public university system more accessible to poor students. He became known as one of Bilbo's "Little Three" defenders who battled the "Big Four" senior representatives, including one Walter Sillers, a planter from Bolivar County in the Delta. Sillers embodied the power and perspective of wealthy landowners, and he grew to detest Bilbo's neophyte floor leader.[15]

Eastland abandoned politics after one term in the state House. His decision was driven in part by political failure—the Bilbo administration he had vigorously supported had not only failed to address the deepening economic crisis in the state but also earned a reputation for graft and scandal. Recognizing that his son faced imminent defeat (indeed, every candidate associated with Bilbo lost in 1931), Eastland's father encouraged him not to run. "I was a boy then," Eastland later recalled of his short-lived retirement from politics at age twenty-six. "My father figured it was time I get married and learn something about business and the law profession." Woods Eastland was concerned that being a small-time, local politician would mean "always scratching a poor man's hip pocket." Jim followed his father's advice, leaving office when the legislative session ended in 1931 and getting married the next year to Elizabeth Coleman, a demure brunette who taught math at Ruleville High School back in Sunflower County. A high school valedictorian, Libby Coleman had grown up within three miles of the Eastland plantation, but she and Eastland did not get to know each other until after the Eastland family moved back to Doddsville in 1930. Without private telephone lines, the two courted via messages sent through one of the Eastland plantation's black laborers, who took them by horseback to the Coleman home. The newlyweds were married in Elizabeth's house and spent their honeymoon on the Gulf Coast, the only guests at their hotel during that Depression-ravaged time.[16]

Although both the Eastland and the Coleman families lived in Doddsville, the new couple started out in Forest, where Jim began his law practice focused on personal injury cases, much like his father's practice. Cotton prices were so low—barely 6¢ a pound—that he could not envision attracting any clients in the Delta. Even in Forest, he recalled, finding clients was so tough that "any fee from chickens to pigs was welcome." By 1934, cotton prices had rebounded. New Deal programs made cotton farming more lucrative, offering the economic incentive to return to Doddsville. Once again, however, it was his father who dictated the course of Jim's life. When Woods Eastland's health began to fail in 1934, he needed his son to assume control of the farm, which by that time had reached nearly three thousand acres and stretched for miles along Highway 442 west of Doddsville. Jim and Libby left Forest for good. Their return made news in the local paper, which warmly noted that "their many friends welcome them back." He set up an office in Ruleville and began practicing law while also running the financial operations of the plantation. Although Jim ran the farm, his father was still the boss. On the family plantation, one former sharecropper remembered, Woods would not allow his son to order his workers around. The future senator "had to listen to what his daddy say," Rosie Cole recalled. "His daddy didn't allow him to mess with his hands [laborers]" even up into the late 1930s. A full six feet tall with slightly sloping shoulders and a slowly retreating shock of brown hair, Jim Eastland was thirty years old by this time, a grown man. He nonetheless remained his father's son. "As you know," he wrote one relative in 1940, "my father is the boss, and I am subject to his orders."[17]

By the mid-1930s, Jim Eastland had settled into his life as a small-town lawyer and planter. He and Libby lived with her mother in the house in which he was born until 1935, when they all moved into a three-bedroom home that had been built for them on Highway 442, just to the west of the Sunflower River bridge. Jim's parents lived directly across the highway in a similarly spacious but not ostentatious home. The young couple began a family—daughter Nell was born in 1933, followed by Anne in 1938, Sue in 1943, and their only son, "Little" Woods, in 1945.

The Eastlands enjoyed a life filled with family and protected from the plagues of the Depression's poverty. Libby had stopped teaching to tend the house and raise the children. A fine bridge player who enjoyed time in the garden, she spent much of her time with the black women who worked in the house—a maid, a cook, a nurse, and a laundry woman—as well as the yard man, who worked outside. The Eastland children enjoyed a "wonderful, happy, relaxed, safe-feeling childhood," Sue recalled. With so many relatives nearby, most of their time was spent with family—obligatory daily visits with both grandmothers, along with nightly family meals. Despite the Depression, planter families such as the Eastlands enjoyed life to the fullest, going to intergenerational parties and dances throughout the region and attending fashion shows in Greenwood. "It was a fun place to be white and to be of a certain social class," explained Anne Eastland. The "secure, small-town feeling" that the children relished was an important part of the world that Jim Eastland loved deeply and would always try to protect.[18]

This feeling of security rested on the distinct line that separated blacks and whites and kept the one race subordinate and subservient and the other privileged and powerful. With whites so heavily outnumbered in Sunflower County and on the farm—the plantation was home to hundreds of black workers—the Eastlands and other planting families relied on rigid boundaries to maintain their sense of safety and supremacy. Theirs was a segregated world, but that term can be misleading because it conjures up urban images of "white" and "colored" lunch counters, waiting rooms, and water fountains. On the plantation, the lives of blacks and whites were intertwined on a daily basis. There was no need for signs or other material manifestations of segregation because the rules were understood—blacks could not challenge the word of whites; they had to defer to white supervision; they could not enter the plantation office. The Eastland parents did not instruct their children on the proper relationship between the races, and they did not discuss their family's role in racial violence. They did not have to. The culture of white supremacy—the separation, the subordination, the social distance—was "just there from the time you decipher your first sounds," Little Woods recalled. This "subliminal cultural conditioning" trained both black children and white children to follow the racial rules without questioning.[19]

Blacks and whites on the plantation inhabited "two worlds that lived side by side," Anne remembered. "There was no interaction at all except in the servant relationship." Black families lived a hundred yards away, but the Eastlands had more social interaction with white families who lived across town or in other counties. Even when blacks worked closely with the family, as Willie Jackson did for decades as a water puller and yard man, they never gained the respect accorded a white visitor. Jackson never had a conversation with Eastland himself and made sure never to touch the Eastland daughters when he took them on horse rides across the plantation. So long as the social hierarchy was understood, whites felt secure enough to develop close relationships with individual blacks, particularly women. The Eastland children adored the black women who nursed them, cooked for them, and helped raise them. At the time, they assumed that the feelings were mutual; looking back from the vantage point of the twenty-first century, however, they are not so sure. "We loved them and they loved us, or at least we felt they did," Anne recalled in a 2001 interview. Sue shared her sense of uncertainty: "I felt like, and it may not have been true, but I felt like all the people on the place were very, very devoted to Mother and Daddy." Sunflower County whites by and large shared this sense of black contentment. "Were the Negroes oppressed in those days?" wrote one white Sunflower County native in 1990. "We didn't think so. We thought they were happy and contented. No other thought ever entered our minds."[20]

The Eastland children may have loved the domestic help as individuals, but they also learned to fear black culture in general. Sunflower County in the 1930s remained a violent, dangerous place, for both blacks and whites. Shortly after James and Libby moved back to the farm, the white plantation manager was murdered in broad daylight by another white man, a disgruntled former blacksmith. Most of the violence, however, was committed by blacks against blacks. In deference to planters' need for labor, white authorities ignored most crimes with black victims. Knife fights, brawls, and other altercations were relatively common among Eastland plantation workers. In his written reports to Eastland about conditions on the farm, the plantation book-keeper would take note if there were "no fights or killings on the place." The children sometimes witnessed violence among the workers, but more often they heard adults tell tales of sordid black behavior, stories that made it seem as if blacks "were children or as if they were not civilized," Anne recalled. "It was understood that they didn't have the same visceral values we had and you had to cut them some slack for that."[21]

Despite the perceived danger that blacks posed, whites could walk with impunity into black homes or through the black crowds that thronged Doddsville's main strip on Saturday nights. They could do so because of the strength of white supremacy, which established strict, if unwritten, rules regarding not only the personal interactions that took place on the plantation but also the public world of politics and social life. Maintaining white supremacy was a primary goal of politics. Planters had an effective monopoly on political power in the region. In the half century after 1890, when Mississippi became the first state to disenfranchise blacks, politics became essentially a white man's game. Political power was skewed toward large Delta planters whose representation was inflated by the area's large, unregistered black population. Despite their numeric superiority, blacks could not wield political power because they faced two almost insurmountable hurdles: the poll tax and the literacy test. Prospective voters had to pay an annual $2 tax for two consecutive years before being allowed to cast a ballot, a provision that limited access to the polls, particularly for people eking out a subsistence existence on the plantation. Even more effective, however, was the subjective literacy test. Those blacks with the means and the temerity to pay their poll tax then had to read and verbally interpret a portion of the state constitution to the satisfaction of the county registrar. "This test is admittedly designed to prevent Negroes from voting," Hortense Powdermaker noted. "No white person in charge of it would admit that a Negro's interpretation was correct. Knowing this, the Negroes make no attempt to qualify."[22]

Though white politicians differed vehemently on economic and social issues, they remained united on race. As the editor of the *Sunflower Tocsin* lectured to white politicians who sought to bring "the

Negro issue" into a campaign, "For the sake of peace, the prosperity of the State, let the negro alone in his contentment, except to encourage him and assist him in working out his destiny" as a manual laborer. For all intents and purposes, by the time Jim Eastland returned to the farm in the mid-1930s blacks in Sunflower County did not vote, hold office, or wield any sort of political power. The brief flowering of black political freedom during Reconstruction had long since faded. "Local self-government is, of course, based on the postulate of white domination," Yale sociologist John Dollard observed dryly in *Caste and Class in a Southern Town*, his extraordinary study of Depression-era Sunflower County. "It is part of the Negro's caste 'place' that he does not vote and does not complain about being unable to do so." Dire consequences awaited any black person who stepped out of that place. Though lynching declined throughout the 1920s and 1930s, the threat remained palpable. Without political power, there was no legal defense against the threat. "No Negro man is safe," Powdermaker wrote, "and every Negro knows it."[23]

The strength of white supremacy kept the Eastland children isolated from the surrounding black majority and insulated from the perceived threats that blacks posed. Yet the Eastlands' livelihood and lifestyle—indeed, the entire plantation world of Sunflower County and the Delta as a whole—depended upon the labor of the impoverished blacks whose cabins dotted the landscape. Without masses of unskilled, relatively docile black workers, there could be no cotton economy, no thriving plantations, no amassed fortunes. Planters recognized their utter dependence upon black labor. Washington County planter Alfred Stone wrote in 1908 that the Mississippi River levees "upon which the Delta depends for protection from floods have been erected mainly by the Negro, and the daily labour in field and town, in planting and building, in operating gins and compresses and oil mills, in moving trains, in handling the great staple of the country—all, in fact, that makes the life behind these earthen ramparts—is but the Negro's daily toil." Black sweat made whites rich. "We must keep the darkies as workers," one white woman explained to Hortense Powdermaker in the 1930s, "because we can't do without them." As James Eastland's own son, Woods, observed, "The lifestyle of the landowners of the Delta was built on one thing: abundant, dirt-cheap labor." That labor came from Sunflower County's masses of black sharecroppers, folks such as the Townsend family up the road in Ruleville.[24]

"LIFE WAS WORSE THAN HARD"

Like James Eastland, Fannie Lou Hamer was reared to assume a fixed place in Sunflower County society. Born Fannie Lou Townsend on October 6, 1917, she was the twentieth and last child of two share-croppers, James Lee and Lou Ella Bramlett Townsend. She lived most of her life only about five miles from the Eastland home in Doddsville, but hers was a different world, one of hunger, disease, and unremit-ting labor. She was born and raised in a rigidly circumscribed world where limited education, economic opportunities, and political power forced black sharecroppers like her into a subordinate role in most as-pects of daily life. Although a global cotton economy depended in part upon her and her fellow sharecroppers, young Fannie Lou's awareness of the universe beyond the plantation was minimal. Lacking opportu-nities to pursue political and educational ambitions, she and many blacks in Sunflower County turned instead to the one institution that offered dignity and hope: the church. Through her Baptist faith, she developed a sense of a larger world beyond the plantation: the king-dom of God, which emphasized justice and freedom.[25]

The Townsends, like the Eastlands, had a family history that bore the scars of Mississippi's tortured heritage of racial violence and eco-nomic exploitation. Fannie Lou's grandmother, Liza Bramlett, was a slave who was raped by a series of white owners and forced to bear twenty of their children. "This man would keep her long as he want to and then he would trade her off for a little heifer calf," recalled Fannie Lou's sister, Laura Ratliff. "Then the other man would get her and keep her as long as he want." Her grandmother's experience was a les-son in coerced integration that Hamer learned as a child and never forgot. Though she did not often speak of her grandmother in public, she did talk directly of the "special plight" of black women. "We was used as black women, over and over and over," Hamer told an audience in

1971. Liza Bramlett gave birth to twenty-three children in all, only three of whom were born of a consensual relationship with a black man. Lou Ella Bramlett, Hamer's mother, was one of them.[26]

Lou Ella married James Townsend in 1891, and the couple raised their six girls and fourteen boys in Montgomery County, Mississippi. In 1919, when Fannie Lou was two years old, the family packed up and moved two counties west to Sunflower County. Though they had moved less than a hundred miles, the Townsends had crossed into a different world. They left behind the rolling hills of Montgomery County and headed across the flat expanse of Sunflower. Today, the drive from the Hills into the Delta offers a stark, sudden contrast as one descends the final, forested hill and sees miles of orderly fields spreading out to the horizon. For the Townsends, the shift likely would have been less jarring, for the thin, newly graveled roads could barely contain the clambering vines and overhanging oaks and cypress that still dominated the view. As their wagon bounced toward Ruleville, they could see stump-strewn cotton fields hacked from the wandering wilderness, fields bounded less by fences than by lines of jungle.

The Townsends were part of a massive internal migration of black southerners that came to be known as the first Great Migration. Sharecroppers had always been mobile—the freedom to pick up and leave a plantation was often the only freedom they had—but the migration that began shortly before World War I was qualitatively and quantitatively different. More than half a million blacks left the South between 1916 and 1919, with another million leaving in the 1920s. Their flight was triggered by two causes, one tiny and one massive—a bug the size of fingernail and a war of unprecedented scale.[27]

Across the cotton South, black sharecroppers abandoned the fields as the plantation system shuddered in the face of a diminutive but deadly enemy: the boll weevil. The intrepid weevil, which had crossed the border from Mexico in the early twentieth century, feasted upon the precious white fiber that lay hidden inside each cotton boll. Its arrival in a particular area triggered a devastating economic chain reaction. A weevil infestation would wipe out a whole year's worth of crops. Faced with massive losses, planters tried all sorts of methods to stave off the weevil—they planted their rows east to west to put more sun on the weevils, they enlisted tenants' wives and children to pick off the weevils one at a time, they planted seeds twice as far apart. Nothing worked. Most planters would not or could not commit the time and money necessary for a collective response to the weevil, a management blunder that led to soil erosion, a loss of fertility, and a further decrease in production. Coupled with floods that swamped Mississippi in 1912 and 1913, the weevil's destruction left sharecroppers with little cotton to pick. Thousands of workers abandoned the fields or were evicted from their land.[28]

While the weevil pushed black workers off the farm, an invigorated defense industry pulled them into factories, encouraging a black exodus to cities north and south. After initially disrupting world markets, the outbreak of hostilities in Europe in 1914 gave American industry a tremendous boost. As demand for war materiel boomed and immigration from Europe fizzled, labor recruiters ran to the rural South in hopes of luring disgruntled or desperate farm laborers from the fields. The *Chicago Defender*, the NAACP's *Crisis*, and other black publications touted the North as a "promised land" of economic opportunity and racial equality compared to the oppressive South, and so many of their southern readers believed them that worried white officials in the South sought to ban the spread of the magazines. Inspired by visions of a better life, more than a hundred thousand Mississippi blacks hopped aboard the Illinois Central Railroad that ran northward through Sunflower County and the Delta and on to Memphis, Chicago, and all points north. Between 1910 and 1920, the percentage of Chicago blacks who had Mississippi roots quintupled.[29]

Yet for all the blacks who fled to factories, many more migrants, such as the Townsend family, simply switched fields. Like the rest of the Delta, Sunflower County was booming when the Townsends moved there in 1919. Largely spared the devastation of the boll weevil, Sunflower County's cotton planters weathered the initial crisis in the global cotton market when the war broke out. "The higher cotton goes the broader grows our smile," gushed the planter-friendly editor of the *Sunflower Tocsin* as cotton prices soared in 1915. By 1917, planters enjoyed greater demand, higher prices, and less domestic competition, but the massive black migration triggered their recurrent fears of a labor shortage. As planters complained of "idlers" who refused to work, they used both sticks and carrots to keep black workers in the fields. A group of planters formed the Self-Preservation Loyalty League, which used patriotic appeals to justify its desire to "compel idlers and vagrants to do their part in the war"; the *Sunflower Tocsin* pondered sterner measures, calling for the Ku Klux Klan to come to the county to force blacks back to work.[30]

But the most effective inducement for workers was money— wages in some areas more than doubled, to $2 per hundred pounds picked. "Cotton picking demands as much money nowadays here as skilled mechanics received just a few years ago," grumbled the *Sunflower Tocsin* in 1919. Native Delta blacks still left the area in search of jobs in the North, but new people were "continually moving in from the hills to fill their places," one reporter noted. Sunflower County may not have been the "promised land" of the North—or even the promised land that it had been just a few decades earlier— but it seemed to offer black migrants such as the Townsends the op- portunity for better pay doing something familiar. Sunflower County's population exploded in the 1910s, growing by more than 60 percent to exceed 46,000 inhabitants—it now was the state's fourth-largest county and had nearly 700 people per square mile. Ruleville's popula- tion more than doubled, to 1,000. Like the Townsends, most of the migrants were black, as were roughly 75 percent of Sunflower County residents in 1920. "There are but few white laborers," acknowledged one county booster. "This field is left to the Negro, practically without competition."[31]

The Townsends arrived in Sunflower County at a particularly tense period in American race and labor relations. It was 1919, the Great War had ended, and thousands of servicemen returned home to a changed economic landscape that featured cities teeming with newly arrived black workers. Economic competition conspired with racial animosity to trigger frightfully violent postwar clashes between blacks and whites. After having fought in Europe to "make the world safe for democracy," many black veterans came home prepared to wage war on racism and inequality in America. "We return from fighting," wrote black leader W.E.B. Du Bois. "We return fighting." The spirit of the "New Negro" rejected the alleged subservience of the older genera- tion, preferring instead to challenge white power directly. From Mar- cus Garvey's United Negro Improvement Association (UNIA) to radical newspapers such as Harlem's *Crusader*, the early postwar period witnessed a seeming revolution in black consciousness. The worried editors of the *Sunflower Tocsin* feared a return to Reconstruction. Whites responded to black militancy with a shocking wave of violence. "Race riots"—the misleading term used to describe white rampages through black communities—erupted in Washington, Chicago, and two dozen other northern cities in the bloody summer of 1919, resulting in more than a hundred deaths.[32]

Black militancy and white violence spread far beyond the urban North. Across the South, white mobs tallied a record number of black lynching victims—eighty-nine in 1919 alone. But that official number masked the magnitude of the violence, particularly in cotton-growing areas such as Elaine, Arkansas, a town the size of Ruleville about eighty miles northwest of Sunflower County. Planters around Elaine sought to retract the economic gains their workers made during the war, and they began wholesale evictions in the spring of 1919. Black sharecroppers and tenants, led by war veterans, fought back by forming the Progressive Farmers and Household Union of America. Their success in uniting black workers frightened planters and white authorities, and violence erupted that October after a white railroad agent was killed during a shoot-out at a black church. Several days of white rioting resulted in the deaths of more than two hundred blacks, almost triple the official number of lynchings for the year.[33]

Sunflower County could not escape the tumult. In January 1921, a young black man, reportedly a nephew of one of the Elaine organizers, was hanged in the county for the alleged crime of molesting a white girl. The formation of a local chapter of Garvey's UNIA that same month made the front page of the *Ruleville Record*, manifesting the fears of the local white community. White leaders worked diligently to promote a docile labor force. "The intelligent, industrious, self-supporting negro is welcome," the Indianola Rotary Club wrote in a brochure designed to promote investment in Sunflower County. Unwanted was "the lazy, lying, crap-shooting, loafing, thieving negro" who undermined white authority.[34]

By 1924, when the brochure appeared, whites' postwar jitters had subsided and boosters touted the stability of the plantation world. "Today a planter owns a thousand acres and upward and the negro tenant tends the crops as in the days before the war," boosters wrote. Indeed, throughout the 1920s the Townsends and other black families in Sunflower County tended the crops much as previous generations had. Farming techniques in the area had changed little since the days of Luther Holbert. Human muscle and animal power drove the county economy, and the family spent its days working the fields without the benefit of the agricultural machinery that was beginning to make its mark on farms in the West. The first tractors had made their appearance in Sunflower County during the war, when high cotton prices and labor costs had encouraged a few adventurous planters to experiment with the machines. Most plantations, however, remained completely dependent on sharecroppers and their mules. As Booker T. Washington once observed, "The Southern economy is based on the Negro and the mule."[35]

Fannie Lou and her family found work on E.W. Brandon's plantation, along the Quiver River a few miles east of Ruleville. "The Richness of the Soil Makes Living Easy and the Folks there make Life Worthwhile," Sunflower County boosters claimed. But life was anything but easy for the Townsend family. As unskilled agricultural laborers, Fannie Lou's parents faced limited economic choices. Sunflower County was cotton country, and 96 percent of the cotton was picked by sharecroppers and other tenants. Because sharecropping did not always provide enough to feed the family, her parents had to find creative ways to make ends meet. To supplement the family's income, Hamer's father worked as a bootlegger and a Baptist preacher, while her mother labored as a domestic in white homes. They also "scrapped" cotton to supplement their income, walking from plantation to plantation after the fields had been picked to scrape the last bits of fiber off the stalk. Done in the cold weather of late fall and early winter, scrapping cotton was particularly difficult, but it could often bring an extra five-hundred-pound bale that provided much-needed cash.[36]

Despite these arduous efforts, Fannie Lou's family, like other black families who lived on Sunflower County plantations, dwelled in wretched conditions. "By any modern standards of hygiene," observed Hortense Powdermaker, "the living quarters on most of the plantations would be considered uninhabitable." The Townsend family rarely had enough to eat. Dinners of unseasoned greens and flour gravy left young Fannie Lou painfully hungry. As she lay on her bed of dry grass stuffed in a cotton sack, she had recurrent dreams about eating cornbread or the rare Christmas treat, apples and oranges. "Life was worse than hard," she recalled of her childhood. "It was *horrible!* We never did have enough to eat, and I don't remember how old I was when I got my first pair of shoes, but I was a big girl. Mama tried to keep our feet warm by wrapping them in rags and tying them with string." The lack of adequate food and clothing led inevitably to disease—pellagra was widespread among blacks in Sunflower County. Though Fannie Lou managed to avoid pellagra, she endured a bout with polio, which left her with a limp that plagued her for the rest of her life and earned her the nickname "Hip."[37]

While James Eastland had a close relationship with his dominating father, Fannie Lou Townsend revered her strong mother, Lou Ella. As an adult, Fannie Lou rarely spoke of her father, but she often recalled the influence of her mother. Despite (and because of) the indignities of life under Jim Crow, Lou Ella Townsend encouraged her child to be proud of herself and her race. "She was one woman in the state of Mississippi who didn't let no white man beat her kids," Fannie Lou remembered later. "Sometimes when things were so bad and I'd start thinking maybe it would be better if we were white, she'd insist we should be proud to be black, telling us, 'Nobody will respect you unless you stand up for yourself.'" Lou Ella carried a gun out to the fields every day, and her willingness to stand up for her children helped protect Fannie Lou from physical abuse.[38]

Yet Lou Ella Townsend could not protect her polio-afflicted daughter from the cotton fields. Like their parents, black children in Sunflower County did not have a choice about participating in the cotton economy. Young Fannie Lou Townsend was no exception—she began picking cotton at the age of six. The year she was "tricked" into picking, the nation was in the throes of a heated debate over a constitutional amendment to outlaw child labor. Sunflower County's planters were adamantly opposed. "It is a far different proposition from the white factory hands of the north and east to the colored farm children of the south," the *Sunflower Tocsin* editorialized in early 1925. "This section cannot endorse anything that cuts out any farm labor." The owner of Fannie Lou's plantation certainly agreed. That spring, he fig-ured out a way to get the young Townsend girl to join her family in the fields. While she was playing near her family's wooden shack, he came up to her and asked innocently, "Can you pick cotton?" Little Fannie Lou answered that she did not know if she could or not. "Yes, you can," he encouraged. He offered to give her a reward of sardines, a quarter pound of cheese, some Cracker Jack, and a gingerbread cookie from the plantation commissary if she would pick thirty pounds of cotton that week. The excited Fannie Lou hurried out to the fields, ea-ger to earn her reward. Her parents did not discourage her, though they insisted that she pick her own thirty pounds—they would not simply give it to her. So Fannie Lou picked and picked, finally reach-ing the magic thirty. She turned it in to the plantation owner, and sure enough he took her to the plantation store to get her reward. As she soon realized, however, the owner now expected her to work every day. Recalling the incident later, she observed, "What had happened was he was trapping me into beginning the work I was to keep doing and I never did get out of his debt again." For the second week, he ex-pected sixty pounds out of the six-year-old, and this time there would be no treats from the store. Fannie Lou was in the fields to stay.[39]

Working in the fields was a grueling experience. As one laborer on the Eastland family plantation remembered, sharecroppers "worked from sunup to sundown on any given day." Rosie Cole, who worked for the Eastlands for several decades, recalled that she had to get up at 2 A.M. to begin preparing the breakfasts and dinners for other work-ers. Typically, the rest of the crew arose at 4:30 A.M. to eat a breakfast of fried okra, salt pork, and tomato gravy before heading out to the field by five o'clock. They worked until roughly eleven, when heat and hunger drove them to the shade for dinner, their midday meal. At about 1 P.M., they returned to work till dark, a workday from "can to can't"—from the time you can see in the morning until you can no longer see at night. "We worked," Hamer recalled. "Wasn't no two ways about it."[40]

Sharecroppers worked, indeed, in conditions that defy compari-son in modern America. Outside all day, they endured the stifling heat and humidity of Sunflower County summers without ever feeling the coolness of air-conditioning. Although county boosters boasted of "head-high cotton," most stalks grew to about waist level. Pickers had to stoop to remove the fiber from the stalks as they trudged down the rows with long croker sacks trailing behind them. Armed with sharp spikes, the stubborn stalk yielded its prize reluctantly. Pickers' fingers quickly became callused as they struggled to remove the bolls swiftly. As the sun faded, the sweaty workers attracted mosquitoes and other pests that could bore through their soaked clothes, and they had no spray repellant to keep the bugs at bay. Fannie Lou always resented picking cotton, but she learned the "art" (as she later described picking) well. By the time she was thirteen years old, she could pick almost two hundred pounds a day—for which she received about a dollar or two of Depression wages. As an adult she became known for her picking prowess; some days she could gather more than three hundred pounds, outpicking many men.[41]

No matter how much she picked, however, she could not extricate herself or her family from the world that cotton made. When Fannie Lou was twelve, her father managed to earn enough money to rent some land and buy mules and a cultivator, thus moving a step up the economic ladder from sharecropping. "We were doing pretty well," she recalled later. Her father had bought a car and begun fixing up the house. But then someone poisoned their livestock. "We knowed this white man had done it," Hamer insisted. "He stirred up a gallon of Paris Green [poison] with the feed. When we got out there, one mule was already dead. The other two mules and the cow had their stomachs all swelled up. It was too late to save 'em." The experience "knocked us right back down flat. We never did get back up again." The motive for the economic sabotage lay not in anything that Hamer's family had done wrong. On the contrary, "that white man did it just because we were gettin' somewhere," Hamer argued. "White people never like to see Negroes get a little success." Returning to sharecropping was a devastating experience, one that burned itself in Fannie Lou's memory; years later, she would tell the story repeatedly to show how whites had derailed her family's economic progress.[42]

The experience ended Fannie Lou's formal education. She had been a solid student at the local school, winning spelling bees and doing well in reading, but she never made it past the sixth grade. Homework always played second fiddle to fieldwork. Her family's poverty made it difficult for her to attend school—during the winter months her family could not always supply the clothing and shoes for her to walk to school. Furthermore, the schools she and other black students had to attend were woefully inadequate. In 1929–30, when Fannie Lou stopped going to school, Mississippi spent about $6 annually per black pupil, less than 20 percent of what it spent on each white pupil; the average value of white schools was ten times higher than the value of black schools. Black children had to settle for hand-me-down books discarded by the white schools, and their facilities often lacked enough basic amenities such as desks and seats. "The colored schools of Sunflower County are in deplorable condition," white officials acknowledged in a 1937 survey.[43]

More damaging to black students, perhaps, was the curriculum, which inculcated children with a sense of black inferiority. In a 1930s study commissioned by the National Education Association, the state teachers colleges surveyed Mississippi textbooks and found that they systematically ignored black contributions to American society and degraded black culture. "The elementary-school course of study ignores the Negro almost entirely," the authors concluded, and in all the English books, "there are no readings from Negro authors, no readings about Negroes, no references to Negro poets, short story writers, novelists, or artists." Slavery was depicted as a "pleasant" experience, and in general "the Negro is simply ignored save when problems of white people bring him to the center of attention, and then his treatment is in terms of the white man's advantage." When black figures did appear in school lessons, they often represented stereotypes rather than reality. As an adult, Hamer recalled reading stories featuring Epaminandus, a silly black boy whose exaggerated features and idiotic behavior made him a laughingstock. The point of this kind of education was to keep blacks in their place. "No matter how much education you give them," one white Sunflower County teacher emphasized in the 1930s, "a million years from now, a nigger will still be a nigger in the South."[44]

White planters' vision for blacks focused on labor, not education; hence the school year deferred to the planting season. When Fannie Lou was "coming up," she only went to school after the cotton was picked and ginned in the fall and before planting time in the spring, essentially during the four months from December until March, when "you didn't have absolutely nothing to do." By contrast, white children in Sunflower County attended school for seven to nine months during the year. The problem with education, as Governor James Vardaman pithily had put it, was that it "only spoils a good field hand." Planters feared that book learning would sow unwanted ideas in the minds of their laborers. John Dollard noted that planters had welcomed black churches on the plantation, but they resisted establishing schools. While churches "helped to keep the status quo by offering an illusory consolation to the Negroes, the school threatened, on the other hand, to make accessible to every human being the ideas of personal dignity which were dangerous to the caste system." Sunflower County planters resisted the establishment of Rosenwald Schools, named for Chicago businessman Julius Rosenwald, who spent millions of dollars building schools for black children across the rural South. Planters feared that the northern philanthropists who funded the schools would be able to influence their workers. Local planters did, however, support schools that trained blacks to fill their appointed role in Sunflower County life. In the Eastlands' hometown of Doddsville, white planters eagerly supported the Delta Industrial Institute, which had been founded in 1917 to train black children in vocational trades and other suitable endeavors. The superintendent gratefully acknowledged planters' "hearty cooperation and financial support" for his school; James Eastland's uncle Oliver sat on the school's board of directors.[45]

Without an education, Fannie Lou had few economic alternatives beyond sharecropping and domestic work. As the youngest child, she was discouraged from following her brothers and sisters who had fled to the North in search of opportunity; she was responsible for taking care of her aging parents, particularly after her father suffered a stroke and her mother was nearly blinded in a wood-chopping accident in the late 1930s. She lived at home and helped her parents sharecrop until she was nearly thirty. Now a grown woman, she stood a stout five feet four inches tall. In her late twenties, she grew close to a tall tractor driver on a nearby plantation, Perry "Pap" Hamer. Five years her senior, the lean, six-foot-three Pap Hamer had made a similar journey from the Mississippi hills to the Delta in search of economic opportunity, only to end up sharecropping. The two married in 1944, and Fannie Lou moved into Hamer's home on W.D. Marlow's plantation in Ruleville, where Pap had worked for a dozen years.

The Hamers did not have children of their own—Fannie Lou gave birth to two stillborn children—but they raised two girls from the community. Dorothy Jean, the elder girl, was the child of an unmarried mother who could not afford to take care of her; Vergie Lee, nine years younger, came to the Hamer home at age five months after she had been scalded when a tub of boiling water spilled, and her family proved unable to provide for her. After the family moved down near the river on the Marlow place, Fannie Lou became a timekeeper, an important post that involved keeping track of the number of hours worked, bales picked, and money owed each field hand. Like her parents, she and Pap supplemented their sharecropper income by hunting, doing work in white houses, bootlegging, and running a juke joint in the winter. They had what Fannie Lou described as a "pretty decent" home, with running water indoors, a bathtub, and an indoor toilet. The toilet never flushed, however, so they still used an outhouse. Hamer found the outhouse particularly degrading after she discovered that Ole Honey, the Marlows' family dog, had its own indoor bathroom in the big house.[46]

As adults, the Hamers could not escape the grinding poverty in which both had grown up. Yet they could not publicly object to their condition without fear of retribution. "There was no protest," Hamer's friend L.C. Dorsey recalled. "There was no saying, I'm not going to take that. There was nobody else you could appeal to. *Nobody else*." Despite their lack of institutional power, black sharecroppers did not entirely acquiesce. Resistance to the planter's power could not be overt and confrontational—blacks had no recourse through the courts or the police, and landowners legally could do what they pleased. Instead, their resistance had to be subtle, covert, quiet. One black informant explained to John Dollard that he, like other blacks in Sunflower County, had "a kind of dual personality, two roles, one that he is forced to play with white people and one the 'real Negro' as he appears in his dealings with his own people." As Hamer told an interviewer in 1975, "Now we have been some of the greatest actors on earth, 'cause we could smile when we would see [white people] coming and they'd get about ten feet and we would say—you know it wouldn't be right to put in the book what we would say." Older blacks in Sunflower County to this day still refer to the "white folks' smile" to describe the behavior that poet Paul Lawrence Dunbar described in "We Wear the Mask":

> We smile, but, O great Christ, our cries
> To thee from tortured souls arise.
> We sing, but oh the clay is vile
> Beneath our feet, and long the mile;
> But let the world dream otherwise,
> We wear the mask![47]

While the Eastlands and other whites saw contentment and happiness, Hamer and her fellow blacks understood a different reality and sought to fight back against it where they could. Hamer used her position as timekeeper to "get back" at the owner, to repay past debts without him ever knowing. She was the sharecropper closest to the cotton balance, and she recorded how much each cropper had picked. She could see how the owner cheated the workers through false calculations and inaccurate readings, and she fought back by using her own weight on the field scales whenever the owner was away, so that the pickers earned more. "So, I would take my 'p' [counterweight] to the field and use mine until I would see him coming, you know, because his was loaded and I know it was beating people like that," she recalled. "I didn't know what to do and all I could do is rebel in the only way I could rebel." This limited, individual resistance helped preserve her strong sense of self, even if it did not ultimately change her living conditions.[48]

Lacking the tangible, worldly power they needed to improve their lives, Hamer and other Sunflower County blacks turned to a source of intangible, otherworldly strength they considered far greater than the plantation owner: God. Across Sunflower County, in Hamer's time and still today, scores of white clapboard churches salted the landscape. These rural churches, often with memberships of just a dozen or so families, bustled with life all Sunday long, their rollicking, three- or four-hour services audible far beyond the thin walls.

Baptized in the Stranger's Home Baptist Church at age twelve, Hamer followed her parents' example. She developed a strong Christian faith that sustained her during difficult times in her childhood and afterward. Religion gave her an alternative to the dismal world of white supremacy, opening up the kingdom of God that promised equality and spiritual fulfillment. No matter how degrading black lives on earth may have been, Hamer believed that all people were equal before God. Her fundamentalist belief in the Bible and the ultimate righteousness of Jesus gave her the power to endure the indignities of Jim Crow.[49]

The black church in the rural South had always been a double-edged sword. As Dollard suggested, Sunflower County planters supported black churches as a means of pacifying their laborers. This strategy had its roots in slavery, when white slaveowners used Christianity (particularly Ephesians 6:5, "Slaves, obey your earthly masters with fear and trembling") to control black anger toward the "peculiar institution." After emancipation, blacks enthusiastically built their own separate religious institutions, but political and economic realities kept the new churches dependent on white goodwill. So long as preachers focused on the afterworld and refrained from political agitation, whites were happy to give churches funding and relative freedom to run their services. "The Negro church could enjoy this freedom so long as it offered no threat to the white man's dominance in both economic and social relations," one black critic noted acidly. "And, on the whole, the Negro's church was not a threat to the white domination and aided the Negro to become accommodated to an inferior status." White anthropologist Hortense Powdermaker acknowledged the church's role in quelling dissent in Sunflower County. "In both its secular and its religious character, it serves as an antidote, a palliative, an escape," she wrote in the 1930s. "By helping the Negro to endure the status quo, this institution has been a conservative force, tending to relieve and counteract the discontents that make for rebellion."[50]

The black church in Sunflower County placed a greater emphasis on brotherly love and forgiveness than on harsh judgment. From sermons, at Sunday school, and in the home, black children learned a philosophy of Christian love that would find an echo in the nonviolent message of Martin Luther King Jr. decades later. "If we hate [whites], we poison ourselves," preachers and teachers stressed to their charges.

"Christ loved His enemies and asked for their forgiveness; we should have Christ within us." Hamer's mother had instilled the same values in her children. "Ain't no such of a thing as I can hate and hope to see God's face," Hamer insisted as an adult. The focus of sermons and Sunday school lessons in many black Sunflower County churches was on the afterlife, not the material world that Fannie Lou and her family had to endure. Black congregants were told to concentrate their energies on earning their way to heaven through peaceful accommodation, not agitation. Having attended numerous black church services in Sunflower County in 1931, Powdermaker placed the responsibility for this mentality on the church leadership. The preacher's "attitude toward his own people still savors strongly of the white masters from whom the Negroes first received their religion," she observed. "It is the white man's concept of the 'nigger' that the colored preacher gives." Preachers encouraged their flocks to be content with their lot in life. As civil rights leader and Clarksdale native Aaron Henry remembered of his church upbringing, "The theory was that the worse off you were on earth, the better chance you had at the pearly gates." Indeed, during the 1930s and 1940s, church leaders did not inspire Hamer or other sharecroppers to challenge white power overtly, a sin that Hamer did not soon forget or forgive. When she became active in the civil rights movement decades later, Hamer often railed against "chicken-eating preachers" and other timid church leaders who she believed held her people back.[51]

While church leaders often preached accommodation, spiritual resistance to the assumptions of white supremacy ran deep. The church did tend to "suppress discontent with mores in general," Dollard noted, but it also was "a center of social solidarity for Negroes." In a world that savaged her sense of herself as a human being worthy of respect, the church offered Hamer a refuge of dignity and decency. "The only thing we've had in Mississippi that we could really call our own is the church," she remembered. Powdermaker agreed: in Sunflower County, "the Negro church is the one institution where the colored people of the community are in full control." It transformed lowly, degraded sharecroppers such as Hamer into proud, enthusiastic parishioners. Hamer and other blacks who toiled all week as cotton pickers or maids in the white man's fields and houses came to church dressed in their Sunday best, ready to assume respected positions—deacon, choir member, church mother. Churches in Sunflower County, Dollard realized, "provide a splendid opportunity for the social and political training of Negroes." Writing in 1933, Benjamin Mays and Joseph Nicholson emphasized the important role the black church played in preserving a black sense of self. "The opportunity found in the Negro church to be recognized, and to be 'somebody,' has stimulated the pride and preserved the self-respect of many Negroes who would have been entirely beaten by life, and possibly completely submerged."[52]

In addition to such intangible benefits, the church also gave Hamer and other blacks, male and female, the opportunity to develop leadership skills, exercise responsibility, and exert influence over other people. The church, Powdermaker found, "provides an avenue for administrative and executive abilities which have little or no other outlet." Clifton Taulbert, who grew up in nearby Glen Allan, remembered, "The church was where leadership skills were honed and practiced." Women played a particularly strong leadership role. Black churches embraced the same patriarchal hierarchy that white churches did, but black women often wielded extraordinary power. "Although the preachers and officers of the church are men," Powdermaker observed, "it is largely the women who run the affairs of the church, and who assume financial responsibility for its maintenance." They also exerted influence in their "invisible" leadership roles, particularly as the venerated "church mothers" or the respected song leaders. Singing helped cultivate community, offer an outlet for suppressed emotions, and pass traditions from one generation to the next. Country churches such as Stranger's Home offered emotional, boisterous services featuring hours of sweaty singing and interactive sermons, and women generally supplied the "amens" and "hallelujahs" that gave the services their emotional power. Many a visitor to a rural church in Sunflower County has been awed by the sense of spirit—even the stiff Yalie John Dollard loosened up and enjoyed the "continuous surge of affirmation" that swelled from the congregation when he spoke at a service. Growing up in the church, Fannie Lou Hamer internalized this confidence and developed a forceful, emotional speaking style that complemented her rich voice and ability to "raise a song."[53]

White planters may have hoped that Christianity would make blacks docile and deferential, but Hamer and other blacks reshaped the religion to provide spiritual and emotional sustenance to endure the hardships imposed by rigid segregation. Ever since slaves first flocked to Christian churches during the 1700s, one historian explains, they "did not simply become Christians; they fashioned Christianity to fit their own peculiar experience of enslavement in America." While whites emphasized Ephesians and Jesus' acquiescence to worldly power, Hamer looked to other parts of the Bible for inspiration. The story that captivated her attention, the narrative that became a running metaphor for her during the civil rights movement, was the book of Exodus. Aside from the parables and life of Jesus himself, no other part of the Bible had a more pronounced influence on her understanding of freedom. Much of what Hamer found attractive and compelling about Christianity was her identification of the Israelites' struggle against Pharaoh and the Egyptians in Exodus with the black struggle against Jim Crow in America. The language and people of Exodus—Pharaoh, the Promised Land, Moses—gave her a conceptual framework for understanding the oppression in which she lived and the freedom she and her people craved. True freedom involved creating a kingdom of God on earth, where all of God's children shared equally in the opportunity to fulfill God's will and enjoy the fruits of His creation. At heart, freedom was economic; it entailed a fair distribution of God's wealth and an equal chance to earn it. At one 1930s Sunflower County church service that Hortense Powdermaker attended, an old man spoke passionately, with nods of approval and accompanying murmurs of support, and emphasized that economic equality, not social equality, was what blacks wanted more than anything else.[54]

By cultivating black self-respect and providing practical experience during a time of rigid white supremacy, the church did more than simply pacify workers such as Hamer; it also provided them with an institutional rock of spiritual resistance upon which more overt political activism could be built. But their deep religious faith could not change the fundamental fact of Sunflower County life: planters such as Jim Eastland and his father had social, economic, and political power. Sharecroppers such as Fannie Lou Hamer did not. Hamer and

Eastland shared the same patch of God's earth, but they certainly did not share it equally. For the planter's son and his family, the lush fields of Sunflower County yielded a stable and secure world structured by natural hierarchy, a contented and comfortable life protected by the economic, political, and social walls of white supremacy. For the share-croppers' daughter and her family, those same fields offered a world of unremitting toil and occasional terror, a life of limitations that con-trasted sharply with the opportunities the Eastlands enjoyed but which offered its own spiritual rewards. For both, the fields produced in abundance the crop around which their lives, and all life in Sun-flower County, revolved: cotton.

3

"Cotton Is Dynamite": New Deals in Sunflower County

Cotton in the twenty-first century is ubiquitous, perhaps the most universally used agricultural product in the world. From T-shirts to X-ray film, from dollar bills to diapers, we use cotton every day. Yet relatively few Americans have ever seen the plant in its natural habitat. Take an autumn drive along sinuous Highway 49 from the Eastland plantation in Doddsville toward Fannie Lou Hamer's hometown five miles north, and you will see snowy fields stretching to the horizon as the year's cotton crop awaits the harvest that will culminate the annual cycle. Six months earlier, the stalks had started out as dark brown, balloon-shaped seeds, about the size of unpopped kernels of corn. Light green shoots bearing their trademark trident leaves burst from the soil just a few weeks later, reaching heights ranging from fourteen inches to six or seven feet. As the days turn humid and temperatures rise in midsummer, pink and white blossoms appear, shadowing the four-seamed, football-shaped bolls that begin to form along the branches. By August, the blossoms fade and the most ambitious bolls pop open to expose the white treasure hidden inside. Pull off the road and pick some cotton by hand—you may be surprised to find that the boll is not soft and clean like the cotton swabs you can buy at the nearby Wal-Mart. Instead, it has several hard seeds hidden amidst fiber, woody chips, and flecks of dirt. Only after the boll spends some time at the gin does the thin fiber emerge straight and pure, white gold ready for its infinite industrial uses.

This plant that you hold in your hand played a starring role in the drama of James Eastland, Fannie Lou Hamer, and the world they shared. Long after she had stopped picking cotton to work on civil rights full time, Hamer described herself as a sharecropper and saw her experiences in the fields as fundamental to her perspective on the world. Eastland, too, saw his connection to the land as a defining characteristic. To the end of his days, he considered himself first and foremost a man of the soil, a planter whose farm was his first love, his refuge. "The best fertilizer is the owner's foot," he believed, and even after he became a U.S. senator he returned to his farm nearly every weekend and spent many afternoons in the plantation office or riding his horse around the fields. Cotton, the crop on which both planter and picker depended, created the context in which they matured as young adults. In Sunflower County, cotton meant "far more to the community than agriculture," anthropologist Hortense Powdermaker suggested in her landmark 1930s study of the area. "It is because of cotton that the slaves were brought here, because of cotton that Negroes now outnumber Whites two to one, because of cotton that the plantation system developed under slavery has been modified to continue 'after freedom.'" And, she might have added, it was because of cotton that Eastland, Hamer, and their neighbors were connected to a global economy beyond their control. Cotton produced a "plantation mentality" that saddled blacks and whites with self-destructive and self-deluding attitudes that helped to ingrain persistent patterns of inequality into Sunflower County life. We need to look closely at this little plant to figure out how it came to wield such great power.[1]

"A DEFIANCE OF LOGIC AND PROBABILITY"

"Cotton obsessed, Negro obsessed, and flood ridden," wrote University of North Carolina sociologist Rupert Vance in 1932, the Delta "is the deepest South, the heart of Dixie, America's superplantation belt." At the Delta's geographic center, Sunflower County was perhaps the most cotton-obsessed place of all, the Delta's own superplantation county. Today, you might find catfish farms or soybean fields alongside Sunflower County's highways, but in 1930 nearly 90 percent of farmland was planted in cotton. Cotton defined life in Sunflower County throughout the 1930s. Powdermaker gave Indianola the fictitious name of "Cottonville" in her anthropological study. In its Mississippi travel guide, the Works Progress Administration (WPA) described Eastland's hometown of Doddsville as little more than a "plantation center for trading and shipping cotton." In the areas south of town, the WPA authors commented, "perhaps more cotton is grown per acre than in any other part of the state." That made Sunflower the most productive cotton-growing area in the most productive cotton-growing state in the most productive cotton-growing country in the world. Little else was grown. "A tenant," remarked one local teacher in the early 1930s, "was compelled to plant cotton up to his doorstep and was not permitted to have his own vegetable patch." The reliance on a single crop drove population growth. Planters felt the need to retain masses of workers year-round, even though the workers spent several months idle, in order to be prepared for the picking season, when every available hand was needed in the fields. As a result, with more than 66,000 residents in 1930, Sunflower County was among the most densely populated areas in the entire South.[2]

Cotton growing in Sunflower County and across the Delta became, in the eyes of planter David Cohn, "a secular religion, a mystique of the soil, an obsession, a defiance of logic and probability." It defied logic and probability partly because it was such a difficult, labor-intensive process. As we have seen, simply surviving in the swampy, snake-infested, mosquito-ridden Sunflower jungle was a challenge, both for whites, who had little natural immunity to malaria, and for blacks, who were forced to work in the stifling heat and humidity. Clearing the land required excruciating, time-consuming labor with handsaws and axes (not until the 1940s did gas-powered chain saws come into use). Teams of men and mules struggled to drain the bogs, saw down centuries-old cypress trees, and burn the remaining stumps to prepare the land for cotton cultivation. James Eastland's mother often talked about the fires—fires that burned all night to make the land ready for farming; Fannie Lou Hamer recalled how as a child she watched her axe-wielding mother fell massive trees "just like a man." Fannie Lou and her siblings gathered the brush and burned it. Even by the time Eastland returned to cotton farming in the 1930s, much of Sunflower County remained dense forest; on any given plantation, large sections of tangled wilderness loomed beyond where the rows stopped.[3]

The year in Sunflower County was not marked by a desk calendar; instead, it followed cotton's cycle of life. The cotton year began in the early spring, usually in March after the last freeze. Whole families of black men, women, and children trooped out of their cabins with their mules to cut down the old stalks and break the land in preparation for planting. They then walked carefully down the rows dropping seeds into the earth by hand, brushing soil over the seeds with their feet. By late April, they had completed most of the planting, and workers began the tedious process of "chopping" the cotton, a process that did not involve touching the crop at all. Rather, field hands used hoes to slash away the relentless weeds and vines that threatened to strangle or overwhelm the valuable and vulnerable young plants. Hamer preferred calling the process "hoeing the cotton." All summer long workers chopped, until the cotton bolls began to appear in mid- to late August. Then came the picking. For months on end, workers bent over the cotton plants and picked the thorny bolls, filling their long croker sacks with hundreds of pounds of fluff. Pickers often wore knee pads and shuffled along on their knees to reach the low-hanging bolls. Because bolls opened at different times, each field had to be picked multiple times; not until late November or even December could the laborers hope to get out of the fields and rest.[4]

Fannie Lou Hamer, like Eastland's workers and nearly all blacks in Sunflower County, was a sharecropper. Sharecropping, which had started out as a seemingly preferable alternative to supervised gang labor, had become by Hamer's time an inequitable system tilted heavily in favor of the planter. The problem, from the sharecroppers' perspective, was an imbalance of power. The Eastlands and other white planters wielded almost dictatorial authority in their local areas. They controlled the judicial system, law enforcement, and labor relations; they managed all aspects of agriculture and kept all financial records; they even determined the diet and amount of education their tenants received. The key to the planters' power lay in the credit system, which trapped sharecroppers and tenant farmers in a crushing cycle of debt. The trap was laid deliberately, Hortense Powdermaker discovered. White planters sought to perpetuate their workers' debt because "the belief is general among white people that the Negro is congenitally lazy and must be kept in debt in order to be made to work." Here's how it worked: At planting time in the spring, sharecroppers had to mortgage their future earnings to receive credit from the planter or a furnishing agent for the seed, equipment, and other items they needed to produce the crop. In Sunflower County, croppers got about $10 a month in credit through the summer and fall. This credit was issued in coupon books (not cash) that could only be used for food and supplies at the plantation's commissary, where prices tended to be 10 to 25 percent higher than in local stores. Local planters charged between 15 and 25 percent interest on their loans, an extraordinary rate justified in the planters' eyes by the risks of advancing money to potentially untrustworthy tenants. At "settlin' up time" near the end of the year, the planter ginned and sold the cotton, then deducted expenses and interest from the cropper's share. The cropper got whatever cash remained.[5]

All too often, there was nothing left—or so the planters claimed. Because the planters controlled the legal system, croppers were unable to challenge the figures in court, and the culture of white supremacy made even informally questioning the figures a dangerous act. A sharecropper who dared to ask about how a particular sum was calculated could be met with an angry retort: "Do you mean to call me a liar?" The word *liar* carried immense cultural weight, and the cropper likely would recognize the veiled threat lurking within the planter's response. (To this day, to call someone a "liar" in Sunflower County is considered socially unacceptable; the term is almost considered a curse word.) Though some Sunflower County planters kept scrupulously fair records, John Dollard found that many others routinely abused their power in an effort to keep workers in debt and thus maintain a stable workforce. Because workers frequently had a negative balance at "settlin' up time," they had no other option than to work for the same employer for another season. "That the debt may be fictitious makes it no less binding on the Negro, who is without legal or social defense," Powdermaker observed. Black sharecroppers only could ask for more

credit to get food and fuel to help them survive the winter. "On Settlement Day the sharecroppers would get what the white man gave
them without any questions asked and walk out pretending to be satisfied," one black man in neighboring Leflore Country recalled. "If
they showed any dissatisfaction, they were usually asked to move for
fear they would spoil the rest of the niggers." Most did not reveal their
resentment. Deeply in debt, they repeated the process the following
spring with little hope of ever breaking the destructive cycle. As
Hamer complained, "It was so many 'its' in cotton; you had to plow it;
you had to chop it; then you had to gather it; then he taken it."[6]

Planters justified this manifestly unequal system by developing a
morally reassuring philosophy of paternalism. Expressed perhaps most
eloquently by William Alexander Percy, a planter in adjacent Washington County, paternalism helped whites explain and justify sharecropping. The paternalist white planter was the head of the plantation
household, the father in charge of his ignorant, sometimes unruly, but
often charming black children. The black worker "is nothing but a
child—a big black child," one observer sympathetic to the planters insisted, "with no heredity of sustained effort behind him, no training,
no background." By this logic, all the stressful responsibility, the
heavy burdens of overseeing a complex agricultural operation rested
upon the planters; the black sharecroppers simply had to work the
land without worry about prices, housing, yields, and the like. Percy
considered himself and others of his class the blacks' "friend and protector," and he believed that "profit-sharing" (as he preferred to call
sharecropping) should be adapted to the industrial North because it
was "the most moral system under which human beings can work together." Like white colonial administrators across Africa and Asia, Percy
lamented the "white man's burden" that he and other white planters
shouldered. "To live among a people whom, because of their needs,
one must in common decency protect and defend is a sore burden in
a world where one's own troubles are about all any life can shoulder,"
he sighed.[7]

Sunflower County whites tended to agree. They strongly defended paternalism not only as essential to the local economy but also
as beneficial to black workers. "The Negro is the best economist
around the place," one large planter argued. "He always gets a living

whether the plantation makes or loses money, but makes money if the place makes it." John Dollard met another farmer who complained that "when times are bad he has to take care of the Negroes first, whether they make anything or not; when times are good he has to make all he can in order to catch up on the bad times." Whites pointed to the short work year that blacks enjoyed—from December to March, workers had little to do. One planter insisted that croppers only work about ninety days a year. "The rest of the time they fish, fool around, attend revivals, and follow other trivial pursuits."[8]

Paternalistic planters such as Woods Eastland and his son, James, made sure that their workers were treated well enough to stay contented with their lot. So long as sharecroppers did not protest their condition or agitate for equal rights, the Eastland plantation was a relatively good place to work. Mack Caples, who labored on the plantation in the 1940s and 1950s, considered James Eastland a "mighty nice man" who talked to workers, loaned them money, and treated them well. "Workers didn't suffer for nothing" on the Eastland plantation, remembered Willie Jackson, another sharecropper. Long after they no longer could work in the fields, black workers could remain in their cabins on the plantation. "If they had been faithful over the years they were allowed to stay there," remembered James Eastland's daughter Anne. "But if they didn't do what you told them to do, you didn't pay their bills or furnish them what they needed."[9]

The Eastlands also offered their workers protection from law enforcement. Like other planters, they received deferential treatment from local police. "We would never send a deputy on a man's plantation without going to the boss man many, many times," a Bolivar County sheriff from the 1950s and 1960s explained. "When we wanted somebody that had done something we would just call the plantation owner and tell him to bring the man in." Field hands recalled that Woods Eastland and, later, his son "wouldn't let the polices come on the plantation" and prevented local officials from enforcing the law against their laborers. If an Eastland hand managed to make it across the Sunflower River and onto the plantation, the cops pursued no further. "Once you made it across the bridge, you was all right," went a common saying around Doddsville. The Eastlands regularly intervened in legal proceedings; decades after the fact, one worker remained grateful to James Eastland for helping get his sentence for a serious crime reduced to six months in jail. They wrote to local law officials to plead a worker's case, and they sometimes took their case directly to the governor's mansion, where family friend Paul Johnson lent a friendly ear. Planters could also requisition laborers from prison when they needed extra hands. As Woods Eastland explained to the governor, "there are plenty of old negroes in the penitentiary that no one on earth objected to their suspension of sentence." This immunity from law enforcement, along with a reputation for producing much of the county's corn whiskey, created the impression that laborers on the Eastland plantation were among the most dangerous in the area. Charles Cobb, who came to Sunflower County during the civil rights movement, noticed that Eastland's workers were allowed to have "the run of the town." "You have to be careful," one African American woman remembered being told as a child. "That's those Eastland plantation folks."[10]

Black workers were protected from local law enforcement and they did not suffer for housing, emergency health care, and food, but that paternalism came at a high cost. By looking to the Eastlands and other planters to provide these basic needs, they became profoundly dependent on the planters' goodwill. "The status of tenancy demands complete dependence," observed black sociologist Charles S. Johnson and two University of North Carolina colleagues who studied cotton tenancy in the 1930s. "It requires no education and demands no initiative." This dependence often cultivated within sharecroppers a "plantation mentality," an outlook on life that encouraged immediate gratification and deference while discouraging individual responsibility and collective protest. Because black workers were not allowed to make decisions or wield any power on the plantation, over time they were conditioned to defer to authority and accept (and sometimes even prefer) powerlessness. Major decisions that affected their lives were made by someone else; they grew accustomed to not having to worry about making those decisions. Having the plantation owner provide life's basic necessities may have gnawed at their souls, but it did satisfy hunger; providing for oneself was far more dangerous, more uncertain. Why cause trouble for yourself and your family when your basic needs were being met? The plantation owners provided a kind of insurance. In return for the security of food, shelter, and a job, you paid with your freedom.[11]

This "plantation mentality" undermined blacks' cultural ability to fight back against white supremacy, often manifesting itself in self-destructive behavior that in turn provided fodder for the white planters to justify their paternalistic treatment of their workers. One "very intelligent Negro" who spoke with John Dollard emphasized that the plantation system "tends to discourage the type of habit necessary to self-improvement in our society." Whites wanted—no, needed—blacks to be poor so that there would always be a ready supply of cheap labor. Thus, the man explained, "it was to the advantage of whites not to encourage thrift or consistency of behavior, because, as long as these qualities are lacking, the Negroes are dependent on the furnish and the landowners are relatively sure of their labor supply." Sociologist Johnson and his colleagues agreed. "Under a system which does not encourage labor and thrift men easily develop habits of improvidence," they wrote. "The tenant who really works on his place, who labors to restore the soil, who repairs and builds, is merely inviting his landlord to raise his rent." One of Dollard's black informants in Sunflower County saw how this process affected black behavior. "The Negroes are shiftless because they have no incentive to improve their farms and homes," he argued. "They do not get anywhere at the end anyway and the improvements go to the white man." Another black informant believed that "the ignorance and shiftlessness is a heritage from slavery days and it is cultivated now by the whites to keep Negroes down." Decades later, when civil rights workers came to organize blacks to fight segregation, they often struggled to overcome the behavioral patterns and the habits of dependence and deference typified by the "plantation mentality."[12]

"THIS SENSITIVE WORLD-WEB"

Planters such as Woods and James Eastland or Fannie Lou Hamer's bosses, E.W. Brandon and W.D. Marlow, appeared to be omnipotent, and they strived to maintain that impression among their sharecroppers. They deliberately and effectively limited the educational, economic, and political opportunities available to Hamer and her fellow laborers, forcing them into dependence and powerlessness. But from a larger perspective cotton growers too were dependent and powerless, unable to control the crop on which planters and pickers alike relied. They not only were fundamentally dependent upon the labor of their black workers but also were at the mercy of fluctuations in global economics, politics, and culture that in turn affected cotton demand and prices. Cotton was a global crop, a "world power" in the words of one contemporary scholar, and the lands that depended upon it were "bound together in a world-encircling web." Control of this white gold slipped from planters' hands as it flowed down the Mississippi River, through New Orleans, and to the vast world markets in which it was ultimately sold. "The Mississippi," planter David Cohn observed, "made each of us a world citizen" and exposed planters and pickers alike to the] dangerous currents of the global economic system. Little wonder, then, that folks across the plantation South often said, "Cotton is dynamite."[13]

Delta cotton planters in the early twentieth century have the reputation of being parochial, backward-looking aristocrats intent on maintaining their privileged status by preserving an anachronistic economic system based on black subservience. Say the words "cotton planter," and we often think of paunchy, wrinkled white men in beige pants and suspenders supervising crowds of overall-clad black men. Indeed, many planters sought to reestablish the labor control that their antebellum predecessors had enjoyed, but they had to work within the framework of legally free labor and increasingly global competition. Far from being anachronistic, cotton farmers such as the Eastlands and cotton pickers such as Hamer were enmeshed in a global economic system that was thoroughly modern and that expanded throughout the twentieth century. This worldwide system had its roots in the Industrial Revolution that transformed first Great Britain in the early nineteenth century and later the United States and much of the Atlantic world. Cotton drove this transformation, for it was the mechanization of the British textile industry that fueled much of the era's extraordinary economic growth.[14]

For nearly three generations after the Civil War, American cotton farmers reaped the benefits of an increasingly interconnected and industrialized global economy. As the U.S. government pushed for an "open door" in China and other nonindustrialized nations, the American cotton industry expanded production, particularly in Sunflower County and the Delta, to meet the boom in worldwide demand. Although they often are associated with the antebellum era, cotton plantations in the South actually reached their zenith in the early twentieth century, when James Eastland and Fannie Lou Hamer were young. These plantations were highly capitalized operations that had enough land and labor to achieve economies of scale and compete in a global marketplace, and they did so through careful, year-round management. American cotton plantations were far and away the most productive and efficient in the entire world, and the United States stood as the world's lone cotton superpower. In the 1890s, the United States produced three times more cotton than the rest of the world combined; even into the 1910s, America alone accounted for 60 percent of the world crop.[15]

But solitary superpowers tend to breed resentment, even among trading partners and allies. As European nations scrambled for economic advantage during the long era of colonialism and industrialization, cotton became one more arena for global competition. Britain in particular pursued an aggressive strategy of both opening up new lands for cotton cultivation and establishing new markets for the sale of finished cotton goods. The chief new areas for cotton cultivation were lands with heavy British influence—India and Egypt—because the British textile industry consumed most of the world's cotton. But in the late nineteenth century cotton fields began to appear as well in the Sudan, Russia, Argentina, Brazil, and China. Although it took decades for the foreign cotton industry to become competitive with the American juggernaut, the presence of foreign competitors ultimately would prove disastrous to cotton planters and pickers in places such as the Mississippi Delta. In Sunflower County, the rise of foreign competition was front-page news. In February 1921, for example, the *Ruleville Record* warned of increases in Indian cotton production and pointedly observed that "English mills are now running 35 hours a week on Egyptian cotton but only 24 hours a week on American cotton." Delta planters kept tabs on world cotton prices, as well as methods and costs of production in India, Egypt, Peru, and elsewhere.[16]

Cotton industry executives abroad wanted to break their dependence on American cotton. "Competition in other parts of the world is the only lever we can bring to bear on America," one British cotton executive in the early 1900s argued. "We must get the Indian Government to produce more cotton in India, and the British Cotton Growing Association to increase production in Africa." But how does one country "get" the people of another nation to increase production? Cotton required certain growing conditions—a subtropical climate with adequate rainfall—that European nations could not meet. The only lands that were suitable for cotton cultivation happened to be inhabited by people who looked very different from the average European cotton executive. To get such people to participate in a capitalist cotton enterprise, cotton executives looked to the world's most successful model of growing cotton: the American South. Like the massive sugar and coffee plantations of the Caribbean and Central and South America, the cotton plantation system in the American South forced masses of low-wage, predominantly nonwhite laborers into producing an export crop for consumption in industrialized nations while offering few rewards for local people. The southern cotton industry offered a template for how a ruling white minority could turn a nonwhite majority into a productive, politically incapacitated labor force. The "formula" included racial subjugation, political disenfranchisement, physical violence, and economic intimidation, all of which had been practiced and perfected in Mississippi and across the South.[17]

Interestingly, one of the best examples of how foreign countries sought to follow the southern model used former American slaves as project consultants of sorts. In the German colony of Togoland, on the coast of West Africa, white colonial officials turned to ex-slaves from Booker T. Washington's Tuskegee Institute to help transform Togolese subsistence farmers into cotton exporters. For eight years beginning in 1901, black Americans traveled to Togo and consulted with German officials and Togolese farmers. While Washington and his Tuskegee emissaries hoped to uplift the Togolese by making them essential to the global economy, German officials focused almost exclusively on maximizing cotton production; the Togolese, meanwhile, preferred diversified agriculture and sought to retain old patterns of production that gave them more control over what they grew and how they grew it. These conflicting priorities created tension and limited production, and over time the Germans relied increasingly on violence and coercion to force the Togolese to grow more and more cotton. Faced with being accomplices in the re-creation of the worst aspects of the plantation South, the black Americans abandoned the project, but German officials continued to push for increased production by any means necessary.[18]

Other European colonial powers followed a similar pattern in sub-Saharan Africa, though without American consultants. During World War I, as cotton prices soared, Belgian colonial officials in Zaire sought to establish a cotton regime that would reduce Belgium's dependence on American and Indian imports. Their method of extracting peasant labor—and peasants' clandestine efforts to resist—bear similarities to the situation in Mississippi: the threat and use of force, as well as social and economic incentives for voluntary participation. A little more than a decade later, in the midst of the Great Depression, Portugal followed a similar strategy. It sought to develop its own sources of cotton in colonial Mozambique, which offered the soil, climate, and non-white labor force that fit the American cotton-growing model. Within four years, Portuguese colonial officials had forced more than 700,000 Mozambiqueans into cotton cultivation. Unwilling to devote the time and resources necessary to creating a "paternalist" culture, the Portuguese relied primarily on brutal violence to create a productive cotton enterprise.[19]

Whether in Mississippi, Africa, or elsewhere, cotton growing enriched the few who had the skin color and status to benefit from the global economy. Sunflower County's cotton producers were part of an international agricultural system that capitalized on the labor of the world's most vulnerable and powerless workers. The riches of the planters, and the fates of their workers, hung upon the cotton prices that swung wildly with the vicissitudes of global politics, world weather, and events in foreign lands—cotton prices, observers noted, were "among the most erratic and fluctuating of all agricultural markets." Analyzing the cotton economy in 1916, James Scherer wrote, "Even in times of peace, the annual cotton crop is so huge that apparently in-significant fluctuations, perhaps caused by some slight disturbance in a remote far-away skein of this sensitive world-web [of cotton], may upset the economic equilibrium of all civilized lands." Planters needed to know much more than how to keep the Negroes down on the farm; they also had to pay attention to how foreign affairs affected their pre-cious crop. As one observer in the 1930s noted, when it came to cot-ton, "every mite of data is concentrated in cotton exchanges where a member need only glance at the blackboard to see whether Sao Paulo, Brazil, has got rain; pink-worm depredations in Egypt; or how many American bales were bought yesterday by the mills of Japan." Planta-tion culture may have been parochial, but economically cotton planta-tions could hardly have been more cosmopolitan.[20]

During the 1920s and 1930s, the world economy and foreign af-fairs became increasingly important to the economic life of Sunflower County as the American cotton industry lost its global preeminence. American cotton growers felt increasing pressure on both the demand and supply sides of their market. Synthetic fibers such as rayon com-bined with changes in fashion to undermine the demand for cotton, while foreign competitors battled to topple America from its domi-nant spot atop the supply market. Upstart nations such as India, China, and Brazil became major players in the cotton textile industry and began to produce lower-quality yarns that required cheaper cotton grown in less-developed nations. Even within the United States, Sun-flower County planters faced competition as cotton farms sprouted in Oklahoma, Arizona, and California.[21]

The Wall Street crash of 1929 only accelerated the decline of American cotton. Congress in its wisdom responded with the Hawley-Smoot tariff, which immediately raised tariffs on imported goods. For planters dependent on cotton exports, Hawley-Smoot was catastrophic—as a senator more than a decade later, James Eastland would point to the high tariffs as the primary cause of southern poverty. The tariff, England's Sir Arthur Salter commented, "was a turning point in world history." Almost overnight, foreign markets shut their doors to Ameri-can imports as other nations responded in kind to the tariff. American cotton became dramatically more expensive compared to its foreign competition, and overseas mills turned increasingly to other sources, including India, Egypt, the Sudan, and especially Brazil. Foreign production of cotton soared—Brazil alone quadrupled its production within a decade. By 1934, for the first time, the United States failed to produce a majority of the world's output of the crop, and five years later it accounted for barely 40 percent of world production. If American cotton growers could not find a way to produce the crop more cheaply, they were in danger of losing their livelihood.[22]

"THE MOST SERIOUS SITUATION . . . SINCE THE CIVIL WAR"

In the Delta, nature added to the woes of planters and pickers alike as a terrible drought struck the area in 1930. "We had no rain for over 100 days," recalled one Sunflower County planter. "We made one-third of a crop, and got one-half the price that cotton had brought the previous year." Even as American cotton became more expensive relative to its competition, cotton prices plummeted, bottoming out at less than 6¢ a pound in 1931, its lowest price in almost forty years and less than one-tenth of what it had been barely more than a decade before. Planters responded by cutting wages to less than 50¢ per hundred pounds of cotton picked—a quarter of what they had offered during the boom days of World War I when Fannie Lou Hamer's family and other blacks were lured to Sunflower County. As sporadic strikes broke out, Walter Sillers, a planter in Bolivar County, feared that cotton growers were "confronted with the most serious situation they have faced since the Civil War."[23]

Desperate farmers reacted to the falling prices by planting more cotton, producing a near-record crop of more than 17 million bales in 1931 that only aggravated the fundamental problem: overproduction. With the cotton economy teetering on edge of collapse, sharecroppers and cotton farmers alike looked to the incoming administration of Franklin D. Roosevelt to alleviate their suffering. Through the New Deal's Agricultural Adjustment Administration (AAA), Roosevelt aimed to solve the problem of rural poverty by limiting crop production, thereby raising prices. Combined with other New Deal agencies, however, the AAA's limits on cotton produced a short-term windfall for the Eastlands and other planters while triggering a long-term agricultural revolution that ultimately would lead to the end of sharecropping as Fannie Lou Hamer had known it.

The Cotton Section of the Agricultural Adjustment Act, passed in 1933, stipulated that the federal government would pay landowners to reduce their crop acreage; the planters would then pass partial payments on to their tenants and sharecroppers. With fewer acres in production, the reasoning went, the supply of cotton would decrease and prices eventually would rise; government payments would relieve suffering in the meantime. But for sharecroppers, the AAA had two drawbacks: first, the crop acreage reduction meant that fewer sharecroppers and tenants were needed to work the land; second, the government sent its checks to landowners rather than the people who actually worked the land. The program assumed that planters would uphold the spirit of the law by honestly reducing their acreage and sharing the federal benefits with their sharecroppers, but with so much federal money flowing into the area, many planters could not resist the temptation to abuse the system. Planters could—and often did—keep the money, evict their sharecroppers and tenants, and turn to low-wage day laborers instead. They also could use the payments as a means of keeping their laborers dependent and docile; workers who did not toe the plantation line could expect to receive nothing at payment time. Even William Alexander Percy, the paternalist planter who extolled the virtues of sharecropping, complained to the AAA that the program underestimated "the amount of dishonesty practiced by landlords in this section."[24]

In addition to the AAA, planters enjoyed easier access to credit through the Commodity Credit Corporation, the New Deal's less visible but profoundly influential "other" CCC. Created by executive order in October 1933, the CCC had been devised by Oscar Johnston, who ran the world's largest cotton plantation in neighboring Washington County. It was intended to be a means of stabilizing prices and bolstering planter revenue. Through the CCC, cotton farmers could secure significant loans by using their crops as collateral. The CCC paid above-market prices for the cotton, thus helping to boost prices as planters held more and more of their crop out of the market. At the same time, the program helped alleviate some of the risks of growing cotton for those planters who could get the loans.[25]

In Sunflower County, as elsewhere in the rural South, the New Deal played into the hands of the large plantation owners who controlled the agricultural programs and who fought to ensure that their workers would neither receive Social Security nor benefit from New Deal legislation that supported labor's right to collective bargaining. The county's planting families had powerful allies in Washington, including the AAA's finance director, Oscar Johnston. They also had economic leverage: federal officials needed their consent to implement any new program. Planters consolidated their power in 1935 with the creation of the Delta Chamber of Commerce (later renamed the Delta Council), a lobbying organization devoted to promoting economic development and protecting cotton planters' interests. Sharecroppers, on the other hand, had neither a voice on Capitol Hill nor the power to force federal officials to listen. Not surprisingly, the AAA did little to relieve rural poverty but helped the planters a great deal. In plantation areas such as Sunflower County, large landowners ensured that the new programs would be to their liking; as one historian notes, "the programs rescued and enriched planter-landlords and inflicted frustration and suffering on the already poor and landless."[26]

With easy access to credit and federal largesse through the CCC and the AAA, planters cashed in, big-time. Between 1933 and 1939, Sunflower County farmers received more than $3 million in acreage-reduction payments. In 1933 alone, the Eastlands were paid $26,000 for not producing cotton. That may not seem like much given the size of the Eastland plantation, but the payments were extraordinary when compared to the amount of money spent on New Deal relief programs. In 1933, relief efforts for the thousands of poor Sunflower County residents amounted to $6,000—less than a quarter of what the Eastlands alone had received. Two years later, spending on relief programs had increased to $32,000, but county farmers received almost ten times that much in acreage-reduction payments. The massive payments to large farmers—particularly the more than $175,000 that went to Oscar Johnston's Delta plantation—attracted criticism from reporters and congressional investigators, but for most of the decade planters were able to fight off attempts to rein in the payments. Not until 1938 did Congress pass limits on large subsidies.[27]

It could hardly get much better for the Eastlands and other planters. In the words of one historian, "The South was planter's heaven by the late 1930s, with generous government subsidies, protection against risk, ready financing for new machinery, and cheap harvest labor to make it all possible." For the Eastlands, the Depression offered an opportunity for growth as they snapped up acreage made available when smaller farmers lost their land. Beginning in 1928, Woods Eastland began a massive expansion of the family farm, adding more than 1,000 acres to the plantation by the time he turned over roughly 2,500 acres to James in 1932. During the next seven years, father and son bought more than 2,500 acres, so by the end of the decade they controlled a plantation that exceeded 5,000 acres, making them the largest landowners in Sunflower County. As the plantation grew, so did the labor force—during the 1940s, more than 150 families, upward of 800 people, resided on Eastland land. By the beginning of World War II, the Eastlands had amassed a cotton empire.[28]

The New Deal's short-term benefits to landowners may have been extraordinary, but its long-term consequences were revolutionary. The New Deal ushered in a new era for Sunflower County and the rest of the Delta, one marked by mechanization and the decline of sharecropping. Before the 1930s, large plantation owners had had little incentive to switch to labor-saving machinery such as tractors. With so much cheap, abundant labor available, they could rely on a multitude of sharecroppers and mules to plant, chop, and harvest their crop. Furthermore, because there was not yet a way to mechanize the harvest, planters needed to keep their tenants on hand for picking in the fall. But the New Deal changed planters' calculus. The AAA, intended to help poor farmers survive the Depression, instead gave large planters the economic incentive to switch to wage labor because federal payments had to be shared with sharecroppers but not with wage laborers. In the 1930s, the number of sharecroppers in the Delta fell by almost 10 percent and the acreage farmed by sharecroppers dropped by more than 20 percent, while the acreage farmed by wage hands increased significantly. The sharecroppers who remained, including Fannie Lou Hamer's family, often were given plots of land too small to make a living on, forcing them to work as wage laborers to supplement their income. Planters who switched to wage labor no longer were responsible for housing, feeding, and clothing their workers all year round; they could consolidate their vast land holdings, use a smaller number of tenants to plant their crop with tractors, and then hire off-plantation day laborers at harvest time.[29]

The switch to wage labor helped pave the way for the fully mechanized cotton plantations that would make most farm laborers such as Fannie Lou Hamer economically obsolete. There remained one major impediment: the harvest bottleneck. For decades, planters had dreamed of mechanizing their harvest, but one unsuccessful attempt after another made a mechanical cotton picker seem like a pie-in-the-sky notion. "A successful cotton picker has been just around the corner for the last eighty-seven years," one wry commentator noted in 1937. The *Sunflower Tocsin* mocked enthusiasts' faith in "the mechanical cotton picker, which is usually perfected in the spring and is a failure in the cotton picking season." Too many factors appeared to impede the process. Critics insisted that a machine could never replace hand labor because of the varying height of cotton stalks, the difficulty of removing the fiber without also removing stalk, and the fact that bolls opened at unpredictable, uneven times. Many knowledgeable observers believed that cotton would always be harvested by hand.[30]

But change was coming. In the 1920s, major companies, including John Deere and International Harvester, raced to develop a practical mechanical picker, but their efforts were eclipsed by the work of a lone inventor with socialist aspirations: John Rust. Having grown up picking cotton in west Texas, Rust wanted to produce a mechanical picker that could relieve sharecroppers of what he termed "the back-breaking slavery of the cotton fields." A cotton-picking machine would force thousands of sharecroppers out of the fields, Rust recognized, and he hoped the machine-induced transformation of the cotton economy would heighten the contradictions of capitalism and push people to accept socialism as a humane alternative.[31]

As Rust demonstrated the effectiveness of his machine to interested audiences across the South in the early 1930s, he provoked widespread fear of the social consequences the picker might trigger. "There is impending a violent revolution in cotton production as a result of the development of the mechanical cotton picker," warned Charles Johnson and his University of North Carolina colleagues. "When it comes it will automatically release hundreds of thousands of cotton workers particularly in the Southeast, creating a new range of social problems." Despite the potential economic benefits, many observers envisioned social chaos. "Nothing could be more devastating to labor conditions in the South than a cotton-picking machine," the *Jackson Daily News* stressed in 1936. "Imagine, if you can, 500,000 negroes in Mississippi just now lolling around on cabin galleries or loafing on the streets of the cities and towns while machines are picking cotton." John Dollard thought a cotton-picking machine might spark a renewed African colonization movement or an effort to create a black state within America. Many sharecroppers saw the machine as a threat. "Every time you kill a mule you kill a black man," one black farmer in Washington County protested. "You've heard about the machine picker? That's against the black man too." The farmer was right to be concerned. Though John Rust did not live to see it, his 1930s invention, enhanced and mass-produced by International Harvester in the next decade, did not so much help sharecroppers and promote socialism as render them economically irrelevant and enhance the power of large planters.[32]

"THE POOREST MEN ARE ON THE RICHEST LAND"

Long-term economic changes can be difficult to discern while they happen, and the slow erosion of the plantation system was not apparent to most folks in Sunflower County during the late 1930s. Indeed, to Fannie Lou Hamer and other sharecroppers, the system only seemed to grow stronger with New Deal dollars. Although the switch to machine picking remained a generation away, sharecroppers and other southern farm workers immediately felt the effects of both the Depression and the ensuing New Deal policies that benefited planters. Sharecroppers by the thousands were forced off the land, and those who remained suffered from extraordinary hardship. Their difficulties captured the attention of outside observers as "the plight of the sharecropper" became a staple in media commentary. "Many parts of the south represent more acute poverty and injustice than that of slavery days," argued theologian Reinhold Niebuhr. "The slave was worth money and the tenant farmer is not. He consequently gets less consideration." The journalists, scholars, and politicians who traveled south to document and publicize the sharecroppers' struggles often were shocked by what they considered a paradoxically impoverished land, a world of fertile fields and poor people, wealthy planters and suffering sharecroppers. The land "ought to give men plenty, but it betrays," wrote visiting white newspaperman Jonathan Daniels. "The poorest men are on the richest land."[33]

This paradox prompted more than just media fascination; it also triggered organized action among sharecroppers and a challenge to the power of the planters. Having promised to help "the forgotten man at the bottom of the economic pyramid," President Roosevelt raised expectations among laborers across America. The early New Deal appeared to bolster workers' rights as Section 7a of the National Recovery Act protected the right to unionize and bargain collectively. But after its initial success, Roosevelt's ambitious program seemed to stall and appeared incapable of lifting the nation out of the economic abyss. As fascists gained power in Germany, Italy, and Japan, America faced homegrown radicalism from both sides of the political spectrum. Charismatic leaders such as Louisiana's populist governor (later senator) Huey Long, conservative radio host Father Charles Coughlin, and old-age-pension activist Dr. Francis Townsend challenged Roosevelt's agenda. Meanwhile, organized left-wing groups, particularly the Communist Party, made inroads not simply among northern factory workers but also among black sharecroppers in the South.

The Communist Party attracted support and condemnation across the South as the economic depression worsened and the party made a concerted effort to organize poor black farmworkers. The party's willingness to address racial issues was extraordinary; almost alone among white Americans, Communists vigorously pursued racial equality. The Sixth World Congress of the Communist International declared in 1928 that the black-majority areas of the South represented an oppressed nation entitled to self-determination, political power, and control of economic resources. The American Communist Party sent

organizers to the South, including a pair who surveyed farm conditions and interviewed sharecroppers in the Delta. Although interested
in building a power base among the poor of both races, the party soon
earned a reputation as a "race" organization for its willingness to work
among and defend poor blacks in the South. In 1931 the Communist-
led International Labor Defense (ILD) supplied critical legal help to
nine black men accused of raping two white women in Scottsboro, Alabama, and Communist Party organizers helped to organize the Share
Croppers Union (SCU) in rural parts of the state. The ILD's highly
publicized success in contesting the men's convictions and the SCU's
quiet progress in organizing sharecroppers horrified southern whites
but impressed blacks, even if they did not share the party's ideology.
Such efforts, party boosters claimed, helped inspire "a rebirth in the
life of the Negro people."[34]

Even closer to home, the Southern Tenant Farmers Union, founded
in 1934 by a pair of Arkansas socialists, successfully organized strikes
among cotton pickers in the Arkansas and Mississippi Deltas. From
its inception, the Union made a firm commitment to crossing the
racial boundaries of Jim Crow. "As long as we stand together, black
and white together in this organization," one founding black member
argued, "nothing can tear it down." For most union members, the commitment to interracial organizing did not stem from altruism or some
enlightened vision of humanity; rather, it grew out of self-interested
realism. Union leaders at the outset emphasized that both races shared
a common enemy—the planters—and they needed to work together to
battle the planters' power. After a slow beginning, the union hit its
stride in late summer 1935, when it called its first major strike. Nearly
five thousand cotton pickers braved violence and intimidation by staying out of the fields to force planters to pay $1, rather than the cus-
tomary 40¢ to 60¢ cents, per hundred pounds of picked cotton. Facing
the prospect of losing the year's crop, many planters raised their rates
to 75¢ (still less than half what they had been during the boom years
of World War I), prompting the union to call off the strike and declare
victory. News of the strike victory spread like wildfire through cotton
country; by year's end, union leaders claimed to have 25,000 members
region-wide.[35]

The union's growth encouraged leaders to establish a model of cooperative economic development in Bolivar County, next door to Sunflower. On more than two thousand acres of farmland, a bit more than half the size of the Eastland plantation at the time, the union established the Delta Cooperative Farm for union members who agreed to work the land cooperatively. Supported by northern philanthropists and activists such as the white theologian Reinhold Niebuhr and the black sociologist Charles Johnson, the cooperative initially attracted thirty families, eighteen black and twelve white, who sought to achieve self-sufficiency through diversified farming, cooperative economics, and racial harmony. It was governed by a five-person council, not more than three of whom could be of one race. Members built their own houses, set up a cooperative store, and started a health clinic. They also provided four extra months of schooling for black children to supplement the paltry four-month program offered by the state. Niebuhr called the farm "the most significant experiment in social Christianity now being conducted in America," and he spoke a language of freedom that Fannie Lou Hamer and other civil rights activists would find familiar three decades later. "Freedom that has no economic base is a bogus freedom," Niebuhr wrote shortly after the founding of the farm. "In a world in which souls are not discarnate there can be no freedom without some degree of power, including economic power."[36]

The Delta Cooperative Farm attracted the attention of John Rust and his brother Mack. With a prototype of their mechanical picker ready to roll through the fields, the Rust brothers saw the Delta Cooperative Farm as the ideal place to demonstrate their invention's revolutionary potential. They planned to create a foundation that would plow the profits from their picker into programs that helped the unskilled laborers who lost their jobs to machines. But the Rust brothers and other enthusiastic supporters could not prevent the Delta Cooperative Farm's ultimate failure. Facing constant harassment from planters, internal dissension, and irresponsibility among its workers, farm leaders by 1941 had abandoned the cooperative venture in favor of a return to sharecropping, and the focus of their effort shifted to Providence Farm in nearby Holmes County. More than two decades later, Fannie Lou Hamer would lead another cooperative farming effort, Freedom Farm, that sought to achieve many of the same goals.[37]

Pushed by the organizing among the poor, as well as by the increasing demands from liberals within his administration, President Roosevelt began taking more aggressive legislative action as he shifted the New Deal's focus from recovery to reform. Beginning in 1935, this Second New Deal included economic measures such as the Wagner Act, which guaranteed unions' right to collective bargaining and created the National Labor Relations Board to enforce the law, and the Fair Labor Standards Act, which established a national minimum wage. Combined with popular programs such as the Works Progress Administration (WPA) and Social Security, the reform effort gained widespread support among laboring classes. Years later, Fannie Lou Hamer recalled Roosevelt fondly for "putting people on jobs." Throughout Sunflower County, blacks viewed federal relief efforts as fair and necessary. "For some Negroes, the government has taken over the role of 'good white folks,' appearing almost more beneficent and more paternalistic than they," Hortense Powdermaker observed. She read a black child's poignant poem: "Say, my Lord knows just how we've been fed / If it weren't for the President we'd all be dead."[38]

The New Deal's new direction captured the imagination of radicals on the left and ignited the fears of extremists on the right. The Soviet Union urged all foreign Communists to unite with the non-Communist left to form a Popular Front. Under the banner "Communism is Americanism," the party allied with labor unions, established front organizations, and actively promoted the New Deal in a wide-ranging effort that made Communists more popular than at any other point in America history. Roosevelt's programs earned support among northern black voters, a growing electoral force that promised to reshape the national Democratic Party. As the decade wore on and left-wing forces seemed to gain power in Washington and support in the South, Eastland and other Sunflower County planters grew apprehensive. They feared that federal money would lure their black workers away from cotton, thereby undermining their ability to secure and retain labor for the plantation. "Planters are having trouble to get labor for spring planting in some places," complained the editor of the *Sunflower Tocsin*. "The WPA and relief offer easier times and better pay, and much of the labor prefer to receive charity than do honest and necessary work." Too many people expect the government to take care of them, the *Ruleville Record* agreed. "Every man and woman who can work and get work should not be given aid," referring not to the Eastlands and other planting families receiving tens of thousands of dollars in federal money but instead to cotton pickers who might pocket $4–$5 a day with the WPA. Among whites in Sunflower County, John Dollard found "a good deal of resistance" to giving blacks federal relief.[39]

By the late 1930s, Eastland's economic philosophy had undergone a total makeover. As a state representative from Forest, Eastland had supported former Governor Bilbo, who during the New Deal was perhaps the South's most economically liberal U.S. senator. As a lawyer in Scott County, he had followed in his father's footsteps as the defender of workers hurt by rapacious corporations. As a young man of the Hills, he had butted heads with the Delta aristocracy embodied by Walter Sillers and other cotton planters. But now Eastland himself was a cotton planter with very different economic interests. He saw the leftward drift of national politics as dangerous, even un-American, for it threatened the essence of the power that he and his fellow planters enjoyed in Sunflower County: an economically and racially stratified society run by the natural leaders of a local community devoted to the single-minded cultivation of cotton. He worried that labor agitators, Communists, and federal bureaucrats were conspiring to "enslave" the South through higher tariffs and worker empowerment. Fearing the loss of the local control that protected and perpetuated planters' power, Eastland grew increasingly involved in politics toward the end of the decade.[40]

Although he insisted that he had retired from politics when he left the Mississippi legislature in 1931, Eastland remained active in the state and local political scene. He helped his father's old college roommate, Paul Johnson, during an unsuccessful bid for the governor's seat in 1935, then again four years later when Johnson won the election. Eastland declined a job offer from Governor Johnson, insisting he was satisfied with tending to his lucrative farm, but his political back-scratching and his father's connections served him well. In June 1941, Mississippi's senior U.S. senator, Pat Harrison, a social conservative who had supported most of the early New Deal, died in office. Governor Johnson originally sought one of the Hederman brothers, the powerful media moguls who controlled the Jackson *Clarion-Ledger*, to replace him, but was rebuffed. He then offered his old pal Woods Eastland the temporary seat. In a story Senator Eastland would tell later, he and his father journeyed the one hundred miles from the Eastland plantation to the governor's mansion in Jackson to meet with Governor Johnson about the Senate seat. As Johnson made the case for having Woods take the seat, the elder Eastland mutely munched on his dinner. Finally, he declined the governor's offer, but suggested in his stead his thirty-six-year-old son: "The boy'll do it." Governor Johnson agreed, and James Eastland was on his way to Washington.[41]

The appointment was "a surprise almost amounting to a shock to even the closest friends of the governor," one Mississippi newspaper reported, and Eastland himself claimed it was "a complete surprise." "My father never talked to me about that," he later recalled. Once again, it was his father who had directed the course of his life. This time, however, the son had the opportunity to forge his own path in a new setting. The world he knew at home depended in part upon the eternal vigilance of local politicians who worked assiduously to protect the white minority from the encroachments of the black majority; it depended as well on hard-nosed public officials at the state and national levels, committed allies who fought labor organizers, Communists, and other radicals who sought to unite the working classes against the planters. Now he had the chance to be one of those men who "stood up for the South."[42]

"NOT ONLY ECONOMIC SLAVERY BUT HUMAN SLAVERY"

Eastland arrived in Washington in the summer of 1941. Slated to serve less than three months, he was to be replaced by the winner of a special election that fall. The election for the full term would be held in November 1942, and Governor Johnson suggested that Eastland wait until then to run for the seat in his own right—that would give him time to build a power base throughout the state. Without having to worry about immediate reelection, Eastland turned his eighty-eight-day term into a campaign to gain statewide name recognition by taking visible stands on issues of great interest to his primary constituents, cotton planters. Although Senator Eastland later gained a reputation as a racist demagogue, he entered the Senate with one issue foremost on his mind: economics. He wanted to challenge what he saw as the anti-South, pro-worker tilt of federal economic policy. At the root of the problem, he believed, was Communism.

Although many Americans associate anti-Communism with the Cold War and the McCarthy era of the early 1950s, the roots of the struggle against Communist influence went back several decades earlier. Even before Woodrow Wilson sent U.S. troops to Russia to battle the Bolsheviks in 1917, American policy makers worked to undermine the power and influence of Communism at home and abroad. The Bolshevik victory magnified American fears of a Red revolution, and in 1919 Attorney General Mitchell Palmer authorized raids on suspected subversives, leading to the first "Red scare" and hundreds of deportations. During the 1930s, conservative critics attacked the New Deal for its alleged Communist influences and worried, particularly after the Spanish Civil War, about a "fifth column" of American socialists who would destroy the nation from within. In 1938, Representative Martin Dies of Texas established the Special House Committee on Un-American Activities to ferret out subversives, responding to—and further fueling—fears of widespread Communist influence. Along with other Americans, Depression-era whites in Sunflower County and the Mississippi Delta worried about the Red menace. As workers in Mississippi began imitating the sit-down strikes pioneered by the Congress of Industrial Organizations in the North in the late 1930s, the *Sunflower Tocsin* in Eastland's home county urged Deltans to "get rid of labor agitators and Communists" and consistently ran anti-Communist cartoons on its front page.[43]

"This is the big battle we have to face at home today," Walter Sillers wrote to Eastland shortly after the latter's appointment to the Senate, and not long before the Japanese attack on Pearl Harbor. "It is more serious and more directly threatening to our nation than the armed forces of the Axis powers, and we must deal with it regardless of whether we are successful or unsuccessful in the present war."

Scion of a planting family in nearby Rosedale, Sillers also served as a powerful state legislator who later would become Speaker of the Mississippi House of Representatives. Although he and Eastland had been at odds during the latter's one term in the state legislature, the two became friends after Eastland began running the farm in Doddsville. Sillers often shared his thoughts with the young planter, particularly concerning "the in-roads being made by the Communistic and socialistic groups who are over and a day hammering at the foundation and institutions of our government." Like "Red" Sillers—a college nickname inspired by his prominent freckles and hair, not his politics—Eastland saw Communism as a threat to a southern way of life built upon white supremacy and economic hierarchy, and he came to the Senate with a profound hatred of "Reds" and the nations that supported them.[44]

When Eastland first arrived in Washington as an appointed senator, he brought with him the anti-Communism of his region and upbringing. His initial reaction to Capitol Hill was one of professed shock about the extent of subversion. Writing his fellow planter Sillers, he fumed about the presence of Communists within the Roosevelt administration: "Walter, I was amazed when I got to Washington to see the Communists in high places in the Government." These subversive government bureaucrats not only were prejudiced against the South in general, he warned, they also were planning a massive redistribution of property in the Delta: "I know that they desire to break up all farms over forty acres and to inaugurate a system of subsistent farming in the South, and especially in our section. I know that our section has been picked as the ideal place to experiment." It was the nightmare that whites in the Delta dreaded most, part of what Greenville newsman Hodding Carter called a "heritage of fear" that the black majority one day "would exchange its position of inferiority and servitude for one of dominance." The Communist demand for redistribution of private property would destroy the plantation system that enriched his family and protected his planter constituents from the "worse than hard" life than Fannie Lou Hamer and other sharecroppers endured.[45]

During his eighty-eight days in office, Eastland sought to show those planters that he would protect their interests by fighting Communism and promoting cotton in world trade. The war in Europe had been raging for several years and consumed more and more government attention, but among planters and observers in the Delta its most noticeable effect was on cotton prices. Shortly after Hitler's invasion of Czechoslovakia and the beginning of the European conflict, the *Sunflower Tocsin* advocated neutrality but continued trade: "If they must fight this country will be glad to sell them what they need to kill each other." Even in late 1941, Delta residents focused primarily on the war's economic impact. "What has happened to the War?" asked the editors of the *Delta Hub*. "The Delta citizen's only interest in it at present is the effect on cotton prices." Representing such constituents, Eastland spent his short time in the Senate fighting to defend cotton farmers from what he believed were Communist-inspired, antisouthern assaults.[46]

In his first major battle, he took on the Office of Price Administration (OPA) over its attempt to put a cap on cottonseed prices. Created to harness the nation's economy for the war in Europe, the OPA sought to prevent a repeat of the price gouging that many Americans had suspected during World War I. Its chief, Leon Henderson, announced in June 1941 that the OPA would put in place a cap of $25 a ton for cottonseed, which was used primarily in the production of oil. For planters such as Eastland, the cap would be a tremendous economic blow. Because they regularly conflated their own interests with those of the entire region, the young senator pronounced the action "a contemptible, malicious stab at the South." Only one-third of any given cotton harvest can be separated out as fiber; the rest is mostly seed. Thus, for each five-hundred-pound bale of fiber, planters also produce roughly half a ton of seed. On a plantation of five thousand acres such as the Eastland farm, a good crop could bring in tens of thousands of tons of seed—a major boon to planters. In May, before he was appointed to the Senate, Eastland had planned to sell his farm's cottonseed at $60 a ton, but word of the OPA's plan sent prices tumbling. Even before he arrived in Washington, he resolved to challenge the ruling, and within the dark cloud of economic loss he found a silver lining of political opportunity. By attacking the OPA and personally challenging Henderson, he could show planters back home that he was willing to buck the federal government to defend their interests.

It was a chance for him to assert himself on his own, in a realm not dominated by his father.[47]

Eastland seized upon the cottonseed issue in early August. Taking the floor in his maiden Senate speech, he spoke from handwritten notes on yellow legal paper and lambasted the OPA's plan for the cottonseed cap. "This attack on cotton is another attempt to crucify the South," he thundered, using the dramatic, religion-tinged language that later would earn him a reputation as a demagogue. The cottonseed cap was bad enough; even more galling, perhaps, was the fact that the Roosevelt administration was allowing Canadian companies to use Brazilian cotton to make American military uniforms. The federal government not only was placing unreasonable limits on cotton producers' income, Eastland argued, it now was subsidizing the very foreign competition that was impoverishing the U.S. cotton industry. Southern taxpayers were thus financing their competitors: "The South is being taxed to dig its own grave," he fumed. His principal targets were Henderson and Treasury secretary Henry Morgenthau, who, Eastland claimed, "is prejudiced against the South and is totally ignorant about all questions relating to cotton and the South." It was not the last time that he and Morgenthau would tangle.[48]

Eastland's efforts, along with similar critiques leveled by other cotton advocates, produced immediate results. The OPA backed away from the cap, and cottonseed prices shot back up to near $60 a ton. The OPA's retreat enriched hundreds of Delta planters and earned Eastland widespread praise among the powerful back home. "You have made many new friends in this fight," one planter wrote the senator. The *Delta Hub* ran a front-page cartoon showing a svelte Senator Eastland wielding a "Southern Pine" club to beat down the corpulent Henderson and effete Morgenthau as he yanked the cotton balance high; an accompanying editorial gushed, "Jim, we are proud that we had a man like you to help us in our time of need." With its imagery reminiscent of the antebellum caning of Massachusetts senator Charles Sumner by South Carolinian Preston Brooks, the cartoon enhanced Eastland's budding reputation as a defiant defender of the South's elite. One person who was less enthusiastic about Eastland's speeches was his father, who feared that his son had indulged in rash rhetoric. "For God's sake lay off of the demagoguery," he wrote his son, "as you would disgust and drive all of the intelligent people of the State away from you."[49]

Emboldened by his success, Eastland continued his well-publicized attacks on administration policy. The cottonseed cap was simply the latest in a string of federal decisions that Eastland blamed for crippling the southern economy. In the second bill he introduced to the Senate, Eastland joined with Senator John Bankhead of Alabama to eliminate what he believed to be the source of the South's economic woes: the high tariff. Like his antebellum hero John Calhoun, Eastland saw the tariff as an abomination that struck at the economic heart of the South. Before the Civil War, he argued, the South had prospered not because of slavery but because of free world trade. After the Civil War, and particularly after World War I, the northerners in charge of the federal government consistently had passed high tariffs to protect northern industries. As a result, the United States no longer dominated the global cotton industry because foreign competitors could produce cheaper grades. "The farmer of the South must work harder, must work longer, and have less in order to pay this tribute to the protected industrialists of the East," Eastland insisted, referring not to sharecroppers but to white planters. "This is not only economic slavery but human slavery, just as bad, just as dark, and just as unjust as ever existed on any continent of this earth."[50]

There is no record of what Fannie Lou Hamer or other sharecroppers thought of this remark, but it reveals a great deal about Eastland and the economic and political philosophy that underlay what would become a forty-year public career. At its heart lay a racially restricted definition of freedom. Though it may seem hypocritical or excessive for a Confederate-admiring white supremacist to condemn tariffs as "slavery," Eastland saw no contradiction between his strong public stands for freedom and the treatment of blacks and workers on his plantation and throughout his home state. For him, freedom meant unfettered economic opportunity for white people. True freedom implied an adherence to the natural hierarchies symbolized on the plantation—landowner over laborer, white over black, male over female—and the unchallenged opportunity for the natural superiors to dictate the course of economic, political, and social life. Government action to protect these hierarchies sometimes was necessary and welcome, so long as it neither hindered the accumulation of wealth nor encouraged changes in social relations. Communists and labor agitators were dangerous precisely because they promised to do both—they not only hoped to overthrow the capitalist system that built massive fortunes but also promoted an egalitarian view of race. Eastland would not stand for such an inverted social order, and he embarked upon a political career to preserve the hierarchical order he knew.

Eastland's success in the cottonseed fight had "hooked him," his daughter remembered. He planned to run for the seat on his own in 1942. Although his Senate stint had earned him plaudits among planters, he still faced an uphill battle against the political machine run by former governor and erstwhile Senate colleague Theodore Bilbo. As Eastland shifted his economic priorities from Hill farmer to Delta planter, he became a target for the Bilbo machine, which sought to undermine his nascent career by supporting Eastland's opponent, Wall Doxey, a former congressman who had won the special election to fill out the remainder of the term. To Bilboites, Eastland represented the enemy: the privileged son of a powerful planter, the appointed lackey of the Delta aristocracy—one letter writer to the *Jackson Daily News* dismissed him as a "planter playboy." Bilbo sought to play up this image of a pampered lawyer by highlighting the thirty-seven-year-old Eastland's decision not to enlist in the armed forces. But these attacks worked to Eastland's advantage by bolstering his reputation among anti-Bilbo forces throughout the state. By virtue of his birth in the Delta and his upbringing in the Hills, he had roots in both major regions—an important political asset. Running at a time when personal ties mattered more than campaign war chests, Eastland parlayed his father's Hill county connections into moderate support among Hill farmers; among anti-Bilbo planters, Eastland had cultivated a reputation as a man that planters could count on. Walter Sillers and other planters vocalized their strong support for Eastland's candidacy. "Jim Eastland and his father are planters and what is to their interest is to our interest," Sillers wrote to a fellow landowner. "We are going to be very much in need of a man in the Senate during this war, and especially when the re-adjustment takes place after the war. If Eastland is there we will have his ear." Planters responded enthusiastically, and money "poured into the campaign," recalled East-land's campaign publicist.[51]

The problem lay in getting Eastland elected. Eastland's attacks on the tariff, his discussions about the importance of foreign cotton markets, his opposition to the New Deal and labor—all of his campaign rhetoric appealed to economically conservative planters but not to the masses of poor white farmers who lived outside the Delta. Since Governor James Vardaman's election in 1903, Hill farmers had dominated Mississippi politics, and Bilbo's brand of New Deal economic liberalism resonated among them. To appeal to such people, Eastland had to undermine their faith in left-leaning economic policies that had held sway through much of the 1930s. He did so by fusing anti-Communism, economic conservatism, and white supremacy into a political philosophy that would not only get him elected in 1942 but also characterize his entire career.

Though the Bilbo machine shared a firm commitment to white supremacy—no white Mississippi politician at the time disagreed publicly about race—Eastland nonetheless used the issue to his advantage. He not only vociferously advocated traditional racial policies such as the poll tax, which he described as the "surest safe-guard of white Democratic supremacy," but also linked his racial rhetoric to his economic rhetoric. Walter Sillers, whom Eastland later would call his most loyal campaign supporter, made this strategy clear. He urged Eastland to position himself as the defender of white supremacy by attacking labor agitation and Communism and telling people "that Communism means social equality and amalgamation and destruction of the white race." The strategy followed the simple transitive property kids learned in middle-school math: if $a = b$ and $b = c$, then $a = c$. By equating the economic liberalism of Bilbo and the New Deal with labor agitation and Communism, and then equating Communism with "mongrelization," Eastland could link economic liberalism with the destruction of the white race.[52]

Eastland's opponent, Wall Doxey, helped the cause by appearing to kowtow to labor unions, the very forces of economic liberalism that Eastland argued were destroying the white race. In October 1941, shortly after Doxey had taken office, a Delta supporter had written the new senator urging him to denounce a proposed strike called by

John L. Lewis, head of the United Mine Workers of America. Doxey wrote back claiming that while he shared the writer's concerns, he did not feel that Senate protocol allowed him to speak on the floor so soon after his arrival in Washington. In the spring and summer of 1942, with the war in the Pacific going poorly for American forces, the Eastland campaign managed to get copies of both letters and circulated them widely to make Doxey appear to be jeopardizing national security by failing to stand up to big labor. Unlike the spineless Doxey, Eastland argued, he would denounce Lewis and his union cronies. He regularly railed against "Traitors in Labor's robes" who were "knifing the country" at a time of war.[53]

Eastland's attacks worked. He won handily, carrying sixty of the state's eighty-two counties, and election observers across the state attributed his victory to his relentless assaults on labor. "Better than any other candidate, Senator Eastland knew of the bitter hatred for labor organizations felt by the farmers and the folks around the courthouse in every town in Mississippi," one journalist wrote. "From the first he made blistering vocal attacks upon John L. Lewis and 'labor.'" Eastland had challenged the old order and won, wrote the editors of the *Forest News Register*, because "folks are tiring of the paternalism of the New Deal." The new senator had his critics, of course—the editor of a Jackson newspaper called his election "the biggest farce ever perpetrated on the people of Mississippi"—but he had earned broad support across the state. The Tupelo newspaper praised the election "of a man who is steeped in the Spirit of the Old South—a man that Lee and Jackson and Jefferson Davis would have voted for had they been living." Walter Sillers congratulated Eastland and urged him to "stand firm for White Supremacy and Southern Democracy" while in the Senate. Eastland left for Washington in early 1943 determined to do more than that.[54]

4

"An Enormous Tragedy in the Making": Revolutions in Sunflower County and Abroad

The five-mile stretch of highway between the Eastland plantation in Doddsville and Hamer's former home in Ruleville has changed dramatically in the seventy-five years since the senator and the sharecropper began their adult lives. The fields have not been paved over with parking lots and strip malls, as so much of America's farmland has been. The two-lane highway has not been transformed into an interstate, and land values have not soared beyond the means of average wage earners. On the surface, the fields look the same, as if Sunflower County remains stuck in time. Cotton still dominates the landscape, though soybean and corn fields, rice paddies, and the occasional catfish pond have muscled their way in. The fields still extend to the horizon, broken intermittently by thin lines of vine-draped trees that mark property lines and bayous. But something is missing, something vital: people. Except for the men who drive the machines that plow, plant, and harvest the crops, the fields you pass in your car are virtually empty.

How different it was fifty years ago! On a visit to the Delta shortly after the end of World War II, war veteran and future congressman Frank Smith marveled: "The white fields are alive with pickers, and bulging wagons and trucks move along the roads towards the gins." During his childhood in the 1940s, James Eastland's son, Woods, remembered, "The countryside was full of people," with a family living on every twenty to forty acres, from Memphis to Vicksburg. Yet even then, discerning eyes could see harbingers of change. "The September visitor can ride through broad white fields bobbing with negro pickers," Smith wrote, "and move on to a neighboring plantation and find the fields empty of all life but a tractor-drawn, mechanical picker." The most visible sign of the slow transformation of Sunflower County, the mechanical picker was one of many subtle but far-reaching economic and political changes in the area during and after World War II. The battle to shape how these changes would affect life in Sunflower County would bring James Eastland and Fannie Lou Hamer into direct confrontation with each other, and their struggles thrust their home to the forefront of the nation's attention. Let's look now at how the senator and the sharecropper responded to the beginning of this era of transformation.[1]

NO MORE "LABOR FOR THE PICKING"

When James Eastland left his plantation for an office on Capitol Hill, Sunflower County as he and Fannie Lou Hamer knew it was firmly in place. He left behind his wife, Libby, their two daughters (a third girl was born shortly after he arrived in Washington), and his ailing parents. Bolstered by the New Deal, the plantation world seemed stable and profitable, at least for planters, and Senator Eastland aimed to keep it that way. Although Eastland later gained a reputation as a racist demagogue, he first distinguished himself among his colleagues with his single-minded defense of planters' economic interests. As one of his planter constituents wrote to him soon after he arrived in Washington in early 1943, by standing up for cotton Eastland could "go down in history as the economic saviour of the Cotton South."[2] Economic concerns topped Eastland's agenda when he assumed office, and they remained his primary focus for years as the war and its aftermath threatened the labor supply upon which his cotton empire rested.

The war had triggered an economic expansion that lifted the national economy out of the doldrums. Sunflower County's planters and pickers both benefited from increasing cotton prices. The federal government abandoned its Depression-era acreage controls in an effort to boost cotton production, and initially planters enjoyed "labor for the picking," a labor surplus that allowed them to increase production without increasing costs. For a brief period, plantations were more profitable than ever. "Cotton is 26 cents in the Delta now," wrote author Lillian Smith after a 1942 visit, "and the general attitude among the planters is that neither Mr. Roosevelt nor God Himself is going to keep them from making some money while the making is good." God may not have been able to stop the planters, but the war did. As they had a generation earlier, wartime exigencies drew black workers away from the fields, and the labor surplus evaporated. Whether they were drafted for military service or they pursued opportunities in defense industries, black workers fled the farms, creating a labor shortage that increased planters' costs and cut into their profit margins. "The area no longer has any surplus, nor any great reservoir, of workers," noted the Delta Council, the planter-dominated regional chamber of commerce of which Eastland was a member. By 1943, Sunflower County had lost more than four thousand workers, a loss of nearly 12 percent of its labor force; going into the 1944 planting season, the county stood nearly a quarter short of the labor needed for production. With all the young men leaving, one observer noted, "we have a much higher percentage of old men, women, and young children working on the farms."[3]

The problem extended into the Eastland household. A frustrated Libby Eastland wanted to find a black nurse for the children so that she could spend more time with the senator's ailing mother, but, as she complained to her husband, "I can't find a negro anywhere." Her frustration with the labor shortage, combined with the stress of raising three girls under the age of ten, put strains on their marriage. Libby grew "dreadfully lonely" and wrote to Jim pleading for him to write and visit more often. She insisted that she and the girls get an apartment in Washington so that they could spend time with him while Congress was in session from January to June. The stress of the job may have been taking its toll on Jim, too. Woods Eastland worried that his son might be drinking too much and regularly implored him to stop. "Hope you are getting along fine," one letter closed, "and for God's sake, lay off of liquor." Though Jim insisted that he did not have a drinking problem, his fondness for Scotch would prompt rumors throughout his Senate career.[4]

While Eastland and other planters struggled to find enough workers, Fannie Lou Hamer and other laborers who remained on the plantation gained increased leverage and bargaining power. The Delta Council may have condemned the "unethical labor recruiting practices carried on by out-of-State agents," but Sunflower County workers enjoyed the competition for their labor. Whereas during the Depression planters eagerly sought to move sharecroppers off the land in favor of wage workers, they now desperately tried to keep their tenants in order to ensure a stable, year-round labor supply. Wages jumped from $1 per hundred pounds of cotton picked in 1940 to $3 in 1944—planters willing to pay high wages found that they had no problem finding workers. The higher wages, coupled with government benefit checks coming to families of servicemen, gave some black tenants the freedom to move to town and work for wages when necessary. "With those checks and the high price they can get for chopping cotton and picking cotton," complained the county extension agent, "these folks do not have to work many days to get enough to live on."[5]

In an effort to retain their access to cheap, abundant labor, planters such as Eastland overcame their rhetorical objections to federal intrusion in local affairs and eagerly sought governmental intervention to protect their labor supply. Their demands at times stood opposed to national security needs. While the military needed soldiers, planters wanted cotton pickers; while the War Manpower Commission sought to place workers in the most essential positions, planters wanted to keep their laborers on the farm; while the Office of Price Administration aimed to keep prices low, planters worked to keep cotton and cottonseed prices high. Though they clashed with the military, planters had friends, not only in Senator Eastland but also within the U.S. Department of Agriculture, which consistently sided with planters. With powerful allies in Washington, planters were able to use the Emergency Farm Labor Supply Program and other federal programs to get cheap labor. Eastland, who had objected to the OPA's attempt to cap cottonseed prices, nonetheless supported the successful effort to limit cotton-picking wages in the Delta. In 1945, when the Southern Tenant Farmers Union and the Congress of Industrial Organizations (CIO) sought an increase to $3.50 per 100 pounds of cotton, Eastland helped push for, and win, a federal ceiling of $2.10—a welcome bit of "outside interference" that saved planters an estimated $15 to $20 million in wages. For Eastland and his supporters, federal intervention in the economy was acceptable, so long as it benefited the right people.[6]

Planters also sought Eastland's help and federal assistance to exploit another pool of labor: prisoners of war. POW camps were sprinkled throughout the nation, and Sunflower County became home to two such camps, one in Indianola and one in Drew. About a thousand German and Italian prisoners captured in North Africa arrived in the county in 1943, and planters saw an opportunity to both meet their labor needs and undercut their black workers' growing economic leverage with a literally captive labor force. The Delta Council urged Eastland to help planters get access to the POWs, and he obliged. Planters all over the county requested and received POWs to work in the fields during picking season; at least twenty picked cotton on the Eastland farm. Guards marched the prisoners to the fields, where they spent their days toiling for $2 per hundred pounds, to be paid to the U.S. government. The prisoners' lack of experience often produced what one observer called "trashy" cotton "with cotton stalks, grass, and mud," but most planters welcomed the inexpensive laborers. "Of course they didn't know what they were doing," remembered one Sunflower County farmer, "but they were an invaluable service to us." The Delta Council agreed. "This labor, though unskilled in cotton picking, contributed appreciably to the labor supply of the Delta and, by the end of the season, was picking per man day enough poundage to be of real assistance in harvesting." Even after the end of the war in Europe in May 1945, planters beseeched Eastland to help them keep the prisoners in the Delta for the duration of the cotton season. Once again, their voices were heard in Washington. That fall, after the dropping of the atomic bombs, German and Italian voices still could be heard on the Eastland plantation and in the cotton fields of Sunflower County.[7]

Eastland's perspective as a Sunflower County planter concerned with protecting access to cheap labor manifested itself in the Senate, where he devoted his energy to attacking labor unions. Eastland feared that union leaders would seize upon the wartime labor crunch to push what he considered to be a Communist agenda of property redistribution and racial egalitarianism. Union workers in urban areas used their increased leverage to protect the hard-fought gains of the 1930s, including collective bargaining rights and the closed shop, and they led numerous wildcat strikes in northern factories. Angry Mississippians wrote to Eastland to complain about "these labor gangsters, strikes, inefficiency, waste and bureaucracy." Eastland shared such concerns, and he spent much of his first two years in the Senate attacking labor unions and organizers to prevent the spread of their worker-friendly agenda. "We are not only fighting the greatest war in all history, but we are fighting a war on the home front," he wrote one constituent. "There is no doubt but that certain bureaucrats with Communistic leanings are attempting to destroy the old American principles that made our Country great." These bureaucrats, he feared, were in league with the CIO, an interracial union that not only sought to organize unskilled black and white workers but also lobbied against the poll tax and in favor of a federal anti-lynching law. Eastland savaged CIO organizers, calling them "aliens" who "desire to destroy our institutions and mongrelize our people." He viewed striking during wartime as traitorous and sought to impugn the patriotism of labor leaders. Among his first actions as a senator was to draw up legislation giving the federal government power to draft striking workers into the army. Indeed, he proposed only three bills in his first year in the Senate; all three sought to limit labor rights and increase management's power to break strikes. Both as a senator and as a planter, he made control of labor his top priority.[8]

"AN INSURANCE OF LASTING PEACE"

Eastland's obsession with labor control led him to become engaged in a struggle that would take him far from the fields of Sunflower County: the early postwar effort to oppose Soviet expansionism. With the fascist opponent defeated, he believed the United States now could focus on the more insidious foe—the Soviet Union and its ideology—and he threw down the gauntlet in Germany. When the war in Europe ended in May 1945, he became deeply immersed in the postwar reconstruction of Germany, which he saw as essential to the preservation of Western civilization. In the face of resistance within the Roosevelt administration and in public opinion, he devoted himself to promoting a lenient reconstruction policy. Upon his retirement more than thirty years later, he recalled that his greatest accomplishment was helping the German people rebuild their nation.[9]

The catalyst for Eastland's reconstruction campaign was an overseas excursion. For three weeks in late May and early June 1945, shortly after V-E Day, Eastland joined other members of the Senate Naval Affairs Subcommittee on a trip to war-ravaged Germany. Walking in the footsteps of Allied liberation armies, the senators interviewed army personnel and compiled statistical reports about the devastation. Even more than the statistics they heard, it was the scenes they saw firsthand that made the deepest impression on Eastland and his companions. Burned-out homes, buildings reduced to ashes, refugees wandering in search of food—the hellish images sickened the senators. Eastland returned to Mississippi pessimistic about the future of Europe, telling reporters that he saw "nothing promising" during his trip. The war had been won, but at a horrific price. Now came the daunting task of reconstruction.[10]

Six of the group's nine members were white southerners. As the rubble crunched underfoot, the men could hardly resist seeing immediate parallels to their own region following the American Civil War, a time of Reconstruction that Eastland considered the most "shameful" era in America history. In their minds, the United States had made grievous errors following the "War Between the States," forcing a punitive peace upon a prostrate South, curtailing the power of the ex-Confederates, and elevating their colored subordinates to undeserved positions of power. "The Republican Party attempted to destroy the white race," Eastland believed, and he proudly recalled how both of his grandfathers joined other whites in "throwing off the yoke of carpetbagger Reconstruction." Now, eighty years later, he was witnessing the end of another terrible war, another war with potentially revolutionary consequences. The horrors Eastland and other white southerners had heard about growing up seemed to be repeating themselves in postwar Europe. In Germany, as in the South during the grim years of Reconstruction, the U.S. army was an occupying force with the power to dictate the terms of peace. In Germany, as in the South, the defeated and suffering people were white, and they faced a challenge from nonwhites—the "Asiatic hordes" from Russia who Eastland believed were bent upon enslaving the German people under Communism. In Germany, as in the South during Reconstruction, the future of white civilization seemed in peril: "Germany has served both as a neutralizing agent and as a barrier between the Oriental hordes and a western civilization 2,000 years old," Eastland argued, "and for the first time in history we find in Czechoslovakia savage, barbarian Mongolian hordes stalking the streets of western civilization as conquerors, and threatening not to stop at Vienna and Berlin but to push on to engulf the very civilization from which we ourselves have stemmed."[11]

Eastland, like his grandfathers before him, sought to take his stand. Believing that only a strong, industrial Germany could resist Communism, he urged economic support and material relief for the German people. His immediate target was the Morgenthau plan, which represented what he saw as the harsh alternative to German reconstruction—the modern equivalent of Radical Reconstruction. The Morgenthau plan, named for Treasury secretary Henry Morgenthau, Eastland's nemesis from the cottonseed fight, emerged in 1944 when the Roosevelt administration began to formulate plans for the postwar world. While State Department officials urged moderation, Morgenthau pushed for punitive measures that would reduce Germany to a "pastoral" state by destroying its industrial capacity and extracting cash reparations. Rather than taking steps to rehabilitate the economy, Morgenthau argued, the occupying forces should allow economic chaos to reign—only then would the German people admit defeat and acknowledge their guilt for causing the war. This "planned chaos" ultimately would yield a pacified Germany unwilling and unable to wage war. President Roosevelt ultimately favored a less punitive course, but Morgenthau's ideas nonetheless found their way into American occupation policy because military officials found it easier to administer a harsh peace than a lenient one. Although the Potsdam agreement in August 1945 gave military officials more leeway to pursue economic rehabilitation, the thrust of occupation policy retained the spirit of the Morgenthau plan.[12]

As winter approached, the effects of U.S. occupation policy generated more and more criticism. A series of reports released in November revealed growing skepticism among military and congressional leaders about the wisdom of the punitive approach. Armed with such documentation, Eastland took to the Senate floor in early December to challenge what he called the "sadistic" American policy of punishing the German people. In characteristic fashion, his lengthy speech focused not simply on the particular details of occupation policy but on grander moral themes. He spoke in global terms, arguing that the policy debate really was part of a much larger struggle to preserve Western civilization. His passionate performance on the Senate floor revealed his vision of the postwar world: a clash of civilizations between East and West, a racial and religious battle between white Christians and Oriental Communists. World War II had been won, but the battle to save Anglo-Saxon civilization had just begun. Germany was no longer the enemy—the new evil in the world was the Soviet Union, which Eastland labeled as a "predatory, aggressor nation" that "follows the same fateful road of conquest and aggression with which Adolf Hitler set the world on fire."[13]

Eastland had seen conditions in Germany firsthand, and he drew upon that experience as he painted a pathetic picture of the landscape. Millions of people were dead, millions more homeless, factories lay in ruins, railroads had been blown up. "No nation in modern history has suffered such catastrophe as Germany endures today," he insisted, echoing a recurrent theme in the white memory of southern Reconstruction. Moreover, Eastland charged, U.S. policy was only making things worse. By pursuing a "policy of vindictive hatred," American leaders were causing "grave hardship, starvation, and human suffering." This human suffering was unacceptable, Eastland insisted, not simply from a humanitarian perspective but also from an ideological one. Starving people were desperate people, and in their quest for survival hungry Germans could very well turn to Communists who would take advantage of the misery, manipulate the population, and assume control of the country. If misguided American policy pushed Germany into the arms of the Soviet Union, America would face an extraordinarily powerful alliance capable of conquering the world. To live up to "our responsibility as a civilized, Christian people," Eastland charged, U.S. policy had to be changed immediately lest it touch off "a prolonged era of pitiless hunger, a program of central European chaos and disorder, to be ultimately presided over by the ghouls of revolution, starvation, and atheism, and resulting in the cremation of Christianity in Europe."[14]

Eastland's voice joined a growing chorus that condemned U.S. occupation policy, and administration officials soon heard the message. A week after his speech, the State Department issued a statement that reflected a shift in policy—American officials would now work to prevent starvation, allow German industrial production, and ultimately give control of the economy back to the Germans. But global events did little to assuage the senator's fears that white civilization was under attack abroad. In a March 1946 speech at segregated Westminster College in Missouri, England's prime minister, Winston Churchill, gravely warned of an "iron curtain" descending upon Eastern Europe. The Soviet Union's rapid expansion in the next two years only seemed to confirm Eastland's fears that Communism was taking over the world. "This is the greatest crisis in the Christian era," Eastland warned as Europe slipped closer to famine and social chaos in the winter of 1946–47. "Oriental Communism directed from Moscow seeks to destroy Christian civilization and western culture. It has made great progress; our danger is greater than at any time in modern or medieval history."[15]

Harry Truman shared Eastland's sense of urgency. He and Eastland got along quite well—Eastland liked to claim credit for Truman's selection as the vice presidential nominee during the 1944 convention—and they both saw the Soviet Union as an immediate threat. Although Truman had toyed with the idea of sharing the secrets of atomic weaponry with the Russians and had even good-naturedly described Stalin as "good old Joe," by early 1947 he supported taking a much harder anti-Communist line and began to lay the ideological and institutional foundation for the Cold War. In a March 12 speech before a joint session of Congress, Truman laid out what became known as the Truman Doctrine. The president neatly cleaved the world into two opposing ways of life, one "distinguished by free institutions, representative government, free elections, guarantees of individual liberty, freedom of speech and religion, and freedom from political oppression" and one that "relies upon terror and oppression, a controlled press and radio, fixed elections, and the suppression of personal freedoms." It was up to the United States to defend the free peoples of the world, he argued, and he urged Congress to appropriate $400 million to support anti-Communists in Greece and Turkey. Major Cold War initiatives followed rapidly. Less than two weeks after the speech, Truman signed an executive order requiring that federal employees take loyalty oaths affirming their anti-Communist beliefs; in May, administration officials announced a plan to spend hundreds of millions of dollars reconstructing the economies of Europe; by July, Congress had passed the National Security Act creating the Central Intelligence Agency, the National Security Council, and the Defense Department. Throughout the world, the United States would confront and contain Communism. The nation had thrust itself fully on the side of "freedom" in the Cold War.[16]

Eastland saw himself as standing squarely with the forces of freedom. He eagerly supported the Truman administration's anti-Communist efforts, both with votes in the Senate and in public speeches. Equating the Soviet Union with Hitler, he urged the United States to avoid a "weak, vacillating policy of appeasement" that would encourage Soviet expansion. Like Hitler, he argued, the Soviets were biding their time, slowly building an empire through insurgencies in small nations. As the only power strong enough to oppose Communist expansion, the United States had the moral duty to do so. He predicted that war would result if America did not stand up to the Soviets' world of "chaos, revolution, and aggression"—support for anti-Communist forces in Greece, Turkey, and other nations was "a program of peace," the only way to forestall World War III. No means should be spared to defeat the Communist menace. "There can be no compromise with Communism," Eastland insisted, "because one cannot compromise with death."[17]

Eastland raged against the Soviet Union's denial of political liberties and abuse of human rights. The Soviet Union denied its satellite countries the right to choose their own governments and "go their own way without coercion and without domination by any other power." He was particularly incensed by Russian prison camps. These slave labor camps forced opponents of Communism—white people, he emphasized, not "Asiatics"—to work in squalid conditions in frigid Siberia. "There is more slavery on the earth today than at any previous time in the world's history," Eastland argued, "because Communism is the greatest of all enslavers." To defeat Communist slavery, the United States had to make a major commitment to rebuild its defeated enemies. As he had in Germany, Eastland insisted that the United States should spend the energy and resources to promote economic prosperity worldwide. "The best weapon against Communism is the establishment of prosperous peoples and strong democratic governments." As he explained in a radio debate in 1946, "Peace, regardless of armed might, cannot be built upon hunger, unemployment, and human suffering." "To win the peace, we must permit [Germany and Japan] prosperity, high living standards, if they can earn them, and freedom to work and prosper."[18]

Economic prosperity through free enterprise was essential to Eastland's understanding of freedom and civilization. It also was essential to his own family's cotton empire. Coming out of the war, the American cotton industry was in shambles, plagued by labor shortages, declining market share, and competition from rayon and other synthetic fibers. Worse still, the devastation in Europe meant that some of the industry's best customers could not afford to import cotton. Cotton farmers feared a future of falling prices. Even as the war raged on they urged Eastland to prevent a catastrophe. "If we don't get into the world market, synthetic fibers—after the war—will put us out of business," one worried planter wrote to Eastland. "Our customers are on the other hemisphere." The Delta Council warned of a "precarious future" for cotton, which was "a paramount problem to the Delta." With the end of hostilities, Eastland saw an opportunity, a way to bolster the flagging cotton industry while helping Europe resist Communism. The solution, as Eastland outlined in a published piece entitled "Let's Prevent Chaos in Cotton," was to use federal money to purchase surplus crops such as cotton and give them, free of charge, to European nations for use in rebuilding their economies. Combined with tariff reductions that promoted free trade, the government-subsidized export of American surplus crops would serve as "an insurance of lasting peace," Eastland wrote, and it would allow American cotton farmers to compete with foreign growers who enjoyed lower labor costs. Federal intervention would stimulate demand for U.S. cotton at a time when global demand was slack. As he had in the effort to cap cotton-picking wages, Eastland laid aside his philosophical objections to "outside intervention."[19]

Other powerful cotton defenders, including fellow Delta planter and founder of the National Cotton Council Oscar Johnston, supported the surplus-export idea. Undersecretary of State Will Clayton, himself a cotton merchant who shared Eastland's commitment to low tariffs and open trade, crafted a plan to implement the surplus-export idea within a comprehensive framework of European recovery, which ultimately took form as the Marshall Plan. Named for the widely re-spected former army general and current secretary of state George C. Marshall, the Marshall Plan committed more than $13 billion in four years to the reconstruction of Europe. The Marshall Plan later was celebrated as an enormously successful example of foreign policy ttatesmanship, but its passage through Congress was by no means as-sured at the time. Congressional Republicans feared an "international New Deal" that would expand federal control of the economy, raise taxes, and increase government power, and many war-weary Ameri-cans were wary of a renewed international commitment. Facing stiff congressional opposition throughout 1947, administration officials desperately needed the support of southern Democrats such as Eastland to pass their plan, and they appealed consistently to the re-gion's economic self-interest, particularly in the cotton industry.[20]

As if to underscore the importance of cotton to the proposed legislation, the Truman administration's first public announcement of the Marshall Plan came not in Washington, New York, or San Fran-cisco, but in May 1947 at the annual meeting of the Delta Council in Cleveland, Mississippi—about fifteen miles from the Eastland planta-tion. (This event is memorialized by a historical marker in downtown Cleveland.) More than two weeks before Secretary Marshall himself would reveal the plan to the national public, the urbane Undersecretary of State Dean Acheson spoke to an audience of cotton planters to assure them that the federal government was preparing to take action to promote and protect foreign trade by rebuilding Europe. Acheson was preaching to the choir. With more than a third of cotton exports going to Western Europe, planters believed that preserving access to European markets was essential to the long-term survival of the cotton economy. The Delta Council enthusiastically supported the Marshall Plan as a way to promote "a more efficient southern agriculture and maintenance of international markets." Both as a planter and as cotton producers' representative in Washington, Eastland agreed; without these "historic markets," he argued, the cotton industry, indeed the entire U.S. economic system, would collapse. With their interests preserved, southerners in Congress joined Eastland in supporting the Marshall Plan, which passed in mid-1948.[21]

Eastland was by no means solely or largely responsible for the passage of the Marshall Plan or the shift toward a lenient reconstruction policy in Germany. Yet his role in both debates revealed his determined effort to shape the direction of postwar American foreign policy toward an active, global commitment against Communism that would include economic intervention to protect cotton farmers. Eastland and his colleagues decisively cast their lot with the growing anti-Communist forces during the critical months following the end of the war, before the rivalry with the Soviet Union had registered fully with the American public. As the Cold War intensified, their unwavering anti-Communist support gave them leverage in their domestic agenda. Although members of Truman's foreign policy corps often found Eastland and other southern segregationists in Congress diplomatically embarrassing, the conservative southern bloc formed an important part of the growing Cold War consensus upon which Truman's policies depended. If President Truman wanted their votes for aggressive foreign policies, they believed, then he would have to bargain with them regarding his proposed domestic agenda.[22]

"AS INIQUITOUS AS THE FREEDMAN'S BUREAU"

Eastland's obsession with Communism and foreign affairs grew from his Sunflower County plantation roots. Planters such as Eastland, one observer noted, depended on a global economy, so they were always "interested in world production, world consumption, and the world price of cotton and of competing fibers." Though he sometimes struck a statesman's pose and belittled domestic concerns, his postwar foreign policy objectives could not be divorced from his domestic agenda to preserve segregation and maintain economic control over his plantation's workers. Indeed, the threats from abroad appeared all the more dangerous because of their potential to wreak havoc at home. The foreign and domestic objectives were inextricably linked through race and anti-Communism; the hierarchical, segregated order he cherished in Sunflower County was what he hoped to protect in the fight against the Soviet Union. For Eastland, the fight against Communism was a fight for white supremacy—much of his hatred for Communism grew from his concerns about its potential effect on black Americans.

Like the Civil War, World War II and the ensuing Cold War had raised the possibility of a world made new, a world in which racial equality would be a foundational principle of domestic and international affairs. He feared that the Sunflower County world that protected his children, the safe, segregated world where white elites dominated the black majority, might be torn asunder by Communist expansion and racial agitation. But Eastland and his allies worked to ensure that America's Cold War posture would not include a dismantling of Jim Crow. As a senator, Eastland sought to protect that world and the freedom for which he believed the United States was fighting in both the "Good War" and the Cold War: a capitalist America where economic hierarchies reflected natural, racial hierarchies. His efforts bolstered both the supply of and the demand for the cotton crop on which his Sunflower County empire rested.[23]

When he returned home from Germany in mid-June 1945, Eastland found an immediate domestic challenge to white supremacy brewing on the floor of the Senate—the fight to establish a permanent

Fair Employment Practices Committee (FEPC). Designed to prevent discrimination on the basis of "race, color, creed, or national origin," the FEPC had been established by executive order in 1941 after a threatened march on Washington by the imposing head of the Brotherhood of Sleeping Car Porters, A. Philip Randolph, and other black labor leaders. An important triumph for civil rights activists, the agency banned racial discrimination by employers and labor unions engaged in federal defense contracts and became the first federal agency since the Freedman's Bureau during Reconstruction to be devoted to race-related issues. To supporters such as black educator Mary McLeod Bethune, the FEPC was "a refreshing shower in a thirsty land," but for Eastland and other white southern Democrats the agency was the ill wind of an advancing storm, an ominous sign of a renewed federal commitment to racial equality. They viewed the FEPC as one face of a multiheaded attack on traditional southern institutions. Like the Civil War, World War II had unleashed powerful forces that threatened to destroy the old world order based on white supremacy. This time, the threat was not confined to the South—it was global.[24]

Rhetorically, intellectually, and politically, white supremacy and colonial rule faced unprecedented challenges worldwide. According to President Roosevelt, the Allies had fought for the Four Freedoms— freedom of speech and religion, freedom from want and fear. Implicit within those freedoms, many activists argued, was a commitment to racial equality; after all, the defeated Nazis and the Japanese had advocated racial hierarchy. Nonwhite peoples the world over saw the war as a war to end colonialism, a turning point in human history when nations would repudiate the doctrines of racism and subjugation once and for all. They gained support from a new generation of scholars, who slowly began to overturn nineteenth-century shibboleths on race and instead offered new theories that showed the biological similarity and equality of humankind. Perhaps the most influential anti-racist scholar, and the one who became Eastland's primary academic target, was Swedish sociologist Gunnar Myrdal, whose epic study of race relations in the United States, *An American Dilemma*, appeared in 1944. Directly confronting American segregation and prejudice, Myrdal argued that the crucial test the nation faced in the postwar era was how to turn American rhetoric about democracy and freedom into reality for black Americans. With the opportunities created by the New Deal and the war, Myrdal was optimistic about postwar racial progress. "America can demonstrate that justice, equality and cooperation are possible between white and colored people," he wrote. "Race relations are bound to change considerably." That was precisely what troubled Eastland and his colleagues.[25]

Black Americans compounded Eastland's fears with rising expectations to match their expanding role in the war effort. As black workers by the thousands fled the rural South and poured into the armed forces and defense industries of the North and West, they increasingly chafed against the constraints of racism and became more assertive in demanding fair treatment, often using the war to highlight the hypocrisy of white supremacy. There was "no difference," A. Philip Randolph commented, "between Hitler of Germany and Talmadge of Georgia or Tojo of Japan and Bilbo of Mississippi." The black-owned *Pittsburgh Courier* launched a "Double V" campaign aimed at defeating fascism abroad and Jim Crow at home, while black activists pushed for anti-poll-tax legislation and a federal law to ban lynching. In 1944, blacks scored two important victories. A landmark Supreme Court decision in *Smith v. Allwright* declared the white political primary unconstitutional—a decision Eastland denounced for showing "an alarming tendency to destroy State sovereignty." Meanwhile, black northerners began to flex their political muscle by helping to derail segregationist James Byrnes's nomination for vice president during the 1944 Democratic convention, a victory that took on extraordinary significance after President Roosevelt's death the next year. This increasing assertiveness did not go unnoticed or unchallenged. Many whites reacted angrily, and racial violence rose during the war. In 1943 alone, 242 racial battles erupted in forty-seven different cities across the country, including full-fledged race riots in New York and Detroit.[26]

To add to Eastland's worries, the new Truman administration appeared willing to push for black equality. Harry Truman grew up in segregated, small-town Missouri, but he took unexpectedly bold stands in favor of civil rights and publicly supported the renewal of the FEPC. Racial discrimination in employment, Truman declared in June, "is not only un-American in nature but will lead eventually to industrial strife and unrest." Buoyed by Truman's apparent support and propelled by the raised expectations from the war, liberal advocates of the FEPC urged Congress not only to fund the FEPC through the end of the Pacific war but also to make it a permanent agency with enforcement power. By late June, soon after Eastland returned from Germany, a bill that included funding for a permanent FEPC reached the Senate floor. Eastland and his colleagues immediately promised an "extended explanation"—a filibuster in all but name—that would outline their objections to the bill.[27]

The June debate over the FEPC marked Eastland's ascension to national prominence. Initially overshadowed by two solid days of "explanation" by his vitriolic Mississippi nemesis, Senator Bilbo, Eastland took over on June 29 for a four-hour speech that outlined in emotional detail his objections to the federal agency. "Flailing his arms and jerking his tie askew," reporters noted, Eastland shouted his objections to the FEPC on practical, constitutional, ideological, and racial grounds. His spirited attack on the agency sent a clear message to the new Truman administration that he and his southern colleagues were not about to give an inch on white supremacy, a victory over Nazism notwithstanding. With his speech delivered before a packed Senate gallery, Eastland not only emerged as Bilbo's equal in demagoguery but also laid out the conservative white South's Cold War argument that fused white supremacy with anti-Communism.[28]

"We cannot legislate to stamp out of one's heart the prejudices which are contained therein," Eastland argued, and thus the FEPC was a misguided attempt to force equality where it did not belong. "The Negro race is an inferior race," he insisted, and the FEPC was part of a gradual effort to destroy "the safeguards which have been erected to maintain the purity and racial integrity of the white race." To illustrate black inferiority, Eastland, who himself had not served, singled out Negro troops during the war for alleged failures. "The Negro soldier was an utter and dismal failure in combat," he charged. Citing unnamed generals as sources, he ridiculed black troops for desertion, insubordination, and cowardice, claiming that "they were lazy, that they would not work," and that they "have disgraced the flag of this country." Based on such purported evidence, Eastland concluded that any effort to achieve racial equality, such as the FEPC, could only lead to ruin.[29]

But the agency was far more dangerous than just another ill-advised liberal project for bigger government, Eastland emphasized. It was the opening wedge in a Communist assault on the United States. "It is all part of the Communist program to destroy America," he warned, "to destroy the American system of economy, to destroy the American system of government, which we love, in order to sovietize our country." How could an agency designed to deter discrimination be a tool of Moscow? The connection was clear in Eastland's mind, and he painstakingly sought to convey his message to his colleagues and the public. It was an argument he would repeat many times during the next two decades, and it became the linchpin holding together his foreign and domestic agendas: Communists thrived on conflict and tension; they worked to create such tension by making otherwise contented people class-conscious and race-conscious; as conflicts erupted, they would then seize the opportunity to topple the American system. Thus, he reasoned, Communists were using the FEPC to pit blacks against whites and provoke racial conflict that would undermine the nation. The Communist Party was "exploiting the Negroes by making special promises such as FEPC, such as social equality, such as racial amalgamation, in an attempt to line the Negroes up under the red banner of Communism and destroy the United States." In Eastland's mind, anyone agitating for racial change was therefore either a Communist or a Communist dupe.[30]

Eastland's fiery speech was an opening salvo in the battle to determine the course of postwar America, an impassioned defense of white supremacy as the basis of American freedom. "Who has won this war?" Eastland thundered. The white soldier has, and "there will be no FEPC, there will be no social equality, there will be no such un-American measures when the soldier returns." The only way to preserve the American system, Eastland insisted, was to maintain racial hierarchy: "The doctrine of white supremacy is one which, if adhered to, will save America." Eastland's speech generated immediate criticism, particularly from the black press and the military—Undersecretary of War Robert Patterson claimed that he had "no knowledge" of the incidents with black soldiers to which Eastland referred—but the filibuster succeeded in paring down the FEPC's budget and preventing permanent status.[31]

The next year, however, Democratic senator Dennis Chavez of New Mexico surprised his colleagues by introducing a new bill that would make the FEPC a permanent postwar agency. "The Senate chamber had been as peaceful as a henhouse at laying time," one reporter noted, but when Chavez placed the FEPC bill on the agenda, "his colleagues realized that a fox had gotten loose in their midst." Eager to catch that fox before it caused too much damage, Eastland vowed to talk "for two years if necessary." Another filibuster was on. Despite criticism from much of the press outside the South—the *Washington Post* dismissed the southerners' effort as a "senseless display of sound and fury" and a cartoon in the *Chicago Defender* labeled the filibuster a "lynching on Capitol Hill"—the filibuster burned for weeks with no signs of abating. With the war in the Pacific over, there could be no more talk of temporary extension; the issue now was whether or not the federal government should retain a permanent peacetime agency dedicated to eliminating discrimination. For the FEPC's supporters, the matter was clear: at a time when the United States sought to exercise global leadership and serve as the world's example of freedom and democracy, the nation must confront and overcome racial discrimination. For opponents, the issue was equally clear: the FEPC sought to stir up racial tensions by forcing Negro rule upon the land.[32]

Eastland and his southern brethren saw this post–World War II period as another potential Reconstruction, another period of racial upheaval that threatened the sacred doctrine of white supremacy. He worked to preserve the prewar racial status quo, much as his grandfathers had toiled to defend white supremacy from any federal attacks before the Civil War and to redeem the South in the wake of the conflict. His language bristled with the rhetoric of the nineteenth century. The FEPC, he charged, was "as iniquitous as the Freedman's Bureau" and sought to punish the South and end segregation. The day after the bill was introduced on the Senate floor, Eastland echoed the antebellum stance of John C. Calhoun when he sent a public telegram to the Mississippi state legislature urging lawmakers to "nullify" the FEPC should it pass Congress. Though the doctrine of nullification had been repudiated by all three branches of government, Eastland insisted that it was "the unwritten law of the Constitution" and praised the antebellum South's nullification efforts.[33]

Like Radical Reconstruction, Eastland charged, the FEPC was an attempt to "mongrelize the races" and "export Harlem democracy" to the rest of the country. But now there was an added danger—Communism—because "with mongrelization comes Marxism," he explained. The intertwined issue at the heart of the debate was the connection between race and Communism. In an emotional colloquy with Louisiana senator Allen Ellender, himself a staunch segregationist, Eastland recommended his solution to the problem of Communism and other agitation in characteristically Socratic fashion. "Does not the Senator think the cure for all the racial agitation is taking the doctrine of white supremacy to the American people?" Eastland asked. After Ellender responded affirmatively, Eastland continued, "And showing the American people the value of race—that race is everything in American life?" Ellender agreed, though he urged Eastland to calm down as he was becoming "a little bit excited" on the matter.[34]

The southerners' passionate commitment to the filibuster ultimately won out. FEPC supporters could not overcome the institutional rules of the Senate, which gave individual senators the right to immobilize the chamber until a two-thirds majority voted to cut off debate. With a solid bloc of twenty-five southern Democrats behind the filibuster, the southerners needed to secure only eight votes from Republicans to keep it going. The bill's backers struggled to muster enough votes to end the filibuster, but they eventually gave up after more than three exhausting weeks of droning speeches. Eastland's hometown newspaper exulted, praising the senator's "brave and fearless fight for decent and democratic government." The FEPC was dead. Less than five months after the filibuster ended, the beleaguered agency quietly closed its cases, never to reopen them.[35]

"THE PEOPLE OF THE SOUTH ARE EXPECTED TO REMAIN DOCILE"

Despite his successes in the early postwar period, Eastland continued to offer apocalyptic warnings about the end of global free enterprise and increasingly shrill denunciations of the growing movement for black equality. To him, perhaps the most disturbing aspect of international

Communism was its effect on black Americans. The very fact that more and more blacks were pursuing civil rights in the late 1940s was evidence that the Communists were gaining ground. While Eastland and the Truman administration shared an anti-Soviet stance, their Cold War strategies diverged on the issue of race. Truman and members of his foreign policy team came to view American racial prejudice as a hindrance, a propaganda nightmare that the Soviets were more than willing to exploit; Eastland saw racial segregation as the hallmark of the American way of life that the nation was committed to defend. The growing rift on race threatened to undermine the Democratic Party's efforts to win the 1948 presidential election.

Like World War II, the Cold War opened ideological and moral opportunities for civil rights advocates to advance the cause of black equality. Truman, Eastland, and other Cold Warriors spoke about protecting "freedom" and "democracy" from Soviet encroachment; black leaders and their allies pointed to the obvious denial of freedom and democracy to black American citizens all across the South. How was it possible, wondered skeptical black activist and scholar W.E.B. Du Bois, to "export democracy to Greece and not practice it in Mississippi"? Despite their defeat in the FEPC fight, black leaders and their allies in 1947 and 1948 continued to push for an expansive definition of "freedom" that would bring an end to the poll tax, lynching, disenfranchisement, and segregation. They took advantage of the postwar posture of the United States as "leader of the free world" as a means of gaining mainstream support for their cause.[36]

The United Nations became one particularly important forum in which to highlight American hypocrisy on race. While Senator Eastland initially had supported the United Nations, he and other southern conservatives quickly soured on the fledgling organization. The United States and white European nations maintained an overwhelming majority in the UN, but nonwhites, including black Americans, challenged the international body to spearhead the drive for racial equality worldwide by helping to dismantle colonial empires and fight racial discrimination in the United States. By February 1946, the UN had created a Commission on Human Rights that promised to protect minorities and attack discrimination. In the organization's first two years, African Americans presented two separate petitions urging an end to American discrimination; the NAACP's 1947 "Appeal to the World," written chiefly by Du Bois, was a scholarly treatise condemning racial practices such as segregation, lynching, and voter discrimination. The petition rejected Eastland's notion that Communism was the major threat to freedom in America and elsewhere. "It is not Russia that threatens the United States so much as Mississippi," Du Bois insisted, "not Stalin and Molotov but Bilbo and [Mississippi Representative John] Rankin."[37]

The Soviet Union did in fact seize upon southern racism as a wedge to split nonwhite nations from the United States. The American Communist Party long had advocated racial equality as part of its platform, and at least since the Scottsboro trial in 1931 it had been active in promoting racial justice in the United States. After the war the Soviet Union self-consciously and opportunistically depicted itself as the champion of nonwhite peoples. The Soviet press trumpeted incidents of American racism to audiences worldwide; postwar lynchings such as the quadruple murder of four blacks by a white mob in Georgia made international headlines. When U.S. secretary of state James Byrnes attacked the Soviet Union for denying voting rights in the Balkans in 1946, his Soviet counterpart shot back that "the Negroes of Mr. Byrnes' own state of South Carolina" were "denied the same right." In their attacks on the United States and Europeans, the Soviets emphasized not only American racism but also the history of colonialism and imperialism. The persistent criticism of American racial practices hampered the Truman administration's ability to project the United States as the "free" alternative to the "slave" system of the Soviets. "The existence of discrimination against minority groups in the United States," observed the State Department's Dean Acheson, "is a handicap in our relations with other countries."[38]

President Truman and many of his senior foreign policy advisors recognized how southern racism undermined their efforts to build a strong anti-Communist alliance, and they began to pursue a strategy that blunted criticism by emphasizing civil rights. In June 1947, Truman became the first president to address an NAACP convention. "Our case for democracy," he told the crowd of ten thousand, "should rest on practical evidence that we have been able to put our own house in order." In October, the President's Committee on Civil

Rights released a comprehensive report, *To Secure These Rights*, calling for a multifaceted attack on racism, including a permanent FEPC, legislation to protect black voting rights, a federal anti-lynching law, an end to the poll tax, integration of the military, and a prohibition of segregation on interstate transportation. The next February, shortly after his State of the Union speech, Truman adopted several of the committee's recommendations as part of his new civil rights agenda, which he outlined in a speech to Congress devoted solely to civil rights. Such dramatic gestures gave the State Department, the Voice of America, and other U.S. agencies positive news to trumpet abroad; they also inspired civil rights advocates and boosted Truman's image among black voters in the North who, the president's political advisor Clark Clifford advised, hold "the balance of power in Presidential elections." White southerners may complain, Clifford assured the nervous president, but ultimately they "can be safely considered Democratic."[39] He was wrong.

Eastland and other white southerners saw the administration's renewed push for black equality as a direct assault on their homeland, one reminiscent of the dark days of Reconstruction but with the added Red tinge of the Cold War. The white southern reaction to Truman's civil rights agenda was swift and negative. Contrary to the claims made within the administration and the national news media, the storm would not blow over quickly. Eastland saw no more reason to compromise on civil rights than he did on Communism. On February 9, a week after the president's speech, he took to the Senate floor to attack Truman's efforts. The same man who condemned Soviet slavery invoked the memory of a slave society to challenge Truman: "If the present Democratic leadership is right, then Calhoun and Jefferson Davis were wrong," Eastland argued. "The people of the South are expected to remain docile while their civilization and culture are destroyed, while their segregation statutes are repealed by Federal action, and while the white race is destroyed under the false guise of another civil-rights bill. We are expected to remain docile while the pure blood of the South is mongrelized by the barter of our heritage by northern politicians in order to secure political favors from Red mongrels in the slums of the great cities of the East and Middle West."[40]

In the face of this brazen attack on the South, Eastland counseled defiance. He proposed a strategy that closely followed the blueprint outlined in Charles W. Collins's *Whither Solid South?*, an intellectual critique of the push for black equality that deeply influenced the senator. An unabashed white supremacist, Collins condemned organized groups that were "attempting to drive the South into a corner of moral isolation on the Negro race question" by calling for "'democracy' which in its very concept condemns in one breath the whole southern system." He urged the white South to withhold its electoral votes from the Democratic Party to throw the presidential election to the House of Representatives, where southerners could ensure the election of a pro-South candidate. Eastland and other white southern politicians adopted this idea as the political stimulus for a states' rights movement, which was one part of what the Mississippi senator dubbed the "Battle of the South" against the "destruction of her social institutions." Whites needed to "act speedily and decisively," Eastland argued, by organizing at the grassroots level and creating a region-wide network of local groups dedicated to the cause of preserving segregation. The people of the South then would "make our case before the people of the North" through a region-wide organization. A month after his speech in the Senate, Eastland proposed this plan to approving representatives in the Mississippi legislature.[41]

Among the white Mississippi Democrats who were Eastland's constituents, the idea of taking aggressive action against the national Democratic Party gained widespread support. Although he was a vocal supporter of the states' rights movement, he was up for reelection and did not take a major leadership role; that task fell to two governors, the winsome, dynamic World War II veteran Strom Thurmond of South Carolina and Mississippi's stern, aristocratic Fielding Wright. Shortly after Eastland's Senate speech, Wright held a mass meeting in Jackson to launch a states' rights movement that would be dubbed the "Dixiecrat revolt"; throughout the spring, they worked with Charles Collins and Deep South politicians to mobilize the white South for a fight against Truman's civil rights agenda. The crux of the matter, Wright explained, was "whether or not the majority of the people were going to let negroes run the country."[42]

By the July 1948 Democratic National Convention in Philadelphia, tensions within the party threatened to tear it apart. Southern states' rights advocates arrived at the convention ready to oppose both a civil rights platform and President Truman's nomination. Liberals, led by former vice president Henry Wallace, saw the first postwar convention as an opportunity to articulate a party vision that combined the economic policies of the New Deal with the racial policies demanded by morality and the Cold War. Truman, meanwhile, hoped somehow to appease all factions enough to maintain party unity for the tough upcoming campaign. The convention was a disaster for the president. Despite his effort to mollify white southerners by adopting a watered-down civil rights platform that was no more ambitious than the one in the 1944 platform, the Mississippi delegation and half of the Alabama delegation walked out in protest. As one states' rights supporter wrote Eastland, "I think Truman's popularity is about on the par with that of a Ku Klux empire at a ball game between Jews and Catholics." Two days later, several thousand states' rights sympathizers staged their own convention in Birmingham. Eastland attended the Birmingham convention, along with his colleague Senator John Stennis and several members of the Mississippi congressional delegation, and he emerged publicly optimistic. Truman will be "hopelessly defeated," he predicted to a Memphis audience six weeks before the election, so voting for the president was a "wasted vote."[43]

But Eastland had to eat crow come November. Hampered by a lack of organizational and ideological unity, as well as a lack of time for campaigning, the states' rights advocates failed to win the regional bloc of electoral votes necessary to throw the election to the House, as Eastland and others had hoped. The Dixiecrats won only four states—Alabama, Mississippi, Georgia, and South Carolina—and President Truman held on to a narrow victory. Eastland, meanwhile, cruised to reelection without facing a serious challenger. Despite the Dixiecrats' defeat, he remained publicly undaunted. The "States' Rights movement will never die," he declared shortly after the election, arguing that the nation is in the "opening phases of a fight—to determine the kind of government we will have in the future—the kind of South we are going to have, the kind of race." The Dixiecrats were the advance guard of a broader movement that he hoped would encompass not only the South but all of white America, a movement to reaffirm the racial and cultural character of the nation. "I think an organization should be set up in every section of the country to present the issues at stake to the American people," he explained to Archibald Coody, a Jackson lawyer who had been friends with Eastland and his father for decades. "The White people of the North are with us; however, they have lost control of their government because they are not organized. If an organization is set up and the issues presented to the Northern people they would be with us." That kind of collective effort would emerge in the next decade, after the momentous Supreme Court decision in *Brown v. Board of Education.*[44]

"NO AGRICULTURAL AREA OF THE NATION IS UNDERGOING SUCH A REVOLUTION"

Fannie Lou Hamer did not vote for or against Senator Eastland in the 1948 election. Thirty-one years old, married, working on the Marlow plantation, Hamer was not registered to vote. Indeed, she did not even know that she had the constitutional right to do so. While Eastland busied himself with trips to Europe, grand speeches on the Senate floor, and appearances with the national media, Hamer's days were consumed with the tasks of planting, chopping, and picking cotton, tasks that her parents and grandparents had spent their lives doing as well. But on neighboring plantations, a new type of worker appeared with increasing frequency, a different kind of laborer that promised to produce more cotton at lower cost than Hamer and her fellow sharecroppers ever could: the mechanical picker. The mechanical picker was a sign of transformation, revolution even. "No agricultural area of the nation is undergoing such a revolution as the Yazoo-Mississippi Delta," observed the planters of the Delta Council in 1946. For generations, Sunflower County planters had depended upon masses of black laborers such as Fannie Lou Hamer to plant, chop, and pick the crop that made them rich; by the late 1940s and 1950s, it had become clear to many observers that this way of life no longer was economically feasible.[45]

Fannie Lou and her husband, Pap, had begun working for Eastland supporter W.D. Marlow after their marriage in 1944, and there they remained throughout the 1950s. They gradually worked their way up the limited ladder of plantation life, with Fannie Lou assuming the responsibilities of timekeeper while Pap drove a tractor. Despite their relative advancement, they endured destitute living conditions similar to those of the field hands on the Eastland plantation. Given Eastland's prominent position as a U.S. senator, his plantation attracted outside observers who detailed the conditions in which his laborers lived in the 1950s. Though life on the Eastland plantation generally was no worse than on other area plantations such as the Marlow farm where the Hamers stayed, the living conditions shocked the reporters who came to visit. Living in "shanties" with bare-board floors, workers enjoyed neither indoor plumbing nor insulation nor windows, and many of their shotgun shacks had leaky roofs and peeling wallpaper made of old newspapers. While the homes generally had electricity from hookups provided through the Rural Electricity Administration, their heating system stood in the center of the main room in the form of a wood- or coal-burning stove. Around this stove were arrayed the various pieces of well-worn furniture and pallets that served the entire family.[46]

In the midst of such deprivation, Hamer struggled to provide for her family. In addition to their two children, the Hamers cared for Fannie Lou's mother, Lou Ella, until she died in 1961. Their five-member household was relatively small by sharecropper standards, but their meager income made life difficult. Though no records show what the Hamer family earned, they lived in a county where 94 percent of black families earned less than $2,000 and the average wage for a full day of chopping cotton was $3. Their income probably did not range far from that of the Eastland workers, who generally were given about $40 per month in "furnish" during the planting and chopping season from March to August. During picking season, they earned roughly $10 per bale of cotton, and a typical family could pick about four bales each month from August to December. At "settlin'" up" time at the end of December, the plantation bookkeeper calculated how much each family had earned after all the "furnish" had been paid off. Ranging from $200 to $500, this money had to last the family until spring.[47]

As meager as their living may have been, the Hamers at least remained employed on the plantation. Thousands of their neighbors, especially their fellow sharecroppers, left the fields to search for opportunities elsewhere. Sunflower County and the postwar South were in a state of flux as people abandoned the countryside in droves. After having reached a peak of more than 66,000 residents in the 1930s, Sunflower County's population—particularly its rural black population—began a steady descent that continued for more than half a century. The war and the Second Great Migration it helped inspire took its toll on the county's black population; during the 1940s, the black population dropped by more than 12 percent even as the number of whites increased marginally. But the following decade witnessed an even sharper decline as the number of blacks in the country dropped by almost 19 percent. By 1960, fewer than 46,000 souls called the county home; the proportion of blacks had declined to 68 percent from more than 80 percent a generation earlier. Sunflower County's experience mirrored that of the rural South in general, as the southern countryside shed more than half of its farming families in the postwar period.[48]

The rapid decline in population, coupled with the wartime labor shortage that had pushed wages skyward, prompted some planters to reconsider the wisdom of their heavy dependence on cheap black labor. As the war wound down, talk of mechanization filled the farm offices and newspapers of Sunflower County and the rest of the Delta. "The Delta cannot expect again the large labor supply enjoyed previous to this conflict," the Delta Council observed in 1944. "Adjustments in farming operations and production may have to be made because of this one factor." The primary "adjustment" many planters pursued was mechanization of the entire cotton-growing process, from planting to harvesting. At the beginning of the 1946 planting season, the first after the end of the war, Fred Hurst made the case for mechanization in a four-part series of articles in the *Ruleville Record*. "The exodus of labor from farms to factories during the war forced farmers to turn more and more to machinery to keep their farms going," he noted, and that process had to continue, given the realities of the global cotton market. "Far-seeing farmers realize that greater economies must be made in the production, marketing, and manufacturing of cotton if cotton is to be able to meet the growing competition of other fibers and bring in enough net income to make cotton profitable." Mechanized pickers not only eliminated "the worry and expense of recruiting hand pickers," he insisted, but also sharply reduced the number of labor hours needed to grow and pick a bale. Planters still skeptical of the newfangled machines found convincing evidence in well-publicized studies conducted at the Delta Branch Experiment Station in Stoneville, just ten miles from Sunflower County, which showed that it took eighty to eighty-five hours for a person to pick an acre of cotton, while a machine could do it in five. Government-financed researchers in Stoneville also helped develop new breeds of cotton better suited to machines, and their findings were widely reported.[49]

The awkward one- or two-row mechanical pickers that began to plod inexorably through fields once picked by hand offered a vivid, visible explanation for the dwindling population. But they were as much a symptom as a cause of the tremendous transformation in southern agriculture. Much of the transformation was driven by changes in the global cotton economy that pushed producers to find cheaper and cheaper ways to grow their crop. World War II and the Marshall Plan had boosted American cotton exports, but southern cotton growers faced a number of serious threats during the decade following the war. First, the market for synthetic fibers such as rayon, acrylics, polyesters, and spandex grew dramatically, driving down the demand for cotton as consumers turned to cheaper, man-made alternatives. Within the cotton industry, American producers continued to lose ground to foreign competitors; by the mid-1950s, U.S. cotton production remained at the same level as it had been in 1920, while foreign growers had more than tripled their production. The main problem for American growers, as cotton expert Read Dunn told a group of worried National Cotton Council members in 1948, was labor costs. Hamer and her fellow pickers may have struggled to survive on $3 a day, but their counterparts in other cotton-growing countries earned only 25¢ to 50¢ a day, making foreign-grown cotton far less expensive on the world market. The solution, Dunn insisted, was mechanization. The labor-intensive Cotton South had to mechanize or risk losing out not only to foreign competition but also to the rapidly expanding, highly mechanized cotton farms of the American West. Whether competing against foreign pickers or Western machines, the net result was the same: southern cotton was becoming relatively more and more expensive to produce.[50]

Global competition combined with policy and technology to encourage mechanization and consolidation. Complex and changing federal policies, beginning with the New Deal and continuing through the soil conservation programs of the 1950s, benefited well-educated, well-financed, large-scale farm operators such as Eastland at the expense of tenants, family-based farmers, and other small-scale operators. Owners of massive plantations could afford to experiment with new technology that promised to cut labor costs and help cotton farmers compete internationally. By 1948, the cost of machine-producing a hundred pounds of cotton had dropped to about $2.65, and the costs continued to decrease as International Harvester and other companies began to mass-produce affordable mechanical pickers—the going price in Sunflower County at midcentury was about $8,000. The Eastland plantation first began selling off its mules and shifting gradually to mechanized picking shortly after the war, even though International Harvester struggled to supply the farm with the machines the senator requested. By 1952, machines already were picking 14 percent of the Delta's cotton crop, according to the Delta Council. In addition, rapid advances in the production of weed-killing chemicals in the 1950s gave planters for the first time a feasible opportunity to mechanize their entire cotton operation, from planting through harvesting.[51]

Together with expanding economic opportunities in the North, these agricultural policies and advances in technology helped create both the "push" and the "pull" necessary to induce thousands of farming families to uproot themselves and take off to the cities or to the North. As more farm hands left, labor became more scarce and thus more expensive, further encouraging planters to switch to machines; labor shortages during World War II had prompted much of the interest in mechanical alternatives to hand labor, and the continued migration of black workers only spurred the shift to machines. The revolution that had started during the New Deal accelerated during the 1950s to the point where, by the end of the decade, sharecroppers such as Fannie Lou Hamer and the Eastland plantation workers were a vanishing breed. Indeed, the number of sharecroppers dropped so dramatically in the 1950s that in 1960 the U.S. Census Bureau stopped including "sharecropping" as an occupational category.[52]

The profound impact of this gradual agricultural revolution cannot be overstated. Within a generation, from the New Deal to the 1960s, the people who had been the economic foundation of the region had become economically expendable. As we have seen, the Delta was built upon cheap black labor. Every aspect of life was rooted in the central fact that large numbers of black workers were essential to the economic development of the area and to the prodigious wealth and power of white elites. Now, fewer and fewer of those workers were needed to run the machines of the modern plantation. Like other planters, James Eastland, a "tinkerer" who sought out new technology whenever possible, welcomed mechanization as a way to loosen his dependence on black sharecroppers. "The farm tractor and the mechanical cotton picker so reduce the number of days the sharecropper is needed that they may be the primary cause of the complete elimination of the ruinous system," two planters in nearby Coahoma County wrote in 1951. "We hope so." These planters saw sharecropping as a way to enrich lazy tenants who "have been lying up all winter and spring in the landlord's house, warming by the fire and eating the food he furnished, until they have gotten fat, insolent, and sassy." With mechanization, planters envisioned an efficient enterprise that could compete in a changing global cotton industry.[53]

And what of the "sassy" laborers? Some observers forecast chaos. There is "an enormous tragedy in the making," wrote Delta planter-pundit David Cohn in 1947. "Five million people will be removed from the land within the next few years. They must go somewhere. But where? They must do something. But what?" Business leaders and moderate politicians such as Delta congressman Frank Smith suggested industrial development to create jobs for low-skilled workers. The Delta contained "a reservoir of workers with potential productivity in the number of persons displaced, or likely soon to be displaced, from agriculture," wrote one researcher who assessed the region's economic resources for the Delta Council in 1949. Others advocated an investment in education. In Sunflower County, the authors of a 1950 study commissioned by a white community group recognized the potential impact of the agricultural revolution and urged county leaders to improve black education to minimize the potential social disruption. "Economically, it is profitable" to devote more resources to black schools, they argued, because with mechanization, "many Negroes now living in Sunflower County will be forced either to move or become self-sufficient." Planters within the Delta Council agreed. "The education of the Negro is of vital concern if he is to be other than an economic liability and it is even more important as we enter an era of mechanized agricultural and industrial development," council members wrote in 1950. But, envisioning a Delta drained of its black laborers, the council two years later urged a reassessment of budgetary priorities. Why should the state spend money on improving black schools in the Delta when "rural areas with a heavy concentration of Negroes at the present time may have few Negroes ten years from now?"[54]

Sunflower County with just a "few Negroes"? That had not been true since the county was founded a century earlier. The very thought would have been virtually unthinkable before World War II. But the war had changed everything, for planters and pickers alike. By the middle of the century, Sunflower County had passed the crossroads, and it was headed down a path that led toward complete mechanization of the cotton growing process. For Eastland, Hamer, and the rest of Sunflower County, this was uncharted terrain, and they spent the next generation wrestling with each other over how to map out the new social, economic, and political landscape.

5

"From Cotton—to Communism—to Segregation!": The Senator's Rise to Power

As you drive into Ruleville from the south on Highway 49, a maroon and cream sign welcomes you to "the home of Fannie Lou Hamer." Slow down and enjoy a respite from the blazing sun as the highway changes briefly into an oak-lined residential boulevard. Just past the fish house, take a left on Oscar Street and park on the next block, in front of Ruleville Middle School. Set in a neighborhood of modest, well-kept homes, the school itself is a modest, one-story structure that exudes a 1950s charm—the sleek silvering lettering on its façade once may have been considered progressively "modern," though hipsters of the early twenty-first century might find it faddishly "retro." Look up as you walk through the doors, and you will see pictures of graduating classes lining the upper reaches of the hallway walls, far above the mischievous hands of teenage students. Look long enough and you might see a white student or two, but in general only black faces smile from the oval frames, just as nearly all the students bustling through the hallways today are black.

Ruleville Middle School once sat in the heart of white Ruleville, a school where the Eastland children and their white friends studied and socialized. Safely ensconced in an all-white neighborhood, the school stood for decades as a symbol of the Sunflower County way of life, a segregated institution supported by the entire white community and protected by the white officials who monopolized political power. You would have looked in vain for a black student's picture in any class until more than a decade after the Supreme Court's momentous 1954 decision in *Brown v. Board of Education of Topeka*. Though the decision had little immediate impact (or long-term impact either, apparently) on the racial composition of Sunflower County schools, *Brown* defined an era and catalyzed the white resistance movement. The decision launched James Eastland's national political career, transforming him from a little-known senator, a farmer-politician with visions of retirement, into the South's most visible segregationist politician, a nationally recognized symbol of racism and resistance.

"BOY, WHAT HAVE YOU GOT TO HIDE?"

Given the *Brown* decision's prominence and the drama of the civil rights struggles that followed it, we may be forgiven for overlooking the half decade before the *Brown* decision. We can forget the sense of cautious optimism about the prospects of self-propelled change in the South following the Dixiecrat defeat in 1948. As Frank Smith, a white moderate from Greenwood who won election as the Delta's U.S. congressman in 1950, wrote, "The climate for a relatively liberal approach to the race issue in Mississippi was better just after World War II than at any time since the Civil War." Provocative writers such as Lillian Smith and William Faulkner, maverick journalists such as Hodding Carter and Harry Ashmore, and populist governors "Big Jim" Folsom of Alabama and Sid McMath in Arkansas were among a number of whites, even in the Deep South, who fought publicly not only for gradual racial change but also for economic reforms such as expanded social programs, improved health care, and collective bargaining, all of which were targeted at the region's poorest citizens, white and black. These cautious southern whites, along with northern civil rights activists in the NAACP, sought to build upon impressive postwar gains in organized sports, the military, and voter registration.[1]

Much of the optimism stemmed from the White House, where a

rejuvenated President Truman began his first full term flush with Democratic majorities in both houses of Congress and eager to spend the political capital he had gained with his extraordinary, come-from-behind victory in November 1948. During his State of the Union address the next January, he outlined his "Fair Deal," an ambitious domestic agenda that would broaden the New Deal and extend the scope of federal civil rights activities. In addition to pro-labor policies such as repeal of the anti-union Taft-Hartley bill, he proposed to boost Social Security benefits and the minimum wage, increase federal aid to education, and pursue national health insurance. He also pledged to act on many of the recommendations outlined in his Committee on Civil Rights' manifesto, *To Secure These Rights*, such as establishing a permanent FEPC, abolishing the poll tax, and passing a federal anti-lynching bill.[2]

But the intensification of the Cold War and the rise of domestic anti-Communism soon impinged on liberals' ability and desire to pursue domestic reform on race or economics. Events in 1949 and 1950 cemented the Cold War and the national security state as seemingly permanent fixtures in American life. Even as Truman articulated his sweeping domestic vision in early 1949, Chinese Communists led by Mao Zedong closed in on Beijing and began to push American-backed Jiang Jeshi and his Nationalist Kuomintang off the mainland. The Communists' overwhelming victory in October came on the heels of the stunning revelation that the Soviet Union had developed an atomic bomb. The news sent Americans and their political leaders reeling. To many, Eastland's apocalyptic warnings about Communist subversion and the potential for invasion no longer seemed so far-fetched. His charges of Communist influence in civil rights or labor movement efforts, which he had been making throughout his Senate career, now gained more salience, as Americans of all political persuasions grew increasingly concerned about the Communist threat. Liberal advocates of the Fair Deal and racial integration became suspect as a new Red scare—led by an irascible, often inebriated Republican from Wisconsin, Senator Joseph McCarthy—clamped down on domestic dissent. By the time Communist North Korea invaded U.S.-backed South Korea in June 1950, the window of opportunity for racial equality and economic rights opened by World War II, the establishment of the United Nations, and the breakup of colonial empires seemed to have slammed shut.[3]

The polarization of international politics helped ensure that Eastland and other Dixiecrats did not suffer for their betrayal of President Truman and the national Democratic Party. Many Cold Warriors, particularly those from the South, rejected Truman's domestic policies and urged more aggressive anti-Communist action abroad and at home. Needing southern support for his foreign-policy agenda, Truman and his allies in the congressional leadership resisted calls to "blacklist" Dixiecrat politicians; instead, they worked to win back the southerners' loyalty by giving them the committee assignments they desired. Eastland requested, and received, the chair of the Judiciary Committee's Subcommittee on Civil Rights, while his courtly Mississippi colleague Senator John Stennis (who recently had won a seat after Senator Bilbo died in office) gained control of the Rules Committee's subcommittee with jurisdiction over the poll tax. With Eastland and Stennis in charge of these important subcommittees, southern newsman Howard Suttle gleefully observed, "the South was never in a better position to bottle-up" civil rights legislation.[4]

The escalation of the Cold War not only enhanced Eastland's ability to prevent domestic reform, it also forced his opponents on the defensive. The pressures of conforming to the domestic anti-Communist crusade took a heavy toll on left-wing activists in both the labor and civil rights movements. Within the NAACP, Cold War divisions deeply split the leadership, as leftists struggled with anti-Communists for the right to speak for the black masses. Prominent left-wing activists such as popular entertainer Paul Robeson and prolific scholar W.E.B. Du Bois attracted widespread attention for their opposition to American foreign policy and domestic suppression of dissent, while mainstream black leaders feared that their effort to secure black political equality would be tarnished as pro-Communist and thus anti-American. At least since the Scottsboro trial in 1931, key NAACP leaders, particularly its pragmatic and well-connected executive director, Walter White, had viewed Communism as an opportunistic, impractical, and dangerous distraction from the cause of civil rights. Their fears stemmed at least in part from reality—the Communist Party did indeed hope to organize poor blacks around its economic agenda of property redistribution, and blacks comprised a disproportionate share of the party's membership—but Communists never attracted widespread support among the NAACP rank and file. Nonetheless, in an effort to inoculate the organization and its cause against segregationist attacks, White led a successful campaign to discredit the black left and trumpet the NAACP's mainstream anti-Communist views. In the same week that the Korean War started in June 1950, the group passed a resolution barring all Communists from its ranks. Though it was strategically prudent and arguably even necessary, the NAACP's decision helped cut ties between the cause of racial equality and the drive for radical economic change, a choice that was not without its consequences.[5]

A similar process occurred within the Congress of Industrial Organizations and the labor movement at large. Emboldened by gains in union membership during the war, the CIO launched Operation Dixie, an expansive campaign to organize black and white workers across the South that Eastland condemned as an attempt by a "carpetbag organization" to "destroy southern civilization." The campaign initially scored important victories, but after 1948 it succumbed to the combined pressures of internal schism and external opposition to the racial and ideological implications of the effort. Communist organizers had been integral to the CIO's success in attracting workers to join the union throughout the 1930s and early 1940s, but in the postwar era anti-Communist union leaders such as Operation Dixie director George Baldanzi sought to isolate them from union activities. Embattled CIO president Philip Murray attempted to maintain an inclusive, politically diverse union, but he faced increasingly rancorous discord within the union in addition to well-financed anti-Communist attacks at the grassroots level in southern cities such as Memphis and Winston-Salem. Like the American Federation of Labor, the NAACP, and other more moderate political organizations, the CIO ultimately decided to purge Communists from its ranks to maintain its viability within the political system. What had been the most radical bastion of the labor movement began to drift toward the mainstream; by the mid-1950s, the CIO had merged with its former nemesis, the AFL, and its vision for reform had narrowed considerably.[6]

While black leaders and labor organizers struggled to establish their credibility as anti-Communists, a determined Eastland kept the pressure on as he immersed himself in the task of ferreting out and exposing domestic Communists. He saw the "loss" of China and the end of America's atomic monopoly, combined with the conviction of suspected subversive (and New Dealer) Alger Hiss, as irrefutable evidence of what he had long suspected: Communist infiltration within the U.S. government and, more broadly, in the entire New Deal effort to reshape American society. Though he had not yet garnered a national reputation like that of his bombastic colleague Joseph McCarthy, Eastland made a name for himself as an anti-Communist through his persistent—critics called them demagogic—investigations as a charter member of the Senate Internal Security Subcommittee (SISS).

SISS has faded from our collective historical memory of the McCarthy era, but for a time it outpaced its better-known House counterpart, the Committee on Un-American Activities. Founded in January 1951, SISS had the authority to investigate allegations of Communist influence in government, unions, universities, and other institutions. It conducted well-publicized probes of the State Department, Communists involved in youth organizations, left-wing schoolteachers, and radical immigrants. Eastland and other SISS members cultivated a close relationship with the ferociously anti-Communist J. Edgar Hoover and his Federal Bureau of Investigation, which helped to turn the subcommittee into Congress' primary investigative unit by the time of the *Brown* decision in 1954. Whereas his committee colleagues followed McCarthy's lead in focusing primarily on suspected Communists in government agencies, Eastland preferred to attack the labor movement. Though he was not chair of the committee, he nonetheless had the power to call hearings, and it is instructive to note that the first two hearings he initiated and for which he served as chair both involved unions that aimed to organize southern black workers. These two hearings, held in Memphis and Washington in August and October 1951, sought to expose the assumed Communist influence in two majority-black unions: the Dining Car and Railroad Food Workers Union (DCRFWU) and the Distributive, Processing, and Office Workers of America (DPOWA). These early SISS hearings reveal how Eastland earned his reputation as an anti-Communist demagogue.[7]

Eastland's foremost concern was that labor organizations, inspired by Communists, were targeting southern blacks in an interracial effort to dismantle both white supremacy and capitalism. In the hearings he conducted, he sought to establish this fear as fact by opening the proceedings with a series of witnesses who testified about the extent of Communist influence in the union and recounted stories of the harassment they received for being anti-Communist. Some of these witnesses, ostensibly employees of the Immigration and Naturalization Service, appeared repeatedly at SISS hearings. They professed to be reformed Communists who could give an inside perspective on the party's efforts to organize black southerners. They corroborated what Eastland already assumed—that Communists actively sought to recruit blacks in a revolutionary attempt not simply to overthrow the U.S. government but to establish, in the words of witness Manning Johnson, "an independent and autonomous Negro republic in the black belt" through "armed rebellion of the Negroes." Johnson, a black former dining car worker who later would accuse Nobel Peace Prize–winning black diplomat Ralph Bunche of being a Communist, gave voice to Eastland's worst fears as he outlined the Communists' plan to establish a "Soviet form of government" in the Cotton South. First, they would "utilize the just grievances of the Negro in order to subvert him." After having infiltrated existing black groups and created new Communist-front organizations to dupe urban black workers, they would use these workers to "organize and gain leadership over the Negro sharecroppers [and] tenant farmers" and overthrow the existing government. Here was the Reconstruction nightmare of "Negro rule," with a twentieth-century Red tinge.[8]

Eastland was a notoriously unforgiving questioner who used his power to crush witnesses, as we can see from the testimony of Lee Lashley, the black president of DPOWA's Local 19. Presiding alone over the hearing, Eastland grilled Lashley for several hours over the course of two days, treating the union president as if he were an intransigent prisoner unwilling to confess his crime or reveal his collaborators. The senator skillfully alternated between being the "good cop" and the "bad cop," sandwiching flashes of anger around seductively sincere signs of gentleness in an attempt to break Lashley's will. "Lashley, you want to tell the truth, do you not?" Eastland soothed early on during the testimony. "I want you to think because you could get in some very serious trouble." But when Lashley remained silent in the face of questions about the union and its activities, the enraged senator accused the witness of having been coached by the union's "New York lawyer," Victor Rabinowitz. "Boy, what have you got to hide?" he roared. Returning to a more kindly tone, he began a line of questioning aimed at undermining Lashley's confidence in his lawyers. "We just want you to tell the truth, and I want you to realize that people who give you advice and try to use you are not trying to help you, but trying to help themselves," Eastland coaxed. "You wanted to tell the truth about this thing and you admitted to these gentlemen that you were a Communist until you got in his [Rabinowitz's] hands, did you not?" Those on the committee were Lashley's true friends, Eastland implied: "You know that we do not want to hurt you."[9]

And so it went for hours. On his second day of testifying, Lashley's steadfast silence began to crack. "This is the first time I have ever been on any kind of witness stand and anything and I tried to do the thing that I know is right," he pleaded. "Personally, I haven't got anything to hide from this court." Seizing upon this opening, Eastland encouraged him to speak freely: "If you have not anything to hide, then that is just absolutely fine. Just tell us the facts, that is all." The senator graciously offered to meet with the witness behind closed doors, without the cameras and microphones. Lashley took the bait. Although no record exists of what was said in that meeting, when Lashley returned to the witness stand he admitted to having been a Communist in the 1940s but insisted that he really did not know what Communism was all about. A satisfied Eastland thanked him for his honesty, but later dismissed him and the other black witnesses as dupes. "I think that the Negro officials who testified here are dumb," Eastland concluded after the DPOWA hearings. "I think that they have simply been used by designing people."[10]

For such "designing people"—white union officials whom he accused of being Communist—Eastland reserved his unrestrained anger. Like Reconstruction-era carpetbaggers and FEPC egalitarians, these cunning northern whites, Eastland believed, cynically exploited unwitting blacks by making false promises of racial equality. He called them to the witness stand in an effort to get them to confess to being Communists—an admission tantamount to treason in Eastland's mind and the minds of many other Americans in the early 1950s. Faced with hostile questioning from the chair, the witnesses refused to answer any questions pertaining to Communism, citing the Fifth Amendment protection against self-incrimination. Their insistence on refusing to answer questions infuriated the senator. "Did you commit some crime?" Eastland demanded of Theodore Bromson, the white general counsel for the DCRFWU. Bromson's continued defiance provoked another outburst: "What are you guilty of? What are you afraid of? Have you betrayed your country? Is that what you are afraid of? . . . Are you an American? Were you born in this country?" Victor Rabinowitz, who also served as Bromson's attorney, objected to such questioning, infuriating Eastland. "Throw that damn scum out of here," he told the bailiff. "Get rid of him." Two burly court officials lifted the lawyer out of his chair and forcefully ushered him from the room.[11]

"PEED ON BY A POLE CAT"

Eastland may have had complete control of the hearing room, but he and other planters could not claim such power over their erstwhile black laborers. The migration of blacks off southern farms, which continued unabated in the postwar era, led many planters to view black workers less as a source of profit and more as a potential source of problems. "Many of the Negroes who have left the farms and have congregated in our towns and cities in agricultural areas have changed their status from an integral part of the economy to that of transient workers," the Delta Council warned in 1949. "For their religious life, their family life, and their usefulness as dependable citizens, this, we think, has been a serious step backwards." Like his fellow planters in the council, Eastland worried that displaced rural blacks would flock to southern cities, only to be enticed by civil rights advocates and labor organizers into joining revolutionary organizations. Freed from their plantation moorings, they could become a menace to white society.[12]

Planter fears rose in direct correlation to civil rights activity. Despite stalled reform efforts at the federal level, activists forged ahead. The NAACP, with its anti-Communist credentials secured after its 1950 resolution, continued to make inroads into communities across the South. It even succeeded in establishing a presence in Sunflower County. In 1951, black leaders in Indianola, headed by a determined and well-named young doctor, Clinton C. Battle, reestablished a local NAACP chapter (a previous, short-lived one had died out in 1948) and began working with white officials on moderate racial reform. Elsewhere in the Delta that same year, another doctor, the flamboyant T.R.M. Howard in the all-black town of Mound Bayou, created the Regional Council of Negro Leadership (RCNL), and two years later an exuberant young pharmacist named Aaron Henry organized an NAACP chapter in Clarksdale. The RCNL and NAACP, though rivals at times, shared a commitment to improving the lives of black Mississippians through political and legal equality. Along with the Mississippi Progressive Voters League, they also shared a leadership and membership rooted in the small number of middle-class blacks who had managed to remain financially independent of local whites. None of the groups tackled the issue of economic rights, and none of them made any progress in organizing plantation workers, for whom the economic and physical consequences of civil rights activity remained too severe. As a result, Fannie Lou Hamer and other sharecroppers had little contact or involvement with the NAACP, the RCNL, or other such organizations during the 1950s. Nonetheless, the NAACP and other civil rights groups managed to register an increasing number of black voters. Between 1948 and 1952, the number of black voters in the state nearly tripled, reaching twenty thousand. "Negro Vote Shows Signs of Becoming a Factor in 1953," ran the headline of an article by Mississippi journalist Bill Minor and he credited black voters with influencing numerous local elections. In Sunflower County, more than one hundred new black voters successfully registered to vote in the first two years of Battle's rejuvenated NAACP branch.[13]

Voting gains paralleled advances in the federal courts. For more than a decade, beginning with *Gaines v. Oklahoma* in 1938, the Supreme Court had been chipping away at the legal foundation of segregation, particularly in higher education. By 1950, with its decisions in *Sweatt v. Painter* and *McLaurin v. Oklahoma*, the Court effectively had invalidated segregation in graduate schools. With the nomination of California's crusading governor, Earl Warren, to be chief justice in 1953, Eastland's friend Walter Sillers lamented, "It looks to me like it is a dead [c]inch that the Supreme Court will declare all segregation laws unconstitutional." To prevent any further federal intervention in their schools, many white leaders in the Deep South began to upgrade black schools in a belated attempt to make good on the latter part of "separate but equal." The manifestly unequal schools that Fannie Lou Hamer and her black neighbors had attended now appeared to be a lightning rod that could attract unwanted legal and social agitation. Mississippi officials authorized a massive increase in expenditures for black schooling, agreeing to equalize teacher salaries and offer equal transportation. Between 1940 and 1952, the amount of money spent per black pupil in the state nearly quintupled, and spending on black students as a percentage of spending on white students increased from 17 percent to 30 percent; given the aggressive building campaign, by 1952 the per-pupil capital outlays for black schools—money for facilities and equipment—actually exceeded outlays for white schools by nearly 40 percent.[14]

In Sunflower County, the poor state of black schools caught the attention of the Inter-Racial Committee, a group of forty-nine relatively moderate whites who sought to foster improved race relations through gradual reform. At the request of superintendent Sam Jones, the group chose seven whites and three blacks to study black schools in the county and make recommendations for improvement. This ten-man Citizens' Committee then commissioned the University of Mississippi's Bureau of Education Research to conduct a study, which highlighted many of the problems that Hamer knew firsthand—poorly equipped, one- and two-room schools, short school terms that deferred to agricultural seasons, inadequately trained and poorly paid teachers, and an excessive pupil-teacher ratio. The bulk of black students attended the elementary grades—86 percent of black students were enrolled in grades one through six—while only 2 percent made it to high school. The report recommended massive consolidation and new construction, challenging Sunflower County to be a "pioneer" in the field of black education before the federal judiciary forced the necessary changes.[15]

Though still dramatically unequal, black schools enjoyed a marked improvement, prompting some grousing among whites. "While the niggers do need, and in order to keep them out of white schools, better

buildings," complained one letter writer to the staunchly segregationist columnist Florence Ogden Sillers (sister of Eastland's friend Walter Sillers), "still there is a waste of money in giving them schools . . .
with all the fol de rols that are unnecessary in order to teach them the
three Rs and something of manual training." With more money going
to black schools, some whites worried that their white schools would
get even worse than they already were. Despite the defiant public
boasts by Eastland and other state officials, white schools in Mississippi were not particularly good compared to schools nationwide, as
the Eastland children discovered. When their father first went to the
Senate, he split his time between Washington and Doddsville; the kids
attended Mississippi schools in the fall, then transferred to Washington schools in January, when Congress began its session. Each winter,
the Eastland children arrived in Washington to find themselves further
and further behind their peers—their mother had to tutor them every
night to catch up. Anne Eastland struggled so much that the head-
master of Sidwell Friends, the private school she attended in Washington, convinced her parents to let her stay in D.C. year-round; she
lived with Mr. and Mrs. Stennis when her siblings returned to Sunflower County.[16]

Despite the sorry state of Mississippi schools overall, Eastland
defended the segregated system with increasing vigor as the Court
took stronger positions against segregated schooling. He began to use
his position on SISS as a powerful means of attacking the liberal
agenda on race and to prevent any potential support in the South for
a decision outlawing segregation. The "point was to create an atmos-
phere in the South that 'exposed' any progressive people in the civil
rights effort as Communists," civil rights activist Jack O'Dell argued.
"So white Southerners who were for civil rights had been called nigger
lovers for years, but now you could call them Communists, and the
segregationists hid behind that." As we have seen, Eastland had
claimed to find Communist machinations behind civil rights measures
long before the rise of anti-Communism and Joseph McCarthy as national phenomena. The difference was that in the early 1950s, the fear
of Communism resonated so strongly among Americans of all political persuasions that any link to the hated ideology could be expected
to harm the movement toward equality or, at the very least, drain

energy and resources from the movement. With the Soviet Union posturing as a vocal (if opportunistic) advocate of racial equality, Eastland and other segregationists believed they had solid evidence that racial liberalism was a sign of Communist subversion.[17]

The more progress civil rights advocates made, the more aggressive Eastland became. In March 1954, as the Supreme Court heard arguments in the cases that would culminate in *Brown v. Board of Education*, Eastland made a preemptive strike against a possible pro-integration decision by targeting the Southern Conference Educational Fund (SCEF) for alleged Communist subversion. The SCEF was an outgrowth of the Southern Conference for Human Welfare (SCHW), an organization dedicated to promoting liberal economic reform through political action. Founded in 1938 by a mix of southern liberals, left-wing organizers, and middle-class activists, the SCHW from its inception included Communists, prompting the House Committee on Un-American Activities to label it a Communist front organization in 1947—Eastland considered it "nothing but the Communist Party" itself. Its offshoot, the Atlanta-based SCEF, likewise had links to Communists, but its mission focused more specifically on eliminating racial prejudice through educational efforts aimed at southern audiences—it sponsored interracial conferences, anti-segregation publications, and lawsuits. The combination of Communist involvement and a commitment to racial equality made the organization a prime target for white supremacists such as Eastland.[18]

Rather than challenging the SCEF directly on its racial or educational agenda, Eastland instead accused it of Communist subversion. In a spectacular set of hearings held in New Orleans in March 1954, Eastland—the sole member of SISS represented—attacked several pillars of southern white liberalism, including Virginia Foster Durr, an aristocratic social reformer and founding member of SCHW, and her husband, Clifford Durr, a prominent New Deal attorney from an old southern family; Myles Horton, the brash founder of the Highlander Folk School, an interracial training school for social justice organizers; Aubrey Williams, the combative president of the SCEF and former head of the Works Progress Administration and National Youth Administration under President Roosevelt; and Jim Dombrowski, the SCEF's executive director. Using the testimony of paid informants (including Paul Crouch, who had appeared in Eastland's earlier hearings in Memphis), Eastland hoped to implicate not only the individuals connected to the SCEF but also by extension the cause for which the organization worked. The hearings featured the physical ejection of Horton from the courtroom, impassioned accusations of perjury and subversion hurled back and forth, and Clifford Durr's lunging assault (followed by a mild heart attack) on Crouch, who had accused Durr's wife of having exploited her kinship to Supreme Court Justice Hugo Black in order to promote Communism. The dirty accusations make "you feel like you have been peed on by a pole cat," a disgusted Virginia Durr noted later. "You know you are clean, you know you are free of all this and yet you smell bad and people don't want to be associated with you." The spectacle generated criticism from observers as well as participants. When asked by the *Montgomery Advertiser* which of the hearing's participants represented the greatest threat to the United States, half of the journalists who covered the hearing named Eastland, while most of the others named Crouch. Crouch was so thoroughly disgraced by the events that he never testified at another federal hearing.[19]

"MONSTROUS CRIME"

A mere two months after the New Orleans hearings, the Supreme Court dropped the bomb that Eastland and other white southerners feared: *Brown*. Much as the Chinese Communists' victory and the Russian's building of the atomic bomb in 1949 had ignited the Cold War and anti-Communism, the *Brown* decision took the struggle for and against black freedom to a new level of intensity. For Eastland and many of his white southern compatriots, May 17, 1954, became known as "Black Monday," a day that would live in infamy; for Hamer and her rural black neighbors, the decision had little immediate impact aside from antagonizing local whites. Overturning its 1896 precedent in *Plessy v. Ferguson*, the Supreme Court ruled in *Brown v. Board of Education of Topeka* that segregated schools were unconstitutional. A generation of careful groundwork by lawyers and activists from the NAACP culminated in the Court's unanimous repudiation of "separate but equal." Accepting the NAACP's legal and sociological arguments and addressing the federal government's national security concerns, the Court declared unequivocally, "In the field of public education the doctrine of 'separate but equal' has no place. Separate educational facilities are inherently unequal." Like Pearl Harbor, the *Brown* decision appeared to many whites in the South as a vicious, unprovoked assault on their way of life, and it galvanized mass white opposition as had no other recent development.[20]

While the *Brown* decision rightly is viewed as an important symbolic victory for advocates of racial justice, in the short term its impact on the lives of southern blacks was minimal. Most visibly, schools remained segregated throughout the South. Despite the Court's unanimous ruling and its follow-up decision in *Brown II* the next year that urged southern school districts to desegregate "with all deliberate speed," few districts complied, particularly in black-majority areas such as Sunflower County. For nearly a decade, not a single child in the state of Mississippi attended an integrated public school; Ruleville Middle School, with its gleaming gymnasium built just a few years before, remained off-limits to black students. A child born in Ruleville in May 1954 would be in high school before Sunflower County schools were desegregated. Indeed, it was not until 1968 that Hamer's daughter Vergie attended school with white children.[21]

More ominously, *Brown* ignited white opposition to all forms of racial progress. In the immediate aftermath of the decision, most white southerners wavered between grudging acceptance and outright defiance. Even in the Deep South, some whites initially expressed resignation rather than rebellion, and they encouraged their compatriots to abide by the law of the land. Delta congressman Frank Smith disapproved of the decision but conceded that the Court "seemingly followed the best course it could in seeking advice from all quarters" and claimed he was "hopeful" about prospects of implementing the decision. But such voices of moderation quickly were drowned out by a chorus led by Senator Eastland and other Deep South white political leaders who vowed massive resistance. "The South will not abide by nor obey this legislative decision by a political court," he flatly declared on the day of the decision. "Integrated schools are desired by neither race in the South." He called for a constitutional amendment protecting a state's ability to regulate "health, morals, education, marriage, and good order" and took to the floor of the Senate to denounce what he often called the "monstrous crime" in no uncertain terms. "To do the things which the Court is attempting to do is beyond the power of government," he insisted, then sounded a note of self-fulfilling prophecy: "It will justly cause evasion and violation of law and contempt for law, and will do this country great harm."[22]

Eastland reacted to the school desegregation decision viscerally as well as politically. He was more than an avowed segregationist with a public record of defending white supremacy; he also was the father of four school-age children, including three girls. Without school segregation, his children would become minorities in their schools, for in both of his homes, Sunflower County and Washington, D.C., black students constituted a vast majority of the school-age population. More nightmarish still in Eastland's mind, his daughters would be in classrooms with black males—a frightening scenario that Eastland and other white southerners assumed would lead inexorably to interracial sex and "race mixing." The fear of "amalgamation" and the perceived loss of "racial purity"—made personal by his daughters' age—animated much of Eastland's reaction to *Brown*. Other whites shared his fear. Speaking of white southerners such as Eastland and his constituents, President Eisenhower told Chief Justice Warren, "These are not bad people. All they are concerned about is to see that their sweet little girls are not required to sit in school alongside some big overgrown bucks."[23]

Eastland's concern for his daughters reflected a hierarchical worldview in which the prospect of school desegregation threatened the control that he wielded over his household and challenged his ability to protect his children, particularly his daughters, from the perceived danger of integration. Like his father before him, Eastland headed a patriarchal household that followed what he believed was the natural order. Despite the pressures of commuting between Washington and Mississippi, he and his wife, Libby, worked hard to provide a stable family life. Libby stayed home and maintained the household, a task made easier by the presence of black domestic workers, but Jim was the recognized head of the household. "When he was home, he was very much in control of the house and of the family," his daughter Anne remembered. Jim Eastland, having himself been a dutiful son, assumed the role of the authoritarian father whose mere presence could inspire awe in his children, though he never used corporal punishment—much the way as a powerful planter he could command respect from his workers without resorting to the whip.[24]

Jim Eastland was "every inch a man's man," his son, Woods, recalled, and he enjoyed the company of men—he often went fishing, took trips to see football games, or sat in the farm office talking politics with his buddies. He sought to develop this sense of manly freedom within his son, whom he allowed wide latitude growing up. With his daughters, Anne Eastland recalled, "he was very protective, controlling." From how they dressed to how they presented themselves in public, Eastland held his girls to high standards. He did not want them running around in shorts, and he imposed a 10:30 P.M. curfew throughout their high school years. On the plantation, he did not allow the girls into the farm office and forbade them from having contact with black men. They stayed off the campaign trail—politics was a man's game—and they were expected to become nurturers and housewives when they got older. To Eastland, the control he wielded over his family members, like the authority he asserted over his workers, was the essence of freedom. Neither the government nor any other institution could tell him how to raise his children or treat his workers, and he wanted to keep it that way. Now, with the *Brown* decision, the government challenged his sense of control by attempting to thrust itself into this protected world. His daughters faced scorn and hostility from their politically aware and often socially liberal Washington classmates, his neighbors faced the specter of being an overwhelmed minority in their public schools, his state faced outside scrutiny and condemnation. The world he knew seemed to be under attack, and he vowed to protect it. As he told supporters shortly after the ruling, "I want for my children, as you want for yours, the same social protection afforded them that you and I have enjoyed in our lifetime."[25]

The Court's decision appeared to give him renewed energy and helped spur him to campaign vigorously for reelection in the fall of 1954. For much of the previous year, political observers in Mississippi whispered about the prospects of defeating Eastland or the possibility of the senator's retirement. Eastland himself encouraged such talk—he told confidants about his desire to spend more time on the farm, and his erratic health seemed to reflect a physical disdain for life in Washington. He never had committed himself to the social scene inside the Beltway and had not bought a house in the area. For more than a year before the decision, he did not make any speeches on the Senate floor. His frequent absences from floor votes attracted critics, particularly thirty-one-year-old World War II veteran Carroll Gartin, the state's lieutenant governor, who emerged as a powerful challenger.[26]

When *Brown* hit the newsstands, Eastland had yet to announce his intention to run for reelection, but the Court's decision gave him a tremendous boost. As Erle Johnston, his campaign's publicist, remembered, "Whether he needed it or not, the U.S. Supreme Court gave Senator Eastland a powerful new plank in his platform." Hundreds of congratulatory letters poured into his office after he denounced the decision. *Brown* offered him the cause, the abiding mission, the dramatic confrontation to save civilization that had driven him in the early postwar years. Now, once again, he could stand alongside the heroes of southern lore and battle foreign forces bent on destroying freedom.[27]

During his reelection campaign kickoff in his boyhood home of Forest that June, he called for a "great crusade" to defend segregation. Fist pounding into palm, index finger jabbing the air, arms pumping furiously, Eastland exhorted county fair crowds, Rotarians, and other white Mississippians to join the crusade. He bragged about how he had suppressed civil rights legislation while chair of the Subcommittee on Civil Rights: "I had special pockets put in my pants and for three years I carried those bills around in my pockets everywhere I went and every one of them were defeated." He reveled in his role as a rebel against the northern establishment. "They said I broke the law, and maybe I did. They said I was arrogant, and so I was. But not a single one of their vicious measures ever got out of the subcommittee." His campaign brochures pledged "an all-out fight against CIO left-wingers and NAACP to preserve segregation in Mississippi," prompting the NAACP to label his reelection effort an "almost 100 percent anti-Negro campaign." Asked by his publicity manager if he wanted to raise other issues during the campaign, he exclaimed, "Hell, no! Stay on segregation . . . segregation . . . segregation!"

Nonetheless, Eastland did have other priorities during the reelection effort, as one of his campaign slogans revealed. To answer critics who pointed to his absenteeism, the senator emphasized his commitment to the three main pillars of his political philosophy: "Name the fight—from cotton—to Communism—to segregation!" On all three fronts, Eastland argued, he had stood firm to protect what he and others labeled the "Southern way of life." He crushed Gartin in the critical Democratic primary and cruised to an unopposed triumph in the November general election. Not surprisingly, perhaps, not a single one of Sunflower County's 114 black registered voters bothered to vote in the election.[28]

"THE TWO-FISTED MISSISSIPPIAN"

Eastland's commitment to defend the white southern way of life reflected and shaped his constituents' desire to resist the Supreme Court decision. Given his public defense of white supremacy and his history of attacking the Court, his response perhaps was predictable; to have accepted the decision casually or called for calm obedience would have been out of character, politically and temperamentally. "The entire future of this country is at issue," he insisted to his audiences, and at stake were "the racial integrity, the culture, the creative genius, and the advanced civilization of the white race." Abetted by a lack of leadership from the White House, the sheer vituperation of his attacks and his ominous warnings about the South's response helped foster a spirit of resistance that during the mid-1950s shattered the middle ground of southern politics and forced white southerners to choose between their country and their race. *South*, a periodical mouthpiece of the white resistance movement, applauded Eastland as "the two-fisted Mississippian who has emerged as the South's leader in the fight to preserve segregation." By insisting that there was "no room for compromise," Eastland helped create the massive resistance to integration that not only blocked racial progress for a decade but also poisoned future efforts at racial reconciliation.[29]

Of course, he was by no means alone in his strident condemnation of *Brown*. One columnist in the *Ruleville Record* told readers flatly, "You and I know that we are not going to permit negroes to enter our white schools in Mississippi, and any wishing to the contrary is like a man in hell wanting a drink of ice water." Two weeks after Eastland's call for a "great crusade," a group of white planters, businessmen, and political leaders met in Indianola, twenty miles south of the Eastland plantation, and formed the Citizens' Council, an organization dedicated to preserving segregated schools by any legal means necessary. The Citizens' Council was founded by Robert Patterson, a local farmer and World War II veteran who had grown up, ironically, with NAACP leader Aaron Henry. Although the council was officially founded on July 11, 1954, Patterson had told Senator Eastland even before the *Brown* decision that he had organized a group of men dedicated to opposing integration. Patterson's group (often mislabeled the "White Citizens' Council") tapped a vein of resentment across Mississippi and the South. Within six months it had established 110 chapters in the state, and by 1956 it boasted a membership of 250,000.[30]

Living amidst a black majority, Sunflower County whites flocked to the Citizens' Council because "we didn't want to lose complete control of everything," one planter recalled. Unlike the Ku Klux Klan and other extralegal groups, the council publicly denounced the use of violence, though its members at times implicitly encouraged it. Council members emerged from the small-town elite, operated openly, and used legal, nonviolent means, particularly the application of economic pressure, to discourage both blacks and whites from supporting racial reform. "Its leadership is drawn not from the pool hall but from the country club," a young Mississippi journalist noted, and "its aims are not couched in violent language but in the careful embroidery of states' rights and constitutionalism." Some council leaders took their preference for local control to an extreme. Asked how the group could support resistance to the stated law of the land, one local council leader bellowed, "This isn't the United States—this is Sunflower County, Mississippi!"[31]

Eastland never became an official council member, but he heartily endorsed the effort—council leaders were "courageous, intelligent, and forthright," he insisted—and he was among their most popular speakers, particularly in the organization's first several years. Like the leaders of the Citizens' Councils, Eastland believed that the key to a successful resistance could be summed up in one word, which he emphasized to several thousand council faithful at a statewide convention in 1955: "organization." While the councils focused on organizing the local elite, Eastland sought to unite resistance efforts at the state and regional levels. He advocated a two-pronged approach that would use the resources of government to present a united southern front and undermine the authority of the Supreme Court. At the state level, he called for a region-wide commission that would spend public money on an expansive public relations campaign to explain the white South's position to the rest of the nation. On the national level, he himself led a public campaign to investigate the Court on charges of Communist subversion. Together, these efforts aimed not only to "stiffen the spine" of white southerners but also to shape white opinion in the North.[32]

Eastland insisted that the nation misunderstood the white South's opposition to the Court's decision. He fundamentally believed that white northerners would join their southern brethren if only they could be made to understand the South's position. While he called for a region-wide public relations campaign, he applauded Mississippi's campaign to create its own state commission. Pushed by Eastland's old friend Walter Sillers, who now was Speaker of the Mississippi House of Representatives, state lawmakers in early 1956 created the State Sovereignty Commission to "resist the usurpation of the rights and powers reserved to this state and our sister states by the Federal Government." With an appropriation of $250,000 for its first two years, the Sovereignty Commission under Governor James P. Coleman at times antagonized hard-line segregationists by emphasizing "practical segregation" and focusing initially on public relations rather than the covert investigations of civil rights groups for which it later became known. It sought to counteract what many white Mississippians perceived as the national bias against the state—many cars sported bumper stickers proclaiming, "Mississippi—Most Lied About State in the Nation." The Sovereignty Commission sponsored a tour of Mississippi by northern news editors, sent advisors to a documentary filmmaking crew to ensure positive coverage of the state, and lavished northern reporters and politicians with reports of the state's progress in race relations.[33]

The Sovereignty Commission's efforts dovetailed nicely with Eastland's work to create a region-wide commission to, in his words, "tell the truth about the South" to white northerners. The "truth," according to Eastland, was a distillation of principles that underlay American freedom: implicit white supremacy based on explicit states' rights. Eastland did not veer from his support of segregation and white supremacy, but in contrast to his rhetoric in the FEPC filibuster, he steered clear of outright assertions of black inferiority. After more than a decade in Washington, he had become more politically savvy, and he began to recognize the national political ramifications of the racist rhetoric that had marked his early career. Race was an underlying motive, the driving force of his opposition to the *Brown* decision, but in his lengthy speeches on the Senate floor, in his campaign pitches, in his interviews, he framed his arguments with appeals to two fundamentally American themes he believed would attract a national audience: anti-Communism and the Constitution. Arguing for the rights of states to determine their own affairs, Eastland linked the Court's decision and the growing power of the federal government to the "international Communist conspiracy."[34]

Eastland's logic was clear: Communists, by definition, wanted to topple the American form of government established by the Constitution. To do so, they not only worked to foment racial discord but also sought to consolidate power in the national government, for a centralized government could more easily be manipulated and overthrown. A major obstacle in their path was the Constitution, which had created a federal structure of government in which power was distributed among the fifty states. Sanctified and protected by the Tenth Amendment, states' rights to all powers not specifically designated to the national government served as a bulwark, Eastland believed, against the predatory dreams of Communists, for it would be virtually impossible to overthrow fifty state governments. "The Communist conspiracy can never succeed in America unless there is first destroyed the powers of the States," he argued in 1955. "It can never succeed until the people are deprived of the power to control their local institutions." States' rights to control their internal affairs were the "core of Americanism," he insisted. To reflect his focus on the legal principles he espoused, the resistance organization he founded was christened with a rather awkward, legalistic name: the Federation for Constitutional Government (FCG).[35]

Established in December 1955, the FCG was an overarching

informational agency that encouraged state government resistance to *Brown*, coordinated pro-segregation efforts nationwide, published a magazine, and created a lobbying front in Washington. In his keynote address at the founding conference of the FCG, Eastland called upon the organization to lead "a crusade to restore Americanism" and emphasized that "our organization will carry on its banner the slogan of free enterprise." One of its first acts was to pass a resolution supporting state efforts to "nullify" Supreme Court decisions and other federal acts considered to be unconstitutional. The FCG got early support— one letter writer to *South* magazine applauded Eastland's organization as "the only thing that will save us from the terrible tyranny that will result when our brain-washed children grow up with their perverted socialistic politics, religion, and morals." The creation of the FCG worried some black activists; black labor leader A. Philip Randolph saw a need for a counterorganization to "neutralize the smearing campaign of the Negro phobists." But from the outset the FCG was an organization of state and national leaders, and it lacked the funding and grassroots base that such a movement needed. Despite Eastland's aggressive salesmanship, the FCG soon was eclipsed by the success of the Citizens' Councils' own regional efforts.[36]

More effective at promoting the white South's cause were Eastland's personal efforts at the national level. Using the Senate floor as a bully pulpit of sorts, Eastland launched a vigorous attack on the Supreme Court that helped catapult him into national prominence. A year after *Brown*, he made what one historian called "the most important speech of the resistance" when he challenged the scientific authorities the Court had used when it rendered its decision. Analyzing the footnotes of the *Brown* opinion, he argued that the Court had based its revolutionary decision on the research and ideas of Communists. One by one, he dissected the scholars whose work had been cited by the Court, focusing not on the content of their work but on their past affiliations to alleged Communist and Communist-front organizations. Not surprisingly, Eastland claimed that these authorities— respected black academics such as Kenneth Clark, W.E.B. Du Bois, and E. Franklin Frazier as well as, most emphatically, the Swedish socialist Gunnar Myrdal—were either Communists or Communist dupes. Given the profound influence of such un-American scholars,

Eastland asked, "Who is obligated morally or legally to obey a decision whose authorities rest not upon the law but upon the writings and teachings of pro-Communist agitators and people who have a long record of affiliations with anti-American causes and with agitators who are part and parcel of the Communist conspiracy to destroy our country?" The answer, for Eastland and his supporters, was clear: no one.[37]

"I MERELY SIT THERE"

The speech—135,000 copies of which Eastland's office reprinted and distributed nationwide—helped raise his stature within the resistance movement, paralleling his rise in the Senate itself. Now in his third term, he began to reap the fruits of the seniority system and play a much larger role within the chamber. In 1955, he assumed the chairmanship of the Senate Internal Security Subcommittee and sought to capitalize upon his growing power by challenging his critics within the news media. Angered by how northern newspapers had been "hassling" him since the *Brown* decision, Eastland called SISS hearings to investigate alleged Communist infiltration of the news media. He issued thirty-eight subpoenas, thirty of which were sent to members of the *New York Times* staff. The "Eastland purge," as it became known in media circles, was roundly condemned by the *Washington Post* and the *New York Times*, but most newspapers remained silent in the face of the senator's attacks.[38]

With the demise of Senator McCarthy in the wake of his attempted smear on the army, Eastland became perhaps the most notorious anti-Communist in the Senate—critic I.F. Stone dubbed him the "Mississippi McCarthy." But Eastland grew to wield far more power than McCarthy ever had. Early in 1956, just a year into Eastland's third term, the death of Senator Harvey Kilgore created a vacancy at the head of the Judiciary Committee, which oversaw nearly 50 percent of all bills considered by the Senate and was among the most powerful committees in Congress. As the most senior Democrat on the committee, Eastland was slated to become chair. Incredulous liberals could not stomach the irony of having the Judiciary Committee headed by a man who urged resistance to the supreme law of the land.

"A public official who openly preaches defiance of the U.S. Supreme Court is in a poor position to rebuke other types of subversive activities," wrote the editors of *America*. The chair of the Judiciary Committee, the *New Republic* argued, "is the one seat of power in Washington where a dedicated opponent of civil rights can do his greatest damage." Civil rights advocates launched an unsuccessful campaign to convince the new Senate majority leader, an ambitious, jug-eared Texan named Lyndon Johnson, to prevent Eastland from taking control. Despite opposition from the NAACP, Americans for Democratic Action, major media outlets, and several Democratic senators—New York senator Herbert Lehman publicly called Eastland "a symbol of racism in America"—Johnson supported the seniority system. Eastland won approval and assumed the chair that March.[39]

A storm of media attention descended upon him following his appointment. His Cheshire-cat grin flashed across the covers of both *South* and *Time* magazines, and viewers nationwide watched the pumpkin-faced senator take questions from Walter Cronkite on the popular *Longines Chronoscopes* television show. Reporters painted portraits of a cigar-chomping segregationist as Eastland began to garner widespread adulation and condemnation. The *Memphis Press-Scimitar* proclaimed Eastland the "South's Mightiest Champion of the White Race," while *Time* labeled him the South's "authentic voice"—but it also noted that he was "one of the most widely disliked men in the U.S." and loomed as the nation's "most dangerous demagogue." *Collier's* magazine placed him on the "frantic fringe" that wants to "reverse the healthy trend toward sound, civilized Americanism," while the NAACP called him an "accessory to murder and treason" and likened him to "a mad dog loose in the streets of justice."[40]

But earning the enmity of liberals and civil-rights advocates only enhanced his reputation among right-wing anti-Communists. "The Moscow Reds have diverted their poisonous attention from Senator McCarthy to Senator James O. Eastland of Mississippi," claimed one anti-Communist newsletter in a favorable review of the senator's work. Back home, one Sunflower County columnist praised the senator for being the "fly in the ointment" of the NAACP. Walter Sillers congratulated Eastland and applauded the senator for prominently displaying pictures of Confederate generals Robert E. Lee, Stonewall

Jackson, and Nathan Bedford Forrest in his Washington office. "To-day you are the stalwart champion and patriot who is courageously leading the fight in defense of that same noble and beloved Southland, as well as the white people of America, against the powerful forces of vicious and tyrannical enemies who would enslave the South." Reviled or revered, as chairman of the Judiciary Committee Eastland could no longer be ignored.[41]

By the middle of 1956, Senator Eastland had learned to wield his tremendous power ruthlessly, developing a well-deserved reputation as an intransigent and effective foe of racial and economic reform. The chairmanship of the Judiciary Committee was a position ideally suited for Eastland, a man born wealthy and reared to assert unquestioned authority over his plantation laborers and household. It gave him not only the ability to alter the nature and course of legislation, partic-ularly in the realm of civil rights, but also the opportunity to do so quietly, behind the scenes—much the way he used his authority as a planter. His vitriolic public speeches had earned him a reputation as a frothing demagogue in the mold of Theodore Bilbo or James Var-daman, but even after two terms in the Senate he was a relatively ob-scure segregationist with little clout to influence policy on a national level. Up until the mid-1950s, he sought to assert power through bom-bast, but that approach had not earned him either the respect of his colleagues or the ability to prevent progress on civil rights. With his ascension to the chair of the Judiciary Committee, however, he came to be seen quite differently. The chairmanship gave him for the first time in politics the authority that he enjoyed on the plantation. He learned to run the Judiciary Committee much the way he ran his farm, and he began to see that, whether in the fields or in the hearing room, true power did not require vitriol or ostentation; rather, it gained strength from deference and dependence. Far from the racist, "red-neck" populism of his Mississippi predecessors, Eastland represented, as one reporter noted, "the epitome of respectability," the gentleman planter who masked his raw power with the outward appearance of graciousness.[42]

Eastland recognized the value of appearing to be fair, generous, accommodating, even powerless. "The chairman is just the errand boy of the committee," he once observed innocently. "I merely sit there."

But political observers knew well that Eastland never just sat there; he used every opportunity to protect his interests. On his plantation, he understood that paternalistic measures helped ensure the loyalty of his workers, who depended upon him for the favors he bestowed. As chairman, he sought to cultivate that same kind of dependence among committee members by using appointments, political favors, and parliamentary procedures to reward loyalty and punish betrayal. He instituted the policy of the "blue slip," for example, which gave senators effective control over judicial nominees from their home states and gave him added leverage as chairman. Eastland "goes out of his way to accommodate the membership and he plays it fair all down the line," his chief of staff, Courtney Pace, explained privately to Archibald Coody. "Because he is so zealous in interpreting rules fairly, they cannot become irked when he uses these same rules himself."

Despite the vehement protests he generated, Eastland managed to stay on friendly terms with most of his Senate colleagues, and his public reputation as a rabid segregationist contrasted sharply with his scrupulously fair and genially polite personal manner. One frustrated political opponent acknowledged that he was "always courteous and gentlemanly in his manner and conciliatory in his approach." He protected his committee members' political bases by working diligently to ensure that their constituents' needs were addressed, yet he refused to give any ground on issues of primary importance to him; in his first ten years as chair, only one of more than a hundred civil rights bills introduced ever made it out of his committee. His magnanimity became a weapon. Eastland "is very seductive in his manner," one exasperated northern senator commented during a debate. "I can well understand how he is always able to keep bills bottled up; because it is hard to refuse him." Within the confines of his senatorial plantation, "the Chairman," as he became known, maintained tight control under the guise of fairness and friendship.[43]

But the control he was able to wield within the Judiciary Committee did not extend far beyond his legislative plantation. Even as he established himself as a national leader of a growing white resistance movement, he and other white supremacists faced mounting challenges in the late 1950s, both internationally and domestically. From the *Brown* decision to the anti-integration riots in Little Rock three years later, international events, which had helped Eastland and his southern colleagues block racial and economic reform during the anti-Communist heyday of the early 1950s, increasingly became a weapon of civil rights activists. Massive resistance in the late 1950s rose in direct correlation to the quickening pace of a global movement against white supremacy.

"AMERICAN RACIAL INTEGRITY MORE IMPORTANT THAN FOREIGN OPINION"

The *Brown* decision not only sent shock waves throughout the U.S. South but also resonated across the globe and helped push race to the fore of international relations. The decision had profound symbolic importance to American foreign policy makers as they struggled to position the United States as the morally superior leader of the "free world." Hoping to bolster the nation's image abroad, the Voice of America immediately translated news of the decision into thirty-four languages and broadcast it throughout Eastern Europe and the rest of the world. *Brown* had its intended effect on nonaligned peoples; as a National Security Council report observed in August 1954, in Africa and India "the decision is regarded as the greatest event since the Emancipation Proclamation, and it removes from Communist hands the most effective anti-American weapon they had in Black Africa." For white supremacists such as Eastland, that kind of assessment threatened to remove from *their* hands one of the most effective weapons against the cause of racial equality: Cold War anti-Communism. Although they would continue to use the brush of Communism to tar the growing civil rights movement, they found their arguments challenged by the seeming consensus among foreign policy makers and civil rights activists that racism and segregation hurt the United States politically in the Cold War, which was being waged more and more within the nonaligned "Third World."[44]

By the mid-1950s, the Cold War had settled into a stable, if dangerous, equilibrium as the hated Soviet dictator Joseph Stalin died, the armed conflict in Korea ended in a stalemate, and Senator McCarthy disgraced himself with an attempt to smear the military with

the Red stain of Communism. The national hysteria over internal subversion subsided, as did the actual threat of Communist infiltration.
The federal government's crackdown on the American Communist
Party crushed the organization's leadership, and much of its remaining rank-and-file membership abandoned the cause in 1956 after the
Soviet invasion of Hungary and Khrushchev's secret speech detailing
Stalin's crimes. The logic of mutually assured destruction—because
both nations had nuclear capabilities, any violent confrontation could
destroy both—helped diminish the prospect of direct superpower confrontation. The battlefield of the Cold War began to move toward Asia
and Africa, where European colonial empires were crumbling in the
face of economic pressure and native resistance. From Ho Chi Minh's
war for Vietnamese independence to the Mau Mau uprising in Kenya,
nonwhite peoples began asserting claims to national self-determination
and wielding influence internationally. Newly independent nations such
as India and Egypt refused to align themselves immediately with either the United States or the Soviet Union, prompting the two superpowers to seek to win their allegiance through economic aid and
diplomatic blandishments. A new breed of Third World leader, embodied by Egypt's Gamal Nasser, India's Jawaharlal Nehru, and, later,
Ghana's Kwame Nkrumah and Guinea's Sekou Touré, aggressively
played the two superpowers off each other in an effort to advance
their national interests.[45]

The United States aimed to gain allies by projecting an image of
itself as a democratic, racially egalitarian country that would defend
freedom—particularly freedom of enterprise—worldwide. But image
alone, civil rights critics argued, would not suffice. As the *Chicago Defender* noted during the Korean War, "There's no doubt that colored
Asia and Africa have their eyes on the United States in these decisive
days, and the total battle against the spread of Communism will stand
or fall on whether the United States is willing to move forthrightly to
accord those fundamental rights to Negro Americans which are everyday guarantees for other Americans." Liberal critics delighted in highlighting the hypocrisy of southern segregationists who championed
free elections for Communist states yet refused to consider applying
those same rules to the South. When Eastland publicly chastised the
Soviet Union for its anti-democratic actions in Poland, the NAACP

congratulated him. "We are happy to join you in urging 'free elections' in Poland," the group chimed, "and in turn we call upon you to join us in urging free elections in Mississippi." *America* magazine specifically targeted Eastland's fusion of segregation and anti-Communism as counterproductive and contradictory. "It seems to be time for the Senator to decide whether to rest his claim to future fame upon racist hatreds, or upon his zeal as a defender of national security," the editors insisted. "One thing is certain, he cannot do both. He is giving Communist propagandists at home and abroad a wonderful chance to paint all who actively oppose them as race baiters and political bitter-enders." By emphasizing how racial prejudice undermined the American cause, activists sought to capitalize upon the Cold War and force segregationist anti-Communists such as Eastland onto the defensive.[46]

Despite the positive press the United States received after *Brown*, newly independent nonwhite peoples looked skeptically at American claims of freedom and democracy while white supremacy still reigned in the South. In August 1955, little more than a year after *Brown*, at least two white men in Money, Mississippi—about thirty miles from Eastland's plantation—murdered Emmett Till, a black Chicago teenager visiting relatives in Mississippi, for the alleged crime of flirting with a white woman. Acquitted by an all-white jury after an hour's deliberation, the unrepentant men later brashly confessed their crime to a magazine reporter. The Till murder and the subsequent acquittal of the killers outraged blacks nationwide, some of whom explicitly used Cold War language to highlight the injustice of the case. Congressman Adam Clayton Powell Jr., one of three black members of Congress, pointedly asked, "This is world Communism's finest hour [—] shall we let them win because of a bigoted few?" The case also generated international coverage and condemnation. Calling the murderers' acquittal "one of those inequities that history does not forgive," one Tunisian publication insisted that "it is not enough for the U.S. to present itself verbally as the champion of liberty and justice"—it had to act aggressively to end injustice in the South. Foreign observers, Communist and anti-Communist alike, recognized the toll segregation was taking on the American effort to win allies in the Cold War.[47]

Black Americans backed up their rhetoric with assertive action.

In December 1955, on the same day that Senator Eastland spoke before thousands of Citizens' Council faithful at a massive Mississippi rally, a diminutive but determined Montgomery seamstress and NAACP member, Rosa Parks, refused to yield her seat to a white man. Parks's nonviolent act triggered a bus boycott that vaulted a stocky, twenty-six-year-old minister named Martin Luther King Jr. into national prominence. The intellectual and urbane King recognized the international implications of the boycott, which continued for more than a year before the Supreme Court struck down Montgomery's segregation statute. "The oppressed people of the world are rising up," King declared, emphasizing that black Americans were part of that global struggle. Some of Eastland's constituents feared just that. "This is the last round up," a worried Archibald Coody wrote Eastland. "If we don't fight to the finish now, we may as well arrange for our mulatto grandchildren."[48]

Twice in late summer 1957, the growing movement for racial equality clashed with the forces of resistance, first in the halls of Congress, then on the streets of Little Rock, Arkansas. Civil rights advocates long had pushed for passage of a federal civil rights bill that would codify the federal government's commitment to dismantling segregation. Not since Reconstruction, however, had the national Congress passed a civil rights bill; the last bill, passed in 1875, eventually had been struck down as unconstitutional. Since then, repeated efforts to pass civil rights legislation, including an effort supported by the Eisenhower administration in 1956, foundered on the shoals of southern resistance, which had been fortified by Eastland's appointment to head the Judiciary Committee. But 1957 was different. Democratic intransigence on civil rights, embodied by Eastland, had been a political liability in the 1956 elections—NAACP lobbyist Clarence Mitchell mused, "Seldom in the long political history of our country has a man been so helpful in defeating members of his own party as Eastland." Worried Democratic leaders, including Senate majority leader Lyndon Johnson, came to see passing civil rights legislation as a political necessity, particularly if Johnson hoped to win the presidency in 1960. Johnson worked to gut the bill to render it a toothless, symbolic measure, weak enough to ensure that southerners would not mount a full-scale defense, and he allied with Vice President Richard Nixon to keep the bill away from Eastland's committee. The strategy worked. Though Walter Sillers and other constituents urged Eastland to filibuster "the outrageous Communist inspired Civil Rights bill," he refused to do so out of deference to Johnson's presidential ambitions. Besides, Eastland explained privately to a friend, the end result was "almost a miracle" compared to the original bill, and he did not want to jeopardize "some of the friends and good will which we did establish in connection with the struggle." In early September, Eisenhower signed the measure. Though the bill was a hollow version of its original self, the Civil Rights Act of 1957 if nothing else showed that southerners in the Senate were not invincible, even with Eastland in charge of the Judiciary Committee.[49]

American foreign policy leaders barely had time to trumpet news of the bill's passage before the federal government's will to enforce it was tested by events in Arkansas. Under court order, nine black students had been selected to attend all-white Little Rock Central High School. On their first day of school, white mobs and Arkansas National Guardsmen blocked their attempts to enter the building. Initially, President Eisenhower proved reluctant to involve himself in the local struggle. As images of state-supported white hooligans openly defying federal law appeared in newspapers and on television screens around the world, criticism mounted, prompting Eisenhower to federalize the National Guard and send troops from the 101st Airborne Division to protect the students and keep peace in the school. The next day, Eastland spoke to a Citizens' Council audience in Belzoni, Mississippi, at which council officers wore black armbands to mourn the death of states' rights. Although the federal government had triumphed by imposing its will on the "peaceful assemblage" outside Central High School, Eastland vowed that white southerners were not ready to accept its actions and forgive the perpetrators—"no more so than that the Hungarians have forgiven the Soviets for the repression in Budapest." Little Rock became a symbol of all that they had feared and predicted about the reach of federal power in the wake of Brown. "The evil of the Brown decision in 1954 has borne the fruit of Little Rock in 1957," Eastland lamented.[50]

The Little Rock crisis did not simply confirm the superiority of federal force; it also manifested the influence of international opinion on domestic affairs. The image of southern whites actively and unrepentantly defying the *Brown* decision gave the United States a black eye in the international community, and the intensity of foreign feeling about the issue convinced Eisenhower and other national leaders that segregation was an increasingly unaffordable burden for the nation to bear. Little Rock was "ruining our foreign policy," Secretary of State John Foster Dulles worried. "The effect of this in Asia and Africa will be worse for us than Hungary was for the Russians." The role of international opinion in persuading Eisenhower to intervene in Little Rock highlighted the difficulty that Eastland and other white southerners faced in the late 1950s and early 1960s as they sought to use the Cold War to destroy the black struggle for equality. Much had changed in ten years. The anti-Communism they had wielded effectively in the early 1950s now could be used against them, for in the court of international opinion white supremacy in the South increasingly appeared guilty.[51]

Combined with the independence movements in Africa and Asia, the increasing relevance of race internationally helped drive many segregationists toward isolationism and unilateralism in foreign affairs. In the postwar South, as we have seen, Eastland and other white segregationists tended to have strongly internationalist views and initially supported the newly formed United Nations. Eastland was a strong supporter of the Truman Doctrine, the Marshall Plan, the North Atlantic Treaty Organization, and other international efforts because he saw such global actions as essential to the fight against Communism as well as an economic boon to cotton farmers back home in Sunflower County. His internationalism assumed that collective security efforts would remain driven primarily by the interests of anti-Communist white nations. But as more and more African and Asian countries gained independence and joined the United Nations, the world body became more aggressive about challenging American racism. Eastland and other segregationists became increasingly disconcerted by what they saw as the federal government's catering to native nationalists. "American Racial Integrity More Valuable than Foreign Opinion," proclaimed a State Sovereignty Commission pamphlet that urged Americans to ignore international criticism of segregation. Internationalist efforts seemed to be driven no longer by white

America's self-interest, Eastland worried, but rather by the misguided desire to appease nonwhite nations to gain their allegiance in the Cold War.[52]

Indeed, Eastland worried that the U.S. government was supporting the wrong kind of freedom worldwide. Instead of defending anti-Communist white nations, Eastland charged, American foreign policy makers were aiding and abetting the rise of Communism, particularly in the Caribbean. For decades, U.S.-backed authoritarian regimes, often led by descendants of the European minority, had ruled much of the Caribbean, including two nations that attracted Eastland's attention in the late 1950s and early 1960s: the Dominican Republic and Cuba. In the Dominican Republic, the dictatorial General Rafael Trujillo capitalized on U.S. policy makers' concerns about both Communism and race to maintain close relations with the United States even as he pursued authoritarian measures at home. Eastland applauded Trujillo's efforts to prevent "Ethiopianization" of the island by stressing Spanish heritage, encouraging European immigration, and blocking Haitian migrants. Twice Eastland visited the island as Trujillo's guest, and he extolled the general as "one of the great men of the free world." But Trujillo's strong-arm tactics to crush domestic dissent during the 1950s clashed with the shifting strategies of the Cold War, and he slowly lost support in Congress, which slapped economic sanctions on the Trujillo regime in 1960. Labeling the sanctions a Cold War "blunder" on par with the loss of China, Eastland argued that undermining Trujillo's regime would "create a vacuum into which Communist power will flow." Instead of catering to native nationalists who sought self-determination, Eastland insisted, America must focus on the true crisis: Communism.[53]

The mistreatment of General Trujillo was magnified in Eastland's mind by the ineffectual reaction of foreign policy makers to Fidel Castro's regime in Cuba, just ninety miles off the coast of the United States. The light-skinned Castro had cobbled together a band of revolutionaries that included various mixtures of European, African, and Indian blood, an interracial alliance that a disgusted Eastland saw as a warning against the dangers of race mixing. Furthermore, once Castro came to power, he sought to nationalize industries owned by foreign capitalists and made overtures to the Soviet Union, proving to

Eastland that Castro was part of the world Communist conspiracy. "The Communist objective," Eastland argued, "is to use the Castro government as a tool in bringing all Latin America under Communist domination." Yet, he claimed, the American diplomatic corps was doing nothing to stop Castro's rise because it feared upsetting minority groups in America and nonwhite nations abroad. The problem of containing Communism in Cuba was exacerbated by the growing presence of Asian and African countries in the United Nations. "If there is a rebellion in Cuba," Eastland feared, "two-thirds of the United Nations could vote sanctions and send armed forces to crack a rebellion." Eastland's foreign policy concerns were tied directly to his domestic worries about the growing civil rights movement. By failing to counter Castro or support Trujillo, Eastland believed, American policy makers were only encouraging the spread of revolutionary ideas to black Americans. In the face of such challenges abroad, Eastland was determined to strengthen resistance at home.[54]

By 1960, Eastland and his fellow white southerners could claim some important successes, particularly on the issue of school segregation. Six years after *Brown*, Eastland noted proudly, "in one manner, form, fashion, or another, it has been combated and successfully resisted in every community where the white people are determined that their children are not going to be forced into public schools with those children of the Negro race." As a new decade dawned, there were no black students at Ruleville Middle School. Indeed, not a single black student in Mississippi was attending a white school. With Eastland safely ensconced atop the Judiciary Committee, white southerners looked forward to continued success at resisting legislative efforts to promote civil rights. Racial egalitarians had been unable to circumvent Eastland's committee and produce serious legislative reform; they could claim only the ineffectual Civil Rights Act of 1957. Eastland's success at blocking legislative action contributed to the growing sense, particularly among younger black Americans, that a more aggressive approach was necessary to gain equality. As Eastland waged war on *Brown* and the movement for racial equality nationally and even internationally, a movement was gathering that would soon bring the battle to his doorstep in Sunflower County. And there that movement would find Fannie Lou Hamer.[55]

6

"No One Can Honestly Say Negroes Are Satisfied": The Sharecropper Embraces the Movement

From Ruleville Middle School, Highway 49 heads north through town. Ruleville has changed a fair bit since the days of Fannie Lou Hamer and James Eastland. The population has swelled as plantation workers abandoned the countryside in the mid-twentieth century, and the town now boasts more than three thousand people, about the size of Indianola a century earlier. As in the rest of America, chain stores, including Dollar General and Double Quick, have replaced family-run businesses. It's gone now, but on the right-hand side of the road there used to be a small convenience store run by Roy Bryant, one of Emmett Till's murderers, who found refuge in Ruleville and lived there until he died in 1994. Few blacks in town lamented his passing.

Once you cross Highway 8, there is a sign that reads "Fannie Lou Hamer Recreational Complex." Before you get to the complex on the left—a squat, nondescript 1970s building with a baseball field and swimming pool outside—there is a brick church. This is William Chapel, the place where Fannie Lou Hamer's involvement in the civil rights movement began back in 1962. Unpretentious in design and function, William Chapel is perhaps the most famous of Ruleville's several dozen churches, at least to outsiders, but today the church struggles to hold on to its diminishing congregation. It earned its fame nearly half a century earlier, when it became the first church in Rule-ville to open its doors to the young organizers of the Student Non-violent Coordinating Committee (SNCC). It was here that Ruleville's first mass meetings were held, here that Hamer first belted out the freedom songs that inspired a generation of civil rights workers. "You can hear her sing in William Chapel if you're standin' in front of East-land's bank" more than half a mile away, SNCC field secretary Charles McLaurin used to tell incoming workers. These workers in turn opened a new world to the black men and women of Sunflower County. Life would never be the same.[1]

LIFE "ALMOST AS MY MOTHER'S WAS"

The southern white backlash against the *Brown* decision and other civil rights measures succeeded in preventing racial progress, but it also spurred the black movement. To some extent, white resistance de-legitimized the efforts of the previous generation of black activists, particularly in the NAACP. The NAACP had pursued a judicial and legislative strategy that emphasized laws and law enforcement as the primary means of achieving equality. While this strategy had produced many important victories, it had become apparent by 1960 that it had reached a seemingly impenetrable barrier, the barrier of white power. No matter how many decisions the NAACP could win, no matter how many responsible bills it could help craft, no matter how reasonable it could seem, the organization still encountered massive white resist-ance that successfully blocked all its efforts. It could win a decision but could not have it enforced; it could get a civil rights bill passed but could not protect it from being hollowed out by opponents; it could purge itself of Communists but could not prevent an illegal assault on its membership and its very existence throughout the South.

By 1960, it was clear that the NAACP's law-based strategy was not making progress because white southerners simply were not abid-ing by the law. Encouraged by Senator Eastland and other leaders of massive resistance, the vast majority of southern whites refused to apply the laws of the United States to black southerners. Blacks, in response, looked to extralegal means of producing change. As the movement turned to nonviolent civil disobedience and direct action, Eastland lamented the rise of "militant" black leaders who had no respect, he claimed, for law and order. Their rise can be attributed in part to the success of his very own efforts at circumventing the Supreme Court and the law of the land.

The new militancy manifested itself through the strategy of nonviolent direct action, which first captured the nation's attention with a dramatic form of protest: the sit-in. Frustrated by their inability to effect change through the traditional channels of democracy, young blacks took to the streets and lunch counters to demonstrate their commitment to change. Unlike previous lunch counter demonstrations in Oklahoma and Kansas two years earlier, a sit-in by four young men in Greensboro, North Carolina, on February 1, 1960, sparked an explosion of sympathetic demonstrations across the region. Over the next three months, about fifty thousand people, mostly college students, descended upon segregated eateries in Richmond, Baltimore, Nashville, Montgomery, and dozens of other southern cities (though none in Mississippi). To capture the spirit of the sit-ins and channel it into productive leadership, Ella Baker of the Southern Christian Leadership Conference (SCLC) called an April meeting of student leaders at Shaw University in North Carolina. Out of this conference grew the Student Nonviolent Coordinating Committee, a loosely structured, student-run organization dedicated to achieving desegregation and political equality through nonviolent direct action and grassroots leadership development.[2]

The sit-in spirit fed off rapid changes that were redrawing the map of the world. A wave of independence was washing away the colonial empires of Asia and Africa; 1960 was dubbed the "Year of Africa" as sixteen different African nations threw off their colonial yokes and waded into the fresh waters of freedom. As more African nations became independent, many black Americans, particularly the young, grew increasingly frustrated with the slow pace of racial reform in what was supposed to be the world's pioneer of democracy and freedom. If Ghanaians could win their freedom from a colonial oppressor, activists reasoned, then surely black Americans could triumph over white supremacy in the South. "American Negroes take courage and hope from an independent Ghana and Guinea; revolts in the Congo stiffen the resolve of Africans in South Africa," wrote the editors of the NAACP's *Crisis* magazine. "Everywhere the colored peoples are resolved that the arrogance and the domination of the whites must go."[3]

The new intensity of the global freedom struggle confirmed for Eastland and his supporters that the worldwide Communist conspiracy was winning. "Student uprisings are taking place all over the world," a worried Virginia supporter wrote Eastland in June 1960, urging the senator to investigate recent student protests. "They follow the same pattern, and there is no doubt that the Communists are masterminding them." In a letter to the senator, Eastland's old friend Walter Sillers linked various world events, including anti-U.S. student protests in Okinawa and Castro's triumphs in Cuba, to the "Communist inspired negro sit-ins and demands for social equality in all spheres of life and activity." In a world beset by protest, segregationists felt besieged.[4]

Yet for all the swirling of events worldwide, Eastland's home remained relatively unaffected. The global freedom struggle may have swept away colonial regimes, but Sunflower County's plantation society seemingly stood calm in the eye of the storm. Fannie Lou Hamer and other black sharecroppers back in Sunflower County, like their counterparts across the rural South, were far less informed about international events than white Americans and far less likely to have an opinion on foreign affairs in general. Although by 1960 television had penetrated much of America, it still was a relatively unknown phenomenon in the rural South. Radios were prevalent on the plantation, but workers seldom had the time to listen to news broadcasts. "Livin' out in the country," Hamer recalled, "if you had a little radio, by the time you got in at night you'd be too tired to listen at what was goin' on." Years after she had joined the civil rights movement, Fannie Lou Hamer looked back on the late 1950s and early 1960s and recalled that her life remained "almost as my mother's was." Like her mother, Hamer too was an impoverished sharecropper who enjoyed few of the economic, educational, or political benefits of living in the "free world."[5]

Hamer was raising her children in a segregated society that placed distinct limits on black educational aspirations. The *Brown* decision notwithstanding, both Dorothy Jean and Vergie Hamer attended separate and unequal schools that lacked the basic resources available to white students. Senator Eastland and other Mississippi politicians liked to point out that in the 1950s the state had spent more on black schools than white schools, and indeed it had, at least in terms of capital expenditures. One observer noted, however, that some of the new schools were "shells"—one recently constructed high school near Sunflower County had no lockers, central heating, ventilators, or other essentials. A decade after the well-publicized effort of the Sunflower County Inter-Racial Committee to call attention to the deplorable state of black schooling in the county, conditions for black students had not markedly improved. In 1960–61, the county still spent two and a half times more per white pupil than per black pupil. One class in Ruleville had seventy-seven students being taught by a single teacher. "We just have nice school buildings," Hamer complained, and there were not even enough of those—only three buildings for eleven thousand black students while the county's four thousand white students enjoyed six buildings.[6]

Hamer's life was similar to her mother's in the realm of politics as well. By 1960, only 5 percent of black Mississippians and 3 percent of blacks in Sunflower County were registered to vote, a mere 161 black registrants at the time of Eastland's reelection campaign. Prospective voters faced a number of serious obstacles. First, they had to confront the hostility of whites who publicly discouraged blacks from even considering registration. From the organized resistance of the Citizens' Council to the arbitrary power of individual planters, whites economically and physically harassed blacks who advocated voting rights. "If any of my niggers try to register," one Ruleville planter boasted, "I'll shoot them down like rabbits." In the Delta, this was not an idle threat. The Reverend George Lee, an NAACP leader in Belzoni, was murdered in 1955 after publicly urging blacks to vote; his friend Gus Courts was severely wounded and forced to flee the state for a similar "offense." That same year, World War II veteran Lamar Smith was murdered in broad daylight in Brookhaven for his voter-registration activities. More common than outright violence was economic intimidation—blacks who advocated voting rights could lose their jobs, fail to secure bank loans, or face a white-inspired boycott of their services.[7]

If prospective registrants could overcome fears of retaliation, they had to go to the county courthouse, where they faced indifferent or hostile white registrars. The Sunflower County registrar, Cecil Campbell, was a strong Eastland supporter. He sent the senator lists of county residents with the black residents crossed out and refused to admit black registrants who came to the courthouse. Determined registrants who managed to make it into the registrar's office then had to take a literacy test that included a section where they had to write a "reasonable" interpretation of a portion of the state constitution to the satisfaction of the registrar. This written-interpretation clause, adopted in response to *Brown* and the NAACP's successful voting drives of the early 1950s, helped reduce the number of black voters on the state rolls from 22,000 in 1954 to less than 12,000 a year later. On the off chance that they succeeded in passing this test, registrants then had to pay two years' worth of poll taxes before they could cast a ballot. The poll tax was necessary, supporters such as Senator Eastland insisted, to pay for schools. Besides, he argued, any person "who does not care enough for the franchise to desire to pay a poll tax as a qualification should not be permitted to vote, because I do not believe that he cares enough about his citizenship." Given these impediments, it hardly is surprising that so few black Sunflower Countians were registered to vote.[8]

Yet such institutional barriers to voting existed only for those blacks who were knowledgeable and dedicated enough to attempt to register. For Fannie Lou Hamer and other sharecroppers, the very idea of voting was an altogether foreign concept—no one she knew voted, and she later claimed that she never knew blacks even had the right to vote until after the civil rights movement came to Sunflower County. Senator Eastland and other segregationists pointed to sharecroppers' ignorance of voting as an explanation for the low numbers of black registrants. Blacks were free to vote, he argued, but their "apathy," not voter intimidation, literacy tests, or prejudiced registrars, accounted for the low levels of black voting. "There is no attempt to discriminate against anyone," Eastland insisted. "Everyone who is qualified votes; as a rule, everyone votes who desires to vote."[9]

The key, Eastland understood, was information. So long as Eastland and his fellow segregationists could control black education and limit the flow of information to blacks, they could keep black aspiration under control and squelch the growing movement for racial equality. Without information about events beyond the plantation, without education about their rights, without knowledge of the freedom struggles in other parts of the world, then Fannie Lou Hamer and other sharecroppers would not desire economic equity, educational equality, or voting rights. To keep a tight grip on the information that Mississippi blacks received, white elites in the state created both institutional and psychological barriers to ideas that did not conform to the economically conservative and racially repressive understanding of freedom that Eastland espoused. Mississippi became, in the words of dissident University of Mississippi historian James Silver, a "closed society" where conformity was the rule—state libraries even banned a children's book that showed a marriage between a light-furred rabbit and a dark-furred one. It was not only blacks who were not free to think on their own; whites too faced serious social and economic retaliation if they did not abide by local customs. In 1956, the Mississippi legislature declared it illegal "to incite a riot, or breach of the peace, or public disturbance, or disorderly assembly, by soliciting, or advocating, or urging, or encouraging disobedience to any law of the State of Mississippi, and nonconformance with the established traditions, customs, and usages of the State of Mississippi." Among the victims of this crackdown on nonconformity was Providence Farm in Holmes County, the successor to the Delta Cooperative Farm; after nearly two decades of quiet interracial living, the farm came under attack in the years after *Brown* and was forced to close down. By 1960, state and local political leaders, in concert with Eastland and other national figures, had actively clamped down on dissenting thought and openly promoted the idea that "the people of Mississippi" were of one mind on matters of politics, economics, and race.[10]

"NOW I CAN WORK FOR MY PEOPLE"

Civil rights activists recognized the particularly difficult task of opening up Mississippi's closed society. For more than a year after the formation of SNCC, the organization studiously avoided the state, focusing instead on building its organizational strength in less repressive areas. Yet Mississippi could not stay isolated for long. The 1960 wave of sit-ins had barely breached the borders of the state—an April "wade-in" at Biloxi beach met with such violence that no other such direct action was attempted—but the next year the Freedom Rides burst through the barriers and forced Mississippians to come, in Eastland's words, "eye to eye with the international Communist conspiracy." A reprise of a 1947 effort, the 1961 Freedom Rides were the brainchild of the Congress of Racial Equality (CORE), which hoped to pressure the federal government to enforce the Supreme Court's decision in *Boynton v. Virginia* that banned segregation during interstate travel. An interracial group of thirteen passengers boarded two Greyhound buses in Washington, D.C., with the intention of traveling throughout the South testing integration in bus terminals until they reached New Orleans. Their early stops in the Upper South were relatively uneventful, but by the time they reached the Deep South, they faced riotous mobs of armed whites who, with the support of local police, firebombed one bus and savagely attacked the passengers of the second vehicle. Dramatic images of the burning bus reached worldwide, and once again race relations threatened to become a debilitating issue for the United States in the Cold War. To white Mississippians, the Freedom Rides represented the first direct assault on their segregation stronghold; Eastland's son remembers that year as particularly "traumatic" as his parents struggled to deal with the impact of the movement on Mississippi. For black Mississippians, the Freedom Rides were an exhilarating (and even frightening) gust of fresh air blowing through their stifling state. For years afterward, local people, black and white, called all civil rights workers "Freedom Riders," even if they were involved in voter registration, Freedom Schools, or other movement activities.[11]

Shortly after the Freedom Riders had penetrated the state, SNCC too pushed its way into Mississippi. It joined forces with the NAACP, CORE, SCLC, and the National Urban League to form the Council of Federated Organizations (COFO), an umbrella group designed to encourage unity and cooperation among the various civil rights organizations. SNCC soon set its sights on Sunflower County. As the home of Senator Eastland, Sunflower was a ripe target, one that offered the opportunity to highlight the lack of freedom in the senator's backyard.

Bob Moses, a soft-spoken, introspective, bespectacled New Yorker who had pioneered SNCC's efforts in Mississippi, sought to expose the senator as a hypocrite by showing the American people and the federal government that the state's black population simply did not have the right to vote. By attempting to register blacks in Sunflower, Moses expected to encounter resistance that would both embarrass Eastland and induce the Justice Department to investigate the voting-rights violations. "The aim," SNCC worker Charles McLaurin recalled, "was to focus on Eastland." In the process, SNCC discovered a sharecropper who would become the senator's antithesis in seemingly every conceivable way.[12]

In late summer 1962, McLaurin, a short, feisty Jackson native with a taste for dark sunglasses, joined fellow SNCC workers James Jones, Landy McNair, and Charles Cobb in an effort to organize Sunflower County. Like most of SNCC at the time, the four men were young—the oldest was twenty-two—black, and, with the exception of Washington, D.C., native Cobb, southern. Their work was usually tedious, often unpaid, and always dangerous. Dressed in the "SNCC uniform" of overalls or jeans, they trooped through the fields and the streets of black Sunflower County avoiding the gaze of potentially hostile whites as they encouraged people to attempt to register to vote. Voting rights were an essential element of political freedom, a necessary first step toward breaking white power over black lives. With the vote, SNCC organizers reasoned, blacks would gain a measure of physical protection as well as a voice in how government funds were distributed. "The vote won't make Mister Charlie love us, but it will stop him from lynching us!" commented Aaron Henry, the head of the Clarksdale NAACP who allied with SNCC when it first came to Mississippi. With enough participation, he continued, black voters could "make a [liberal New York senator Jacob] Javits of an Eastland." More public and confrontational direct action campaigns such as sit-ins and Freedom Rides had been effective in attracting attention to the movement, but in Delta counties such as Sunflower they simply were too dangerous. Furthermore, they had little relevance to the lives of most Delta blacks, who were too poor to eat in restaurants or use integrated public facilities such as waiting rooms or hotels. As Charles Cobb put it, "The last thing on your mind is whether or not you can

get a hamburger at the one Woolworth's, if you can find one up there."
Voting rights, by contrast, promised to translate directly into visible,
material change.[13]

Progress in voter registration came slowly at first. Blacks conditioned to defer to their white bosses often refused even to listen to
talk of change, and they encouraged their friends and relatives to steer
clear of "dat mess"—a dismissive catchall phrase for civil rights work.
Others simply nodded politely, with no intention of ever going to a
meeting. But word spread, and slowly more and more blacks began
coming to the evening mass meetings, if only to find out what all the
commotion was about. One curious woman was the powerfully built
timekeeper from the Marlow plantation in Ruleville, Fannie Lou Hamer,
who attended one of the first mass meetings held at Ruleville's William
Chapel. Hamer had been following news of the sit-ins and Freedom
Rides, but "until then I'd never heard of no mass meeting," she later
recalled, "and I didn't know that a Negro could register and vote." She
learned of the meeting from her friend Mary Tucker, an elderly neighbor who was among the few people in Ruleville who had allowed civil
rights workers into her home. Hamer was initially reluctant to go. According to Tucker, Hamer told her dismissively, "Tuck, they taught us
that mess in school and that's turned me off like that." But Hamer
changed her mind and, with permission from her husband, Pap—who
promised to let her go only "if we picked enough cotton that day"—
she joined Tucker at William Chapel on Monday, August 27.[14]

The meeting revolutionized both Hamer's life and SNCC's efforts in the Delta. SNCC leaders Bob Moses, James Forman, and
Reggie Robinson and SCLC's James Bevel led the congregation in
"freedom songs," traditional religious hymns and spirituals whose
words had been changed to reflect the movement's goals. Hamer, who
had never heard freedom songs before, was mesmerized. She listened
intently as Bevel, a charismatic, Nashville-educated, and somewhat
eccentric preacher who often wore a yarmulke, read from Luke 12:54
and exhorted his listeners to read the signs of the times the way they
could read lightning in the sky—and the signs of the times indicated
that segregation must go. He finished his fiery speech by calling for
volunteers to join him on a trip to the courthouse to register to vote.
An enthusiastic Hamer raised her hand "up high as I could get it." Re-

No pictures survive from the lynching and burning of Luther and Mary Holbert in Sunflower County in 1904, but the brutality of their murders was not unique. Across the South in the early twentieth century, white mobs tortured, mutilated, and burned black victims such as Jesse Washington (pictured), whose charred corpse was photographed in Waco, Texas, in 1916. GILDERSLEEVE, VISUAL MATERIALS FROM THE NATIONAL ASSOCIATION FOR THE ADVANCEMENT OF COLORED PEOPLE RECORDS, LIBRARY OF CONGRESS PRINTS & PHOTOGRAPHS DIVISION (LC-USZ62-38918)

Forest High School Class of 1922. James Eastland sits in the front row, third from the right. FOREST PUBLIC LIBRARY, FOREST, MISSISSIPPI

"The Richness of the Soil Makes Living Easy and the Folks there make Life Worthwhile," claimed Sunflower County boosters in a 1924 brochure that featured this picture of cotton being picked by hand. Cotton drew settlers to the area beginning in the mid-nineteenth century, and it remained the engine of the Sunflower County economy throughout the twentieth century. HENRY M. SEYMOUR LIBRARY, INDIANOLA, MISSISSIPPI

A black woman uses a hoe to clear weeds in a Delta cotton field, 1937. Fannie Lou Hamer and other sharecroppers worked from "can" to "can't"—from the time you can see in the morning until you could no longer see at night. DOROTHEA LANGE, FARM SECURITY ADMINISTRATION–OFFICE OF WAR INFORMATION PHOTOGRAPH COLLECTION, LIBRARY OF CONGRESS PRINTS & PHOTOGRAPHS DIVISION (LC-USF34- 017305-C)

Three International Harvester cotton pickers march through the fields of Hopson Plantation, just north of Sunflower County, 1939. Labor shortages during World War II and afterward made mechanical pickers more economically feasible for planters. Within a generation, hand-picked cotton was a thing of the past in Sunflower County. MARION POST WOLCOTT, FARM SECURITY ADMINISTRATION–OFFICE OF WAR INFORMATION PHOTOGRAPH COLLECTION, LIBRARY OF CONGRESS PRINTS & PHOTOGRAPHS DIVISION (LC-USF34-052533-D)

As a temporary senator appointed to an eighty-eight-day term in 1941, Eastland earned plaudits from Mississippi planters with a highly publicized attack on Treasury Secretary Henry Morgenthau's plan to cap cottonseed prices. *DELTA HUB*

Senator James O. Eastland's official portrait, taken shortly after he won election to the U.S. Senate in 1942. He was so unknown in the chamber that the Library of Congress misidentified him as the "Senator from Michigan." LIBRARY OF CONGRESS PRINTS & PHOTOGRAPHS DIVISION (LC-USZ62-63253)

The Pepple School in Sunflower County was typical of the one- and two-room plantation schoolhouses that Fannie Lou Hamer and other black sharecroppers attended. Built amidst the cotton fields, these schools had no indoor plumbing and few educational amenities. JOHN E. PHAY COLLECTION, SPECIAL COLLECTIONS, UNIVERSITY OF MISSISSIPPI

A 1949 report conducted by researchers from the University of Mississippi found that the segregated county school district offered black students a woefully inadequate education beset by overcrowded classrooms, poorly equipped schools, short school terms that deferred to agricultural seasons, and inadequately trained and poorly paid teachers. JOHN E. PHAY COLLECTION, SPECIAL COLLECTIONS, UNIVERSITY OF MISSISSIPPI

TWENTY CENTS MARCH 26, 1956

TIME
THE WEEKLY NEWSMAGAZINE

MISSISSIPPI'S
SENATOR EASTLAND

$6.00 A YEAR   REG. U.S. PAT. OFF.   VOL. LXVII NO. 13

With his ascension to the chairmanship of the Senate Judiciary Committee in 1956, Eastland became the focus of national media attention. *Time* magazine labeled Eastland the "spiritual leader of the segregationists," "one of the most widely disliked men in the U.S.," and the nation's "most dangerous demagogue." *TIME*, 12 MARCH 1956

Eastland with his trademark Cuban cigar. Even after Fidel Castro took control of Cuba and the United States placed an embargo on Cuban imports, Eastland received a package of cigars from an anonymous supporter every month. MISSISSIPPI VALLEY COLLECTION, SPECIAL COLLECTIONS, UNIVERSITY OF MEMPHIS

Fannie Lou Hamer speaks to potential voters during her 1964 run for Congress. "I'm showing people that a Negro can run for office," Hamer told a reporter during her campaign. "All my life I've been sick and tired. Now I'm sick and tired of being sick and tired." BERN KEATING COLLECTION, SPECIAL COLLECTIONS, UNIVERSITY OF MISSISSIPPI

Blacks vote in a Freedom Vote, Sunflower County, 1964. Often barred from voting by local officials, blacks participated in mock elections ("Freedom Votes") organized by the Student Nonviolent Coordinating Committee. BERN KEATING COLLECTION, SPECIAL COLLECTIONS, UNIVERSITY OF MISSISSIPPI

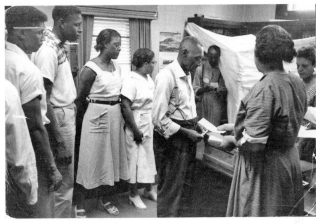

Hamer testifies before the Credentials Committee during the Democratic National Convention, 1964. Hamer's powerful testimony riveted television viewers and vaulted her into national prominence, but it failed to persuade Democratic Party leaders to seat an integrated delegation from the Mississippi Freedom Democratic Party. WARREN K. LEFFLER, U.S. NEWS AND WORLD REPORT COLLECTION, LIBRARY OF CONGRESS PRINTS & PHOTOGRAPHS DIVISION (LC-U9-12470B-17)

Hamer speaks before a crowd of supporters, Washington, D.C., 1965. Along with Annie Devine and Victoria Gray, Hamer had contested the results of their 1964 congressional races, but Congress refused to unseat the white representatives who had won the official election. "We'll come back year after year until we are allowed our rights as citizens," she told the crowd. ASSOCIATED PRESS

As the civil rights movement achieved its greatest legislative victories in the mid-1960s, Eastland faced harsh criticism from Mississippi conservatives, particularly for his close relationship with the Kennedy family. MISSISSIPPI DEPARTMENT OF ARCHIVES AND HISTORY

"Give a man some ground and he'll never be hungry no more," Hamer insisted. To put that philosophy into practice, she built Freedom Farm, an cooperative venture that was part farm and part social service agency, providing food crops, subsidized housing, child day care, help with utility bills, and even college scholarships for local students. PHOTOGRAPH BY LOUIS H. DRAPER

A flyer from Fannie Lou Hamer's 1971 campaign for state senate. Despite repeated defeats, Hamer continued to run for elected office until she suffered a nervous breakdown in 1972. MISSISSIPPI DEPARTMENT OF ARCHIVES AND HISTORY

Elect
INFORMED

SINCERE

CAPABLE

MRS.
Fannie Lou
HAMER
STATE SENATOR
District 11 – Post No. 2
BOLIVAR AND SUNFLOWER COUNTIES
NOVEMBER 2, 1971

As Hamer's health deteriorated in the early 1970s, she grew increasingly frustrated with the lack of black economic progress and worried that the future for black children in Sunflower County was bleak. "It seems to me we are just going backward," she lamented in 1973. PHOTOGRAPH BY LOUIS H. DRAPER

In the early twenty-first century, a generation after their passing, it is the sharecropper, not the senator, who remains visible in Sunflower County. Visitors can make their way to the Fannie Lou Hamer Recreational Complex, the Fannie Lou Hamer Day Care Center, a landscaped gravesite, and other sites honoring the civil rights legend. PHOTOGRAPH BY AUTHOR

flecting on that moment years later, Hamer acknowledged, "I guess if I'd had any sense I'd a-been a little scared." But she recognized that she had been waiting for this moment for years. Her decision to volunteer "wasn't no bolt out of the blue," she recalled. "I would get out in the fields and I was always talkin' to folks about conditions." So when she heard the civil rights workers talking about voting, "I could just see myself votin' people outa office that I know was wrong and didn't do nothin' to help the poor. I said, you know, that's sumpin' I really want to be involved in."[15]

Four days later, on August 31, Hamer joined a group of seventeen other volunteers and journeyed to the courthouse in Indianola to attempt to register to vote. The twenty-five-mile trip gave the hopeful voters plenty of time to consider the consequences of what they were about to do, and when they pulled up to the courthouse, Charles McLaurin recalled, "most of the people were afraid to get off the bus." Before fear could paralyze them, however, "this one little stocky lady just stepped off the bus and went right on up to the courthouse and into the circuit clerk's office." The bold pioneer, McLaurin soon learned, was Fannie Lou Hamer.[16]

Hamer's courage did not translate into success in the courthouse. The registrar told her to copy and interpret a portion of the state constitution, which she was unable to do. "I could copy it, but I sure couldn't interpret it, for up to that time, I hadn't even known Mississippi *had* a constitution," she later recalled. Disappointed, the group returned to the bus and began driving back to Ruleville, only to be stopped by the police a few minutes later for riding in a bus that was "too yellow"—the officer claimed that the bus, which was used regularly to transport workers to the fields, looked too similar to a school bus. On this pretense, the officer arrested one of the SNCC workers and fined the driver, then escorted the entire group back to the jail in Indianola.[17]

By the time Hamer returned to Ruleville that evening, news of her attempt to register had reached her plantation boss, W.D. Marlow. An enraged Marlow confronted Hamer and her husband, demanding that she withdraw her application or leave. Apparently, other whites were "worrying" Marlow about allowing an employee to register, and he in turn "worried" Hamer about her application. Hamer refused to disavow her desire to vote, telling her boss that she had gone to the courthouse to register for herself, not him. Faced with what he perceived to be direct defiance, Marlow made good on his threat and threw her off the plantation; still in need of Pap's labor, he waited until the end of the picking season before firing him as well.[18]

Hamer stayed with friends and family, moving about regularly to avoid harassment and limit the potential of bringing harm to her benefactors. Being associated with SNCC was dangerous. As Charles Cobb recalled, "If it's possible to feel violence and tension in the air, you could certainly feel it in the Delta of Mississippi in the late summer and fall of 1962." One house where Hamer stayed was sprayed with gunfire in early September, just days after she had left it—a shooting the mayor of Ruleville claimed was "prefabricated" by civil rights workers in an effort to win sympathy. "That was a rough winter," Hamer recalled, as she and her husband moved around for months until they could find a black homeowner who would rent to them. "And it was *so dangerous.*" But the violence also inspired her, for she interpreted it from a religious perspective. "I walked through the shadows of death," she later told people, citing Psalm 23. "They shot sixteen times in [my] house—and it wasn't a foot over the bed where my head was— but that night, I wasn't there. Don't you see what God can do?"[19]

Forced off the plantation and into desperate poverty, Hamer ironically became free to challenge the system more directly than she ever had before. "There was nothing they could do to me. They couldn't fire me, because I didn't have a job. They couldn't put me out of my house, because I didn't have one. There was nothing they could take from me any longer." The key to the plantation owners' power was their stranglehold on access to land and jobs; blacks in Hamer's situation traditionally either had to acquiesce to the system or leave. Through the movement, she had options. Being kicked off the plantation, she told one SNCC worker, was "the best thing that could happen. Now I can work for my people."[20]

Stuck with admittedly "nothing else to do" and few prospects for local employment, she began to work actively with SNCC, COFO, and SCLC. At the invitation of Bob Moses, she attended a SNCC conference at Fisk University in late 1962. It was a crash course in movement strategy and tactics, and the sharecropper who normally would have been trudging through chilly cotton fields now found herself in workshops on politics and voting, learning about nonviolence and communication. She returned to Ruleville determined to take another stab at registering to vote. She studied the state constitution and in early December, on her second attempt, she passed the literacy test. "Mrs. Hamer returned with joy in her eyes," wrote one SNCC worker after Hamer learned that she had passed. Just a few months earlier, she had not even known she had the right to vote; now she was a fully registered voter with a basic understanding of voting laws and her state constitution. It was an extraordinary accomplishment—but she was only the sixth new voter registered since SNCC had begun organizing in Sunflower County.[21]

Emboldened by her success, Hamer started teaching citizenship classes around the county and gathered names on a petition to help poor black families get federal commodities. She later became perhaps the oldest field secretary in SNCC and earned an irregular paycheck—$10 a week, if the organization could spare it—that supplemented support from movement friends such as Amzie Moore, an economically independent activist from nearby Cleveland, and the federal food stamp program. She also began receiving support from northern organizations such as Operation Freedom, which offered financial assistance to activists who had been targeted for their civil rights work. With this diverse array of support, she was, for the first time in her life, financially independent of the plantation owner. She had gained both the freedom to resist and the economic power to fight on.[22]

In her organizing work, Hamer spoke—and sang—the language of the rural black South. It was less a matter of grammar than of worldview, a way of conceiving events that derived more from the biblical Moses than Marx, Camus, or the other philosophers that appealed to Bob Moses and other secular SNCC workers. The movement's emphasis on freedom fit naturally into her understanding of the Bible as a text that spoke directly to the black experience in America. She readily adapted her faith to the movement, particularly through the freedom songs that permeated SNCC activities. Confronted with hostile registrars or jailers or young toughs, Hamer responded with prayer and song. Her deep, rich voice rang out in mass meetings, on picket lines, and in the jailhouse. "Her booming voice, scolding, singing, or laughing, was freedom itself," recalled volunteer Tracy Sugarman. As in church, her ability to "raise a song" won her respect and helped establish her as a leader, someone to whom others could turn for inspiration and guidance. Singing gave her a power to influence others that her gender, economic status, and education level could not. By framing the movement within the familiar language of the Bible, she helped overcome the fear and skepticism with which many rural blacks viewed it.[23]

Her religious faith combined with her personal experiences to give her a sense of economic freedom that differed sharply from that of Senator Eastland. Hunger, both real and metaphorical, drove her to insist that freedom implied being paid adequately and having enough money to provide a decent living for one's family. "So many times as a child, I have gone hungry and now as an adult, I'm still hungry," she wrote to supporters in 1963. "I'm sick of being hungry, naked and looking at my children and so many other children crying for bread." Her experiences growing up in poverty, combined with her hand-to-mouth existence as an adult sharecropper, cultivated within her a powerful sense that without economic rights blacks would continue to suffer. Like Senator Eastland, she used hyperbole to dramatize her own suffering, claiming that "only a person living in the State of Mississippi knows what it is like to suffer; knows what it is like to be hungry; knows what it is like to have no clothing to wear." Before the movement, she explained, she had "just barely existed, not really lived" because as a sharecropper, she could not afford basic things necessary for survival. "No one can honestly say Negroes are satisfied," she insisted. "We've only been patient, but how much more patience can we have?"[24]

This kind of appeal, coming from someone who personally had felt the ravages of economic inequality, helped Hamer inspire supporters nationwide. Indeed, one of Hamer's most important contributions to SNCC was her ability to articulate the depths of Delta suffering to people outside the region. As a public speaker, she became an invaluable part of SNCC's ongoing fund-raising efforts. Any organization, even one as thrifty as SNCC, depended on a steady flow of funds to perpetuate itself and continue its mission. Because SNCC was dedicated to working with the most impoverished blacks, it faced an in-

herent funding problem: the people whom it served almost by definition could not afford to finance its operations. Delta blacks simply did
not have the financial power to challenge the injustice of their living
conditions. What SNCC could do was organize national resources, in
terms of both money and people, to benefit isolated southern blacks.
In essence, the organization sought to counter white southerners' monopoly on economic power with nonsouthern financial force. During
the early 1960s, SNCC relied heavily on northern philanthropists,
foundations, and individuals. Like other SNCC leaders, Hamer took
regular fund-raising tours to the North to keep the organizational cof-
fers full. At church gatherings, social club meetings, fund-raising dinners, and other venues, Hamer told her story to sympathetic audiences
throughout the North. From her efforts came many of the funds that
allowed SNCC to continue its work.

SNCC members viewed her as precisely the kind of grassroots
leader they wanted to cultivate, and her presence gave their efforts au-
thenticity and inspiration. "Her coming on the scene gave the movement a new spirit," Charles McLaurin recalled. "It added new fire to
the movement." As a sharecropper-turned-voter, she became a vivid
symbol of what SNCC believed Mississippi blacks could achieve; as a
candid and forceful speaker, she articulated the moral imperative of
the movement often more effectively than SNCC's organizers could;
as an older woman in an organization run by twenty-somethings, she
commanded respect within SNCC—everyone in the informal organization referred to her as "Mrs. Hamer"—and became the Mississippi
movement's spiritual anchor. "She represents the dream," commented
white SNCC volunteer Jane Stembridge, "the reason we came and are
staying."[25]

"NEGROES IN THE SOUTH ARE SATISFIED"

Hamer may have reinvigorated the movement in Mississippi, but her
growing prominence within movement circles did not shield her from
the frustrations of organizing, nor did it diminish white resistance. Although she herself had been a sharecropper, her experience after her
first registration attempt soon diverged sharply from that of her neigh-

bors. Where she had broken free of the plantation owner's power by finding support in SNCC, they were still in the same powerless position she herself had held a year earlier; where she now traveled the country speaking to integrated audiences, they remained geographically and culturally isolated on their plantations; where she began to act aggressively to confront white racists, they stayed stuck in deferential patterns of behavior. In her work as a SNCC field secretary, she encountered many sharecroppers and other poor blacks who felt that they simply could not take the risks that she was taking. Jobs on the plantation, menial though they may have been, were better than eviction, and jobs only grew more and more scarce as planters continued to mechanize operations. The Eastland plantation, for example, employed only about four hundred people in the early 1960s, about half what it had supported during the 1940s, and even that total was higher than average; most farms made do with only a quarter of the labor they once needed. To sharecroppers desperate to hang on to the only job they knew, registering to vote was threatening. Hamer and other voter registration workers spent their days canvassing the county encouraging people to register, but they often met with little success. "Some days it would be disgusting," she observed. "Some very disappointing."[26]

Black sharecroppers' fear of getting involved with the movement stemmed from their realistic assessment of white resistance. From the vantage point of early 1963, when Hamer began working seriously for SNCC, it was by no means clear that the movement was making progress in Mississippi or anywhere else. In the face of the Freedom Rides, voter registration, and other movement efforts, Eastland and other Mississippi whites remained firmly in control, offering a combination of righteous indignation, moral condemnation, and aggressive counteraction. The success of massive resistance to the *Brown* decision had prevented all but the most token school integration, and segregationist leaders hoped to resist the latest drive for equality through a similar campaign of official intransigence combined with a public relations effort aimed at white northerners. Egged on by constituents who taunted him as "Judas Jim" for working with the new administration of John Kennedy, Eastland used his position as a powerful Washington insider to attack the new direct-action protests as part of a Communist campaign to destroy a peaceful South. In addition to his public efforts on the Senate floor, he diligently worked behind the scenes, using federal and state resources to subvert the movement.[27]

Senator Eastland worked aggressively to keep the Kennedy administration focused on controlling Communism, not on stopping segregation. As chair of the Judiciary Committee, he had the power to frustrate or facilitate President Kennedy's domestic agenda, and he made it abundantly clear that the price of his cooperation was going slow on segregation. John Kennedy, a Massachusetts Brahmin who had worked with Eastland in the Senate, and his precocious younger brother, Robert, the attorney general, shared the southerner's commitment to aggressive anti-Communism, and the three men developed a close working relationship during the Freedom Rides. Viewing the crisis through a Cold War lens, the Kennedys above all wanted to avoid any violence that could harm America's international reputation; Eastland, meanwhile, sought to prevent federal intervention and protect the state's control over civil rights enforcement. The Kennedys fumed privately at the Freedom Riders, and they enlisted Eastland's help in preventing white violence in Mississippi. As Robert Kennedy recalled, "I talked to him probably seven or eight or twelve times each day about what was going to happen when [the Freedom Riders] got to Mississippi and what needed to be done." Eastland helped broker a deal between the administration and Mississippi governor Ross Barnett, whereby the federal government agreed not to intervene so long as local authorities prevented violence. When the Freedom Riders reached Jackson, they promptly were arrested and escorted to the city jail.[28]

Eastland's growing power in Washington helped him to get the ear of the president, and he benefited as well from his close association with the director of the Federal Bureau of Investigation, J. Edgar Hoover. As chairman of the Judiciary Committee, Eastland officially had authority to oversee the FBI, but he never exercised that power and prevented others from doing so. Instead, he cultivated a mutually beneficial working relationship with "the Director," as Hoover was known. Appointed in 1924 in the wake of the Teapot Dome scandal, the dapper, square-jawed Hoover had built a career out of high-profile criminal and anti-Communist investigations, and by the early 1960s he was one of the most widely respected—and feared—public officials in the country. The Washington, D.C., native and third-generation civil servant shared with Eastland not only a profound hatred of subversives but also an abiding commitment to segregation. As the civil rights movement intensified, the two men worked to expose what they believed to be the Communist origins of the protests. Hoover gave Eastland and his Senate Internal Security Subcommittee access to FBI files, and the senator used this information in his public denunciations of the movement. He also passed along useful tidbits to officials in Mississippi. Through Eastland, one former Mississippi state legislator recalled, the FBI "kept us well informed on who was coming to this state and what to expect."[29]

Eastland's primary conduit for inside information on the movement was not the FBI, however, but the State Sovereignty Commission (SSC), Mississippi's publicly supported investigative agency. The SSC had served primarily as a public relations operation under the governorship of James Coleman, working to improve Mississippi's reputation in the rest of the nation. After the 1959 election of the dour, humorless segregationist Ross Barnett, whose success was partially attributed to Eastland's support, the agency focused less on image building outside the state than on undermining movement efforts within its borders. With Barnett's blessing, the SSC hired investigators to scour the state for signs of "subversive" activity, which included everything from membership in the Communist Party to writing a letter to a newspaper supporting integration. One investigator, former FBI agent Jack Van Landingham, unearthed a petition protesting Senator Eastland's 1954 hearing in New Orleans. Noticing the presence of several Mississippians and "known Communists" on the petition, Van Landingham proceeded to "identify each of them, where they are from, their business, and so forth in order that check may be made of their present activities along both a subversive line and also in their efforts to promote integration in Mississippi." Anyone, black or white, involved in civil rights activities or who expressed pro-integration sentiments became a target. Participation in a Jackson sit-in prompted an investigation of Professor John Salter of Tougaloo College; a letter from the Reverend Dennis Hale of Picayune, Mississippi, to Eastland expressing support for integration was circulated back to the SSC, and the commission conducted an investigation. As Hale later recalled, investigators asked him, "Do you want your children to go to school with niggers?" When he responded that he did not mind his children attending integrated public schools, they continued, "Do you want your children to marry niggers?" The agency's sleuthing of subversives led journalist Bill Minor to label it the "KGB of the cotton patches."[30]

Eastland had strong personal ties to the agency, primarily through its public relations director and future head, Erle Johnston. Johnston had cut his political teeth as a publicist during the senator's first election campaign in 1942, and he directed publicity during Eastland's 1954 reelection. While Eastland supplied the SSC with information from FBI files and other government agencies, Johnston reciprocally shared the results of his agency's efforts with the senator. Johnston's office did much of the investigative legwork on which Eastland relied when he made speeches about the extent of Communist infiltration in the civil rights movement. This mutually enhancing, publicly funded investigative cycle gave Eastland important information on movement activities.[31]

Armed with such information, Eastland conducted a rhetorical campaign aimed at white northerners. Like civil rights leaders, Eastland recognized the necessity of federal force to the movement's success. Without the federal government's power, the movement could not succeed; without pressure from the white North, the federal government would not act. What had been true during the first Reconstruction, Eastland believed, would be true in the second: once the northern public lost interest in pursuing racial equality, the federal government would leave the white South to tend to its own business. "How long did it take the South to win the war?" Eastland joked. "Eleven years, wasn't it?" Hence, in much of his public rhetoric in the early 1960s, Eastland aimed less at galvanizing southern white resistance and more at undermining northern white support. He fundamentally believed that white northerners shared his basic racial prejudices and that they ultimately would sympathize not with black activists and their bearded radical allies but with the besieged white southerners. Convinced that many white northerners supported the movement only because they knew little about it, he sought to "expose" it as an extremist, Communist-inspired effort to destroy not simply segregation but the entire structure of American society. His basic argument was threefold. First, the movement unfairly targeted whites in the South for practices and feelings shared by white northerners; second, it failed to win the support of black southerners; finally, and most importantly, it was driven by Communists. Thus did Eastland take the battle to the North.[32]

Eastland wanted northern whites to understand why white southerners resisted black equality. Do not be so smug in your condemnation of us in the South, Eastland warned, because we are only doing what you too would do in our situation. The point was not hypothetical. As Eastland repeatedly emphasized, anywhere that blacks had become a majority or near-majority of the population, whites in the North responded much as white southerners had—by creating de facto segregation in neighborhoods, schools, and public areas. As exhibit A, he pointed to Washington, D.C. Up to the early 1950s, Eastland's field campaign manager Frank Barber recalled, "every school in the District of Columbia was segregated, every restaurant was segregated, every hotel was segregated; the entire city was a segregated southern city." But integration proceeded quickly following the *Brown* decision. Within several years, the proportion of white students in the public schools had dropped precipitously, as white parents by the thousands pulled their children out of integrated schools and placed them in the many private institutions in the area, most of which had only token integration. Given the resistance of northern whites to school integration, Eastland argued, it was unfair of northern politicians and activists to focus their attention on segregation in the South: "Why are these people not interested in putting their own house in order rather than scuffling for a few racial votes to get reelected in the North?" Unlike their northern white counterparts, who could send their children to elite private schools, white parents in Sunflower County and other parts of the rural South would not have the luxury of sending their children to schools where they would be in the majority.[33]

Eastland sought to verbalize the visceral fears of blacks that Sunflower County whites understood implicitly but which white northerners could ignore so long as blacks were not a large percentage of the population. To do so, he seized upon the issue of urban crime, a major and growing source of racial tensions north of the Mason-Dixon Line. The wave of black migration from places such as Sunflower

County during and after the war crashed down in northern cities such as Chicago, New York, and Detroit, where disputes over employment, housing, and education often divided along racial lines and crime became a racial issue. Northern cities such as Washington were being overwhelmed by increasing criminal activity, Eastland argued, to the point where whites in the nation's capital were "an oppressed race." There had been so many muggings, homicides, "and let me emphasize the crime of rape" that "any white woman walking on the streets of Washington tonight is a prey to vultures."[34]

Though politicians and pundits dismissed such arguments as sensationalistic or demagogic, Eastland hoped to strike a chord with average whites in the North. The enthusiastic response he sometimes received from northern audiences convinced him that many northern whites shared the same resentments toward the movement. During one appearance at Hunter College in New York, the incredulous liberal editors of The Nation fumed at the welcome Eastland received. "Shouts of 'Right,' 'Yes, yes!' and 'You tell 'em' gave the gathering a flavor of an old-fashioned revival meeting as the man from Mississippi drove home the gospel that the NAACP and the Communist Party were working hand in hand to destroy segregation and, thus, the nation." Even as momentum built for civil rights legislation, he remained confident that northern whites were on his side. "[T]hose agitators from northern cities who are urging Freedom Riders to invade the South would be astounded if they knew of the true sentiments of the majority of white people throughout the North," Eastland wrote Walter Sillers. "I am rapidly coming to the conclusion that the NAACP, CORE, and other radical groups of like kind are pushing too hard and, as a result, are moving the mass of decent white people to our way of thinking."[35]

Not only were northern whites truly on his side, Eastland argued, so too were black southerners. Unlike the "outside agitators" who sought to stir up trouble, southern blacks, he insisted, recognized that it was in their best interest to preserve segregation and maintain a good relationship with their white neighbors. "There is racial peace and harmony in the South," he insisted a month after the sit-ins began. "Negroes in the South are satisfied." Yet, given his family history, Eastland knew that black discontent seethed below the placid surface of Sunflower County race relations and could erupt in violence; given his experience as a planter, he understood the importance of maintaining the image of omnipotence and control as a means of discouraging dissent; given his extensive political efforts to block racial and economic reform, he recognized that white supremacy was not a natural or inherent fact of life—it had to be protected vigilantly. In short, he knew that blacks in Sunflower County and throughout the South lived in conditions that easily could provoke anger and retaliation. In this light, his paeans to the "satisfied Negro" appear to be part of a calculated effort to maintain white supremacy by creating a false image of tranquility. But he was both cunning and sincere. Like many planters and other elite whites, Eastland came to believe that the patterns of deferential behavior they demanded from black workers represented blacks' true feelings. Having grown up surrounded by deferential blacks, Eastland could not imagine that most blacks truly wanted integration and equality. Much like their Civil War–era predecessors, many whites in the South professed shock and disbelief that "their" blacks could possibly be dissatisfied with their lot in life. The only reason for the protests of the civil rights movement, then, was that they were being forced by "outside agitators," the most devious of whom were Communists.[36]

Furthermore, Eastland could point to numerous examples of blacks who truly did not support the movement. In an effort to "divide and conquer," Eastland and other segregationists highlighted black supporters of segregation. Though such tactics often took the form of "My maid says . . . " and "This old Negro told me . . . ," some Mississippi blacks came out quite vocally against the growing movement. Local newspapers that generally ignored civil rights activists gave widespread attention to blacks who dissented from movement orthodoxy. Blacks such as Major Hughes Alonzo Robinson enjoyed easy access to the white press to explain why they disliked the protests. Black educators in particular feared that integration would spell doom for the extensive network of black schools, which not only served as centers for the black community but also provided thousands of relatively well-paying and secure jobs. The same held true for black colleges in the state. President J.H. White of Mississippi Valley Vocational College was an outspoken critic of the movement and even served on the payroll of the State Sovereignty Commission. Some blacks who had supported efforts to gain political equality recoiled at the prospect of sit-ins and other forms of civil disobedience, which they interpreted as the ill-mannered rebelliousness of adolescence. Others agreed with Eastland's assessment that the movement was an un-American effort directed by Communists. Percy Greene, the controversial editor of the *Jackson Advocate*, Mississippi's largest black newspaper, condemned the sit-ins, Freedom Rides, and all such demonstrations. Like Eastland, whom he had befriended in the 1940s, Greene believed that Communists aimed "to create friction between the different racial groups that make up this country with the hope of using the Negroes as the opening phalanx in their hope for revolution." Though often motivated by sincere concerns about the movement's means of achieving equality, these black opponents nonetheless gave Eastland and other segregationists ample ammunition against their movement foes.[37]

But perhaps the most potent weapon in Eastland's arsenal remained anti-Communism. The late 1950s had been a relatively quiet time for Red hunters—one Eastland staffer acknowledged that by 1958 "we weren't hunting too many Communists because I guess we couldn't find too many." In the early 1960s, the Cold War heated up again and thrust itself back onto center stage in American politics and culture. The downing of a U.S. spy plane over the Soviet Union in May 1960 shattered the relative peace of the Eisenhower years and precipitated a series of increasingly confrontational events during the first two years of President John Kennedy's administration. From the Bay of Pigs invasion to the Berlin Wall to the Cuban missile crisis of late 1962, Kennedy aggressively challenged his Soviet counterpart Nikita Khrushchev, pleasing Senator Eastland and other staunch anti-Communists in Congress. Eastland sought to turn this renewed anti-Communist vigor against the civil rights movement. Citing what he considered the worsening U.S. position abroad, he argued in 1961 that all Americans "should cease to foment internal strife and discord, and should concentrate on the major problem of winning the cold war, and winning it quickly."[38]

The primary cause of internal strife, in Eastland's mind, was civil rights. He insisted that the Freedom Riders and other movement activists were following the Communist playbook by fomenting racial hatred and domestic dissent where none had previously existed. The

Freedom Riders were "agent provocateurs" who had been sent by the Communist Party "for the sole purpose of stirring up discord, strife, and violence." CORE, which was "carrying on the fight for a Soviet America," had timed the Freedom Rides to coincide with high-level meetings in Europe "to embarrass the Government of the United States in the handling of international affairs." America could ill afford this kind of agitation, and the federal government had no business encouraging it. "What this country needs today is unity and not dissension," Eastland argued, and any group that protested racial conditions within the United States was giving aid and comfort to the enemy in the Cold War.[39]

Eastland was not simply inventing the Communist charge to destroy the movement, though he certainly understood the political benefits of tarring the movement with the Communist brush. As we have seen, he and other conservatives successfully used anti-Communism to force the Congress of Industrial Organizations and other labor unions away from a more radical economic critique of American capitalism. It made strategic sense to cast one's opponents in the Communist camp, where they could not hope to win the support of the American people. Yet the strategy gained credence from the actual presence of Communists within the movement and the Communist Party's active support of the movement's goals. Although Communists involved in civil rights were neither numerous nor powerful, the Communist Party USA (CPUSA) unabashedly supported the movement and could point to several decades of defending integration and black equality, a record of interracial activism that Eastland knew well. At the CPUSA's 1957 conference, the party issued a ringing endorsement of the growing global movement against white supremacy and insisted, "*The question of Negro freedom, then, is the crucial domestic issue of the day*, and a factor of growing international consequence."[40]

After the sit-ins, many Communist organizers gravitated toward the movement because it was the most visible agent of change within American society. Although the NAACP remained avowedly anti-Communist, other civil rights leaders and organizations were less ideologically rigid. Martin Luther King Jr. retained a close advisor despite the man's connections to Communism, and CORE did not purge its members with past Communist affiliations. SNCC neither embraced nor excluded Communists. Its "freedom of association" policy welcomed anyone sincerely commitment to its mission, and it attracted young people with a wide range of opinions, from Communist to black nationalist to integrationist. At a time when few Americans were willing to take the risks inherent in direct action, SNCC leaders chose not to exclude Communists for both philosophical and practical reasons. On principle, they did not want to impose an ideological litmus test or create barriers that would exclude a minority the way blacks traditionally had been excluded from American society. Practically, the movement needed experienced organizers and activists, and many of the Communists were veterans of protest.[41]

Thus, Eastland did not have to fabricate his allegations about Communist involvement in the movement. Critics may have disagreed with his emphasis and motives, but they could not deny the presence of Communists. Indeed, Eastland may have had a more thorough sense of who was involved in the movement than supporters did. Through the FBI, the State Sovereignty Commission, and his own internal security committee, Eastland had access to a wide range of investigative resources, and he trained them all on the movement. He also got help from state officials in other southern states, as in October 1963 when Louisiana police gave him the records of the New Orleans–based Southern Conference Educational Foundation. In the years since Eastland's 1954 attempt to undermine the organization, SCEF had continued its interracial work, though it was forced to spend more and more of its budget defending itself against charges of Communism. Louisiana state authorities repeatedly sought access to its membership lists, donor records, and other information but had been unsuccessful going through legal channels. Undeterred, they chose an illegal route, conducting a weekend raid on the SCEF offices and carting away the organization's files. Aware that the SCEF lawyers would secure an injunction on Monday to prevent the use of the files, that Sunday the New Orleans police spirited the files across state lines into Mississippi and the hands of Senator Eastland. Eastland used the files to confirm connections between people he believed were Communist and the civil rights movement.[42]

Eastland's struggle to nip the movement in the bud had the support of a vast majority of white Mississippians. He won reelection in 1960 without even token opposition and earned plaudits from the white press throughout the state, with the exception of a handful of maverick newspaper editors such as P.D. East in the town of Petal. The influential Jackson *Clarion-Ledger* joined his effort to expose the alleged Communist influence in the civil rights movement. Shortly after the Freedom Rides began, the editors called for a full investigation of the movement to be conducted by Eastland and his Senate Internal Security Subcommittee. Sunflower County's major newspaper, the *Enterprise Tocsin*, regularly published information purporting to show the influence of known Communists on movement strategy. The movement may have entered Mississippi, but the state's white defenders were far from willing to concede defeat.[43]

"I COULD HEAR THEM LICKS JUST SOUNDIN'"

White resistance to the movement did not simply take the form of rhetorical objections, clandestine investigations, and public denunciations. At its base, it relied on violence. The movement's successes in the early 1960s both angered and frightened white opponents; they responded by retaliating ever more fiercely. The threat of physical violence loomed over all movement activities, and civil rights workers had serious cause for concern about their safety. The most visible outburst of violence erupted in the normally serene university town of Oxford in September 1962, just weeks after Fannie Lou Hamer's first registration attempt.

With the help of NAACP lawyers, a steely black Air Force veteran named James Meredith won the legal battle to desegregate the University of Mississippi, perhaps the most iconic symbol of white power and privilege in the state. Unwilling to see "Ole Miss" sullied by integration, white Mississippians rallied behind Governor Ross Barnett, who declared in no uncertain terms that "no school will be integrated in Mississippi while I am your governor." On the Senate floor, Eastland rose to congratulate Barnett "for interposing himself and frustrating the execution of an illegal and unconstitutional order directed at Mississippi by judicial tyrants who are blind and intoxicated

with the alleged power usurped to the Federal judiciary by an unbri-
dled Supreme Court." Behind the scenes, Robert Kennedy and Barnett negotiated a deal to enroll Meredith quietly, with the protection
of a small contingent of federal marshals, but the duplicitous Barnett
publicly encouraged defiance. As word spread that Meredith was
scheduled to arrive at Ole Miss on September 30, thousands of segregationists descended upon Oxford. Barnett backed away from his
promise to keep the peace, pulling the state highway patrol away from
the scene that evening even as rioters began pelting federal marshals
with bricks, Molotov cocktails, and eventually bullets. The outnumbered marshals used tear gas to try to disperse the crowd, but order
was restored only after the arrival of more than twenty thousand army
troops sent by President Kennedy. When the smoke cleared the next
morning, two people had been killed and more than 160 wounded.
Meredith enrolled later that day and in 1963 became the first black
graduate of the University of Mississippi.[44]

The bloody clash in Oxford may have been a defeat for the segregationists, but it did not curtail white violence in the state. Indeed,
violence against civil rights workers surged in 1963, and it soon ensnared Fannie Lou Hamer. In early June that year, Hamer had the opportunity to travel to Charleston, South Carolina, with six other black
Mississippians for an SCLC citizenship school run by the legendary
Septima Clark. Hamer and her fellow activists, all of whom had been
chosen for the trip by SCLC's Annelle Ponder, learned strategies to
help teach people how to pass literacy tests in order to register to vote.
After a week in Charleston, the group boarded a Greyhound bus and
headed home to Mississippi on Sunday, June 9.

The trip was relatively uneventful until the bus reached Columbus, Mississippi, just across the Alabama border. In Columbus, the
group changed buses and encountered an irate white driver who apparently knew about their movement work. He knocked the civil rights
workers to the ground as they stood waiting to board the bus and, after Hamer and her colleagues took the man's name and badge number
(as they had been trained to do), he forced them to the back of the
bus. The bus continued on Highway 82 toward Winona, a small town
in Montgomery County near where Hamer was born, but along the
way the bus driver stopped several times to make phone calls. By

the time they reached Winona, the nature of those phone calls became clear: a number of police officers joined a crowd of whites that had gathered by the terminal. Several members of Hamer's group got out to get some food and use the restroom, and within minutes they had been arrested and thrown in a waiting patrol car. Hamer, who had stayed on the bus, came out to investigate what was going on, and she wound up being kicked, cursed, and arrested. The entire group was whisked to the Montgomery County jail, where things quickly got out of hand. The police had chosen the county jail, rather than the city jail, Hamer believed, "so we could be far enough out, they didn't care how loud we hollered, wasn't nobody gon' hear us."[45]

Arriving to find "white folks appear[ing] from everywhere with guns," the members of the group were interrogated and then separated and thrown in cells. That's when the beatings began. The police first targeted June Johnson, an enthusiastic fifteen-year-old from Greenwood who had pleaded with her mother to be allowed to go on the trip. Despite her youth, the officers beat her mercilessly for several minutes before moving on to Annelle Ponder, the group leader. Listening in a cell nearby, Hamer "started hearing screaming like I had never heard before." At least three police officers, along with another white man not in uniform, peppered Ponder with antagonizing questions and demanded that she show them respect. "They really wanted to make me say yes, sir," Ponder recalled, "and that is the one thing I wouldn't say." They made her pay for her boldness, beating her with blackjacks, a belt, fists, and open palms. "She never would say yessir," Hamer remembered, "and I could hear when she would hit the flo', and then I could hear them licks just soundin'."[46]

Hamer's turn soon came. "Get up there, fatso," one officer told her. "You, bitch, you, we gon' make you wish you was dead." It was not an idle threat. What followed, Hamer recalled, "was the mos' *horrifyin'* experience I have ever had in my life," an exercise in racial and sexual brutality that scarred her literally and figuratively. She was thrown facedown on a bunk bed in a room with five white men and two black prisoners who were forced to participate in the beating. Given a long blackjack, the first prisoner beat Hamer "till he give out," at which point the second prisoner was ordered to start beating her. She tried to protect herself from the blows, but "they beat my hands till they turned *blue*." As she struggled, her dress worked its way up her body and she attempted to pull it down, but one of the white men watching nearby stepped in and pulled it back up. The ordeal continued until the prisoners grew tired. A bloodied Hamer "was hard as a bone." Barely able to walk or sit down, she returned to her cell. Her body would never fully recover.[47]

The next day, Hamer and the rest of her group were convicted of disorderly conduct and resisting arrest. They remained in custody—without medical treatment—for two more days before Andrew Young of SCLC could bail them out. Upon leaving the jail, they learned that a white supremacist from Greenwood had gunned down Medgar Evers, the intense World War II veteran who had spearheaded the NAACP's Mississippi efforts. Evers's murder, combined with her own savage beating, served to strengthen Hamer's resolve. The day after her release, she was interviewed about the incident by staff members of the Southern Regional Council, and she bristled with indignation. "Something is going to have to be done! It really is!" she insisted. "I don't know how long we can keep on going like this . . . somethin' got to break!" Her frustration bubbled over as she thought about how long she and her people had been suffering. "And just keep on saying *wait*—and we been waitin' all of our lives, and *still* gettin' killed, *still* gettin' hung, *still* gettin' beat to death—now we tired [of] waitin'!"[48]

The increasing violence reflected the fact that, by the summer of 1963, the movement was gaining momentum. In Birmingham, Alabama, a peaceful protest march met with a vicious police response, as nonviolent black protestors were savaged by police German shepherds and blasted by high-power water hoses. Images of peaceful protestors set upon by dogs and hoses appeared in newspapers across the globe, and once again international pressure induced the federal government to take stronger action against flagrant southern racism. On the same June night that Evers was murdered, President Kennedy made his most forceful defense of the movement and its goals. He called for a strengthened federal civil rights bill that would ban segregation in public facilities, send federal voting observers to areas where less than 15 percent of eligible black voters were registered, withhold federal funding from racially discriminatory programs, and create a new Fair Employment Practices Committee. Later that summer, he supported the March on Washington for Jobs and Freedom, an interracial protest highlighted by Martin Luther King Jr.'s powerful "I Have a Dream" speech.

That fall, movement leaders in Mississippi sought to attract national attention to blacks' lack of voting rights. Hoping to destroy Eastland's claim that blacks were too apathetic to vote, SNCC and other civil rights groups in the state, which had joined forces through the Council of Federated Organizations, organized a "Freedom Vote" to coincide with the state's gubernatorial election in November 1963. The Freedom Vote was a mock election in both senses of the word. It was not a real election because few blacks had yet gained the official right to vote, and the ballots they cast in the Freedom Vote did not count in the official tallies. But by participating in the ritual of voting, blacks highlighted the unrepresentative nature of the official election. Dismissed by Eastland and other whites as a publicity stunt, the Freedom Vote attracted more than 83,000 black participants and helped educate them about the voting process—"quite a turnout," Clarksdale NAACP leader Aaron Henry commented, "for a people who Senator Eastland said were too lazy to even register." The campaign failed to attract widespread media coverage, however, and the few stories that did appear focused on the dozens of white students from northern colleges who had traveled to Mississippi to help canvass voters. Without media attention, civil rights organizers could not attract the northern support necessary to counter white segregationist power.[49]

The Freedom Vote, combined with Evers's murder and the beating Hamer suffered in Winona, underscored a fundamental problem facing the Mississippi movement: it lacked the power to protect blacks who challenged the system. Courageous local people could march to the county courthouse, they could hold protest rallies and mass meetings, they could put their bodies on the line. They could not, however, enforce the laws of the United States. That power rested with state and federal authorities. As Hamer put it, "My tax money go just like anybody else's, but still we don't have *no protection*." Given white Mississippi's official refusal to abide by U.S. law, black Mississippians needed the federal government to step in and enforce the law of the land, forcefully and consistently. Whether the federal government would act decisively depended on which side could convince Americans outside the South that their cause was morally right. As they looked ahead to the turbulent year of 1964, both Eastland and Hamer recognized that they had to struggle to win the ear of the North.[50]

7

1964: Confrontations

From the William Chapel parking lot, stroll down Lafayette Street. Back in 1964, when Sunflower County became the focal point of national attention and civil rights agitation, Fannie Lou Hamer lived in a rented three-room white frame house about twenty feet off this narrow road. The street was not paved then as it is today, but many of the rectangular, shotgun houses date back at least two generations. Stand beneath the outstretched arms of a pecan tree on a summer's day, and even in the shade the beads of perspiration begin to form. Under these trees, Hamer played host to a sweaty mass of "outside agitators" who streamed into the state in 1964 to work with the Student Nonviolent Coordinating Committee on the Mississippi Summer Project, also known as "Freedom Summer." Hamer's home at 626 E. Lafayette Street, with its faded wallpaper and worn-down linoleum floors, became an unofficial headquarters of SNCC's efforts in Sunflower County that summer. With a pot of beans cooking on the stove and a bag of field peas waiting to be snapped, she welcomed the young activists and schooled them in the ways of rural Mississippi.[1]

Hamer and her brood likely were watching the television on the evening of June 25, shortly after three civil rights workers had disappeared from a jail about 130 miles away in Philadelphia, Mississippi. In a CBS News Special Report, Walter Cronkite and his team of reporters investigated the disappearance, but they could not resist venturing northward into Sunflower County to juxtapose Hamer with her neighbor James Eastland. The senator and the sharecropper appeared to be perfect foils for each other, highlighting the vast differences of race, class, and perspective that separated the two neighbors and, by extension, white and black Mississippians. After reporters interviewed Hamer about her tortuous efforts to become a voting citizen and how she had been forced to leave her plantation, the program jumped to the heavy-jowled face of her state's fifty-nine-year-old senior senator. "There is no attempt to prevent them, as a rule, from registering," Eastland insisted. Asked to explain the charges of intimidation, bombings, and economic threats, he denied any wrongdoing, arguing that such accusations were made by "some agitator" who "doesn't live in the state and knows nothing about it." Viewers were left to ponder how he might account for Hamer, the lifelong Mississippi sharecropper who lived a stone's throw from the Eastland plantation and was becoming, by the summer of 1964, the senator's widely recognized nemesis. Indeed, 1964 was the year that Sunflower County took center stage in the national drama over black freedom.[2]

"WE HAD KENNEDY STOPPED"

The stage for the dramatic confrontations of 1964 was set shortly before Thanksgiving the year before. With Congress in recess for the holiday, James and Libby Eastland were driving home from Washington to Doddsville on the afternoon of November 22, 1963. They had reached New Market, Virginia, just a few hours from D.C., when they heard the news that sent America reeling: President John F. Kennedy had been assassinated. Turning the car around, a shocked Eastland drove back to the capital to find a nation in mourning and a changed political landscape. "No single event in my lifetime has more profoundly shaken and stunned the people of this country and the world," he observed in a remembrance on the Senate floor two weeks later. Though they had differed on many issues, Eastland and Kennedy had sat next to each other in the Senate chamber for several years, and they maintained an amicable relationship. In a time of intensely heated political disagreements, personal relationships still flourished in the halls of Congress. The Delta planter respected the fact that the

Massachusetts scion "was motivated by ideals and convictions that left no doubt in his mind that the courses of action that he pursued were for the best interest of the people."[3]

However sincere Kennedy's convictions and however genuine Eastland's sorrow, the senator also recognized the political implications of the president's death. Kennedy may have been a popular president who brought glamour to the White House, but Eastland knew that he had not been a terribly effective legislator. "Kennedy didn't know how" to get bills passed, Eastland recalled. "We had his whole program bottled up." Indeed, Eastland and his congressional allies had stymied the inexperienced Kennedy. It had been nearly four years since the Greensboro sit-in sparked civil rights demonstrations across the South, nearly three years since Kennedy took office with the support of black voters, nearly six months since the president made an impassioned speech calling for a far-reaching federal civil rights bill, yet no legislative action had been taken. Eastland had reason to boast.[4]

At the time of his death Kennedy was not well regarded by civil rights advocates, particularly the younger radicals in SNCC. Fearful of alienating Eastland and the southern wing of the Democratic Party, the Kennedy administration discouraged civil rights demonstrations and sought primarily to minimize confrontations that could undermine America's Cold War image. It had taken the president nearly two years to honor his "stroke of a pen" campaign pledge to end discrimination in housing, and his administration only halfheartedly enforced existing laws. Attorney General Robert Kennedy often antagonized activists by equating the nonviolent protests of the movement with the violent extremism of the Klan. Despite the presence of civil rights stalwarts such as John Doar and Harris Wofford, the Kennedy administration overall had failed to live up to the promise racial egalitarians had seen in his election. As black author James Baldwin commented after the assassination, "Let us not be so pious as now to say that President Kennedy was a great civil-rights fighter."[5]

Despite their frustration with Kennedy, civil rights supporters mourned the loss of the president and worried about his successor. Lyndon Johnson, after all, appeared to be a typical southern politician when it came to racial matters. A native of central Texas, he had campaigned against President Truman's civil rights efforts when he won election to the Senate in 1948. He had orchestrated the evisceration of the Civil Rights Act of 1957 and had earned the support of his conservative southern colleagues during his 1960 presidential run. Little in his career suggested that Johnson would do anything to support the civil rights movement.

But Johnson defied appearances. Having grown up in poverty, he harbored an abiding desire to address economic inequity in America. His experiences as a young teacher in an impoverished Mexican American community left a deep impression upon him, and during his senatorial career he pursued an economically liberal agenda that often put him at odds with conservatives such as Eastland. Though he never publicly supported civil rights, he sometimes deviated from the traditional southern course. He was one of only three southern senators who did not sign the Southern Manifesto in 1956, and the fact that he had allowed any civil rights bill, even a toothless one, to pass the Senate gave some white southerners reason to doubt his loyalty to segregation. Eastland, who had worked with Johnson for a dozen years in the Senate, recognized that the new president presented a formidable challenge to segregationists. As a masterful legislator, Johnson knew how to manipulate bills and agendas in order to achieve the results he desired. As a southerner, he could stand up to the southern delegation on race in a way that a Massachusetts liberal could not. And as the successor to a slain president, he had the sympathies of the nation behind him. When Johnson took office, Eastland feared that he might not follow the traditional Southern course. "We had Kennedy stopped," he told his friend Erle Johnston, head of the State Sovereignty Commission. "But I'm afraid we can't stop Johnson."[6]

Eastland was right to worry. Immediately upon assuming the presidency, Johnson embraced the Kennedy agenda on civil rights and added a vigorous attack on poverty. Though it took skeptics by surprise, Johnson had given hints of his newfound position on civil rights several months earlier. At a Memorial Day speech in Gettysburg, Johnson urged Americans to see the black struggle for freedom as a moral issue, not a legal one. "The Negro today asks justice. We do not answer him—we do not answer those who lie beneath this soil—when we reply to the Negro by asking, 'Patience.'" It was Johnson who, behind closed doors, had urged President Kennedy to reframe civil rights in moral terms. Two weeks after Kennedy's assassination, the new president met with Martin Luther King Jr. and outlined a multipronged strategy to reenergize his predecessor's moribund civil rights bill and ram it through Congress. He was determined to succeed where Kennedy had failed, and he poured his incomparable energies and powers of persuasion into the cause of passing comprehensive civil rights legislation. As King commented after the meeting, "It just may be that he's going to go where John Kennedy couldn't."[7]

SNCC too redoubled its political efforts after the Freedom Vote and Kennedy's death. Over the course of many staff meetings in late 1963 and early 1964, the organization considered a plan to bring hundreds of volunteers, primarily white students from northern colleges, to spend the summer working on voter registration and education projects throughout Mississippi. Getting black Mississippians, particularly the masses of black laborers in the Delta, registered to vote would be the primary thrust of the summer, not only because the ballot promised to undermine segregationists' political power, but also because voting was a basic element of citizenship that Americans across the country could recognize as essential. The proposed Mississippi Summer Project, which would be coordinated by the Council of Federated Organizations, was designed to dramatize the plight of Mississippi blacks on television screens and radios around the country. If Americans knew the truth about what was happening in the state, advocates surmised, then they would demand that the national government intervene on behalf of black Mississippians. Getting outside attention was essential. Reporters, policy makers, and northerners simply were not going to pay attention if all the civil rights workers were black. Bringing masses of young civil rights volunteers to the state was a dangerous gamble, but some activists recognized that the anticipated violence could work to the movement's advantage. "The death of a white college student would bring on more attention to what was going on than for a black college student getting it," explained Dave Dennis, who was the summer project's assistant director. "We didn't plan any of the violence. But we just wanted the country to respond to what was going on."[8]

Although they recognized the practical logic of bringing in white students, many of SNCC's staff members, most of whom were black and southern, had misgivings about the plan. They feared that well-educated, highly skilled white students would come to dominate important positions and would undermine the organization's efforts to cultivate leadership among local blacks. But Fannie Lou Hamer, Bob Moses, and other SNCC veterans embraced the plan. The involvement of whites was not just a practical necessity, Hamer argued; it was a philosophical imperative. SNCC could and should embody its ideals of integration. "If we're trying to break down this barrier of segregation, we can't segregate ourselves," she insisted. After much heated discussion, the organization decided to pursue the project.[9]

As a prelude to the upcoming summer voting efforts, COFO initiated a political challenge to the state's all-white congressional delegation. Running black candidates against white incumbents would dramatize blacks' lack of voting rights and help educate and catalyze potential black voters. The organization tapped Hamer to challenge Jamie Whitten for the Democratic Party's nomination to the Second Congressional District. Whitten, a Tallahatchie County lawyer, was a solid segregationist who had faithfully served white planting interests in Congress for nearly a quarter century. More than 300,000 potential voters lived in his district, yet a mere 31,345 had voted for Whitten in the previous election, when he had won his twelfth term in Congress. Hamer had no illusions about her prospects for success, particularly given that even a decade after the *Brown* decision only 114 of her home county's 13,524 blacks were registered to vote. The long odds did not deter her. Like the Freedom Vote the previous fall, her spring campaign focused less on winning the election than on educating voters about their rights. "I'm showing people that a Negro can run for office," Hamer told a reporter. "All my life I've been sick and tired. Now I'm sick and tired of being sick and tired." She launched her campaign in Ruleville on March 20 and began acting like a traditional political candidate—traveling the circuit of small towns, talking to small groups of voters, urging people to support her. Unlike most candidates, she spoke not only about her specific grievances against her opponent but also more generally about the power of politics to transform lives and improve living conditions. Political participation, she and her SNCC compatriots believed, was the key to breaking white power. The actual result of the primary—Whitten breezed to an easy triumph that June—was less important than the process of showing blacks the connection between political participation and economic survival.[10]

Hamer made this connection tangible during SNCC's clothing drive that year. At SNCC's request, northern supporters began sending boxes of canned food and clothing to help needy families in the Delta. Many of the shipments came directly to Hamer's home, and she often would distribute them with political considerations in mind. She was not about to reward people who "never even been once to Indianola to try and register to help themselves!" When Ruleville mayor Charles Durrough tried to cause chaos by telling local residents that Hamer was passing out free clothing, she turned it into a political opportunity. More than four hundred blacks showed up on her doorstep, but Hamer refused to pass anything out unless the recipients registered to vote. Many of them did. "Folks up North want to help us free ourselves, and that's why they send these boxes," she argued. She wanted people to understand that SNCC's political organizing was responsible for the clothing and food, and if they wanted to enjoy the benefits they needed to become active politically as well.[11]

Having taken the first steps toward political independence herself, Hamer had little patience for people who were unwilling to put themselves on the line. She knew very clearly what the stakes were. Unlike the Freedom Summer volunteers or even the full-time SNCC workers, she and her family had to live with the consequences of her political activity. On the day she registered as a congressional candidate, Pap Hamer became a voter for the first time in his life. The very next day, his plantation owner, Sydney Levingstone, fired him. Her daughter Vergie applied for a job that year, but once her prospective employers found out who her mother was, they rejected her application.[12]

The consequences were not just economic. The threat of physical violence was a constant companion on a campaign where, as one SNCC worker put it, "a primary consideration is whether the candidate will get killed." The same night that Hamer began her congressional campaign, two civil rights workers, Mendy Samstein and George Greene, traveled to Ruleville to give her some leaflets to use in the campaign. They were arrested by two Ruleville policemen, one of whom was the brother of Emmett Till's murderer. The cops brought them to the station and interrogated them at gunpoint about why they were spending so much time in "niggertown." When Samstein replied that they were working to encourage blacks to participate in politics, one cop sneered, "We don't have any nigger politics in Ruleville." Freedom Summer would change that forever.[13]

"I QUESTION AMERICA"

Freedom Summer was an aptly named endeavor, for freedom became the most oft-used and hotly contested of ideas that summer. Segregationists and civil rights activists alike used the word in many different contexts, some fun—one of the cats in the Greenwood SNCC office was named "Freedom," the other "Now"—and others more serious. For Fannie Lou Hamer and the people with whom she worked in SNCC, freedom was the all-encompassing idea that united the various aspects of the organization's efforts, from voting and education to basic dignity and economic justice; Hamer believed that this expansive understanding of freedom meshed with professed American ideals and Christian teachings. Eastland, too, embraced freedom as the central motivation in his drive to destroy the movement. Emphasizing the freedom of individuals, businesses, and states to determine the course of their own affairs, he rejected the movement's dependence on federal coercion and its connection to left-wing economic ideology. Throughout the summer, both Eastland and Hamer appealed to those outside the South, particularly whites, hoping to convince a national audience that they were on the right side of the freedom struggle.

As SNCC's plans for the summer seeped out, Eastland warned that civil rights activists were "proposing to swarm upon Mississippi like a flight of locusts." White Mississippians braced for an "invasion," and a siege mentality took hold across the state. State officials hired more police officers and bought heavy weaponry, including a $13,000 fifteen-passenger armored van known as "Thompson's Tank" in honor of Jackson's mayor. They also intensified their investigations through the State Sovereignty Commission. The Ku Klux Klan, which had been dormant in Mississippi since the 1920s, began organizing in all parts of the state and soon reached a membership in excess of seven thousand, while a new terrorist group, Americans for the Preservation of the White Race, sprouted up in Natchez and spread across the state. For many whites, the summer project's emphasis on black voting and its focus on organizing among the landless poor raised fears of a potential revolution reminiscent of Reconstruction. When civil rights activists spoke of elementary fairness and basic justice, many white Mississippians imagined property redistribution, a frightening prospect that promised to destroy the economic basis of white power and wealth. "What are we going to do when the Negroes take over again?" worried one white farmer in the Delta who feared a second Reconstruction. "Land confiscation isn't all that hard if you have political control."[14]

White fears were amplified by news from Washington, where congressional liberals—the modern equivalent of the hated Radical Republicans—pushed for passage of a federal civil rights bill to outlaw segregation in all public venues and give the federal government the power to withhold money from segregated school districts. Since the previous June, when President Kennedy had first called for an expansive civil rights bill, Eastland had worked with the State Sovereignty Commission and segregationist leaders such as John Satterfield (whom *Time* labeled "the most prominent segregationist lawyer in the country") to plot a counterattack. With funding from the Sovereignty Commission and a reclusive, racist millionaire named Wickliffe Preston Draper, they created the Coordinating Committee for Fundamental American Freedoms (CCFAF), which orchestrated a massive public relations campaign to convince Americans that the civil rights bill was in truth a "$100 billion blackjack" intended to force a socialist government upon an unwitting public. For a time, the CCFAF was the biggest lobbying group in Washington, and the Johnson administration and its congressional allies viewed it as a major threat to the success of the bill. But as Eastland had feared and Martin Luther King Jr. had predicted, Lyndon Johnson proved far more politically nimble than his predecessor. He skillfully used the outpouring of national sympathy to create the political momentum necessary to pass the landmark civil rights legislation. To avoid the quicksand of Eastland's Judiciary Committee, Senate leaders tied the chairman's hands by setting a deadline for the bill to be reported out of committee. Eastland called the bill the "most monstrous and heinous piece of legislation that has ever been proposed in the entire history of the U.S. Congress," and he labored with his southern colleagues to delay the bill and strip it of its more important features. His efforts failed, and the Civil Rights Act of 1964 passed Congress in early June just as Freedom Summer was getting started. "The America that we have known is being swept away," the senator lamented with characteristic drama. "Freedom and liberty are being destroyed."[15]

Before President Johnson even signed the bill into law, the rhetoric of resistance turned into the reality of violence. Civil rights organizers knew that their work could provoke violence, and at the summer training sessions in Oxford, Ohio, they sought to dispel volunteers' sense of the summer as a romantic, noble adventure. Hamer herself went to Oxford in early June to tell volunteers about her beating in Winona and warn them that they could face similar violence. "We didn't tell 'em no lies," she recalled. "We prepared 'em for exactly what it was like, and it was like you going into combat." The first casualties came in late June, when three civil rights workers, James Chaney, Andrew Goodman, and Michael Schwerner, vanished after investigating a church bombing near Meridian. The subsequent search for their bodies only turned up black victims of previous crimes. As the nation turned its attention to rural Mississippi, Eastland told President Johnson that the disappearance was a "publicity stunt." Like other white Mississippians, he insisted that the incident was a hoax, but the specter of violence haunted the entire summer.[16]

In Sunflower County, tensions ran high. Many local white residents ignored the volunteers, who, sniffed one local historian, "were quite unkempt in their appearance" and whose "social contacts were limited almost entirely to the black community." Other whites made it abundantly clear that they objected not only to the civil rights workers' presence but also to black cooperation with them. "If our local colored citizens are not satisfied with what we have given them," wrote a white columnist in Sunflower County's major newspaper, "then they are free to pack up and leave and go to any place they think they will get better treatment." Such veiled threats mixed with open violence as bottles crashed regularly through windows of host family homes and into cars parked outside, harassing phone calls threatened both the hosts and their guests, and white terrorists firebombed William Chapel, where most mass meetings were held. "Violence hangs overhead like dead air," one volunteer wrote. Eastland nonetheless insisted publicly, "I don't think there is any problem here."[17]

Despite the violence, Sunflower County became a central front in SNCC's efforts. Some activists targeted the Eastland plantation for registration work, hoping to strike a symbolic blow against the senator on his own turf. Contrary to their expectations, Eastland and his white managers did not harass them. "They didn't pay any attention," one civil rights worker recalled in amazement. Instead, the senator himself invited some activists to come inside his home, which they refused to do. Perhaps Eastland could act so welcoming because his plantation workers understood that they were not to support the movement. "If you was on the plantation you couldn't take part," remembered Earline Tillman, who worked on the senator's farm. "If you took part you'd have to move. You wouldn't fool with it." At home with a newborn child that summer, Anne Eastland remembered that despite all the talk about how activists were going to "stomp down our cotton," life was peaceful on the plantation. "It was like being in the eye of the hurricane."[18]

Five miles north, Fannie Lou Hamer was in the midst of the storm. She threw herself into the summer project, and her home became the "nerve center" for the forty outside volunteers who stayed with local blacks in Ruleville. For Hamer, Freedom Summer was an expression of God's will, "the beginning of a new Kingdom right here on earth." The young volunteers were "Christlike" in their willingness to help black Mississippians. "If Christ were here today," she wrote later, "He would be just like these young people who the southerners call radicals and beatniks." The volunteers, most of whom had been drawn to the project for more secular reasons, often found her faith both incomprehensible and inspiring. One Ruleville volunteer wrote that she had wanted to "gag" after a particularly long prayer of thanksgiving. "To watch her [Hamer] limp around here, encouraging the prayer sessions in which we remember Sen. Eastland and Gov. Johnson and all the brutal people they sanction, is almost too much to take," another volunteer observed. "But it's also a never-failing source of courage and determination." Hamer's concept of Christian love, her sense of Christian universalism, and her eternal hope for redemption underlay her understanding of freedom and separated her from the mostly secular college students. Despite a lifetime of segregation, the beating in Winona, and the constant harassment during the summer, she refused to indulge in anti-white rhetoric or actions. "The white man's afraid he'll be treated like he's been treating the Negroes, but I couldn't carry that much hate," she insisted to a reporter that June. "It wouldn't have solved any problems for me to hate whites because they hate me. Oh, there's so much hate. Only God has kept the Negro sane."[19]

Hamer spent much of the summer on the road, speaking at mass meetings in the state and fund-raisers across the country in an effort to generate national support for federal intervention in Mississippi. Eastland, meanwhile, targeted the same national audience for precisely the opposite message. Working closely with the Mississippi State Sovereignty Commission, Eastland became the most visible spokesman for a coordinated, region-wide effort to undermine public support for the movement by linking civil rights to Communism. In July, he unleashed a verbal attack on Communists in the movement from the floor of the Senate. Arguing that the Communist Party "of course has never had any aim but to exploit the Negroes and their problems for the benefit of the party's objectives," Eastland insisted that "it is to the interest of the Communist world conspiracy to promote and foster discontent of every possible kind." Ever the avid observer of civil rights organizations, the senator recognized the shift in Mississippi away from the NAACP and toward SNCC, and he sought to highlight this new direction as a turn toward Communism. "[T]he older Negro organizations have been pushed toward the background, while brashly new and far more militant groups have come to power," he observed, and "these new Negro leaders are almost naive with respect to Communism." In the 1950s, Eastland had seen the NAACP as a radical threat; by 1964, he viewed it as a safer alternative to SNCC.[20]

Eastland zeroed in on several activists in Mississippi who had been the targets of investigations by the Internal Security Subcommittee and the Sovereignty Commission. Unlike Joe McCarthy, Eastland did not simply cite exaggerated numbers; he enjoyed naming names and "exposing" people such as Larry Rubin, a white volunteer from Pennsylvania who had dropped out of Antioch College to work with

SNCC on voter registration. Arrested in Holly Springs, Rubin was found to have an address book with the phone numbers of several left-wing organizations. The little book found its way into Eastland's hands, and he mentioned it on the floor of the Senate to "prove" that Communists were running movement activities. "In Eastland's mind and in the mind of a good many Mississippians, if you showed left-wing connections, this was automatically proof of some kind of conspiracy," Rubin later recalled. "Automatically proved you were running things." After Eastland's speech singled him out, Rubin was subject to more harassment and a beating by a local farmer.[21]

Eastland also targeted the lawyers who had come to Mississippi "to participate in the invasion under the banner of civil rights." His speech had been timed to bolster court hearings in the Sunflower County town of Drew, where local officials had charged a civil rights worker with having employed a Communist as an attorney. Eastland detailed the alleged Communist affiliations of the attorneys, including Frank Pestana, Maynard Omerberg, George Crockett, and other "Communist legal eagle[s]" and "legal carpetbagger[s]" associated with the Southern Conference Educational Fund or the National Lawyers Guild. Together with the Sovereignty Commission's investigations, Eastland's public revelations spurred local law enforcement agencies to harass civil rights workers. A day after Eastland's speech, a similar investigation got under way in Indianola, prompting Sunflower County SNCC worker Jerry Tecklin to mutter, "It wasn't enough that they killed Goodman, Schwerner, and Chaney, they're creating a red hysteria that may lead to a repeat performance."[22]

By the time Eastland launched his attack, movement workers had shifted gears away from voter registration, which had netted twelve hundred new voters, toward a drive to get an integrated delegation recognized at the Democratic National Convention, to be held in August in Atlantic City, New Jersey. The delegation would represent the Mississippi Freedom Democratic Party (MFDP), the political arm of SNCC and COFO founded that April as a way to channel black political energy into an alternative party. After having attempted unsuccessfully to gain access to the state's official Democratic Party precinct meetings, MFDP leaders planned to challenge the composition and legality of the all-white Democratic Party. Activists held their own precinct meetings throughout the state and elected a slate of sixty-six delegates, including Fannie Lou Hamer, who served as vice chair. By juxtaposing the MFDP's grassroots delegation with the official one, civil rights leaders hoped to use the national forum to manifest the difficulties black Mississippians faced in attempting to participate in the political process, as well as the absurdity of segregationists' claims that blacks were satisfied and apathetic. "When we went to Atlantic City," Hamer recalled, "we went there because we believed that America was what it said it was—the land of the free."[23]

The contrast between the two delegations could hardly have been more stark. The MFDP delegation included two white members but was overwhelmingly black, while the state delegation had no black representatives whatsoever; the MFDP promised to support the Johnson administration, while many of the official delegates did not hide their preference for the Republican candidate, conservative Arizona senator Barry Goldwater; whereas the MFDP strongly promoted the new, administration-backed civil rights bill and defended the Supreme Court's civil rights decisions, the state delegation officially condemned both. The MFDP delegates arrived in Atlantic City convinced not only of the moral righteousness of their cause but also of the political wisdom of their strategy. When confronted with the indisputable evidence of the state delegation's lawbreaking and political betrayal, MFDP members reasoned, the convention delegates, party officials, and indeed the nation at large would have no choice but to support the challengers. "The issue was simple in our unpolitic minds," wrote Aaron Henry. It essentially boiled down to "the simple principle that we were right and they were wrong."[24]

Once in Atlantic City, the MFDP delegation's immediate task was to convince members of the Credentials Committee to recognize the alternative party, despite objections from the White House and the Mississippi attorney general's office. In a decision that ultimately would undermine his relationship with much of the civil rights community, President Johnson made clear to party leaders that he would not risk losing southern white support by seating the MFDP. Most southern white Democrats already had turned to Goldwater as a result of Johnson's successful push for the civil rights bill, but the president hoped to retain the image of unity at the convention. While Johnson exerted personal pressure on committee members to refuse recognition, the Sovereignty Commission helped the Mississippi attorney general provide written evidence designed to undermine the MFDP's credibility. The state officially opposed seating the MFDP on the grounds that the party was run by nonresidents of the state, its delegates represented only forty of eighty-two counties, and its organizers were affiliated with Communist-front organizations. Many of the state's arguments technically were true, but they were overwhelmed by the MFDP delegation's powerful testimony before the committee. After a series of witnesses testified about the obstacles black Mississippians faced when trying to vote, Hamer captured the attention and pricked the consciences of convention delegates and national viewers alike. As she had been doing at fund-raising meetings all year long, she recounted the horrible beating she suffered in Winona, as well as the daily harassment she endured for being involved with the movement. Bristling with indignation, on the verge of tears, she challenged committee members to support the MFDP:

> All of this is on account we want to register, to become first-class citizens. And if the Freedom Democratic Party is not seated now, I question America. Is this America, the land of the free and the home of the brave, where we have to sleep with our telephones off of the hooks because our lives be threatened daily because we want to live as decent human beings, in America?[25]

Hamer, one historian has written, "shook the political establishment like Jesus and the money changers." Her stunning testimony angered Johnson, who attempted to cut it short by hastily calling a press conference in order to deflect attention from the sharecropper-activist. But the national networks replayed her performance during prime time, prompting a flood of telegrams from supporters across the country. Determined to quash the challenge and silence "that illiterate woman," Johnson, after repeated consultations with Senator Eastland, sent his prospective vice presidential nominee, Minnesota senator and civil rights stalwart Hubert Humphrey, with instructions to negotiate a compromise. Assuming his place on the ticket was at stake, Humphrey offered to seat two preselected MFDP delegates, Aaron Henry and Ed King—one black, one white, both college-educated and middle-class—and allow the rest of the delegates, almost all of whom were black and not formally educated, to be "guests" of the convention. Hamer adamantly refused to accept the administration's deal: "We didn't come all this way for no two seats!" she thundered. Reflecting later on her unyielding stance, she observed simply, "We felt that we had a right—as it was us, as it was our own delegation, and the delegation was from Mississippi—we had a right to make our own decisions."[26]

The proposed compromise strained the coalition. Swayed by arguments made by Hamer, Bob Moses, and other MFDP leaders, a majority of the delegates refused to accept the president's compromise; Hamer warned Henry that she would "cut [his] throat" if he dared accept it. The Democratic National Committee then refused to recognize the MFDP as the official Mississippi delegation, and Hamer and many of her fellow delegates returned home disillusioned with the political process and angry with moderate national civil rights leaders and Mississippians who had advocated compromise. "The strange thing to me," she recalled later, was that "everybody that would compromise in five minutes is the people with a real good education," referring to Aaron Henry, among others. "Them folks will sell you—they will sell you, your mama, they mama, anybody else for a dollar." She had stood firm in the face of pressure, she had remained true to principle, she had refused to compromise; like Senator Eastland, she earned admiration and contempt nationwide for her unyielding stance. Yet, like Eastland, she had failed to achieve her objective, and she was disgusted with the outcome. Freedom would turn out to be far messier and more complicated than Hamer had imagined.[27]

"SO VICE-VERSA WHAT I'D HEARD THAT I COULDN'T HARDLY BELIEVE IT"

The experience in Atlantic City was both an end and a beginning. It was the culmination of many months of canvassing, registering, and voter education; it was the finale to a dramatic summer that witnessed three murders, thirty-five shootings, and scores of beatings; and it marked the high point of the mass media's fixated attention on race in Mississippi. But it also was the start of a new chapter in Fannie Lou Hamer's struggle for freedom. "That's the beginning of my learning of politics," Hamer recalled later. She learned that moral suasion had its limits and, as she put it, she "found out that Christian love alone wouldn't cure the sickness in Mississippi." Going into the convention, she and many others within the MFDP had been utterly convinced of both the righteousness of their cause and their chances of success. After all, they had played by all the rules of the American system, they had worked nonviolently to register voters, and they diligently had documented evidence of voter intimidation and harassment. And yet they had lost. Their moral claims had failed to overcome the entrenched power of the white Democrats, who had violated the rules of the system and used violence to intimidate potential black voters. "We learned the hard way that even though we had all the law and all the righteousness on our side—that white man is not going to give up his power to us," Hamer recalled. "We have to build our own power."[28]

After Atlantic City Hamer began to see the struggle for black freedom in the Delta in broader terms, particularly during her first experience overseas. In mid-September 1964, shortly after the Atlantic City convention, entertainer and movement supporter Harry Belafonte arranged for Hamer and ten other SNCC leaders to visit the African nation of Guinea as a way to relieve stress and reinvigorate the organization after the difficult summer. Hamer had never been out of the country before, and she later recalled being somewhat nervous about the trip because she had always heard that Africa was "just wild" and that "everybody in Africa was savages and really stupid people." The reality of life in Guinea was "so vice-versa what I'd heard that I couldn't hardly believe it." Reared in the Delta, where blacks had to step off the sidewalk if a white person passed them, Hamer was astonished by what she witnessed in the newly liberated African nation. From pilots and stewardesses on the airplanes to bank tellers and government officials in the cities, everyone in a position of skill or authority was black. She had grown up in the "land of the free," the nation that proclaimed itself the "leader of the Free World," but until she went to Guinea she had never seen free black people. For the first time in her life, she saw a society in which blacks had both freedom and power, where blacks made the decisions that affected their lives.[29]

The Americans were received as honored guests of Guinea's president, Sekou Touré. After having been rebuffed the month before by the U.S. president, Hamer was particularly moved by Touré's warm welcome. "You don't know what that meant to me," she told a reporter several months later. "Here I have been in America, born in America, and I am 46 years pleading with the President for the last two or three years just to give us a chance—and this President in Guinea recognized us enough to talk to us." Touré urged the SNCC members to see the connections between their work in the American South and the struggles for independence and decolonization in Africa. To Hamer, the connections were simple and clear: the Guineans were experiencing the full freedom—political rights, educational access, economic opportunities—that black Americans were denied.[30]

While in Guinea, Hamer saw how the U.S. government sought to capitalize on the civil rights movement as a weapon in the Cold War. Touré's socialist government had remained steadfastly nonaligned in the Cold War, and the United States sought to win the popular African leader's allegiance by highlighting how much progress the South was making on civil rights. Hamer and Bob Moses happened upon an article published by the United States Information Agency that featured a picture of Moses at the Democratic National Convention. The article outraged the soft-spoken Moses, particularly when Guineans seemed to accept the premise that the United States was making great strides toward integration. "People be brainwashed there," Hamer lamented afterward, and both she and Moses condemned the government's transparent attempt to use the movement to make the nation look good in the eyes of the world. Already feeling betrayed by the president and the national Democratic Party after Atlantic City, the experience only fueled Hamer's growing sense that the federal government was not truly on the side of the freedom struggle.[31]

Hamer also objected to what she believed was another propaganda tool used by the U.S. government to gain Cold War allies in

Africa: the Peace Corps. Established by President Kennedy in 1961, the Peace Corps aimed to improve the nation's image abroad by sending young Americans to spend two years volunteering in Third World nations. Hamer ran into a Peace Corps group on a plane and met with some volunteers in Guinea, and she grew incensed at the arrogance of their mission. In language similar to Senator Eastland's advice to northern civil rights workers, Hamer recalled telling the white volunteers that "before [you] would be able to clean up somebody else's house you would have to clean up yours; before [you] can tell somebody else how to run their country, why don't [you] do something here." With her growing pride in her African heritage—and her increasing resentment toward American arrogance—Hamer had little use for young people who spent their energy working abroad rather than at home.[32]

Hamer's experience in Guinea both infuriated and inspired her, stoking her anger at the nation of her birth and fanning her impatience with America's slow progress toward freedom. As much as she enjoyed her visit, she never entertained any notion of relocating to Africa, instead insisting that "it is our right to stay [in America] and we stay and fight for what belongs to us as American citizens." As with Senator Eastland, her awareness of international issues reinforced her sense of urgency and mission back home. "The *world* is looking at America," she noted after her return, and the country is "really beginning to show up for what it is really like." Like Eastland, she came to see Mississippi and the South as a test case in the laboratory of freedom. But the results she hoped to achieve were profoundly different from those of her planter nemesis. She wanted black Mississippians to accomplish in America what black Guineans had accomplished in Africa. Indeed, Guinea's success as an independent nation, she insisted, "shows what black people can do if we only get the chance in America."[33]

"A MONUMENTAL TRIUMPH OF SPIRIT"

Hamer returned to Sunflower County that fall determined to help black Americans get that chance at the ballot box. Despite her anger and disillusionment after Atlantic City, she and her MFDP allies did not abandon electoral politics or grow paralyzed with cynicism. Instead, they sought to use legal means to undermine the political foundation of white supremacy in the state. The Democratic Party had proved unwilling to challenge the legality of Mississippi's elections. Now, the MFDP would turn to Congress itself. For much of late 1964 and early 1965, Hamer and her party were consumed with what became known as the congressional challenge.

Having lost the June primary election to congressional incumbent Jamie Whitten, Hamer joined other MFDP candidates Victoria Gray of Hattiesburg, Annie Devine of Canton, and Aaron Henry of Clarksdale in seeking to get black candidates' names on the ballot for the general election in November. Their chances of victory in the election were slim to none—even after a summer of organizing, less then 3 percent of black Mississippians had successfully registered to vote— but getting their name printed in black and white on an official ballot would be a symbolic triumph. The state of Mississippi had no interest in helping the MFDP succeed, and it refused to grant the candidates' request. First the state election commission ruled that they could not appear as Democrats because they had participated in the Democratic primary. MFDP workers then gathered thousands of signatures on a petition to run as independents, but the commission tossed many of the signatures out, arguing that they belonged to unregistered voters.[34]

Unable to get on the ballot, Hamer and the MFDP focused on building support for another Freedom Vote in November. COFO coordinated the effort, with staff members from SNCC and CORE joining several dozen student volunteers to organize the mock election. Workers and voters alike faced harassment and intimidation perhaps even greater than the year before. Sunflower County was particularly brutal. Hamer complained of a "reign of terror directed against Negro citizens who seek to exercise their right to register and vote." During the last week of October alone, a worker was beaten on the steps of the county courthouse in broad daylight, a local activist's home was firebombed, the Freedom School building was torched, and a rally was broken up by baton-wielding police. Despite the violence, more than sixty thousand voters cast their ballots statewide to register their support for MFDP candidates. Not surprisingly, Hamer won her district easily, gaining 33,009 votes to just 59 for Whitten. In the regular election, however, Whitten and the four other white candidates (three Democrats, one Republican) coasted to victory, setting the stage for a radical attack on the legality of Mississippi's elections.[35]

Even before the votes were in, MFDP leaders had decided to contest the results of the state's official congressional elections. Using a Reconstruction-era law that had been designed to help newly enfranchised ex-slaves challenge the seating of plantation owners, the MFDP argued that Congress should not seat Mississippi's congressional delegation. Its argument boiled down to this: Mississippi's representatives had not been elected by "all the people," as required by the Constitution. By preventing blacks from voting, the state had violated the compact to which it had agreed upon returning to the Union after the Civil War. Therefore, the elections were invalid and the representatives held their seats illegally. Congress should bar the Mississippi delegation, the MFDP argued, and offer the seats to the three MDFP congressional candidates, Hamer, Devine, and Gray.

It was an audacious plan, one that promised not only to energize the party's staff and its base of supporters but also to thrust Mississippi back on the national stage and appeal to allies across America. "Nothing could be clearer than the mockery of the regular elections held in Mississippi," MFDP lawyer Arthur Kinoy noted, and the MFDP wanted America to agree. The party planned a nationwide campaign, setting up support committees in eight northern cities and renting an apartment on Capitol Hill in Washington for Hamer, Gray, and Devine. The three women joined Kinoy and fellow MFDP lawyer William Kunstler in early December to file the official challenge with the U.S. House of Representatives, and they spent much of that month lining up congressional support.[36]

As in Atlantic City, MFDP activists found reason to hope for success. The national elections had moved Congress significantly to the left. Although he received only 6 percent of Sunflower County's official vote, President Johnson trounced Barry Goldwater nationwide and his coattails brought in a large Democratic majority. In addition to having more liberals in Congress, MFDP activists felt that the weight of logic and morality lay on their side. Clearly, Mississippi's five congressmen had not been elected by a true majority of their constituents. As Hamer argued in her petition to Congress, "widespread terror and intimidation" as well as registrar fraud left only 3 percent of her district's black citizens registered to vote. How could Jamie Whitten claim to be the district's representative when he had won the votes of barely 10 percent of the people in his district? Whitten, like the rest of official white Mississippi, dismissed the challenge as "a completely unofficial action" that "can only be taken as a publicity gimmick, for propaganda purposes." Hamer did "pretend to be a candidate" in the Freedom Election, Whitten argued, but that was a mock election with "no color, sanction or authorization of law whatsoever."[37]

The first stage of the challenge came to a head on January 4, 1965, the day the new Congress would be sworn in and seated. Hamer joined more than six hundred Mississippians who traveled to Washington to dramatize the challenge and attract national attention. "The American people have got to realize that Mississippi is a part of American society and that what happens there has a bearing on the whole country," Hamer told reporters. She joined the throng in the galleries to watch the action on the House floor. As each member was sworn in, Representative William Fitts Ryan of New York jumped up to protest the seating of the Mississippi delegation. He was joined by several dozen of his colleagues, far more than the MDFP had expected. Because House rules required that contested members stand aside, the Speaker of the House told the five Mississippi representatives to wait. Though Congress eventually voted 276–148 to seat the delegation pending a formal investigation, it was a symbolic triumph for the MFDP, "a monumental victory of the spirit," as William Kunstler put it. The party of disenfranchised black Mississippians successfully had dramatized the hypocrisy of their state's electoral system. "We did it," whispered Victoria Gray as the white representatives stood aside. "Even if just for this moment, we did it."[38]

That moment marked the high point of the challenge. In the months that lay ahead, more than a hundred lawyers came to Mississippi to gather evidence to support the MFDP's claims, but their efforts ultimately proved futile. Worse still, the challenge exacerbated deep divisions within the civil rights community that had been growing for years and soon would tear the movement apart. While nearly everyone in the civil rights community agreed that the Mississippi delegation had been elected unconstitutionally, activists split on the question of whether Hamer, Devine, and Gray should be seated in their stead. The younger activists, usually associated with SNCC but also present in CORE and SCLC, tended to insist on having the women seated. Older and more moderate leaders, generally in the NAACP and the Urban League, disagreed. They argued that the white representatives should not be seated and that new, legal elections should be held to find replacements.

The legal disagreement over the challenge only masked deeper divisions. "In some ways," wrote Fred Powledge in the *New York Times* in early January 1965, "it is a microcosm of the disagreement that has penetrated the movement during the last year, a disagreement that some observers feel is sapping much of the drive's energy." Traditional leaders and moderates feared that the younger activists were too radical, too confrontational, too impatient. The presence of Communists in the ranks of militant organizations, moderates insisted, only alienated other Americans. Worse still, they warned that militant activists were building up hopes for immediate, revolutionary change; when the change failed to happen right away, blacks' hopes would be dashed and disillusionment would set in. The result could be catastrophic. "There are people who want a race war to start," worried a young white volunteer who had been in Mississippi the previous summer. The radicals, meanwhile, dismissed the criticism as the carping of traditional leaders who were too accommodating, too passive, too patient. "It's pretty horrifying when you have black people saying to other black people, 'Accept more tokenism,' but that's what this is all about," complained one activist. These divisions only hardened as the movement moved into 1965.[39]

8

"This Is America's Sickness"

Downtown Ruleville today bears a ghostlike resemblance to the bustling town center that it was in the mid-1960s. Though its population of three thousand is about 50 percent higher now than it was then, the surrounding rural population has disappeared, taking with it much of the vitality of the downtown shopping district that catered to rural customers. Vestiges of its past linger, from the digital clock above the former Bank of Ruleville to the wooden awnings that offer strolling Saturday shoppers a bit of shade. The Piggly Wiggly remains, its plastic mascot's head a relic of past grandeur that has since been eclipsed by the Super Wal-Mart and other chain stores in Cleveland, ten miles away. A handful of variety shops and liquor stores hang on, but most of the storefronts are empty, their occupants having left long ago when local businesses failed in the face of boycotts and chain store competition. Even the Bank of Ruleville, a community institution for decades, no longer exists, swallowed up by the larger Delta Southern Bank at the turn of the twenty-first century.

For more than four decades, James Eastland owned a small office above the Bank of Ruleville on Floyce Street overlooking Ruleville Memorial Park. "Senator Eastland's Office Upstairs—SMILE" read the sign as visitors entered the building. Like his home, the office was simple and lacked ostentation. It was here that a young Eastland practiced law, here that he had first gotten the call from Governor Johnson that led to his initial appointment to the U.S. Senate, here that he returned on weekends to receive visitors, read mail, and take care of business matters. The plantation was big business and Eastland was keenly aware of the importance of economic power, an issue that came to dominate the civil rights movement in Sunflower County in the years following the drama of 1964. Fannie Lou Hamer, perhaps even more than the senator, understood the importance of economic power as well. Her testimony in Atlantic City had made her a national figure, her trip to Africa had broadened her horizons, her congressional campaign and challenge had brought her to the threshold of political power, but she still was a poor former sharecropper who struggled to make ends meet. As reporters packed their notebooks and left Sunflower County to follow the civil rights movement as it achieved its top legislative accomplishments in the mid-1960s, Hamer remained at her home on 626 E. Lafayette Street in Ruleville.[1]

"SOMEBODY DONE NAILED US TO THE CROSS"

Hamer emerged from the tumult of 1964—Freedom Summer, Atlantic City, Africa, the congressional challenge—with little faith in the federal government and the willingness of the American people to push for racial change on the basis of morality or appeals to conscience. The underlying premise of her work in 1964 was that the American people would force the federal government to rectify the situation in Mississippi if only they understood what truly was happening there. "I used to say when I was working so hard in the fields, if I could go to Washington—to the Justice Department—to the FBI—get close enough to let them know what was going on in Mississippi, I was sure that things would change in a week," Hamer noted. "Now that I have traveled across America, been to the Congress, to the Justice Department, to the FBI, I am faced with things I'm not too sure I wanted to find out." The problem was much larger than her state or even her region. "The sickness in Mississippi is not a Mississippi sickness. This is America's sickness."[2]

And America, she believed, was gravely ill. "This thing they say of 'the land of the free and the home of the brave' is all on paper,"

Hamer told *Freedomways* magazine in 1965. "It doesn't mean anything to us." Rather, she called her part of America, Sunflower County, the "land of the tree, home of the grave." Nowhere in America did whites truly want black freedom, she concluded bitterly. Like Senator Eastland, Hamer considered northern whites duplicitous when it came to race. "There is so much hypocrisy in America," she lamented, pointing out that the threatening letters she received in the months after her testimony in Atlantic City did not come from Mississippi—they came from Philadelphia, Chicago, and other northern cities.[3]

Hamer's skepticism about America grew even as the civil rights movement earned its most important legislative victories. President Johnson's landslide victory over Barry Goldwater in the 1964 presidential election generated the momentum needed to pass a whole series of federal programs, collectively termed the Great Society—Medicare and Medicaid for indigent seniors and children, Job Corps for disadvantaged youth, expanded welfare for impoverished families. Less than a year after the Civil Rights Act, a massive campaign in Selma, Alabama, pushed Congress to pass the Voting Rights Act of 1965, a staggering achievement that had been inconceivable when Hamer stepped on that bus to Indianola not even three years before. Within two years of its passage, the percentage of eligible black Mississippians registered to vote soared from 7 to 60 percent. Even workers on the Eastland plantation registered to vote. The wall of massive resistance erected in the 1950s seemed to crumble as the movement earned the legal and political guarantees of equality that had eluded black Americans since their arrival in the country. In Mississippi, changes were apparent as the state legislature stopped funding the Citizens' Council and some whites appeared to acquiesce to a new order. Resistance to civil rights had "brought us nothing but trouble since 1961," one white Mississippi businessman commented in early 1965. "A lot of us are ready to try something else." SNCC veteran Charles Cobb remembered, "After '64 Mississippi became a part of America."[4]

Hamer recognized the vast impact of the changes. The threat of violence, so palpable in 1964, had subsided somewhat by the next year. "It's different now," she told a friend in the summer of 1965. "Sunflower is just not as bad as it used to be." Though she still encountered intimidation—white people would follow her around as she registered voters—she no longer was arrested or physically harassed. Yet Hamer insisted that the situation remained dire because the new laws had not addressed the economic difficulties faced by poor blacks in rural areas such as Sunflower County. Voting had not improved black Mississippians' daily lives. "Many people in the North think things are getting a lot better in my state," she told supporters. "But things look different in Mississippi." Civil rights struggles had been cast in black-and-white terms, both racially and morally, but by 1965 it had become clear that the roots of inequality that trapped blacks lay deeper than Jim Crow laws. In the Delta, one observer noted in 1966, "economics is supplanting race as the basic problem." Indeed, just as the "problem of the color line" was becoming the center of attention in America, the problem of the dollar line became paramount to Fannie Lou Hamer and other civil rights activists.[5]

Described by one reporter as "the worst Delta winter in recent memory," the winter following the passage of the Voting Rights Act hit Mississippi hard, with record low temperatures across the state. The cold weather exacerbated the economic problems that Fannie Lou Hamer and her poor neighbors faced. For many rural families, basic survival was at stake. One Department of Agriculture study of Washington and Sunflower counties found that 60 percent of families received less than two-thirds of the minimum dietary allowances recommended by the federal government. "Children with the great swollen bellies that mark the protein deficiency disease called kwashiorkor dot the countryside," wrote one reporter. "These children live in Mississippi on a diet of cornbread, grits and Kool-Aid."[6]

Hamer believed that any movement for "freedom" had to address the fundamental economic difficulties such families endured. She had joined the movement because she was hungry not just metaphorically but literally—she knew what it was like to go to bed on an empty stomach, and her adopted daughter Dorothy Jean suffered from chronic malnutrition. She devoted herself to the voter registration fight precisely because she saw it as a way to gain the power necessary to achieve economic opportunity. Hence, her calls for ending racism and opening up the political process consistently were coupled with efforts to improve the economic lot of black laborers. She believed, as she expressed with other MFDP leaders, that "racial equality is only the first step in solving the basic problem of poverty, disease and illiteracy confronting American Society."[7]

Shortly after the congressional challenge, Hamer helped bring publicity to the efforts of the Mississippi Freedom Labor Union, which sought to organize Delta farm workers to improve pay and working conditions. Founded in neighboring Bolivar County in early 1965, the MFLU explicitly incorporated calls for economic justice within the chorus of "freedom." The union, Hamer explained, would use "strikes, picketing, boycotts, collective bargaining, and non-violent direct action to make the people we work for meet our demands." The MFLU organized strikes throughout the mid-Delta in spring 1965, and Hamer spoke at union meetings to rally the troops. With the union, she advocated a broad program that reflected her sense of what full economic freedom meant: no child labor; sick leave and free medical care; full compensation from the government for those who had lost their jobs; health and accident insurance; equal employment practices in wages, hiring, and working conditions; and a federal minimum wage law to apply to farm laborers. Working from sunup to sundown, cotton choppers and pickers earned roughly $3 or $4 a day; the MFLU called for $1.25 an hour, which would yield $10 daily, plus $7.50 in overtime pay. But planters who grudgingly had begun to accept political changes were adamant about resisting pressure to change economically. As one striking MFLU woman noted with frustration, "They told us to take off those freedom buttons 'cause we had all the freedom we was going to git."[8]

But Hamer's efforts to win economic freedom encountered resistance even more formidable than the white power of segregationists: the white power of cotton. The cotton economy upon which the region depended had become stagnant by the mid-1960s, and black laborers' economic base, sharecropping, essentially had disappeared. The revolution in agriculture triggered in the 1930s hit the Delta fully three decades later, just as black southerners finally were achieving political and legal equality. Low-skill agricultural jobs—the only jobs for which most Delta blacks were trained—simply vanished as the cotton industry underwent massive changes. Demand for cotton continued to spiral downward as synthetic alternatives gained in popularity and foreign cotton growers became increasingly formidable competitors.

Cotton farmers had no choice, Eastland told planters in the National Cotton Council in 1962, but to focus on *"greatly reducing the cost of producing cotton."* Increasing agitation from the MFLU and other labor organizations only spurred planters to move more rapidly as they consolidated their holdings, mechanized their operations, and turned to chemicals to control weeds and pests.[9]

The pace of change picked up. Throughout Mississippi, the average farm size tripled in twenty years, to nearly 150 acres in 1970; in Sunflower County, the consolidation was more pronounced—the average farm exceeded 550 acres by the end of the 1960s, and more than 130 farms contained more than 1,000 acres, including Eastland's mammoth plantation, which now covered 5,800 acres. As large planters consolidated their operations, they achieved economies of scale that allowed them to switch to expensive but increasingly efficient technological alternatives to hand labor. The most visible changes could be seen from Delta highways as chemical-spraying crop dusters buzzed overhead while bulky machines lumbered through the fields once picked by hand. "Cabins in the cotton are being replaced by diesel-powered tractors, six-row equipment, two-row cotton pickers, chemicals, and airplanes," noted B.F. Smith, president of the Delta Council. The pace of mechanization increased dramatically in the mid-1960s: while less than three-quarters of Delta cotton was picked by machine in 1964, by 1966 mechanical pickers accounted for 95 percent of the crop. The Eastland plantation turned to mechanical pickers gradually, but by the mid-1960s the transformation was complete— there were only two mules left on the plantation and the number of jobs had been cut by more than half.[10]

With machines picking the cotton, there was little need for black labor. As one planter put it, "Negroes went out with the mule." Some activists believed the advance of technology was part of a larger plot to encourage black migration out of the state. After all, the jump in mechanization coincided with the civil rights movement's major gains in the state. "Mechanization of farms (plantations), usage of agricultural sprays, etc. provide the excuse and the agency to force the Negro to leave Mississippi," one Ruleville civil rights volunteer fumed in a letter home. Sandra Nystrom and Eleanor Holmes Norton condemned the "deliberate and inhumane state policy of getting the Ne-

groes to leave the state now that they are showing some signs of political organization and potential strength and are no longer necessary as
part of the system of virtual slave labor which has for generations supported the gracious and luxurious traditions of the South for a few
whites at the top of society." Whether mechanization stemmed from
global economic forces or from conspiratorial planters, the situation
for black workers was dire. "There's a lot of people that can't pick cotton, because the machines are gonna be picking the cotton," Hamer
worried. "But these people still got to eat."[11]

Technology combined with policy to worsen the job outlook for
rural laborers. The same year that the Voting Rights Act opened political avenues to black southerners, the federal farm bill closed off many
economic opportunities. Like the AAA during the New Deal, this legislation was intended to shore up the cotton industry by lowering supply and thus raising prices, but it also had the effect of causing a
dramatic reduction in the amount of land cultivated and thus the
amount of labor needed. The 1965 farm bill, for which Eastland served
as President Johnson's floor manager in the Senate, offered cash payments from the federal government to cotton farmers who agreed to
slash their cotton acreage by up to 35 percent; in addition, farmers
who agreed to cut their acreage received subsidies of about 10¢ per
pound on the cotton they did grow. Hence, a farmer with a one-hundred-
acre allotment could get more than $16,000 from the federal govern-
ment, a tidy sum compared to the less than $1,000 annual income
black farm laborers earned. Yet, as one incredulous critic noted, in the
bill "not one cent was earmarked for worker relief, relocation, or re-
training!"[12]

For James Eastland and other large Delta planters, the farm bill
was a free lunch: seventy-seven Sunflower County planters received
more than $25,000 apiece in 1967. With about 5,800 acres, of which
roughly a fourth was allotted to cotton, Eastland received nearly
$170,000 in federal payments in 1967, and he sold the cotton that he
did produce for an estimated $280,000. The reduced acreage allowed
farmers to use their best soil for growing cotton while substituting
other crops on the "buckshot" soil that produced lower yields of cotton; the result was an increase in the average yield per acre—on the
Eastland plantation, yield averaged 945 pounds, compared to the

county average of 750—and that in turn led to larger federal payments because the payment formula was indexed to yield. Walker Percy, adopted nephew of planter-philosopher William Alexander Percy, noted the irony of planters who "voted for Roosevelt, took federal money, got rich, lived to hate Kennedy and Johnson and vote for Goldwater— while still taking federal money." Movement critics attacked the largesse. "What such guarantees to individual plantation owners mean is that the federal government is subsidizing segregation," wrote one writer in *Freedomways* magazine. "It is not merely looking the other way—it is in fact financing the perpetuation of segregation."[13]

As planters made the economically advantageous decision to cut their acreage by the full 35 percent, they had less need for labor. Within a year, agricultural employment dropped by nearly one-third. To make matters worse for black workers in the Delta, Congress attempted to alleviate rural poverty by passing a 1966 bill that fulfilled the MFLU's demand of a minimum wage for agricultural workers, albeit at $1 an hour. Combined with the farm bill, the minimum wage law seemed to provide what one reporter called "cures that kill." Farmers across the Delta responded to the new law simply by replacing their remaining workers with machines. Economically, it made little sense to do otherwise—as one reporter observed, "Southern plantation owners have for years read balance sheets the same way as businessmen in Chicago or New York." Planters who had been paying roughly 30¢ an hour now faced an immediate tripling of their labor costs; machines that previously may have been more expensive than hand labor suddenly had become a cheap alternative. Herbicides became twelve times less expensive than weed-chopping workers. "They'll burn this cotton down before they'll pay that dollar-an-hour," one black woman lamented. Eastland may not have been willing to burn his cotton, but he did refuse to pay higher wages. "We simply cannot, at present price levels, pay these wages, notwithstanding that sociologists may well argue that such wages are necessary to provide a fair standard of living." The only laborers needed now were the minority, primarily men, who had the skills to run the machinery—about 25,000 jobs in a Delta with hundreds of thousands of low-skilled black workers.[14]

On the Eastland plantation, workers such as Atley and Irene Taylor and their nine children faced a bleak reality. Where once the farm had supported nearly two hundred families and more than six hundred workers, the farm now only needed forty tractor drivers and supervisors to work the reduced acreage; where once the Taylors and other workers were indispensable to the plantation, now they were economically expendable. Like their boss, the Taylors viewed the minimum-wage law as an economic burden. "A dollar an hour ain't worth nothing when, maybe they give you one day, and then you're off for two weeks," complained Irene Taylor. "It would have been better if it had been 50 cents a day if you work every day." Although they no longer had jobs to do, more than sixty families remained on the Eastland plantation and continued to enjoy free housing and access to interest-free loans. Dozens of families fled the plantation in pursuit of economic opportunities, but Eastland did not evict anyone, and many tenants chose to eke out a meager living from Social Security, food stamps, and other federal programs. "People need a place to live," explained Eastland. "We pay their rent and their water and part of the electricity. It's a dead economic loss to us. When they die, we burn down the shacks." Some of the workers, including Woodrow Wilson, remained on the plantation into the twenty-first century. The senator's paternalistic concern for his workers "would seem incomprehensible" given his political opposition to the movement, journalist W.F. Minor observed, but it won him gratitude from his laborers. "He's good enough to let me stay in the house," acknowledged Charlie Edwards, a seventy-five-year-old laborer who had worked for three decades on the plantation. "I couldn't hold him responsible for my welfare."[15]

Edwards and other Eastland hands may not have blamed their plantation boss, but others did, including Fannie Lou Hamer. "He's never done anything to help anybody, not Negro people," she charged, claiming that she had helped get food stamps for impoverished families on the senator's plantation. But the problem was larger than one particularly powerful planter. Blacks across the Delta may have had more federal protection to help them vote, but they did not have much access to food or jobs. "Good jobs is what we need," Irene Taylor insisted; another Eastland plantation worker went so far as to write

President Johnson asking for a job. "Somebody done nailed us to the cross," complained an aged Sunflower County tenant farmer who had lost his job. "Don't know who it is, but I believe it's the government."[16]

"WE WILL HAVE TO UPSET THIS APPLECART"

The solution, Hamer argued, was revolution. "The only way we can make [freedom] a reality in America is to do all we can to destroy this system and bring this thing out to the light that has been under cover all these years," she emphasized in 1965. She believed that blacks needed to push harder for their own freedom, and to do so, she insisted, "we will have to upset this applecart." In tone and substance, Hamer's increasingly strident public rhetoric paralleled a shift in the black freedom struggle at large. The riots that had swept through Harlem in the summer of 1964 spread to other cities in 1965, and it became clear that black Americans across the country were less willing to abide by the tenets of nonviolence in their struggle. By 1966, the calls for "freedom now" had been replaced by what SNCC leaders Stokely Carmichael and Willy Ricks had demanded during a rally in Greenwood, Mississippi: black power. With Carmichael's ascension to the chairmanship of SNCC and the founding of the Black Panther Party, many activists in the black struggle nationwide embraced a more confrontational approach and began advocating the use of violence in self-defense. For black Mississippians, particularly in rural areas, nonviolence long had been understood as a political strategy rather than a way of life, and nonviolent civil rights workers often were relieved to know that their rural hosts kept guns ready for their protection. While she never advocated violence, Hamer considered the Panthers to be "our children" and did not believe in turning the other cheek: "I keep a shotgun in every corner of my bedroom and the first cracker even look like he wants to throw some dynamite on my porch won't write his mama again."[17]

Hamer's calls for revolution stemmed not from Communist influence or ideology, as Eastland and other segregationists insisted. Rather, they grew out of her desire to create the kingdom of God, an egalitarian society in which people of all races had the freedom to enjoy the fruits of their labor. She remained a committed Christian universalist even in the face of mocking derision from other activists. "I still believe and people make fun of me for saying this, but I believe in Christianity," she told *Movement* magazine in 1967. Even as she joined other activists in becoming more rhetorically revolutionary, she rejected the racial separatism that many black nationalists had begun to advocate. She objected to SNCC's decision in 1966 to expel its white membership and become an exclusively black organization, and she chastised young activists for becoming "cold" and "unloving." Her commitment to interracial organizing led some separatists in the organization to dismiss her as "no longer relevant" and not at their "level of development."[18]

Patronizing comments notwithstanding, Hamer's conception of the dimensions of the freedom struggle was broadening geographically as well as ideologically. After her trip to Africa had exposed her to the world beyond America's borders, Hamer became more willing to speak out on international events, particularly the Vietnam War. Like Eastland, she came to see the civil rights struggle in her native state as a crucial battleground in a global struggle for freedom. The war in Vietnam, she believed, highlighted the nation's hypocritical treatment of colored peoples at home and abroad, and it fueled her resentment toward the federal government.

In time Vietnam would become the emblem of a generation, the very name conjuring up images of conflict and entanglement. But few Americans knew or understood much about the serpentine Southeast Asian nation in August 1964, when Congress nearly unanimously passed the Gulf of Tonkin Resolution authorizing President Johnson to use force to defend anti-Communist South Vietnam against perceived aggression from Communist forces in North Vietnam. Though the United States had supported anti-Communist forces in South Vietnam since the Truman administration, not until after Lyndon Johnson took office did large numbers of Americans go to fight in Vietnam. By the time Congress passed the Voting Rights Act in August 1965, Johnson had authorized a massive bombing campaign against North Vietnam and 50,000 American soldiers had landed in South Vietnam, with another 115,000 to arrive by the end of the year.

The nationalist struggle for Vietnamese independence, which had been waged since the end of World War II, now thrust itself to the forefront of America's consciousness.[19]

The steady escalation of U.S. involvement in Vietnam paralleled the growing black frustration with the lack of racial progress at home, and civil rights activists such as Fannie Lou Hamer became increasingly vocal in their critiques of American policy in Southeast Asia. She was ahead of the curve. Though the war later drew criticism from all segments of American society, in its early years it was quite popular among both blacks and whites, and criticism of U.S. involvement was deemed traitorous. Hamer spoke out against it even before SNCC had issued its official statement on the war.[20]

Like other Americans who viewed the war skeptically, Hamer objected to the war both on philosophical and practical grounds. She considered the war an unnecessary distraction from the more important struggle for freedom in America. The war in Vietnam was just the latest conflict in which the federal government sent blacks to fight for freedoms they did not enjoy at home. "I used to question this for years—what did our kids actually fight for?" she wondered in early 1965. "They would go in the service and go through all of that and come right out to be drowned in the river in Mississippi." On Eastland's plantation, workers such as Charlie Edwards, whose son was serving in Vietnam, shared similar concerns. "He doesn't mind fighting for his county 'cause he was born here and he's been here all his life," the elderly Edwards explained. But "I'd think if I went and took all that punishment, you know, and then came back home and couldn't have a decent bed to lay down in and not a decent job, I don't think I'd feel like this was my country, no space for my part or for me." In Mississippi, not a single black official served on the state draft boards, fueling black discontent over the war.[21]

The freedom struggle was in America, not overseas, Hamer argued, and she was no more interested in having well-equipped American soldiers fight in the jungles of Vietnam than she was in having well-intentioned Peace Corps volunteers working in the jungles of Africa. Americans, Hamer believed, should stay home and fix the problems in the United States before they intervened elsewhere. As she told one crowd of supporters, "I sent a telegram to LBJ and told him to please bring those troops out of Vietnam where they have no business anyhow, and bring them to Mississippi and Louisiana." She supported SNCC's position, announced officially in January 1966 after a SNCC staff member and navy veteran was killed while on duty in Vietnam: "Our country's cry of 'preserve freedom in the world' is a hypocritical mask behind which it squashed liberation movements which are not bound and refuse to be bound by expediency of U.S. cold war policy." As the anti-war movement grew, Hamer became actively involved, attending rallies and giving speeches against the war. "I just don't think nobody with any decency should go to a racist war like that," she explained.[22]

On a practical level, Hamer feared that the war would drain resources, human power, and energy from the civil rights struggle. Even before the escalation of the war, it had been hard enough to get the federal government's sustained attention, let alone the monetary resources needed to counteract generations of segregation. Now, with the war consuming millions of dollars monthly and drafting legions of young men, it became harder to focus the government's attention on continued injustice in Mississippi. Activists marveled at the irony of the federal government's willingness to send troops to Vietnam to promote democracy while, in the words of one writer, it "is apparently baffled by the logistics of dispatching federal registrars a few hundred miles to achieve the domestic variety of self-rule." Indeed, after the dramatic summer of 1964, Mississippi did not again become the focus of national attention. Hamer understood what President Johnson later came to realize: "that bitch of a war," as Johnson termed the conflict in Vietnam, made it impossible to pursue the War on Poverty and the other measures of the Great Society. The willingness of the federal government to abandon civil rights in favor of the war only deepened Hamer's cynicism about institutions and power.[23]

"A CRITICAL TESTING GROUND"

For Senator Eastland, opposition to the war, combined with talk of revolution and growing violence in the cities, revealed the civil rights movement to be at heart a Communist effort to destroy America.

After years of duplicitous talk about nonviolence and democracy, East-land argued, movement activists now were showing their true colors. Eastland's critics often asserted that his virulent anti-Communism simply served as a mask for his fundamental racism, that he raised the issue of Communism as a politically expedient means of preserving white supremacy. But Eastland argued, as he had since he entered the Senate, the opposite: he believed that efforts to pursue racial justice simply served as a mask for his opponents' fundamental desire to overthrow capitalism, that activists raised racial issues as a politically expedient means of promoting Communism. While some moderate white Mississippians began to acquiesce to the new political reality, Eastland became even more aggressive about tying the movement to Communism. In February and March 1965, as the protest movement in Selma, Alabama, came to a head, he launched his most concerted attack to date, speaking out three times on the floor of the Senate to name names of Communists in the movement and to discredit north-ern civil rights workers, the Mississippi Freedom Democratic Party, and Fannie Lou Hamer herself. "They tried to brand me a commu-nist," Hamer laughed, "and I know as much about communism as a horse do about Christmas."[24]

"Communist forces both inside and outside the United States are pressing for a Negro revolution in this country," Eastland began in early February 1965, and he then laid out his argument about the movement's Communist connections. First, he insisted that he did not believe that all or even most movement activists were Communists. Rather, they were dupes, naive innocents who did not realize that "they were part and parcel of the Communist conspiracy." Like the black union members Eastland had interrogated in the Memphis hear-ing fourteen years earlier, these impressionable young people had been led astray by cunning Communists, including his old nemesis Victor Rabinowitz, the avowed Communist and union lawyer who now was helping the MFDP. Eastland singled out other attorneys, par-ticularly those associated with the National Lawyers Guild (NLG). Founded by New Dealers in 1937, the NLG was an interracial bar association that had worked closely with the Communist Party in its early years and refused to bar Communists even after it was the target of investigations by the House Un-American Activities Committee. Several NLG attorneys, including Arthur Kinoy, Morton Stavis, and Benjamin Smith, had come to Mississippi to help collect evidence of voter intimidation.[25]

Under the influence of such experienced Communist operatives, Eastland argued, young activists became apostles of a revolutionary doctrine that alienated local people, white and black. The "freedom houses" that activists had set up were "Communist indoctrination centers" replete with left-wing literature and pro-Communist paraphernalia. Even the physical appearance of activists gave clues to their Communist predisposition, Eastland argued. At a SNCC conference in late 1964, one-third of the attendees sported beards, the senator claimed, and his sources revealed that "some of those who wore them were heard to state that these beards were directly connected with the Castro movement and were symbolic of that movement, and several of the beardwearers declared they would not shave until the revolution was successful." Such radicals had come to Mississippi, bringing with them not only unwanted ideas about race and economics but also deviant social behavior and sexually transmitted diseases. Because the activists were so aberrant, Eastland maintained, they could not win the allegiance of local blacks. He estimated that 95 percent of the black residents in Sunflower County did not support the movement, and he insisted that the MFDP was a "carpetbag outfit" that was "sponsored, organized, and developed by nonresidents of Mississippi."[26]

These carpetbaggers had focused on Mississippi because Communists had targeted the state as a focal point of the worldwide revolution. "The Communists know, and Communist leaders have stated publicly," Eastland argued, "that they cannot succeed with their program of racial demonstrations on a national basis unless they can succeed in Mississippi." The Communist tide that Eastland had fought against in Germany two decades before had now reached his own home, and he insisted that the white people of Mississippi would stand strong: "They know what they face; they know what they are fighting for—not only to protect their own way of life, and their own freedoms, but to turn back the concentrated and focused power of the world Communist conspiracy and all its helpers, witting or unwitting, on what the Communists themselves have termed a critical testing ground." In Eastland's mind, it was up to the white people of Mississippi to protect the leader of the free world.[27]

As overwrought as they might seem in retrospect, Eastland's attacks on SNCC and the MFDP in early 1965 were not a lonely, desperate cry from the sinking ship of segregation. Instead, they were part of a broad assault waged not simply by southern segregationists but also by mainstream conservatives, moderate civil rights groups, and, increasingly, white liberals. A widely publicized piece by influential conservative *Washington Post* columnists Rowland Evans and Robert Novak appeared on the day of Eastland's third and final speech, and it argued that "SNCC is substantially infiltrated by beatnik leftwing revolutionaries and—worst of all—by Communists." This criticism from the right came on the heels of the NAACP's public withdrawal from the Council of Federated Organizations and NAACP chief Roy Wilkins's accusation that "Chinese Communist elements" were present within SNCC. SNCC chairman John Lewis dismissed the charges as "part of a conspiracy," and he refused to apply an ideological litmus test for membership or hiring, emphasizing that the group would "accept anybody who [was] willing to go into the Mississippi Delta or the Black Belt to work for freedom." SNCC's refusal to purge Communists only fueled its critics' desire to destroy the organization.[28]

Eastland's charges of a Moscow-directed movement indeed were exaggerated, as the senator himself must have known from his reading of FBI files and SISS investigations. Having been broken in the early 1950s, the Communist Party USA never fully recovered and had minimal influence within the movement. Yet, despite his critics' justified complaints about his selective and demagogic use of information, he did offer substantial evidence to back his claims. The product of years of (often illegal) investigative work by SISS, the FBI, and the Mississippi State Sovereignty Commission, his list of names and his methodical explanation of each person's background and beliefs were largely accurate; he may have known more about individual members within the movement than movement leaders themselves did. Furthermore, by 1966 Eastland's warnings about Communist involvement in the movement only seemed to become more true. Official Communist Party members were never numerous or in positions of leadership, but they indeed were migrating to the movement in an effort, FBI director J. Edgar Hoover surmised, to be relevant again. The American party's Soviet funders hoped to capitalize on the movement's successes, and they increased the party's annual subsidy fourfold during the early 1960s, reaching $1 million in 1965.[29]

More importantly, those within the movement who were not Communist Party members became increasingly frustrated with the limited gains of the struggle and openly began to espouse Marxist ideology, advocate the overthrow of capitalism, and defiantly quote Karl Marx, Fidel Castro, Mao Zedong, and other Communist leaders. Rather than hiding their affiliations with Communism and left-wing revolution, radicals within the movement brazenly embraced them. The increasing militancy of the movement led Charles Morgan of the American Civil Liberties Union to muse, "Would to God there were Communists in SNCC. They would be a moderating influence." These militant activists seemed to vindicate anti-Communists such as Eastland, and Gallup polls suggested that his fears of Communist involvement in the movement were shared by a large segment of the American public. Despite, and because of, the movement's progress, the politically crippling connections to Communism threatened to hamper its long-term success.[30]

"THE GREEDY, RUTHLESS, VIOLENT FACE OF BLACK POWER"

Communism and black power stood front and center as Eastland ran for reelection in 1966. He encountered a political world vastly different from the one in which he had run six years before. In 1960, he had won reelection for a fourth term without even token opposition in a state that remained closed not only to black political participation but also to white moderates and Republicans. By 1966, the combined effects of the Civil Rights Act, the Great Society, and the Voting Rights Act had hatched a social and political revolution. President Johnson, whom Eastland had supported for the Democratic nomination in 1960, had become the most aggressive civil rights president in American history. With Johnson's blessing, federal dollars poured into Head

Start, the Job Corps, legal services for the poor, and other Great Society programs, and in early 1966 he called on Congress to pass expansive new civil rights legislation that would ban racial discrimination in housing and jury selection and impose hefty penalties for violating a person's civil rights. Johnson's boldness at the national level mirrored the increased civil rights activity at the local level. In Mississippi, blacks flocked to register at county courthouses as the Mississippi Freedom Democratic Party organized oppositional campaigns at all levels of government. The Justice Department estimated that by election time nearly 25 percent of the state electorate could be black. While some white politicians sought to capitalize on new black voters—one Delta sheriff boasted, "Give me 500 Negro votes to start with and there ain't a man in the county who could catch me"—Eastland neither wanted nor could win black votes. He "represents something disgusting to the Negro—his image is a great white father, the white plantation owner," one black voter commented. "It is unthinkable that a Negro would vote for Eastland."[31]

For the first time since 1954, Eastland faced a serious electoral challenge. From the right, Republican representative Prentiss Walker attacked the senator for being too cozy with the national Democratic establishment, particularly Robert Kennedy, who recently had emerged as a popular spokesman for liberal causes. Walker spoke for many white conservatives who, angered by the success of the movement, sought to blame Eastland. "It seems the white people have become serfs," Ann Sullivan wrote the senator. "The Blacks have gone above the law." H.J. West, who called himself "a *former* supporter," complained to Eastland that whites were "being run over by these *damn* burr heads" and the senator had not done enough about it. From the left, MFDP candidate Reverend Clifton Whitley opposed Eastland on nearly every public policy issue possible, calling the segregationist senator "an insult to me personally as well as racially." Although only 11 percent of Sunflower County blacks were registered—a fact that critics attributed to Eastland's ability to block federal registrars from coming to his home county—statewide nearly 50 percent of the black population now was able to vote. The growing number of black voters multiplied the strength of the MFDP and struck fear into conservative white Democrats. One State Sovereignty Commission investigator reported in

June 1966 that MFDP candidates had received "an alarming number of votes" in the Democratic primary and that Whitley had defeated Eastland in two Delta counties. The widespread organizing effort led by movement activists, the investigator warned, would lead to MFDP victories in areas where blacks were in the majority or "where the whites are too apathetic to exercise their privilege to vote."[32]

The attacks from both left and right made Eastland "frantic" and left him "riddled with doubts," national reporters observed, and his opponents within Mississippi became more brazen in their attacks on him. Rather than shrinking from or denying charges of being "Communist," some activists embraced the taboo label in an effort to embolden blacks and remove a rhetorical weapon from the hands of their opponents. In a widely publicized July 1966 letter to the *Jackson Daily News*, civil rights worker Phil Lapsansky proudly asserted that he was a Communist and challenged Mississippians to join him to help unseat "the old plantation master from Sunflower County." "There is a revolution afoot here to destroy the naked rule of the rich, which has made Mississippi the poorest state in the nation," Lapsansky insisted, and it would "destroy the vile racism nurtured by Eastland and his ilk that blinds men to their common interests in struggle."[33]

Lapsansky's boldness, like Fannie Lou Hamer's increasingly revolutionary rhetoric, may have played well in activist circles, but it also suited the needs of the state's senior senator. In what Mississippi's largest newspaper proudly dubbed America's "most anti-Communist state," self-proclaimed Communists generated little public sympathy or support among blacks or whites. Indeed, though he railed against "militants," Eastland recognized how beneficial the radical activists could be to his cause, and he capitalized upon their rhetoric as he sought to motivate white voters. He lumped all advocates of racial justice, from the MFDP to Martin Luther King Jr. to the Black Panthers, under the catchall phrase "black power," which became a code word for extremism, anti-capitalism, and violence. He then linked black power to both Communism and Reconstruction to form a potent rhetorical weapon designed to turn white voters against the movement. Lapsansky and other activists became spokesmen for his reelection campaign. "Who's against Jim Eastland?" asked one campaign brochure, and it provided excerpts from Lapsansky's letter, along with other attacks on the senator from King, MFDP chair Lawrence Guyot, and other "black power advocates." The MFDP is "an arm of the Communist conspiracy," he told supporters in Indianola. "We are at war with the Communists all over the world and see and deal with them right here in Mississippi." By attacking Lyndon Johnson and belittling King, radicals in the movement "have repudiated their white liberal lackeys, they have torn off the peaceful mask of nonviolence and have exposed the greedy, ruthless, violent face of black power." The more radical the movement became, the more Eastland believed that it worked to benefit conservatives. The militants "are turning the cycle the other way," he told one crowd of supporters. "It is now running in our favor." To ensure that those conservatives did not bolt to the Republican Party and vote for his opponent, Prentiss Walker, Eastland raised the specter of Reconstruction. As he told a state convention of county supervisors, the lesson that white southerners learned in Reconstruction was that one-party rule was necessary in the South because "in division there is weakness and in unity there is strength."[34]

Eastland believed that the increasing militancy of the movement helped kill the 1966 civil rights bill, which withered that fall in the face of a Senate filibuster and dwindling northern support. He hoped the militants would help unleash a white backlash not only in the South but also among northern whites that would parallel how white southerners had responded to *Brown*. In his efforts to shape that national white opinion, he again benefited from changes in movement strategy. After the passage of the Voting Rights Act, many movement activists and leaders, particularly Martin Luther King Jr., recognized that the legal structure of southern Jim Crow had been torn down, and they began to shift their focus away from the segregated South to the urban North, where millions of blacks lived in squalor despite legal equality. King himself set up an office in Chicago and began organizing a campaign to improve living conditions in the slums, part of an effort that focused increasingly on the inequities produced by America's capitalist economic system. King's move, combined with chronic rioting in the cities of the North and West, pulled national media attention away from the South, particularly rural areas such as Sunflower County, toward urban hot spots.

This change in battleground delighted southern conservatives. As Eastland explained to members of the Citizens' Council in their weekly newsmagazine, the move north boded well for the white resistance movement because "now those who spawned and nurtured this movement as long as it was aimed at the South find themselves the victims of their own creation." For too long, Eastland argued, northerners "had sown the wind of racial turmoil throughout the South" from afar, but they now would be "reaping the terrible whirlwind of violence" in their own cities. For Eastland and other white southerners, it was an article of faith that whites in the North shared their distaste for integration. "The people [in the North] are for civil rights when it applies to the South," he told supporters. "They are not for civil rights when it applies at home." The North now would have to face its own Reconstruction, he predicted: "the racial skirmishes in the South were only a prelude to the tragic era which has now opened in the North."[35]

Convinced that northern whites shared his philosophy, Eastland harbored visions of a national movement against black equality. He explored the idea of using the State Sovereignty Commission to fund the mobilization of white ethnic groups in the North. The idea, he explained to commission head Erle Johnston, was to donate Sovereignty Commission money to Polish, Hungarian, and Italian American groups in the North for a campaign to get "anti-discrimination" legislation passed to protect white ethnics. Such an effort, Eastland believed, would highlight the absurdity of civil rights legislation targeting blacks and would galvanize northern whites to resist the movement. Eastland and Johnston also discussed pressing lawsuits to get federal courts to apply to schools in Washington, D.C., and other cities in the North the same standards of "racial balance" that were being enforced against southern schools. Putting such pressure on northern whites, they hoped, would help manifest the terrible burden southern whites had to bear.[36]

Eastland's appeals to the North did not rest solely on race, however. As important, and perhaps more effective, were his arguments about the economic nature of freedom. Emphasizing how increasingly militant activists were targeting private property owners and the capitalist system itself, he became more explicit in his defense of free enterprise as the essence of freedom. "Subversive leaders," he wrote a supporter in October 1966, "openly and defiantly are attempting to destroy our system of free enterprise and democracy." The word *freedom* in the preamble of the Constitution, Eastland explained, meant the right to own and control property. This right was being attacked by both civil rights legislation and riots, with the result, he emphasized, that "there has been more property destroyed in the United States during the revolutionary outbreaks of the past two years than there was in Russia when the Communists took over." Individual freedom, the freedom to do what one pleases, particularly with one's property, was the antithesis of collective civil rights, Eastland insisted. "I have seen the lights of individual freedom going out across this land with every extension of Federal power, and I have seen the dark night of despotism slowly descending upon this nation while individual freedom has been sacrificed in the name of 'civil rights.'" The failed 1966 civil rights bill was a prime example of how liberal activists hoped to undermine free enterprise. "We defeated not merely a civil rights bill," Eastland crowed after the bill died, "but a move to destroy the right of the American people to own property."[37]

The civil rights bill's defeat presaged a troubling election season for liberal Democrats and movement supporters. Eastland coasted to victory, garnering more than 60 percent of the overall vote, while conservatives nationwide gained seats in the House and the Senate. Eastland viewed the results cautiously, pleased by his victory and the defeat of numerous liberal incumbents but also troubled by the continued militancy of the civil rights movement. He recognized, too, that the movement largely had succeeded—there would be no rolling back of blacks' voting gains, no retraction of the integration laws. The major battles of the movement may have been lost, as the Civil War had been lost, but Eastland hoped to win a long-term victory, as the white South had during Reconstruction, through unyielding opposition to the changes the movement had wrought. One early test of how much lasting change the movement would effect came as President Johnson waged his massive War on Poverty.[38]

"INSTRUMENTS OF POWER"

A centerpiece of the Great Society, the War on Poverty was an ambitious series of federal programs aimed at lifting millions of poor Americans out of destitution. Congress established the Office of Economic Opportunity (OEO) to coordinate a vast array of programs, from Head Start to the Job Corps. Under Sargent Shriver, the indefatigable, idealistic brother-in-law to the Kennedy family, the OEO became the most aggressive agency working on behalf of the poor. The OEO sought to give poor people the opportunity for "maximum feasible participation" in the anti-poverty programs that benefited them. In Mississippi, this participatory approach was "downright revolutionary," one journalist wrote, and it triggered a fierce battle that pitted Fannie Lou Hamer and her civil rights allies against Senator Eastland and the white power holders in the state.[39]

The controversy focused on the OEO's primary anti-poverty program, the Child Development Group of Mississippi (CDGM), one of the country's first Head Start programs. Launched with a federal grant of $1.5 million in the summer of 1965, CDGM offered preschool education, medical care, and food to six thousand poor children, and the centers became a vital source of federally funded employment for hundreds of teachers and child care assistants. Fannie Lou Hamer and other movement activists initially were wary of the group because of its federal funding and its founding by northern whites—ironically, they had come to share Eastland's distrust of outsiders, for they feared that their grassroots political movement would be co-opted by whites or corrupted by the infusion of federal cash. They also worried that CDGM would drain energy and resources from the MFDP and the political movement. But from the beginning CDGM organizers cultivated close connections to the MFDP, and movement activists, especially Hamer, came to see the new agency as a political opportunity. The CDGM and the movement "were one and the same," one black teacher commented. "It was the same people." Thirteen of the agency's original fifteen staff members had movement experience, and the agency itself was headquartered at Mount Beulah, a former black college that had become the home base of both the MFDP and the

Delta Ministry. CDGM staff saw themselves as an extension of the movement, and they viewed their work with poor children as a political organizing tool.[40]

CDGM's large budget, its hiring of civil rights veterans, and its open support of the movement all made the anti-poverty group a prime target for Eastland. "Dollars are powerful tools in the hands of Communists or those who blindly accept the guidance of Communists," he warned, and he depicted CDGM as a Communist effort to use poverty programs as "instruments of power." Working closely with the State Sovereignty Commission, Eastland and his Senate colleague John Stennis launched a vigorous attack on CDGM in an attempt to pressure the OEO into denying funding to the anti-poverty group. With two informants on CDGM's staff, the Sovereignty Commission had regular access to the inner workings of the CDGM, and it dutifully passed along its findings to the senators in Washington. Hence, Eastland knew embarrassing details about what was going on behind CDGM's closed doors, and he did not hesitate to reveal them. In one case, an informant told the Sovereignty Commission about how CDGM staff members threatened rioting and violence if the OEO pressed the Mississippi group to account for its budget; the commission then urged Eastland to take the matter directly to the OEO to "get some more mileage against the CDGM grant." Both Eastland and Stennis used their senior positions within the Democratic Party to manipulate CDGM's weaknesses and pressure the OEO to crack down on CDGM—with Stennis as chair of the Appropriations Committee and Eastland heading the Judiciary Committee, the Johnson administration could ill afford to alienate the two men.[41]

In addition to applying pressure privately, Eastland publicly assailed CDGM for mismanaging its federal grant, funding civil rights activities, and using federal funds to bail activists out of jail. By supporting such a subversive organization, Eastland maintained, the executive branch of the federal government had joined the judiciary and the Communists in the global struggle against freedom. Although the Cold War foe remained dangerous, the more insidious enemy came from within. "The enemy of our freedom now no longer threatens us across international boundaries," he warned. Rather, "he now looks out at us from beneath the dome of our Capit[o]l and from behind the doors of the numerous welfare agencies and other bureaus." The war against the Communist enemy had changed fronts. More dangerous than Cuban guerrillas or Vietnamese nationalists, "our enemy carries a briefcase full of welfare forms and he is armed with coercive lawsuits and he is backed by the might of the U.S. Treasury as his arsenal." A disinterested observer might have pointed out that the might of the U.S. Treasury also backed the white planters of Sunflower County, to whom it appropriated more than $10 million in 1967.[42]

Though critics dismissed Eastland's charges as the predictable ranting of a desperate segregationist, his allegations about CDGM's civil rights activity, more so than his descriptions of Communist influence in the movement, were largely true. Hamer and other activists hoped that the anti-poverty program could help give poor blacks the economic independence and patronage potential to build a powerful, grassroots political movement that would transform Mississippi. CDGM staffers were indeed using federal money to advance their movement-inspired agenda; Head Start programs ostensibly designed for children were used as political leverage to encourage people to support movement goals; federal funding sustained activists at a time when other sources of money were drying up. As one journalist sympathetic to the program wrote, "Without CDGM many local civil rights leaders would have had to quit 'the movement,' leave the state or starve." CDGM staff members did not see the connections between the movement and the organization as a problem. Indeed, as one internal staff memo suggested, some staffers were concerned that they were not doing *enough* organizing and should set up a separate organization to do so without restriction. In a sense, movement activists were trying to do for their poor black constituents what Eastland had been doing for his rich white constituents for decades: use the resources of government to reward supporters, punish enemies, and build power through the distribution of material benefits and federal largesse. This was precisely what Eastland feared. He recognized in CDGM much more than a simple effort to alleviate child poverty, just as he saw in MFDP much more than a simple effort to exercise the right to vote—both were part of a larger movement to reshape his state along egalitarian lines, a movement that would destroy his base of power.[43]

To blunt the segregationists' criticism, which threatened a whole array of anti-poverty programs, OEO encouraged the formation of a moderate, biracial alternative to CDGM called Mississippi Action for Progress (MAP). MAP attracted high-profile, middle- and upper-class board members such as white newspaper editor Hodding Carter III, white planter LeRoy Percy, and black NAACP leader Aaron Henry; despite her prominence, Hamer, with her links to CDGM and MFDP, was not invited. With MAP in place, OEO stripped CDGM of its funding in early October 1966 and showered the new organization with cash. "Poverty gold is falling over Mississippi," one reporter wrote, as more than $12 million flowed from OEO to MAP. The move away from the controversial, activist-dominated CDGM and toward the moderate MAP further alienated Hamer from the federal government and white liberal allies. She denounced MAP, saying angrily that "we aren't ready to be sold out by a few middle-class bourgeoisie and some of the Uncle Toms who couldn't care less." Dismissing the anti-poverty programs as "awful" and "a whole lotta junk," Hamer argued that they had been designed as a means of quelling discontent, a way to satisfy the hungry masses without addressing their deeper needs.[44]

Other observers agreed. Writing in the *New Republic*, scholar Christopher Jencks explained how many potentially liberating anti-poverty efforts, like the New Deal programs of a generation earlier, wound up controlled by local whites. It worked something like this: black activists demand that the federal government fund a community action program they can control. Officials in Washington express an interest in the program but insist that local white leaders too must be involved, thus angering the activists, who may even abandon the idea. The officials then encourage white participation and fund the program. It looks like the original, activist-inspired program, but whites are in charge. "The local white elite preserves its ultimate control over poor Negroes' lives," Jencks wrote, "but concedes them more food, money and training." Jencks likely would not have been surprised to learn that the State Sovereignty Commission aided and abetted this process of co-optation. By mid-1966, Sovereignty Commission head Erle Johnston began working to persuade local white leaders to get involved in the poverty programs as a way to reap the federal windfall. Yet even by the late 1960s, the combined effect of federal social programs was limited—in 1967, Sunflower County received only $4 million in social program spending, less than $120 per person. Hamer and other black activists wanted more than concessions and federal money—they wanted control of local politics in order to control the distribution of resources.[45]

Political participation promised potentially revolutionary economic benefits, particularly at the local level, where property taxes and land appraisals were controlled by planter-friendly officials. During Reconstruction, reformers had sought to change the appraisal system to bring property assessment in line with market values, but planters and their political allies frustrated their efforts. By the late 1960s, the state still used a Depression-era appraisal system by which local officials routinely undervalued property to keep taxes low. In 1967, Senator Eastland's 5,800-acre plantation, with a market value of between $400 and $500 an acre, was appraised by the county tax assessor at only $32.08 an acre; as a result, Eastland paid less than $8,700 in property taxes. What if, one liberal writer imagined, a black candidate could unseat the local tax assessor? Eastland's property, along with other plantations, could be reappraised, creating a harvest of new tax revenue that could be invested in community services and relief programs that would benefit the black community. The MFDP made the case clear in its political handbook: "If we would elect a tax assessor, he could list the land closer to its sale value. Then we could use the money to pay for good school[s], roads and bridges." If blacks were elected as county supervisors, they could redirect federal money to job training for idle field hands. The possibilities for economic transformation and social change were breathtaking, and they encouraged Hamer and the MFDP to persist in their electoral efforts to dislodge local politicians.[46]

"WE AIN'T DOIN' NOTHIN' SYMBOLIC"

As CDGM succumbed to outside pressure in 1967, a bright political opportunity burst open in the town of Sunflower. In the three years following the MFDP's challenge in Atlantic City, the combined forces of grassroots activism, the Voting Rights Act, and federal judicial action dramatically reshaped the political landscape of Sunflower County. In April 1965, two years after the Justice Department had initiated the lawsuit on behalf of Hamer and other black defendants, a federal court order in the case of *Hamer v. Campbell* acknowledged widespread discrimination against prospective black voters in Sunflower County and ordered recalcitrant registrars to open the political process to all voters irrespective of color. A subsequent, protracted legal battle resulted in another federal court order for new elections in the towns of Sunflower and Moorhead, to be held in May 1967.[47]

Sunflower offered a perfect recipe for MFDP success. Located just eight miles south of the Eastland plantation, the town was home to fewer than seven hundred residents, about 70 percent of whom were black. It was a "small, dreary plantation town," one journalist wrote, that "resembles, in miniature, all the black communities in the rural South: the dusty, unimproved roads, the dilapidated shacks, the rundown churches." Blacks constituted a majority of Sunflower voters, a result of months of diligent MFDP canvassing, and party leaders were optimistic of their chances for electoral success. The town's cheery name and its proximity to Eastland's farm acted as a magnet for national press attention. Hamer went on speaking tours to the North, where she raised money for the National Committee for Free Elections in Sunflower, a New York–based organization that attracted high-profile supporters from Martin Luther King Jr. and Harry Belafonte to John Kenneth Galbraith and Howard Zinn, as well as fifteen U.S. representatives. A congressional delegation even visited Sunflower in April. With all the attention focused on the rural town, "Sunflower had become a symbol," one observer noted. "To win an election here would be to achieve a victory over racist oppression everywhere."[48]

Hamer saw the election as a chance to earn something tangible. "If we could win the election in Sunflower County it would give hope to all the peoples who have been struggling so long and ain't saw nobody win nothing," she explained. "Peoples need a victory so bad. We've been working here since '62 and we haven't got nothing, except a helluva lot of heartaches." She knew the heartaches personally. Not only had she been brutalized in Winona and threatened repeatedly in the years since, she also lost her daughter Dorothy Jean in September 1966 in a horrifying example of racism's human toll. During childbirth, the twenty-two-year-old Dorothy Jean began hemorrhaging and needed urgent medical treatment. Two hospitals refused to treat her because she was black, so Hamer wound up driving her more than a hundred miles to Memphis. Dorothy Jean died en route. Fannie Lou and Pap Hamer adopted Dorothy Jean's two daughters, Jacqueline and Lenora.[49]

Hamer and the MFDP poured their hearts into the Sunflower election, doing everything from canvassing through the night to making appeals to the U.S. attorney general. For mayor, the party ran Otis Brown, a twenty-one-year-old former Freedom School teacher and county chair of the MFDP, against incumbent W.L. Patterson, as well as a slate of black candidates for the board of aldermen. Brown distanced himself from the controversial Stokely Carmichael and pledged not to pursue "black power." His ambitious platform called for more industrial jobs, improved services for the poor, and a curfew to keep young people off the streets. In a sign of how much the political terrain had shifted, Patterson actively and publicly campaigned for votes among the "good Negroes." As election time approached, the MFDP's prospects for victory appeared strong. If black voters turned out in high numbers, party workers told supporters, surely the MFDP would win. "If we stand together, we cannot fail!"[50]

More than 98 percent of eligible voters turned out, including all but four of the black voters. Yet despite the black majority among registered voters, despite the months of voter education and preparation, despite the national attention bestowed upon the election, the MFDP lost badly—not a single movement candidate won, and Patterson was reelected as mayor with more than 60 percent of the vote. It was clear that a significant number of black voters had backed the white candidate. The victorious Patterson pointedly thanked "all my Negro friends who crossed over and voted for me," an assessment that grated on movement activists. "We've been raped," fumed MFDP head Lawrence Guyot, "and our dear white brother isn't the only rapist."[51]

MFDP activists attributed the split in the black vote to voter intimidation—the white chief of police stood prominently outside city hall, and what one reporter termed "ominous groups of whites" clustered menacingly by the exits to the voting area—and the illegal exclusion of a black election official to help illiterate voters cast their ballots. A more disturbing possibility, one almost inconceivable to many movement workers, was that black voters had preferred the white candidates on the basis of personal relationships, deference, or merit. Like Eastland and his allies, some activists could not believe that local blacks could think or act for themselves—any vote against the MFDP thus must have been due to white intimidation, fraud, or self-hatred. Other people within the movement recognized that fewer and fewer local people supported movement activities; one internal SNCC report warned that, unlike two years earlier, in 1967 community support for a new project in Sunflower County "would be questionable" because "people are said to be afraid of SNCC." One resigned MFDP worker conceded, "There are no excuses this time. We had all the organization, money and talent we could use. We simply didn't have the votes."[52]

The devastating results of the Sunflower election, combined with the frustrating loss of CDGM, led Hamer to become increasingly antagonistic toward blacks who did not support the movement, particularly middle-class blacks who challenged activists for leadership roles in the black community. The movement had vanquished legal segregation, and many blacks who initially had scorned Hamer, SNCC, and "dat mess" sought to capitalize on the newfound opportunities. Now that the major legislative goals had been reached, now that the most horrific harassment was disappearing, now that token integration seemed likely even in Mississippi, Hamer feared that she and other grassroots people were being shoved aside by "respectable" blacks who had stayed on the sidelines during the rough early phase of the movement.

Like Eastland, Hamer saw her struggle as a battle between good and evil where there could be no in-between. Unlike Aaron Henry, who had opposed Hamer at Atlantic City and had followed a pragmatic course of action that involved compromises and alliances with white moderates, Hamer considered anyone, white or black, who did not identify with the MFDP and support its agenda either racist, ignorant, or a sellout. Influenced by the rhetoric of her MFDP colleagues, she began to sprinkle her speeches and interviews with condemnations of the "bourgeois," and she vented her anger toward the "Uncle Toms and Nervous Nellies" within the black community. She lashed out at "middle-class Negroes, the ones that never had it as hard as the grass roots people in Mississippi," and she singled out teachers and ministers for scorn: "Sometimes I get so disgusted I feel like getting my gun after some of these school teachers and chicken eatin' preachers." She saw the moment of opportunity receding, her dream of a grassroots movement that truly would help poor black Mississippians fading.[53]

By the late 1960s, Hamer faced a paradox, an enduring irony of the movement in which she had invested so much of herself: the more success the movement had, the more difficult it became to sustain its spirit. As poor people in the Delta finally gained voting rights and access to federal resources, many of them lost their hunger, both literally (federal anti-poverty programs relieved physical hunger and suffering) and figuratively (once people's basic needs were met, they felt less compelled to take political or personal risks). Hamer claimed she knew many people who became "meek as ducks" once they became involved in the federal programs or gained a crumb of political power. "They see that they gonna make them some pretty good money and they tend to get quiet," Hamer seethed. "I think [the poverty program] was directed for that purpose." Indeed, by making salaried jobs available to black Mississippians, federal programs gave blacks more of a stake in the system and offered them an opportunity to live a stable, middle-class life. That many activists condemned people for taking advantage of such opportunities, Aaron Henry believed, reflected misplaced ideological priorities, which "did not emerge from the cotton fields of Mississippi" but instead arose from "highly educated people who came here and lived and worked with the people for a short period of time." Hamer certainly had emerged from the cotton fields and was not highly educated, but unlike most of her Sunflower County neighbors, she had had a transformative movement experience that had revolutionized her ideology. Most black Mississippians had not become as radical, Henry argued, and they did not want "to destroy the middle class but rather to join it and be like them, to share in the comforts conferred by that status." The movement's inability to reach out to those blacks was a failure of imagination and helped explain why it had difficulty sustaining itself.[54]

After the loss in Sunflower, Hamer began to shift her priorities. The bitter lesson of the Sunflower campaign, one reporter noted, was that electoral politics had "failed as a method of lifting people out of the oppression under which they live." Lela Mae Brooks, a black Sunflower native who had lost her bid for an alderman's seat, angrily warned, "It can be Viet Nam right here; in Sunflower; in Mississippi." As one succinct Sunflower teenager put it, "Fuck the votin'; time we fightin'." Hamer, like her fellow MFDP activists, was bitter. "I'm tired of folks comin' and tellin' us to be nice. That we got a symbolic victory," she muttered after the results came in. "We ain't doin' nothin' symbolic; we doin' this cause our lives are at stake!" The failure of the CDGM and the inability to elect black candidates in Sunflower pushed Hamer to see the limits of political freedom. "Walking around with a ballot for the next hundred years ain't going to get us nowhere, if we don't have an economic base." Like Eastland, Hamer came to see economic power as the most important element of freedom. In the Delta, that meant land.[55]

9

"The Pendulum Is Swinging Back"

So much changed on the surface of Sunflower County in the twenti-eth century. Forest gave way to farmland, hand labor yielded to ma-chines, gravel lost out to asphalt, family-run general stores surrendered to corporate chains. But underneath it all lay one constant: the land itself, the deep, rich soil that first had lured white and black settlers to the area and seduced them into braving predators and pestilence in hopes of earning a fortune. Though agricultural scientists have boosted its production with performance-enhancing chemicals, Sun-flower County's soil in the twenty-first century remains a marvel of nature. Farmers still grouse about the relative difficulty of growing crops on the crumbly "gumbo" or "buckshot" soil inland, but they can hardly complain about the sandy loam soils along the county's streams that continue to produce ever-greater yields of cotton, soybeans, corn, and rice.

The land also remains a source of great wealth and power, as James Eastland and his family knew well. By the late 1960s, he was among the richest members of the Senate, and his plantation had nudged close to six thousand acres. Despite the political revolution of the civil rights movement, he remained firmly in power and had be-come an institution atop the Senate Judiciary Committee. He and other white landowners in Sunflower County retained the ability to frustrate black efforts to achieve substantive equality. Economically, the county's blacks seemed to be moving backward by the late 1960s.

The agricultural revolution spawned during the New Deal had left the county's blacks largely landless, jobless, and unskilled, despite their movement successes. So long as whites in the county controlled the land, Fannie Lou Hamer figured, blacks would remain economically dependent, if not on the planters then on the government. Though she continued to fight for political power, Hamer returned to her roots in the late 1960s and early 1970s and channeled her waning energy into the land.

"GIVE A MAN SOME GROUND"

"Now the Movement has dissipated, and the whirr of television cameras is seldom heard in the Mississippi Delta," wrote Nashville journalist John Egerton after a visit to Hamer's home in 1969. "But what was started there in the early 1960's didn't stop when the Movement moved on; in big ways and small, black citizens who have caught a vision of freedom still reach for it." Hamer certainly continued reaching. Part of what had drawn Egerton to Sunflower County was Hamer's latest venture, an ambitious project to implement a poor people's agricultural cooperative. Called Freedom Farm, the endeavor was Hamer's attempt to wrest economic control away from Eastland and other white planters, an effort to achieve economic independence and inspire political action through collective enterprise. "The cotton is gone," Hamer lamented, referring not to the crop itself but to the jobs it formerly had provided masses of black laborers. The Delta's sharecropping economy no longer could sustain its black population, she realized, "so we going to have to build some kind of economic base." Blacks "need to see something concrete, something that touches and is gonna change their lives," Hamer explained. "Only then will they act." Freedom Farm offered a tangible expression of Hamer's definition of "freedom," an alternative culture based on Christian love rather than on material acquisition. Freedom Farm was Hamer's effort to create the kingdom of God on earth, a re-creation of the communal society that early Christians enjoyed in the Book of Acts (2:44–45): "All who believed were together and had all things in common; they would sell their possessions and goods and distribute their possessions to all, as any had need." This was freedom—poor people in control of their own lives, working to support themselves, helping each other in a cooperative environment that stressed communal needs rather than individual desires.[1]

By giving poor people access to their own land and the fruits of their own labor, Hamer hoped to free them economically and psychologically from the "plantation mentality" that crippled many black Mississippians and kept them dependent on white paternalism. The nearly limitless power that planters wielded during Jim Crow not only had corrupted those in charge, it also had created a sense of powerlessness among sharecroppers that undermined their willingness and ability to take responsibility for themselves. As civil rights leader Bob Moses explained, there was "a deeply entrenched habit of deference to as well as genuine fear of white power" among blacks. This deference and fear often prevented blacks from being able to imagine themselves wielding power as whites had. The black man in Mississippi "has been trained from infancy to subservience," observed University of Mississippi professor and civil rights supporter James Silver. "He has been taught by his parents, who have done this in order to protect him; he has been taught that he is inferior." Hamer's mother had made an explicit effort to instill racial pride in her children, and Hamer's movement experience had bolstered her self-confidence, but she believed that other blacks lacked basic self-respect. "So many of our people," she lamented, "seem like they don't want to be anything but white."[2]

One solution to this problem, Hamer argued, was to give blacks the responsibility and the knowledge they had been denied. The movement had taught blacks how to organize and assert power politically, but by the late 1960s Hamer recognized the glaring need for economic know-how. "The black community must have trained economic heroes as it has black political heroes," she told supporters. "*These men* MUST *know economic*." The most direct way to learn economic basics was to give people the chance to be financially responsible for their own lives. "For two years I went around the country beggin' money to buy food stamps," Hamer recalled of her fund-raising ventures on behalf of the poor. "I got $20,000, but folks still needed food." The lesson was clear. "You can give a man some food and he'll eat it. Then he'll be hungry again," Hamer argued. "But give a man some ground and he'll never be hungry no more."[3]

The problem, of course, was that the ground in the Delta was controlled by white planters. In Sunflower County, one observer estimated that only 71 blacks out of a population of nearly 25,000 owned any land at all, and the white-dominated power structure remained, in the words of one journalist, "an oppressive pattern virtually undented politically by the civil rights laws or economically by the poverty program." Having spent her childhood watching her mother clear the forests that became cotton fields, Hamer felt a powerful moral imperative to reclaim the land. "We must buy land immediately," she told northern supporters, "or our people will die forgotten."[4]

If not forgotten, many Mississippi blacks at least would die far away from their native land. Even as the movement broke down Jim Crow, full mechanization had made most black labor expendable, and blacks continued to flood north in search of opportunity. By 1970, the black population in Sunflower County had dipped below 25,000, a drop of nearly 25 percent in the previous decade. The median black family income in the county was a dismal $2,523, less than a third of white income, and more than 70 percent of black families lived in poverty. Some whites actively promoted migration. "What we've got to do, and what's going to be our salvation, is to encourage Negro migration away from here," one young white planter argued in 1964. "We are educating our Negroes for jobs in the north," remarked a Delta school superintendent. "The northern liberals have long evinced a tender-hearted concern for our Negroes. Well, we're sending them on up north to see what those tender hearts will do with them all." Eastland never advocated migration—he once claimed that if all the blacks moved out of Sunflower County, he would move with them—but he too recognized the economic bind in which farm workers had been placed. Though he supported an emergency fund of $25 million worth of free food for impoverished people, he did not believe that such a "free dole" would solve the long-term problem. "If the agriculture industry is completely mechanized, other methods must be found to employ agricultural workers," he argued in 1968. Even attracting industry would not solve the problem because "the vast numbers of these agricultural workers are unskilled for industrial work." Yet the senator offered no comprehensive solution.[5]

Hamer did. Through Freedom Farm, Hamer hoped to keep black families on the land that they had worked for so long. "I would not advise Blacks in the South to migrate to the North to change their situation," she insisted—they should stay put and develop their economic resources at home. Because few resources existed for blacks at home, Hamer sought to create them. The most successful of several black entrepreneurship ideas that arose in Mississippi around the time, Freedom Farm was an ambitious undertaking that aimed to teach poor people in Sunflower County how to wield economic power. It began with a small, communal "pig bank." Any poor family could borrow a pregnant sow and care for it until it gave birth, after which the family would return the sow to the bank and keep the piglets to raise for breeding and food. Started in 1968 with a donation of five boars and fifty gilts from the National Council of Negro Women, the pig bank helped provide ham, bacon, and pork for families accustomed to making do with chitterlings and other meat scraps. The idea blossomed into a self-sustaining operation. Within five years, it had produced thousands of pigs for hundreds of local families.[6]

The pig bank was just the beginning. Even as she initiated the pig bank, Hamer began raising money to purchase land that would become the core of a full farming operation. She contacted Lester Salamon, a teaching fellow at Harvard University, and in early 1969 the editor of the *Harvard Crimson*, James Fallows, wrote an article encouraging readers to send money to help the Freedom Farm. Wisconsin-based Measure for Measure also contributed early funding, and Hamer and the Freedom Farm Corporation (FFC) soon had about $8,000, enough money to get started. Unable to find available land near Ruleville—one observer claimed that "not even the poorest white landowner in Sunflower County would part with his deed if it meant selling to Freedom Farms"—Hamer located a forty-four acre plot of land nineteen miles northwest of town, accessible only by a gravel road that cut through cotton fields. The land was owned by C.B. Pratt, a black farmer with financial troubles, and the FFC secured the land by agreeing to pay Pratt's back taxes. While some whites undoubtedly frowned upon the prospect of a self-sustaining black-run cooperative, Freedom Farm benefited from local white help from the beginning. Much of its legal work, for example, was carried out by Pascol Townsend Jr., a city attorney from Drew who had objected vociferously to the movement during the summer of 1964 but who later befriended Hamer. Less than two years after the initial land purchase, FFC used donations from Washington, D.C.'s American Freedom from Hunger Foundation, singer Harry Belafonte, and other outside sources to buy 640 more acres from a white landowner, Paul Silverblatt, for a discounted price.[7]

By early 1971, Freedom Farm encompassed nearly seven hundred acres of poorly irrigated land in northern Sunflower County, about one-third of all the land owned by blacks in the area. The farm was worked communally and run by a small staff that included Hamer and Joseph Harris, a SNCC worker in his late thirties described by one observer as Hamer's "indispensable right-hand man." Anyone who needed food could join the effort and reap the collard greens, sweet potatoes, butter beans, cucumbers, corn, squash, okra, and other food crops while helping to harvest cotton and soybeans, cash crops that would pay the mortgage, salaries, and other expenses. Poor whites, too, could benefit from Freedom Farm because, Hamer argued, "hunger has no colour line." Hamer sold memberships in the cooperative at $1 apiece, but she never was willing to turn anyone away for lack of money. Thirty families bought memberships, while another fifteen hundred families shared in the harvests without paying a penny.[8]

Hamer envisioned Freedom Farm to be far more comprehensive than just a farm—she wanted it to meet all the needs that poor people might have. It became part farm, part social service agency, providing subsidized housing, child care, help with utility bills, and even college scholarships for local students. It also employed as many as thirty-two people. One enthusiastic journalist reported that the farm meant "houses, jobs, a new security, a new dignity for many in the Delta." The housing program was particularly successful. "We decided to organize everybody who lived in a shack—which was most of us," Hamer remembered, "and teach them how to take advantage of low cost [Farmers' Home Administration] and farm mortgages." The

Freedom Farm Corporation helped thirty-five poor families with down payments on FHA-subsidized homes, and it built 70 two-bedroom homes with affordable mortgages of between $38 and $100 a month. Hamer herself got a new home, which her friends and neighbors had insisted on building as an inspirational example to other poor families.[9]

Hamer harbored plans to open an African garment boutique to add an entrepreneurial dimension to the project, and she emphasized the critical importance of giving poor people experience in governing the operation. "Community living and group decision making is local self-government," she told supporters. "It is this type of community self-government that has been lost over the decades and thus created decay in our poor rural areas in the South and our Northern Ghettos." As one sympathetic observer noted, the entire venture was a repudiation of the capitalist ideal that stressed individual accumulation in favor of "black socialism" that emphasized collective uplift and racial pride. In a truly free society, Hamer believed, every person's needs would be met and limits would be placed on individual wealth. "Individual ownership of land should not exceed the amount necessary to make a living," she argued. Freedom was best expressed through communal living and collective action.[10]

Grand visions did not translate into lasting change, however. Despite significant financial help and sympathetic media attention from northern supporters, Freedom Farm never managed to become a successful, self-sustaining operation. Part of the difficulty, Hamer's friend L.C. Dorsey believed, was that Freedom Farm was trying to get blacks to return to the land at a time when they had been freed from agricultural labor and had no desire to go back. The entire idea of a cooperative enterprise was "very foreign," she explained, and working on the farm "was more of the same backbreaking work that they'd been doing all the time." To such people, the freedom for which the movement had struggled implied liberation from the fields.[11]

Freedom Farm also suffered from management problems that surfaced immediately, a product of the very paternalism and exploitation the program was designed to overcome. Because blacks rarely had been allowed to make decisions on their own behalf, they had little management experience. From a lack of accounting to poor long-term planning, the farm suffered from its leaders' inability to run an efficient operation, and these problems only grew over time as the enterprise fell deeper and deeper into debt. As early as 1971, the farm's board of directors feared that Freedom Farm would go bankrupt. Within a year, the board overhauled the organization to replace the "informal operation" with more professional management, and it separated the farming operations from the social service programs and political activities that Hamer pursued. The problems persisted, however, and Hamer's deteriorating health prevented her from being able to rectify them. After the sudden death of farm manager Joseph Harris in August 1974, the farm essentially collapsed. The directors began selling off the land, and within two years Freedom Farm was no more.[12]

Even the best manager would have had difficulty in transforming Freedom Farm into a successful economic venture. Simply put, labor-intensive, handpicked Freedom Farm cotton could not compete with its machine-harvested, chemically chopped cousin. By the time the operation was launched, small family farms were becoming a thing of the past, both in the Delta and all over rural America. In Sunflower County during the 1960s, the farm population dropped by more than 50 percent and the number of farms decreased by almost half, yet total farm acreage actually went up because farms were getting bigger. Agriculture was fast becoming the domain of large-scale operators and the cost-saving technology they could afford, in part because federal agriculture policies were tailored to suit the needs of large-scale cash-crop farmers such as Senator Eastland, who by 1969 was worth an estimated $3 million. One such policy was the federal subsidy program that paid farmers *not* to cultivate land in an effort to artificially boost prices. In 1968, as Freedom Farm struggled to get off the ground, the Department of Agriculture paid 340 farmers in Sunflower County more than $6.8 million to limit cotton production; the Eastland family plantation alone received nearly $170,000. (As word of these extraordinary subsidies spread, liberals in Congress placed a limit of $55,000 per recipient on federal farm payments, but large operators simply evaded the law; Eastland, for example, created six individual partners—himself, his wife, and his four children—each of whom was eligible to receive the maximum payment.) Without the luxury of being able to withhold land from production and without powerful friends in Congress and the Department of Agriculture, Hamer and Freedom Farm could not take advantage of the federal farm program.[13]

Such external forces exerted pressure on Freedom Farm, but the cooperative venture also suffered from internal difficulties that sapped the energy of its leaders. "Freedom Farm failed," suggested Ron Thornton, the manager of a similar cooperative venture in neighboring Bolivar County, "because of the plantation mentality." Unaccustomed to wielding economic power or managing their own affairs, many Freedom Farm families proved unwilling or unable to live up to the responsibilities that communal living demanded. From the beginning, Hamer refused to set conditions or work requirements for families to receive the benefits of Freedom Farm, envisioning an operation where everyone would contribute according to his or her abilities and would receive according to his or her need, as the early Christians had in the book of Acts. In practice, however, many families ignored the difficult, time-consuming labor during spring and summer and pitched in only when the harvest was at hand. Others simply came and got food because they were hungry, even if they contributed nothing to the overall condition of the farm.

The result was predictable: poor harvests and a lack of long-term maintenance that undermined not only the economic viability of the enterprise but also the collective spirit that sustained it. It was precisely how long-standing white planting families such as the Percys and the Eastlands might have wanted it. Economic changes destroyed sharecropping and the civil rights movement tore down segregation, but the plantation experience lingered. Thanks to the movement, blacks had both the will and the chance to work for themselves, but due to the limited schooling, constricted worldview, and abysmal skill level produced by a century of segregation, they often could not take advantage of the opportunity. When Freedom Farm presented poor blacks with the chance to own land and work cooperatively, too many took advantage of the system by harvesting crops but not helping out in other ways. It was as if they were conforming to the very stereotypes about blacks that the Percys and the Eastlands not only had concocted but also helped create and perpetuate. Ironically, in its attempt to free poor people from local white domination, Freedom Farm itself became dependent on outside white contributors for survival. When that support dwindled after 1972, Hamer's dream shriveled.[14]

"A HAPPY, CONTENTED POPULATION"

Like Fannie Lou Hamer, James Eastland also harbored visions of a better world. Unlike Hamer's dream of an egalitarian, cooperative agricultural community, however, Eastland's ideal was capitalist and white-dominated, a world where social harmony reigned because everyone—blacks and whites, workers and managers, women and men—understood their respective places and duties. The safe, segregated world of his childhood had disappeared, and by the late 1960s it was clear that even continued resistance to civil rights efforts would not restore it. As the new reality of Delta life sank in, Eastland became somewhat wistful about the passing of the old order and sought a return to the kind of life he had known. He found it halfway around the world, in Rhodesia.

To Eastland, Rhodesia was the "bright spot" on a "dark continent," an island of stable white minority rule in a sea of Communism, decolonization, youth protest, and other attacks on the traditional world order. Located in south-central Africa, landlocked Rhodesia had broken apart in the 1960s when the British government dismantled its colonial empire. While Northern Rhodesia gained independence in 1963 as the black-controlled state of Zambia, whites in Southern Rhodesia (called simply "Rhodesia") requested independence as a white-dominated nation. Led by Ian Smith, white Rhodesians, who accounted for roughly 5 percent of the population but controlled half of all the land, feared the loss of their privileged status within Rhodesian society, and they resisted the idea of native black self-government. In November 1965, after the British refused to recognize Rhodesian independence because the proposed regime would not guarantee the United Nations mandate of majority rule, Smith unilaterally declared independence. Great Britain responded by slapping economic sanctions on the new nation, and the UN Security Council followed suit in December 1966. Eager to defuse the situation and maintain British support for the war in Vietnam, the United

States quickly agreed to abide by the sanctions but refused, along with the British, to send troops or weapons to opponents of the Smith regime.[15]

Eastland and other American segregationists applauded Smith's firm stand for white rule in Rhodesia, and they angrily denounced American complicity in the policy of economic sanctions. "Never in the history of American diplomacy has the cooperation of the American Government been pledged to such an unworthy cause," Eastland argued. Within months of Rhodesia's declaration of independence, more than a dozen pro-Rhodesia organizations sprang up in the United States, mostly based in the South. The Rhodesian Information Office was particularly effective in publicizing and promoting the Smith regime through newsletters and organized tours. Eastland became one of independent Rhodesia's most vociferous congressional supporters and excoriated American foreign policy in Africa. "Every time a group of partially-educated, half-savage tribes has constituted an alleged government and declared its country free and independent," he fumed, "we have been pressured by an unreasoning fear of world opinion into immediate recognition of that government." The United States supported "new, unstable, little so-called countries" but could not bring itself to support the stable white nation of Rhodesia. It was clear, Eastland insisted, that American policy in Africa was based on one principle: "increased power for the blacks; but no increased power for the whites." He worked to reverse the travel ban that had been leveled against Rhodesian representatives, encouraged Rhodesians to come to Mississippi to speak, and pushed lawmakers to extend full diplomatic recognition to the nation.[16]

Eastland's spirited defense of the white regime manifested the racial and economic priorities embedded within his conception of freedom. Eastland repeatedly called upon the federal government to recognize the new state, in the "interests of the United States and Western Civilization." The bold white Rhodesians were building a civilization in the African wilderness the same way heroic American pioneers had hacked their way through the wilderness of the New World. Much as Americans had two centuries before, Eastland argued, these white settlers were throwing off the shackles of British domination and were committed to creating a free, democratic nation. Only hypocrites would demand that white Rhodesians allow black Rhodesians to vote, participate in government, and have equal access to land; after all, few Americans would be willing to give their land back to the Indians from whom it was taken. Ian Smith was akin to George Washington, Eastland maintained, and the white Rhodesians were latter-day Americans sacrificing for their freedom.[17]

Aside from racial and cultural ties to Rhodesia, Eastland emphasized the Smith regime's ideological and material support for the United States in the Cold War. Unlike other nations such as Nigeria, Rwanda, and Upper Volta, Rhodesia was a "friendly, peaceful, non-Communist country" that protected American interests in Africa, and thus it was part of the "free world." Indeed, Eastland argued, the Smith government was a better friend to the United States than its supposed ally, Great Britain, was. Where Great Britain had withheld support from the American effort to blockade North Vietnam, Rhodesia had offered not only to adhere to the blockade but also to send white Rhodesian troops to Vietnam. Furthermore, the African nation provided more than 60 percent of America's supply of chrome, a critical material in the production of missiles. Sanctions would hurt U.S. defense contractors by forcing them to buy chrome at higher prices from the world's other large producer, the Soviet Union. The Cold War imperative was clear, Eastland insisted: the United States had to support its anti-Communist friends and lift the sanctions. In early 1966, he offered a resolution that called upon Congress to cease the "inhumane, illegal, arbitrary, unfair, harmful, and costly" economic sanctions, compensate Americans harmed by the sanctions, and resume the "policy of honorable self-interest" toward Rhodesia.[18]

While Eastland decried the sanctions, Hamer and other civil rights activists belittled the U.S. government's efforts to counter white Rhodesians' power grab. Along with its British allies, the Johnson administration steadfastly refused to support the use of force against the Smith regime, preferring instead to pursue diplomatic means to end the crisis. This nonviolent approach contrasted sharply not only with the massive military undertaking under way in Vietnam but also with the American response in the Congo just a year earlier. When Congolese rebels kidnapped two thousand white foreigners in November 1964, the United States immediately sent American planes to aid Belgian forces in a successful rescue effort. But when millions of black Rhodesians faced an illegal, undemocratic regime bent on preserving white supremacy by force, the administration took a hands-off approach. Hamer insisted that the government was allowing "a handful of white folk" to take over because officials simply did not care about Africans. "They wasn't worried about it, cause it was all black folk," she complained. "You know, let them be killed." Even after a full-scale war broke out between Smith loyalists and African guerrillas in August 1967, the Johnson administration continued to oppose force in Rhodesia, and the white-dominated government remained in power.[19]

By the late 1960s, Rhodesia had become a pariah state. In a world where the political current flowed toward majority rule and self-determination, Rhodesia stood like an immovable boulder. Impressed by the nation's resilience, Eastland decided to see one of the world's last bastions of white supremacy for himself. Traveling at his own expense in early 1969, he spent three weeks touring Rhodesia, as well as South Africa. He returned with glowing reports. "The future of Rhodesia is indeed bright," Eastland gushed to readers of the Jackson *Clarion-Ledger*. Waxing lyrical, he wrote, "In this land where wild beasts and uncivilized natives roamed the dense jungles less than a decade ago, brilliant cities rise on remote mountaintops and productive crops burst forth." Like the turn-of-the-century boosters who had touted the Delta as a planter's paradise, Eastland extolled the virtues of the white-run African nation.[20]

Coming from the Delta to the heart of black-majority Africa, Eastland could not help but make parallels to his native land. "A close-up look at Rhodesia," he observed, "gives one the impression it is much like our native Mississippi," though the similarities were closer to Sunflower County rather than the state as a whole. Not only was the climate similar—thus supporting an agricultural economy built on cotton—but Rhodesia, with a population of four million blacks and barely a quarter million whites, "bears the earmarks of the same situation we in Mississippi face." Like white Sunflower Countians, white Rhodesians were heavily outnumbered, yet they wielded control over the economy, government, and social institutions of the land. Their steadfast determination to hold on to power inspired Eastland, who insisted that "its people, the backbone of this fine country, are as near

like Mississippians as any other place I've been." Socially, economically, and politically, Rhodesia resembled the Sunflower County of the
1920s, before the civil rights movement, before mechanization, before all the vast changes that had transformed his home.[21]

Always the planter, Eastland was particularly impressed with the
Rhodesian cotton economy. Like the Delta planters of his childhood,
white Rhodesian cotton farmers enjoyed unrestricted access to large
tracts of land and could draw upon vast pools of cheap black labor. Because native black Rhodesians largely subsisted outside the capitalist
economy and commanded abysmally low wages, labor-intensive farming methods remained economically viable. Mechanized farming had
yet to make its way to Rhodesian cotton fields, so bolls still were
picked by hand—an advantage that made Rhodesian cotton superior,
in Eastland's mind, to the rougher variety produced by machines on
his plantation in Sunflower County. White planters in Rhodesia did
not have to worry about their black workers registering to vote or en-
gaging in demonstrations because there was no organized black movement for social justice; whites enjoyed the superficial serenity of legal
domination that Delta planters had lost.

The perceived absence of racial problems in Rhodesia made a
deep impression on the traveling senator. Rhodesia "is making a frank,
honest approach to the problem of the Black Rhodesian," he told his
constituents. From the funding of government housing in specifically
black areas of the cities to constitutional protections for blacks, the
Rhodesian government, Eastland argued, was fulfilling its paternal obligation to care for blacks. Walking the streets of Rhodesia, he felt safe
and secure, just as he had back in Doddsville growing up. "Rhodesia
has safe streets—a land where policemen carry no guns, where families walk the streets alone at night, and where I, myself, could see firsthand a happy, contented population." Because blacks knew their
place, he believed, they did not feel compelled to challenge righteous
white authority. The result, in Eastland's mind, was clear. "Rhodesia
has an ingredient which is sadly lacking in America," he opined nos-
talgically. "This is racial harmony."[22]

"GET UP AND WALLOP HIM"

Eastland's Rhodesian dreams clashed with the harsh reality he faced when he returned back home to Sunflower County. No matter what illusions he and other white segregationists may have harbored before the movement, by the late 1960s they too could see that American blacks, and Americans in general, were not the "happy, contented population" he claimed to have witnessed in Rhodesia. The continual unrest in American cities, the murders of Martin Luther King Jr. and Robert Kennedy, and the violence outside the Democratic National Convention in Chicago generated widespread anxiety about growing lawlessness in American society. Kennedy's death hit the senator particularly hard, as the two men had worked closely together for more than a decade, despite their political differences. Eastland himself came perilously close to tragedy in the summer of 1968, when he was aboard a plane that was hijacked by an emotionally disturbed young man who sought to divert the airliner to Cuba. Though the situation was resolved peacefully, it underscored Eastland's sense that the nation was careening out of control. America itself had been hijacked, the senator believed, by a motley collection of Communist revolutionaries, civil rights activists, and federal bureaucrats.[23]

Throughout the 1960s, Eastland felt as if he and his conservative allies had been battered by the tremendous changes in American society, changes that promised to revolutionize the way political power, social mores, and economic relations were structured in Sunflower County and the world around it. Having been unable to block the legislation and court decisions that dismantled the legal edifice of Jim Crow and opened unprecedented opportunities for blacks across the South, he remained vigilant for the opportunity to counterattack. "When somebody comes along and hits you and knocks you down, then just continue to lie there," the senator often told staff members. "And while you're there, just grab a stick and hold it. 'Cause sooner or later that son of a bitch is going to come right back by you. And then you can get up and wallop him." Grabbing the stick of his Judiciary Committee chairmanship, he waited for the chance to wallop the institution he blamed for much of the mess: the Supreme Court. As self-styled radicals loudly and often violently demonstrated in the streets, the planter-politician pursued a quietly revolutionary agenda behind the closed doors of the Senate, a strategy aimed at eroding the judicial bedrock that underlay the liberal legislative triumphs he opposed.[24]

For much of American history, the judiciary had been the most socially, politically, and economically conservative branch of the federal government. Not until Franklin Roosevelt's second term, when the president attempted to pack the Court with sympathetic justices, did the Court begin a slow process of reorienting the direction of its decisions toward more liberal goals. With Dwight Eisenhower's appointment of California's three-time Republican governor Earl Warren as chief justice in 1953, the Court accelerated its pace of change, charting an unprecedented course in American jurisprudence that invigorated liberals and infuriated conservatives across the nation. The Warren Court redefined the role of the judiciary and upended precedent in a wide range of areas, from political apportionment and anti-Communist investigations to criminal defendants' rights and the separation of church and state, as well as school desegregation. With its broad interpretation of the Constitution and its willingness to intervene in controversial political issues, the Warren Court was overstepping its bounds, Eastland argued: "Reading into the law something that is not there is the same as writing the law." He sought to restore the Supreme Court, and the judicial branch as a whole, to its traditional conservative role. Where protestors took to the streets to express their displeasure with the political and economic system, Eastland instead turned inward, to the Judiciary Committee he ruled so rigidly.[25]

Widely known within Congress simply as "the Chairman," Eastland by the late 1960s had become a Judiciary Committee institution, a man both loved and hated, but always respected, for the ruthlessly effective way in which he ran the committee. From the assignment of senators to the committee to the number of committee staff a senator could hire to the questions a member could ask in a hearing, he had "absolute control over every aspect of the Committee," liberal senator Edward Kennedy acknowledged. "A political debt is never paid off," Eastland told staff members, and he worked to help fellow committee members of both parties get reelected—so long as they did not challenge his authority. "He uses power as skillfully as anyone I have ever known," one liberal senator marveled; frustrated critics agreed, but they found his power maddening. "His is not the ennobling power to shape bold national policies," complained columnists Jack Anderson and Les Whitten, "but the negative, petty power to frustrate and delay the proposals of others." Eastland's intransigence was legendary. "Once in position he has proved almost impossible to move," Senate minority leader Mike Mansfield observed, "and indeed it requires nearly the entire Senate to budge him." Eastland proudly publicized Mansfield's comment in his campaign literature.[26]

As the chairman, Eastland was in a unique position to help shape the long-term course of the federal judiciary because all presidential nominees had to be vetted through his Judiciary Committee. In effect, he served as a gatekeeper of the confirmation process by which the Senate approved or disapproved the president's judicial appointments. Eastland served on the Standing Committee on the Federal Judiciary of the American Bar Association (ABA), a nonpartisan panel that rated all candidates for the federal bench and played an increasingly important role in the nomination process during the 1950s and 1960s. He also was the sole recipient of an official FBI background report on each nominee, and he had the power to set the timetable and agenda for hearings. He used his power to ensure the appointment of lower-level federal judges who would toe his line on race and economics—men such as Harold Cox, a 1961 appointee who became notorious for his strident efforts to block any civil rights measures, and Charles Clark, a desegregation foe appointed by Nixon to stanch the flow of liberal rulings from the Fifth Circuit Court of Appeals. (Contrary to oft-published historical accounts, Eastland and Cox were not college roommates—they were friends, but Cox was a few years older. He was in law school at the University of Mississippi while Eastland was an undergraduate.)[27]

Clark's nomination revealed how Eastland manipulated his power to produce the results he desired. The Nixon administration originally sought to appoint Judge William Keady to the Fifth Circuit, but Eastland objected to Keady's recent rulings on school desegregation cases. Instead, Eastland pushed Clark, who had represented several school districts that sought to delay federal desegregation orders. Knowing

Clark would encounter resistance among liberals on his committee, Eastland delayed voting on his nomination until Moratorium Day, when liberal senators were away making speeches against the Vietnam War. In their absence, he called a hearing, voted on the nomination, and reported it to the full Senate, where it was approved.[28]

Although actively involved with lower-level nominees to the federal bench, for the first decade of his chairmanship Eastland played a relatively reserved role in the Supreme Court nomination process, generally deferring to the president's wishes even over personal objections. He had not blocked President Kennedy's nomination of Arthur Goldberg in 1962 or President Johnson's nomination of Abe Fortas in 1965, although both men were avowed liberals who promised to become solid members of the Warren Court's left wing. But the accumulation of grievances during the 1960s, along with rumblings of right-wing resentment at Eastland's passivity in the nomination process, led him to abandon his reservations.[29]

The first indication that Eastland would use his influence to block or delay Supreme Court appointments came in 1967, when Johnson nominated the first black justice for the high court, Thurgood Marshall. As the NAACP's chief counsel in the *Brown* case, Marshall had earned the everlasting enmity of white segregationists in the South, but his moderate legal approach also had won little admiration among black activists in SNCC. President Johnson hoped that the historic nominee would sail through the confirmation process, but Chairman Eastland had other ideas. First, he delayed all action on the nomination for a full month, allowing Marshall's opponents to muster a series of attacks on the nominee's character and judicial ability. He then opened hearings at which he, Strom Thurmond of South Carolina, and Sam Ervin of North Carolina challenged Marshall on his judicial philosophy and charged him with being racist against whites. After the hearings closed, Eastland delayed the committee's vote for another eleven days; when Marshall won an 11–5 vote in committee, Eastland joined other southern senators in a "mini-filibuster" to publicize their objections, though they eventually yielded and the Senate easily approved the nation's first black Supreme Court justice.[30]

Eastland was only beginning to flex his political muscles on judicial nominees. After the Marshall nomination, the next big test came in the summer of 1968, when the controversial Chief Justice Warren announced his retirement. Warren's surprise announcement, which had come just two months after Johnson's own decision not to run for reelection, struck many conservatives as a transparent attempt to give the outgoing Johnson an opportunity to extend the liberal dominance on the Court. When Johnson decided to elevate Justice Abe Fortas to chief justice, Eastland and other conservatives turned the promotion into a referendum of sorts on the Warren Court and its liberal rulings. "At the heart of the matter," *Newsweek* magazine reported, was that "there plainly are many Americans who have rallied to the conservative outcry that the Court has gone too far, too fast." Eastland, who objected to Fortas's public linking of black civil rights with the Jewish struggle for justice, agreed. Warning the president privately that Fortas's promotion would force a prolonged debate that would "tear this country apart," he first sought to derail Fortas's promotion by stalling, telling Johnson that he would let the justice out of his committee "at my own time." He then took the unprecedented step of having Fortas sit before the Judiciary Committee for a series of hearings, the first time a nominee for chief justice had to do so.[31]

During four days of hearings, Eastland joined his southern colleagues in peppering Fortas with questions about his judicial philosophy and his advisory relationship with the president, making it increasingly clear that their real target was not Fortas himself but the Warren Court and its judicial approach of flexible constitutional interpretation. Eastland crystallized his objections to such "judicial activism"—an issue that would divide liberals and conservatives for another generation—by asking Fortas if the Constitution retained its "original meaning," or "do you believe that provisions of the Constitution and laws should be reassessed and reinterpreted by the Court in light of changing social and economic conditions?" Fortas's response that the words of the Constitution were not "simple and clear and unmistakable in their meaning" only confirmed the senator's fears that as chief justice Fortas would continue the Warren approach. The drawn-out hearings and ensuing filibuster wore down Fortas and his backers, and shortly before the November elections the beleaguered nominee requested that the president withdraw his name from consideration. It was the first time since 1795 that the Senate had blocked a nominee for chief justice, and according to one observer, Eastland's opposition from atop the Judiciary Committee was "the outcome determinant."[32]

The Fortas nomination fracas launched a new era in the judicial nomination process, one in which ideologues swapped sides as liberals sought to protect the Warren Court's legacy and conservatives demanded a radical break from its precedents. As chair of the Judiciary Committee, Eastland generally had more power to delay and block nominations than to push his own favored candidate, but in 1971 he was able to shepherd a controversial conservative nominee through his committee and the Senate as a whole, despite objections from a wide range of liberal and civil liberties groups. This youthful nominee ultimately had the most profound long-term impact on turning the Court toward Eastland's conception of freedom. His name was William Rehnquist.

At forty-seven, Rehnquist was the youngest nominee since William O. Douglas thirty years earlier, but he had built a solid reputation as a brilliant lawyer. As an assistant attorney general who frequently testified on Capitol Hill, Rehnquist had grown close to Eastland, and the aging senator took him under his wing, treating him almost as a son. After two justices retired due to terminal illnesses in mid-1971, President Nixon nominated Rehnquist along with Virginia judge Lewis Powell, a highly respected conservative magistrate whose age—he was sixty-four—helped lessen opposition to his nomination. Rehnquist, on the other hand, drew considerable fire from liberal groups that challenged him as a "right-wing zealot" who was "out of tune with the times" and offered only "a lonely Western voice echoing the arguments of the Deep South." Knowing that Rehnquist's critics supported Powell, Eastland, with Nixon's backing, tied the two nominees together. "You will not get Powell without Rehnquist," he told liberals on his committee; their confirmations would be "double or nothing." One potential stumbling block was the ABA. Fearing that the influential lawyers' group might give Rehnquist an unfavorable rating, Eastland let it be known that if the committee did not approve Rehnquist, he would force all twelve members to explain themselves under oath. Eastland's pressure helped ensure that the ABA, by a 9–3 vote, approved his favored nominee. Armed with ABA approval, the chairman then pushed the confirmations of both Rehnquist and Powell through his committee simultaneously, and both men won approval in the full Senate.[33]

"DO NOT PATRONIZE US ANY LONGER"

Rehnquist's confirmation sharpened the rightward turn of the Supreme Court, which by late 1971 had four new members without ties to the Warren era. Although the Court under Chief Justice Warren Burger would not prove as ideologically conservative as Eastland and others might have liked, it nonetheless began a slow process of backtracking away from some of the more controversial Warren Court rulings. Most significant for Eastland was the Court's shifting position on school desegregation, the issue that initially had thrust the senator into the national spotlight in the 1950s.

Soon after his return from Rhodesia in the spring of 1969, Eastland and other conservative whites in Sunflower County and across the rural South faced the day of reckoning they had been avoiding since the *Brown* decision in 1954. For ten years following *Brown*, southern schools, particularly in rural areas, remained almost completely segregated. Following the Civil Rights Act of 1964, which forbade segregation in school districts that received federal funding, southern school boards passed "freedom-of-choice" plans that eliminated all references to race in school assignments and gave parents and children of all races the freedom to choose which schools to attend. Ostensibly race-neutral, these plans effectively corralled and limited desegregation efforts for years, as the few black families who dared to exercise their freedom to attend white public schools faced physical intimidation and economic harassment. Some white parents rejected even the token integration that accompanied freedom of choice, and they organized private white schools, dubbed "segregation academies" by critics. Several were established in Sunflower County, including Indianola Academy and North Sunflower Academy (north of Ruleville), but the majority of white students remained in the public schools for several more years. In the face of continued resistance to desegregation, federal courts became more forceful in mandating integration, and in two key cases, *Green v. County School Board of New*

Kent County, Virginia in 1968 and *Alexander v. Holmes County, Mississippi, Board of Education* a year later, the Supreme Court declared that integration had to be accomplished immediately.[34]

The court rulings angered Eastland. He charged that schools and children bore an unfair burden of federal court rulings and had become "pawns in this monstrous sociological experiment" carried out by the judiciary and the Department of Health, Education, and Welfare. The courts may have destroyed freedom-of-choice plans, Eastland argued, but "there is another even more precious freedom of choice which until now they have not destroyed. And that is the freedom to choose whether one will attend the public schools at all." As a result, Eastland pointed out, "there will be total segregation, because all of the white children will go to the private schools, which are open to any white child, and hence the destruction of public education in that area." His words were not an idle threat. The *Alexander* ruling came down in the middle of the 1969–70 school term, and during the Christmas holidays school districts across the South scrambled to come up with feasible integration plans. In Sunflower County, U.S. district judge William Keady ordered the Indianola school district to abandon its dual school system and offer fully integrated schools within two weeks. The result was chaotic and dramatic: essentially all the remaining white students and teachers in the public schools, along with a fair bit of school property, left en masse, flooding the local academies. Almost overnight, the public schools turned from white to black, and remained so for decades. "The decision came down on a Friday, and by Monday all the whites were over at the academy," remembered Isabel Lee, the only black member of the Indianola school board. As white students left the schools and public school enrollment dropped across the Delta, black teachers and administrators often found themselves demoted or fired, and formerly black schools were sometimes closed.[35]

"Is this progress?" Eastland wondered aloud in a speech on the Senate floor on February 9, 1970. He had risen to speak in support of his fellow Mississippian, Senator John Stennis, who had introduced an amendment to the Elementary and Secondary Education Act that would require the federal government to combat school segregation "without regard to the origin or cause of such segregation." Like Stennis, he was convinced that if whites in the North faced full integration of their schools, they would rebel too. What upset Eastland most was that white southerners were being forced to do what he felt no white people anywhere in the country would accept. "The truth and the fact is that almost no white parent wants his child to attend a school where Negro students are in the vast majority," he argued. Using his second home of Washington, D.C., as an example, he emphasized that white parents in that black-majority city had fled to the "safe" suburbs of Maryland and Virginia rather than place their children in a minority position in school; those who remained in the city limits sent their children to private schools just as Sunflower County whites did. "I do not condemn them for this," Eastland insisted. "In my judgment, they have every right to act in the best interests of their children." Eastland himself had sent his children to private, white-majority (though not always segregated) schools in the Washington area, and he knew that most of his colleagues did likewise. He challenged them to think about how they themselves might react if forced to send their children to black-majority schools filled with the offspring of the lower classes. Which congressman "would wish to be forced to send a child, not to school, but into real physical danger; not to a first-rate facility where the child can prepare to assume a position in our society, but into an environment which guarantees inferior education which will penalize the child through all his days?" It was a question few whites in any part of the country would answer honestly, either in 1970 or in the early twenty-first century.[36]

Northerners often pointed out that the reason federal courts targeted southern school districts was not sectional discrimination but rather the difference between the de jure segregation of southern law versus the de facto segregation that resulted from northern housing patterns and demographics. Such distinctions were "meaningless," Eastland contended. The "so-called fortuitous" housing patterns that allow for de facto school segregation in the North "did not just happen," Eastland noted, anticipating a line of argument that future historians later documented in careful studies of Detroit, Boston, and other northern cities. Rather, "they exist because the law sanctioned or permitted them to grow." Indeed, for generations whites in the North had built a legal infrastructure that supported the development of segregated housing patterns that in turn led to segregated schools. "My friends of the North, and East, and West," Eastland warned, "do not patronize us any longer. Your people feel the same way about this as I and my people. Your people do not want it and will not have it. We only ask the same privilege."[37] Whites in the South, Eastland insisted, wanted what whites across the nation already had: the freedom to send their children to whichever school they wanted.

On the same February day that Eastland spoke for the Stennis amendment, one liberal northern senator shocked observers by agreeing with the senators from Mississippi. Senator Abraham Ribicoff, a Jewish Democrat from Connecticut, had become increasingly frustrated by the federal government's unwillingness to challenge the growing de facto segregation in northern and western suburbs. Northerners had shown "monumental hypocrisy in its treatment of the black man," Ribicoff argued, and he chastised his fellow liberals for ignoring the fundamental cause of school segregation, "the dual society that exists in every metropolitan area—the black society of the central city and the white society of the suburbs." Ribicoff's speech infuriated liberals who feared it would spark a retreat from desegregation, while conservatives pounced on the opportunity to divide the opposition. Throughout the early 1970s, Eastland, Stennis, and their allies continued to press the issue of consistent enforcement, calculating that if northerners had to abide by the rules they foisted upon the South, they would abandon their civil rights plans—as one Jackson editor claimed, "Eastland is out liberaling the liberals to beat them at their own game." Their hypothesis soon would be tested, courtesy of the Supreme Court's 1971 ruling in *Swann v. Charlotte-Mecklenburg (NC) Board of Education*. In its momentous "busing" decision, among the last before Rehnquist joined the Court, the high court ruled that school districts had to achieve racial balance in all their schools, even if it meant busing students from one side of town to another. Busing became a national political firestorm that quickly spread from San Francisco and Denver to Ferndale, Michigan, and Boston as whites across the North and West marched, protested, and sometimes rioted to prevent black students from being bused to their neighborhood schools. "In many parts of the North," influential columnist Stewart Alsop wrote, "this ruling has aroused passions as fierce as those the 1954 integration ruling aroused in the South." It was as if Eastland had written the script.[38]

Unlike Eastland, whose children had all graduated from high school long before desegregation hit Sunflower County, Fannie Lou Hamer and her family had been on the front lines of the school integration fight for several years. Her fourteen year-old daughter, Vergie, had been one of the first black students to attend a previously all-white school in Ruleville. When white students abandoned the public schools after the *Alexander* ruling, Hamer joined Carver Randle of the Indianola chapter of the NAACP in filing suit in federal court to force the Sunflower County school district to come up with a more effective desegregation plan and to protect black teachers and administrators from losing their jobs. The case, *Hamer et al. v. Sunflower County*, was decided in June 1970, and Hamer could claim victory. Judge Keady ruled that the county district had to merge schools by September (as the Indianola district had in January), and he followed the Hamer group's recommendations to use nondiscriminatory practices in the hiring and firing of school personnel.[39]

Yet, as Hamer recognized, legal victories did not change reality on the ground. Even by fall 1970, when the full effect of the *Brown* decision finally hit the rural schools of Sunflower County, the county schools were already more than 85 percent black due to white flight to the academies. Little desegregation was even possible in Sunflower County when the Supreme Court's busing decision took the nation by storm in 1971, but the furor over busing nonetheless angered Fannie Lou Hamer and other integrationists. For decades in the South, children had been bused to school to preserve school segregation, but whites nationwide now found the idea of "forced busing" objectionable. "Why, white kids were bused in Ruleville. Black kids were bused, too," Hamer noted sardonically. "Kids were bused right by the black school, and black kids were bused by the white school." But the real issue was not busing per se, as Citizens' Council director William Simmons wryly observed. "It's the destination of the bus." With their passionate objections to busing, whites across the nation revealed their unwillingness to allow their children to attend a school that included a significant number of black students. Hamer found herself reluctantly agreeing with Eastland, as Senator Ribicoff had. "It's no different" in other parts of the country, she lamented. "I thought that if we could just let the people in the North know how bad things were down here, they would do something about it. But things get bad up there, and when you start talking about busing, they get worse."[40]

While Hamer despaired, Eastland continued to push for uniform enforcement of federal desegregation laws. As much as he personally objected to the idea of busing—he, along with President Nixon and other conservatives, called for a constitutional amendment to ban the practice—Eastland recognized the immeasurable boost the Court's ruling had given his cause. The widespread opposition to busing among whites across the nation, he contended, had driven home to northern whites the "double standard" on civil rights that had unfairly demonized the South. "The pendulum is swinging back toward conservatism," he boasted in May 1972, "and it is our job to see that it swings back far enough." The key, he emphasized, was "to keep the heat on the north."[41]

By 1974, the Supreme Court itself had begun to back away from school desegregation. In its *Milliken v. Bradley* decision, the Court prohibited busing across school district lines, allowing suburban whites to avoid integrating their schools with inner-city blacks. The decision launched a generational process of retreat away from the goal of integrated schooling, and William Rehnquist, joined by three other Nixon appointees that Eastland had supported, provided the necessary votes. By virtue of his powerful position atop the Judiciary Committee and his uncompromising positions on the judiciary, Eastland had helped turn his nemesis, the Supreme Court, into the bulwark of conservatism that it traditionally had been before Franklin Roosevelt. Eastland later listed the packing of the Court among his top career achievements. It was a Second Redemption of sorts to follow the Second Reconstruction. The civil rights activists that Eastland labeled "modern Thaddeus Stevenses" now faced the same fate that their predecessors had.[42]

10

"Right on Back
to the Plantation"

The Eastland plantation still leaves a large footprint in Sunflower County. Now run by Senator Eastland's son, Woods, it stretches for about three miles on either side of Highway 442 west of Doddsville. The land is contiguous, so you could walk from one end of the plantation to the other, though you would need your swim trunks. Less than 40 percent of the land is good cotton-growing soil; the rest is buckshot used mainly for rice and soybean planting these days. Like most plantation owners in Sunflower County, Eastland no longer lives on the land and is not involved in the day-to-day operations of the farm. He serves as president of Staplcotn, the nation's oldest cotton marketing cooperative, and lives in a comfortable home in Indianola nearly twenty miles to the south. Woods Eastland is quite a different man from his father. Naturally affable like the grandfather for whom he was named, Woods grew up primarily in Washington, D.C., and attended a lightly integrated, though exclusive, prep school before leaving home for Vanderbilt University and the University of Mississippi Law School. Three years in the Navy exposed him to confident, capable, and non-deferential northern blacks, "a liberating experience," he recalled, that helped him adjust to and succeed in a new world that his father never understood.[1]

There are few traces of Freedom Farm left, but the modest brick home where Fannie Lou Hamer spent her final days still stands in Ruleville. Like the local post office, the street has been renamed in her honor, though until recently the signs managed to mangle her last name—perhaps "Hammer" was more fitting for a woman whose strength and resilience helped destroy legal segregation. Yet the misspelled signs somehow seem symbolic of what happened to Hamer's movement in the generation after her death. Things just did not turn out the way she hoped they would. Her children and grandchildren, literal and metaphorical, continue to inhabit a world that is largely separate and unequal from the world of Eastland's children and grandchildren. This postmovement world grew out of the 1970s, a crucial decade during which the contours of a new—but in many ways familiar—Sunflower County took shape.

"MAC, WE AIN'T FREE YET"

Much changed in the fifteen years after Hamer's first mass meeting at William Chapel, even in Sunflower County. By the mid-1970s, massive resistance had given way to cautious white moderation, along with a healthy dose of resignation. Whites addressed the former sharecropper as "Mrs. Hamer," blacks registered and voted without intimidation, and her hometown even sponsored a Fannie Lou Hamer Day. "Everything the white Southerner once said would never happen has happened," noted Hodding Carter III, the white Delta newsman who became a spokesman in the Carter administration. "Mind-boggling" changes had occurred, another white Deltan wrote in *The Nation*, "fundamental, deep and damaging to the psyche of many of the state's residents, who have had to see their old comfortable standards collapse." In 1971, William Waller won the governorship without having to resort to "nigger-baiting," ending an era of vicious racial rhetoric in political campaigns. Boycotts had demonstrated the strength of black economic power, and merchants became more attuned to their black customers' needs. Mississippi State University even had a black quarterback on its football team, as well as a black "Mr. MSU"—important developments in a football-crazy state. Many young whites, in particular, sought to move away from resistance. "Integration, alone, is not the problem," one white senior at a Jackson high school observed. "People who resist are the problem."[2]

The pillars of James Eastland's world seemed to have collapsed, not only in his home state but across the globe as well. "There can be no compromise with communism," Eastland had warned three decades before, "because one cannot compromise with death." Yet a Republican president he supported took the initiative to open relations with Communist China and seek détente with the Soviet Union; "containment" became "constructive engagement," the "life-and-death struggle" fizzled into "peaceful coexistence." The war against the Communists in Vietnam ended disastrously for the United States, which abandoned its South Vietnamese allies in 1973 after its humiliating failure to defeat a militarily inferior force. The American economy, the juggernaut that had witnessed nearly thirty years of unprecedented growth, suffered from a combination of stagnation and inflation, an unprecedented condition of "stagflation" that was exacerbated by an oil embargo imposed by Arab nations. Even cotton, the economic basis of Eastland's wealth and his way of life, no longer commanded the kingly respect it once enjoyed in the global economy as competition from polyester and other synthetics whittled cotton's market share to historically low levels in the mid-1970s.[3]

Yet as Eastland watched his world unravel, it was Hamer who found the new order most upsetting. "It seems to me we are just going backward," she lamented in 1973. Despite the years of protests, despite the risks she endured, little had changed for Hamer. Her world, and the world of most Sunflower County blacks, remained remarkably segregated and limited. From church and school to work and politics, blacks and whites lived very different, very separate lives. What had happened? Was this the freedom for which she had fought? To Hamer, freedom always had broadly encompassed politics, education, economics, and psychology. In each area, she feared, the lives of her grandchildren would be as circumscribed by circumstance as hers had been. "Mac," Hamer confided to her longtime friend and admirer Charles McLaurin in 1976, "we ain't free yet."[4]

Residual racism remained a constant and formidable barrier to progress—it would take many decades for the generations of white people weaned on white supremacy to die off—but black voters no longer faced legal obstacles to their participation in the political process. Yet the 1970s did not witness the revolution for which Hamer had hoped. Hamer lost a campaign for the state senate in 1971, her third bid for office, and health problems prevented her from running again. Despite the movement, many blacks remained unregistered, and even registered black voters sometimes did not go to the polls. "We are in the majority," complained one frustrated black activist in Sunflower County, "but it seems the more elections there are, the less we become involved." Black candidates often faced formidable odds in at-large, majority-black voting districts, not the least of which was a tendency among some black voters to defer to white candidates. Robert Clark, the first black since Reconstruction to serve in the Mississippi House of Representatives, found it difficult to win support among Sunflower County blacks for his campaign for U.S. Congress in the early 1980s. Only after Clark had won support from important local whites did black voters warm up. "They live with those white folk," he explained. "They depend on the white folk." Legal barriers had fallen, but psychological obstacles remained. "Our fight now is a mental fight more than anything else," commented black Sunflower County activist and lawyer Johnnie E. Walls Jr.[5]

By the end of the 1970s, only 7.3 percent of elected officials in the state were black. But even having more black politicians in office did not necessarily translate into the kind of progress Hamer wanted. As movement activist Hosea Williams noted with frustration, some black officials were "trying to accomplish the same thing that white officials had, which was to get rich and to gain power, to control and exploit the masses." Instead of ushering in an era of empowerment for poor blacks, as Hamer had hoped, the movement had opened opportunities primarily for upwardly mobile blacks. By the 1980s, the only blacks involved in local politics, remarked the black president of the Sunflower County Voters League, are "retired teachers, independent entrepreneurs, and young people determined to go their own way." The masses of poor, undereducated blacks—the people Hamer had sought to mobilize—remained distant from the world of politics.[6]

Part of the difficulty in achieving political gains stemmed from the lack of progress in education. Black candidates often lacked the experience and educational background that voters of any race considered a prerequisite. Black voters did not always vote solely on the basis of race; they too expected black candidates to possess basic levels of education. As Eastland plantation worker Charlie Edwards explained, "By the colored man voting, there's a chance for some colored man, what's got the learning and education, to hold some office." But black educational aspirations remained unfulfilled. The Freedom Schools of the 1960s had proven to be short-lived, and public school desegregation led almost immediately to school resegregation, as whites fled to racially exclusive academies such as Indianola Academy, North Sunflower Academy, and Central Delta Academy—in its first twenty-five years of existence, Indianola Academy enrolled only one black student. The public schools quickly became the "black" schools. "Whites just moved out and gave [the schools] to them," recalled one white Sunflower County planter who had been in the Citizens' Council. Yet whites did not abandon their positions of authority within the school system. "The whites don't mind teaching in our school," Hamer fumed, "but they won't send their kids there." Indeed, throughout the 1970s, the school boards, administrators, and a significant percentage of teachers in Sunflower County schools were white. Across the state, desegregation led not to integration and black empowerment but to white flight (in majority-black areas), token integration (in majority-white districts), segregated tracking (within integrated schools), and often the firing of black teachers and administrators.[7]

Along with the lack of educational improvement, economic stagnation worked to undermine political progress. Economically, poor black residents were perhaps worse off than before the movement, and they remained vulnerable to economic pressure even after racial barriers to political participation fell. With the end of sharecropping and the development of fully mechanized agriculture, economically secure whites were no longer dependent upon black laborers. By the time Woods Eastland returned to run the family farm in 1975, the plantation employed just eighteen people on 5,800 acres. Five years later, only 880 agricultural jobs remained in the entire county, a decrease of nearly 50 percent in a decade. The white landowners who for generations were desperate to keep their black laborers on the plantation now had little use for them. Like workers in other industries who lost their jobs to automation and capital flight in the 1970s, Hamer and black farm laborers became economically expendable and lost political leverage.[8]

To add to Sunflower County's economic woes, industrial development in the area lagged, and many rural towns lost their tax base as planters decamped for regional centers such as Indianola, Greenwood, and Memphis. The result could be seen on the streets of rural towns: people now were not only poor but also idle. With idleness came increases in a host of social problems including crime, teenage pregnancy, and drug use, which further limited black political gains. Drug addicts and petty criminals were less likely to become interested in politics, and large numbers of black men began filtering through the penal system and thus became ineligible to vote—Mississippi was one of a small number of states that permanently barred many ex-felons from registering at all.[9]

The economic stagnation hit home with the Hamers. While Fannie Lou battled health problems, her husband, Pap, struggled to make a living for the family. He cobbled together a "hoe hand crew," a small group of young men who would chop cotton on a piecemeal basis. Pap found work for the crew wherever he could, often on the Eastland plantation. Pap Hamer and the senator's son, Woods, talked regularly about the dismal economic conditions workers faced. "Nowadays are just like the 1930s," Pap told Woods. "Back then nobody had any money and you couldn't buy anything. Nowadays everybody's got a pocketful of money but you still can't buy anything." The persistent economic deprivation led Eastland plantation worker Earline Tillman to dismiss the importance of the movement. While she appreciated the efforts made by Hamer to achieve political equality, Tillman felt the movement changed little in Sunflower County: "I don't see how it affected my life."[10]

The political, educational, and economic stagnation contributed to perhaps the most difficult obstacle to overcome, a major roadblock that remained on the path to full freedom: the "plantation mentality" that still crippled many black Deltans. At the height of its success, the movement had given many black participants the psychological power to fight against an oppressive system. People who were "seeing and feeling dignity," as Hamer termed it, refused to accept the subordinate status they had been assigned. The key, Hamer pointed out, was for people to "decide in their mind they just ain't going back to [the old ways] no more and be willing to fight for something different." With apathy and complacency, Hamer warned, "we can drift right on back to the plantation," back to the mentality of dependence. By the 1970s, going back to the plantation was not economically feasible; instead, many unskilled black laborers turned to the federal government. Where once the plantation owner had provided housing, medical care, and food, now government programs offered assistance such as welfare, housing subsidies, Medicare and Medicaid, food stamps, and Social Security. Poor black families still remained dependent; it was only the source of their dependence that had changed. People who relied on government programs were not free, Hamer believed, because instead of relying on themselves to make their lives better they looked elsewhere. The purpose of the movement was to teach people "to be independent and work for what they get and stop getting so many handouts," Sunflower activist Annie Mae King explained. "That is what has ruined people now." The plantation mentality still reigned, though the "plantation" was now the government.[11]

As the movement gave politically empowered blacks more access to federal largesse, material conditions improved for black families and basic needs were met. Fewer children went to bed hungry, fewer people lacked access to basic medical care, fewer families lived in substandard housing. The results were slow but impressive. Yet the progress had its costs as well. Complacency often set in as Sunflower County blacks achieved an unprecedented (though still impoverished) level of material comfort. Hamer's friend Annie Devine recognized the dilemma of depending on federal money to relieve poverty: "On the one hand people need the money; on the other hand so many people have become satisfied with the situation as it is now, there's not much drive to better the community." The civil rights movement was in some ways a victim of its own success. The very achievements it had struggled to attain sometimes undermined people's willingness to work for social change.[12]

The inability of the movement to achieve the full freedom that Hamer had envisioned gnawed at the aging former sharecropper. Never completely healthy, particularly after the beating she had suffered in Winona in 1963, Hamer saw her health deteriorate rapidly in the early 1970s. She had contemplated running against Senator Eastland in 1972, but she suffered a nervous breakdown in January of that year and grew increasingly ill and depressed. With the collapse of Freedom

Farm in the mid-1970s, she retreated to a more private life at her modest home in Ruleville. Though she had been accused of using the movement for personal glory and material gain, Hamer's activism did not benefit her economically—her fund-raising prowess extended only so far as the boundaries of the movement, and she survived on disability payments and donations from friends and family.[13]

Ultimately, it was her heart that gave way, but her entire body was wracked by breast cancer, diabetes, and hypertension that combined to kill her. After a radical mastectomy failed to stanch the spread of the cancer, she succumbed on March 16, 1977. Still several months from her sixtieth birthday, she died virtually penniless and was buried in a weedy field that had been part of her failed cooperative farm. Her funeral at William Chapel attracted hundreds of former movement activists, government officials, and other well-wishers. Andrew Young, a former activist who recently had been named ambassador to the United Nations, eulogized her as the spiritual leader of Mississippi's freedom struggle, a woman whose decision to challenge segregation "shook the foundation of our nation." As her tombstone read, she was "sick and tired of being sick and tired," and now at last she could rest.[14]

"I WOULDN'T TAKE BACK ANYTHING"

If funeral guests leaving William Chapel had crossed the highway, turned on Front Street, and walked about half a mile, they might have come across the little room above the Bank of Ruleville that still served as the local office of Senator Eastland. Although his health too had declined by 1977, the seventy-two-year-old Eastland nonetheless remained in office and continued to fight for the conservative, anti-Communist vision of freedom that had been his hallmark since entering the Senate more than three decades before. As guests paid their final respects to the fallen civil rights legend, Eastland pondered running for a seventh term.

Hobbled by hepatitis, malaria, and other maladies, Eastland rarely ventured to the Senate floor for speeches and made infrequent speaking tours of his home state, but he continued to wield extraordinary power as chairman of the Judiciary Committee. By virtue of his seniority, he also became president pro tempore of the Senate, a symbolic post with little actual power that nonetheless twice placed the Mississippian "a heartbeat away" from the presidency. Eastland had built a successful career upon his uncompromising rhetoric and tactics, and he could scarcely conceive of how to do things differently. But as he contemplated running for a seventh term in 1978, he began to consider ways to burnish his image among people he had spent much of his career opposing: black voters. The fact that Eastland, even Eastland, sought to mend fences with the black community was for many observers a testament to the profound transformation the movement had wrought.[15]

Eastland had powerful backing for his reelection bid—President Jimmy Carter and Vice President Walter Mondale supported him, as did business interests that did not want to see Senator Edward Kennedy take control of the Judiciary Committee—and his seniority in the Senate remained a powerful deterrent to replacing him. But he also faced serious obstacles. In a state where nearly 30 percent of registered voters now were black, his long-standing record of opposition to civil rights hung like an albatross around his political neck. Shortly after Eastland's reelection in 1972, Aaron Henry had dismissed the senator as a "lost cause" who remained stuck in a "plantation tsar philosophy" and never could "overcome his past image and become acceptable to blacks." Too old, too rigid, too uncompromising—Eastland offered little hope for the kind of reconciliation that had preserved the careers of George Wallace, Strom Thurmond, and other segregationist politicians.[16]

Yet Eastland defied expectations, and it was Aaron Henry himself who provided the opportunity. As Eastland assessed his electoral chances in 1977, he recognized the changed political terrain. "He was a political realist," recalled William Winter, a former Eastland campaign worker who was elected governor of Mississippi in 1979. "He sized up a political situation and moved to be the beneficiary." Eastland met with Henry to see what kind of support he could expect from black voters. The NAACP leader minced few words. "Your chances of getting support in the black community are poor at best," he told the senator. "You have a master-servant philosophy with regard to blacks." Shockingly, the normally reserved Eastland began to weep. "Do you realize you never did invite me?" he sobbed. Taken aback by what he later termed a "Paul on the road to Damascus transformation," Henry agreed to endorse Eastland's bid for reelection and help the senator get black support.[17]

Henry enlisted other NAACP leaders, including Charles Evers, in his effort to win black support for Eastland. Praising Eastland's recent voting record, Henry challenged NAACP members, "What more do you want?" At the annual Mississippi Democratic Party's Jefferson-Jackson Day dinner in 1977, Eastland sat with black party members. "This is a new experience for us, breaking bread with Jim Eastland," Henry marveled, adding playfully, "Remember, it was just as hard for Senator Eastland to be around some of us as it was for some of us to be around him." Bill Minor, a veteran news reporter who had covered the movement, could scarcely believe his eyes. "Thinking back to many a White Citizens Council whoop-de-doo when Eastland was the centerpiece of fervent segregationist adoration," Minor wrote in his syndicated column, "one is bound to think of the Millennium and believe anything is possible in this world of ours." Eastland further confounded critics by speaking at a banquet to raise money for a black industrial college and hiring his first black staff member.[18]

The extraordinary prospect of Eastland winning an election with black votes would not come to pass, however. Although his chances had improved with the endorsement of Henry, Evers, and other black leaders, he still found significant resistance among black voters. As black activist Owen Brooks wrote, "To ask Black people in this state or anywhere in this country to support James Eastland's Candidacy for re-election is the same as to ask the masses of Black South Africans to support [South African prime minister Balthazar] Vorster and his regime or Ian Smith in Rhodesia." He also heard rumblings from within the white political establishment. In early March 1978, former governor Bill Waller announced that he was considering a run for Eastland's seat and even criticized the senator as a "six hour a week man" who was not physically up for the job. Facing the prospect of a long, grueling campaign—he preferred the politics of personal relationships rather than the mass media politics required of 1970s politicians—Eastland ultimately chose not to seek reelection at all. Citing family concerns, he bowed out of the race. Eastland's eleventh-hour steps to earn support among blacks failed to win over critics who welcomed his retirement. The senator was about "35½ years too late," quipped black politician Henry Kirksey; Eastland's calling it quits was "the greatest service he has ever performed for the people of Mississippi," the *Delta Democrat Times* in Greenville editorialized. Eastland's handpicked successor, a relatively unknown district attorney named Maurice Dantin, easily won the Democratic primary, but that was no longer a guarantee of victory in the general election. Independent (but quasi-Republican) black candidate Charles Evers carried much of the black vote, allowing Republican congressman Thad Cochran to win with 45 percent of the vote. With Cochran's election, Mississippi became a two-party state for the first time since Reconstruction.[19]

Eastland retired to the family plantation in Doddsville, and he embraced his return to country living. Without electoral considerations to keep in mind, the hard-bitten segregationist nonetheless continued to soften his position on race. He refused to apologize for his past stances—"I wouldn't take back anything," he insisted—but he cultivated an unlikely relationship with Aaron Henry. The two became, in Henry's words, "about as close as two people can be in terms of friendship." Eastland sent hefty contributions to the NAACP, the organization he sought to destroy a generation earlier, and he thanked Henry for "helping me see the whole picture."[20]

Like Fannie Lou Hamer, Eastland did not fare well out of the public eye. Though he enjoyed the plantation life, his health declined swiftly following his retirement. He lived quietly with his wife, Libby, seeing friends and taking visitors on tours of the plantation. He remained an "interested observer" of politics but refused to become actively involved in any campaigns. Cataract surgery in 1982 failed to restore his normal eyesight, and he became increasingly dependent on his family and friends. He was "embarrassed by physical weakness," his daughter Sue recalled, and "it was hard for him to have us stronger." Following a choking incident that sent him to the hospital, Eastland died of pneumonia on February 19, 1986. Governors, senators, and even former political opponents made their way to Ruleville to pay their final respects. Eastland's funeral, Bill Minor commented, was "an assemblage of raw political power under one roof that hasn't been matched in my career." More than five hundred people crowded into the United Methodist Church to hear Larry Speakes, former Eastland staff member and chief spokesman of the Reagan administration, eulogize Eastland as a "patriot of the first order" who had a "spotless reputation." It was the "end of an era," Speakes observed. Eastland, the "godfather to generation after generation of the state's political leaders," had passed.[21]

Although they did not attend the funeral, workers who remained on the Eastland plantation remembered him fondly. "He never told anybody to move, no matter how old," Wiley Caples remarked. "You can't find a white man like him today." In the last decade of his life, Eastland had improved housing on the plantation, replacing many tenants' tar-paper shacks with brick homes in which he allowed workers to live rent-free. After the senator's death, his son continued the practice and let elderly workers live on the plantation until they too passed away. The Eastland farm was "about as good a plantation as you could live on," recalled Woodrow Wilson, an elderly laborer who remained on the plantation into the twenty-first century. "Nobody suffered on this place for nothing."[22]

SUNFLOWER COUNTY, 2004

James Eastland and Fannie Lou Hamer have followed quite different paths in death, just as they had in life. In the early twenty-first century, a generation after their passing, it is the sharecropper, not the senator, who remains visible in Sunflower County. "Welcome to Ruleville: Home of Fannie Lou Hamer" proclaim signs on the highway leading to her hometown, and visitors can make their way to the Fannie Lou Hamer Recreational Complex, the Fannie Lou Hamer Day Care Center, and other sites honoring the civil rights legend. Her gravesite includes an ornate headstone surrounded by trees, landscaping, and a gazebo donated by a variety of public and private groups. Beyond Sunflower County, too, she has earned widespread admiration and adulation. The state Democratic Party honors her at its annual Jefferson-Jackson-Hamer Dinner, while the Democratic National Convention in 2004 paid homage to Hamer and the Mississippi Freedom Democratic Party's challenge forty years earlier. Presidential candidate

Bill Clinton quoted Hamer during his nomination speech in 1992, and her visage adorns countless books and office walls. She has become a widely recognized symbol of courage and determination in the face of adversity.

Eastland, meanwhile, largely has been forgotten, save by Mississippi history buffs and students of the civil rights movement. No signs proclaim Doddsville as the home of the former chairman of the Senate Judiciary Committee; the University of Mississippi Law Library and a federal courthouse in Jackson are among the only sites in the entire state to honor him. Shortly after his retirement, the University of Mississippi Foundation commissioned a $13,000 portrait of Eastland to be hung in the U.S. Capitol, but it could raise only $3,000 from the senator's friends and supporters for the project. His gravesite consists of a barely visible headstone set amidst the family plot in Forest. Young people growing up in Mississippi, even in Doddsville, today know little about the man whose power was the stuff of legend and whose plantation remains to this day. Even members of his family sometimes seemed eager to distance themselves from him, or at least his reputation. When I first moved to Sunflower County in 1994, my roommate happened to get introduced to one of the senator's granddaughters. The young woman, who had graduated from an elite Eastern college, quickly emphasized that times had changed and she was *not* what her last name implied.[23]

Hamer has earned her spot among the heroines of America history, and she deserves the recognition she has gained. At a time when fear gripped her fellow sharecroppers, she boldly chose to wrestle, in the words of her favorite biblical verse, "against principalities, against powers, against the rulers of the darkness of this world, against spiritual wickedness in high places" (Ephesians 6:11–12). She courageously proclaimed her rights as an American citizen and became an integral part of a movement that destroyed the most glaring contradiction of American society. When it came to civil rights, Hamer, not Eastland, clearly stood on the right side of history. Eastland's uncompromising stance on segregation, coupled with his deft use of the power inherent in his socioeconomic and political positions, forced civil rights advocates such as Hamer to turn to ever more confrontational and dangerous methods in order to win black equality. His unwillingness to bend in the face of moderate and moral demands contributed to the frustration and rage that fueled much of the late 1960s militancy he deplored. His inability to see beyond race blinded him to the possibility that Hamer and other black citizens of this nation had every right to share in the constitutional guarantees, the economic prosperity, and the freedoms he championed. For his unrepentant role in retarding racial progress and his contribution to the mistrust that continues to hamper efforts at racial reconciliation, Eastland has earned our scorn.

Times changed indeed. Sunflower County at the turn of the twenty-first century appeared in many ways to be the nightmare that Eastland had feared. Whites had lost their stranglehold on political power in the county, which remained overwhelmingly black despite decades of out-migration. Even into the 1980s, no black person held a major political office, but the barriers soon began tumbling. Shortly after Eastland's death in 1986, irate blacks in Indianola flexed their political muscle by staging a three-week boycott of the local schools to protest the majority-white school board's selection of a white superintendent for the public school system. The boycott led to the appointment of Robert Merritt, Sunflower County's first black superintendent since Reconstruction, and in the following two decades three more black appointees have assumed the job, while a black superintendent won election to the county school district post as well. By 2004, after a burly former Air Force intelligence officer named Arthur Marble became the first black mayor of Indianola and a cheerful highway patrolman named James Haywood became county sheriff, black officials ran most of the major towns and institutions in the county. A black woman, Sara Thomas, represented Sunflower County in the state House of Representatives, and a black man, Bennie Thompson, represented the area in the U.S. Congress. Blacks served as police chiefs, town aldermen, county commissioners, school board members, and city inspectors, and in every other local public office. The depth and breadth of black political power was unprecedented. Even during Reconstruction, Sunflower County blacks had not made such extensive gains.

In the world outside of politics, too, life in Sunflower County differed dramatically in 2004 from the time when Eastland and Hamer were alive, and certainly from the world in which Luther Holbert and the original James Eastland lived a century before. Whites could not expect blacks to acknowledge any kind of social superiority or defer respectfully in daily interaction. Where once black adults had to step off the sidewalk if a white person was passing by, black strollers, particularly young people, dominated city streets and public events. Although there remained a fair bit of intra-race violence in the area, white-on-black crime was almost unheard of in twenty-first century Sunflower County. White neighborhoods in Indianola, Ruleville, and other towns (though not the town of Sunflower) now included black families, some of whom were well-to-do. Outsiders accustomed to white-majority suburbs often expressed surprise at the level of daily interracial interaction—in grocery stores, post offices, government buildings, and other public areas blacks and whites talked, laughed, and did business together. People interacted on an egalitarian basis that Eastland would have found unimaginable and intolerable.

One place where blacks and whites did not interact was in school. The public schools that Eastland had fought so desperately to preserve as bastions of white supremacy had become almost entirely black by the 1970s, and they remained so into the twenty-first century. Very few white families sent their children to public schools, particularly after the early grades—only 2 percent of Sunflower County public school students were white in 2006. Bill Minor, the veteran white journalist who had covered five decades of Mississippi politics, noted angrily that white flight "has been one of the most damning examples that real racial integration is not part of what white Mississippi wants." The "segregation academies" that sprang up after integration had become community institutions, as children of academy alumni followed in their parents' footsteps through segregated school hallways. The divisions were perhaps most visible on the pages of the Indianola *Enterprise Tocsin*, which regularly and without irony juxtaposed pictures of the all-black sports teams and graduating classes from Gentry High School with their all-white counterparts from Indianola Academy. Whole generations of white and black children grew up almost completely isolated from one another, leading black attorney Carver Randle to propose an exchange program between the white and black schools, akin to a foreign exchange program. Ironically, there had been far more interracial interaction among children half a century earlier, when kids, particularly boys, had spent countless hours playing outside together. When I began teaching in the 1990s, my elementary school students had had so little experience with white people that they wanted to touch my hair and skin to see what it felt like.[24]

Eastland would have taken little comfort in knowing that his dire predictions about the consequences of school integration had proven true. Throughout the 1950s and 1960s, Eastland argued that the civil rights movement demanded of white southerners an act that no white people or wealthy people anywhere in the country would accept: placing white children in schools where they would be a racial minority and placing wealthy children in schools where they would be outnumbered by children of laboring classes. If wealthy white northerners faced the same predicament, he insisted, they would respond as he and other wealthy white southerners had: with resistance and flight. In the fifty years after the *Brown* decision, things played out as he had called it. From Washington, D.C., to San Francisco, in no area where racial minorities or working-class people were a majority or near-majority of the population did a significant proportion of privileged white people live in the same neighborhoods or attend the same schools as racial minorities or lower-class people. Indeed, public schools in the North and West actually became more racially and economically segregated in the generation after the movement; schools in the Northeast were the most segregated in the country. Wealthy parents in the early twenty-first century paid exorbitant prices for houses in neighborhoods where they could avoid sending their children to schools where poor children predominated. In effect, they used their wealth to achieve what white supremacy had done for Eastland and his generation. As a result, many schools across the country were as segregated along lines of race and class as the schools in Sunflower County.[25]

The resegregated schools were one way in which life in Sunflower County a generation after Fannie Lou Hamer's death had come to resemble the nightmare that she had feared. Instead of attending integrated schools that offered a variety of top-quality educational programs, black children growing up in Sunflower County in the early twenty-first century did time at institutions that were as likely to blunt their creativity and curiosity as inspire them to excel academically. In some ways, the problems of the de facto segregated schools were even more difficult to overcome than the de jure segregated schools of generations past because the school system was no longer the only employment outlet for talented and ambitious blacks. As the movement broke down barriers to blacks across the nation, many black educators left Sunflower County and the education field for greater opportunities elsewhere, depleting small, rural communities of their minuscule black middle class. "Sunflower County is a great place to be *from*," went the saying among many successful black expatriates who returned to the area for family reunions.

With white families and middle-class blacks leaving the public schools, community interest in the public school system dissipated. A vicious cycle emerged: as more middle-class families left the local public system in favor of "quality education" in private schools or opportunities elsewhere, the public schools attracted less money, teaching talent, and community support, which in turn made a quality education more difficult to provide. Thomas Edwards, the black superintendent of Sunflower County schools, remarked in 1999 that the biggest obstacles his schools faced were not poverty and discrimination but the lack of qualified teachers and minimal parental involvement in the schools. "If we could get more parents involved," he believed, "it would make a big difference." By the turn of the century, with graduation rates hovering below 60 percent, the Sunflower County school district fell to Level I, the lowest possible rating by the state Department of Education (DoE); in 2003, the DoE ranked two Sunflower County schools among the ten worst schools in the state. In 2006, the average score for Sunflower County students taking the ACT, a standardized test akin to the SAT, was an abysmal 15.7 out of 36 (equivalent to less than 700 on the SAT)—a score far too low for acceptance at most colleges. The public schools continued to suffer from low expectations and stagnant achievement levels, and even after the segregationist impulse waned, the wretched state of the schools served to keep whites and middle-class blacks away. More than two decades of educational reform, initiated statewide by Governor William Winter in the early 1980s, did not fundamentally alter the problem.[26]

Much of the responsibility for the disastrous state of the schools certainly must be laid at the feet of wealthy parents, particularly the vast majority of white families who abandoned the public system and had little incentive to invest their time and energy or support tax increases to support the public schools. But the black majority could not escape its own complicity. In the same way that private academies allowed white families to remain ensnared in a segregated worldview long after the end of legal segregation, the plantation mentality remained firmly implanted in many black people long after the old plantation system had crumbled. Black teachers, principals, and superintendents may have run the schools, but their power did not necessarily produce positive results for black students because the black leaders and parents themselves often were trapped by their own complacency. Low achievement was acceptable not simply because expectations were low but also because many people, particularly those in positions of power, had little sense that higher achievement was possible or even desirable. Using logic that would not have been unfamiliar to plantation owners, some local leaders argued that encouraging young people to achieve at high levels and attend top colleges was dangerous, for it could lead to the young people leaving the area. On more than one occasion, I dealt with high school counselors who did not send transcripts, recommendations, and other required material to college admissions offices because they did not want students to leave the state for college. Such officials were aided and abetted by many black parents who excelled at the art of making demands but refused to shoulder basic parenting responsibilities. Young people learned early on that many of the adults in their lives only paid lip service to the idea that success depended on working hard and excelling academically.[27]

The schools were not the only part of Sunflower County life that would have disappointed Hamer. The political revolution that had swept so many black officials into office failed to alter the fundamental dynamics of power in the area. Most of the political gains were achieved not by the poor blacks whom Hamer had represented but by the middle-class blacks she had ridiculed and attacked as "Johnny-come-latelys" to the movement. They were the ones who bought big houses on the white side of town while the vast majority of blacks remained impoverished and isolated in slumlike conditions. The pattern of economic marginalization that had been set by the early 1970s re-

mained essentially unchanged. Estranged from the land their ances-
tors had worked for generations, a large percentage of blacks relied instead on government largesse in the form of welfare payments, Social
Security checks, and disability payments to eke out a living.

An underlying cause of the stagnation—in education, in politics,
in the economy—was much larger than Sunflower County and even
Mississippi as a whole. It was cotton. As we have seen through the
lives of Eastland and Hamer, life in Sunflower County revolved
around that fluffy fiber that enriched the one, impoverished the other,
and knotted the county to the global economy. Cotton created the
plantation world in which Eastland and Hamer came of age, a world
built upon brutal yet paternalistic white supremacy; uneducated, deferential, and abundant black labor; and the global preeminence of
American cotton. That world began to crumble in the mid-twentieth
century as international economic and political forces, government
policy, and the civil rights movement undermined its racial and economic foundation. While Hamer and her civil rights allies struggled to
slay Jim Crow, Eastland and his fellow planters fought not only to resist the movement for black equality but also to remain competitive in
a ruthless global cotton economy. Sunflower County emerged from
this turbulent time as a new world of politically empowered blacks and
fully mechanized cotton farms.

This transformation liberated the county's black majority from
the shackles of sharecropping and Jim Crow, but it also rendered
black laborers economically expendable. Hamer and her black neighbors now had unprecedented legal rights and protection, but they lost
economic leverage as consolidated cotton operations such as the Eastland plantation required fewer and fewer laborers. They were free, but
free to do *what*? More cotton was grown more efficiently than ever—
the 2004 crop broke all previous records—but only a tiny fraction of
the black majority benefited from cotton or its ancillary industries.
While some educated blacks fled the area in search of opportunities
beyond Sunflower County, many of their less-educated neighbors,
nearly half of whom did not graduate from high school in any given
year, hit the job market unprepared for the world of work. They often
found themselves unable to compete for the few low-skill jobs that

remained in the area, as employers preferred Mexican immigrants who worked harder for less pay and with fewer workplace disruptions than their American peers.

By the early twenty-first century, it was clear that the civil rights movement had not upended the patterns of racial separation and economic inequality that had marked Sunflower County at the turn of the twentieth century. Black efforts to capitalize on the movement's opportunities largely had been unable to overcome the economic advantages Eastland and other white planters gained during the crucial years of the 1930s and 1940s, the limited educational achievements and deferential plantation mentality ingrained in many blacks during the Jim Crow era, and the recalcitrance of white power holders. Sunflower County, like much of the South, had been transformed yet remained resiliently separate and unequal. That was the reality that I entered in the 1990s, and it is the reality in which young Sunflower Countians, white and black, are growing up in the early twenty-first century.

Notes

PREFACE

1. "Initiative, courage, and selflessness . . .": Linda Reed, "Fannie Lou Hamer: New Ideas for the Civil Rights Movement and American Democracy," in Ted Ownby, ed., *The Role of Ideas in the Civil Rights South* (Jackson: University Press of Mississippi, 2002), 75; "heroic and unlettered": Howell Raines, *My Soul Is Rested: Movement Days in the Deep South Remembered* (New York: G.P. Putnam's Sons, 1977), 19; "extraordinary in any demographic category": David L. Chappell, *A Stone of Hope: Prophetic Religion and the Death of Jim Crow* (Chapel Hill: University of North Carolina Press, 2004), 71.

2. "spiritual leader . . .": *Time*, 26 March 1956, 26; "a virulent racist": Jeff Woods, *Black Struggle, Red Scare: Segregation and Anti-Communism in the South, 1948–1968* (Baton Rouge: Louisiana State University Press, 2004), 43; "a ranting demagogue . . .": John Egerton, *Speak Now Against the Day: The Generation Before the Civil Rights Movement in the South* (Chapel Hill: University of North Carolina Press, 1994), 220; "narrow-minded, arbitrary, arrogant . . .": David Chandler, *The Natural Superiority of Southern Politicians: A Revisionist History* (New York: Doubleday, 1977), 300.

1. SUNFLOWER COUNTY, 1904

1. Marie Hemphill, *Fevers, Floods, and Faith: A History of Sunflower County, Mississippi* (Indianola, MS, 1976), 347–48.

2. Story of Dodd brothers: Hemphill, *Fevers, Floods, and Faith*, 347; white woman's recollection: "Townsends Recall Early Formative Days of Delta," *Jackson Daily News*

(1969) in "Mississippi—Sunflower County, Doddsville," Sunflower County Library Vertical Files.

3. The account of the confrontation between Eastland and Holbert that follows in this chapter is a synthesis of a variety of newspaper accounts from the time, particularly those published in the *Memphis Commercial Appeal, Vicksburg Evening Post, Greenville Daily Democrat,* the *Daily Picayune,* and *Greenwood Commonwealth.*

4. Fant quoted in Neil McMillen, *Dark Journey: Black Mississippians in the Age of Jim Crow* (Urbana: University of Illinois Press, 1989), 201–6; Hortense Powdermaker, *After Freedom: A Cultural Study of the Deep South* (Madison: University of Wisconsin Press, 1993, orig. 1939), 173.

5. "famous cotton delta of Mississippi": "Moorhead, Miss.: A Prohibition Industrial Colony," Moorhead Improvement Company (Rand McNally, n.d.), Sunflower County Library Vertical Files; "pure soil, endlessly deep . . .": David Cohn, *Where I Was Born and Raised* (New York: Houghton Mifflin, 1948), 25; amazed geologist quoted in David M. Oshinsky, *"Worse than Slavery": Parchman Farm and the Ordeal of Jim Crow Justice* (New York: Free Press, 1996), 111; "thickest timber I have ever seen": Helen Dick Davis, ed., *Trials of the Earth: The Autobiography of Mary Hamilton* (Jackson: University Press of Mississippi, 1992), 52.

6. Effects of de Soto: Mikko Saikku, *This Delta, This Land: An Environmental History of the Yazoo-Mississippi Floodplain* (Athens: University of Georgia Press, 2005), 77–78; Native American settlement of area: Sherry Mills Donald, "A History of Sunflower County, Mississippi," master's thesis, University of Mississippi, August 1968, 2–4, in "Mississippi—Sunflower County, History," Sunflower County Library Vertical Files.

7. R.W. Parks, "A Personal Experience—and the Early History of Drew," in "Mississippi—Sunflower County, Drew," in Sunflower County Library Vertical Files.

8. Twenty percent cleared: Dunbar Rowland, ed., *Mississippi* (Spartanburg, SC: Reprint Company, 1976, orig. 1907), 2:754; "land of unlevied small rivers . . .": Ruby Sheppard Hicks, *The Song of the Delta* (Jackson, MS: Howick House, 1976), 5; swarms of mosquitoes, settlers trickling in: *Commercial Appeal,* 6 July 1955.

9. Early history of cotton: Stephen Yafa, *Big Cotton: How a Humble Fiber Created Fortunes, Wrecked Civilizations, and Put America on the Map* (New York: Viking, 2005), 9–17; first cotton gin in Mississippi: Rowland, *Mississippi,* 1:570, 572.

10. "same amount of labor . . .": "Moorhead, Miss.: A Prohibition Industrial Colony"; "richest soil in the world": Rowland, *Mississippi,* 2:754; differences in soils: Woods Eastland, interview with author, 16 February 2005; Willie M. Pitts, interview with author, 8 February 2005; "black sheep": "BAWI, a Story of Progress in the Delta," *Lion Oil News* 9, no. 3 (April 1952), 3.

11. "pioneers with means": David L. Cohn, *The Mississippi Delta and the World: The Memoirs of David L. Cohn,* ed. James C. Cobb (Baton Rouge: Louisiana State University Press, 1995), 3; "plantation frontier": James C. Cobb, *The Most Southern Place on Earth: The Mississippi Delta and the Roots of Regional Identity* (New York: Oxford Uni-

versity Press, 1992), 7–28; population statistics: Mississippi Power and Light Company, "Mississippi Population 1960–1800" (Jackson, MS: 1962), 68.

12. For more on the general progress made during Reconstruction, see Eric Foner, *Reconstruction: America's Unfinished Revolution* (New York: Harper & Row, 1988). Mississippi progress during Reconstruction: McMillen, *Dark Journey*, 37; Sunflower County progress during Reconstruction: Hemphill, *Fevers, Floods, and Faith*, 94.

13. For more on the extent of black progress during this time period, see John C. Willis, *Forgotten Time: The Yazoo-Mississippi Delta after the Civil War* (Charlottesville: University Press of Virginia, 2000), 1–3.

14. Hemphill, *Fevers, Floods, and Faith*, 86.

15. For a gripping account of how terrorists overthrew biracial government in Mississippi, see Nicholas Lemann, *Redemption: The Last Battle of the Civil War* (New York: Farrar, Straus, Giroux, 2006); for a detailed, critical look at the rise of the Ku Klux Klan, see Nancy MacLean, *Behind the Mask of Chivalry: The Making of the Second Ku Klux Klan* (New York: Oxford University Press, 1995); David Chalmers, *Hooded Americanism: The History of the Ku Klux Klan* (Durham, NC: Duke University Press, 1987); for a more benign interpretation, see Hemphill, *Fevers, Floods, and Faith*, 89.

16. For more on the global cotton boom, see Timothy Curtis Jacobson and George David Smith, *Cotton's Renaissance: A Study in Market Innovation* (Cambridge: Cambridge University Press, 2001), 59; cotton statistics, see David Goldfield et al., *The American Journey: A History of the United States* (Upper Saddle River, NJ: Prentice-Hall, 1998), 723.

17. Rowland, *Mississippi*, 2:754; John A. Robertson and Tom W. Conger Jr., *Early History of the Town of Ruleville Mississippi in the Heart of the Mississippi Delta* (Parchman, MS: Magnolia State Enterprises, 1993), 24; Hemphill, *Fevers, Floods, and Faith*, 107; Lula Kemp et al., "Historical Research Project, Sunflower County, Assignment #23," in "Mississippi—Sunflower County, Doddsville," Sunflower County Library Vertical Files.

18. Hiriam Eastland: Deloris Pickering Sanders and Lynda Harvey, eds., *Scott County Mississippi: 1870 Census* (n.d.), 11. Although most historical documents record the name as "Hiram Eastland," James O. Eastland insisted that it was "Hiriam." Letter from James O. Eastland to J.C. Ruppenthal, 16 October 1941, University of Mississippi, Special Collections and Archives, James O. Eastland Collection, File Series 1, Subseries 7, Box 1, Folder 3; "The Eastland Family Tree," by Orin Eastland, 1882, Archives and Special Collections, University of Mississippi, James O. Eastland Collection, File Series 1, Subseries 2, Box 1, Folder 15; Eastland's first purchases: Hemphill, *Fevers, Floods, and Faith*, 343; Eastland's bequeath: Dan W. Smith Jr., "James O. Eastland: Early Life and Career, 1904–1942," master's thesis, Mississippi College, 1978, 7.

19. Gov. Claiborne quoted in Rowland, *Mississippi*, 1:572; Sen. Beveridge quoted in Gary Nash and Julie Roy Jeffrey, *The American People: Creating a Nation and a Society* (New York: Longman, 2000), 521; rise of cotton kingdom: Robert Brandfon, *Cotton Kingdom of the New South* (Cambridge, MA: Harvard University Press, 1967), 115.

20. Kristin L. Hoganson, *Fighting for American Manhood: How Gender Politics Pro-*

voked the Spanish-American and Philippine-American Wars (New Haven: Yale University Press, 1998), 36–37.

21. Hamer quoted in Jerry DeMuth, "Tired of Being Sick and Tired," *The Nation*, 1 June 1964, 549; early history of sharecropping: Foner, *Reconstruction*; late-nineteenth-century cotton boom: Brandfon, *Cotton Kingdom*, 115; $25 an acre: Willis, *Forgotten Time*, 157–158.

22. "Moorhead, Miss.: A Prohibition Industrial Colony."

23. Planter class retains power: Cobb, *Most Southern Place on Earth*, viii–ix, 69–124; Delta as worst region for lynching: Terence Finnegan, "Lynching and Political Power in Mississippi and South Carolina," in W. Fitzhugh Brundage, ed., *Under Sentence of Death: Lynching in the South* (Chapel Hill: University of North Carolina Press, 1997), 194; newspaper quoted in Willis, *Forgotten Time*, 153; after 1901 no whites lynched: Willis, *Forgotten Time*, 157.

24. Vardaman background: William F. Holmes, *The White Chief: James Kimble Vardaman* (Baton Rouge: Louisiana State University Press, 1970), xi; Vardaman quoted in Oshinsky, *"Worse than Slavery,"* 87.

25. Cox story background: Lula Kemp, "Historical Research Project, Sunflower County: Interesting Interviews Assignment 13," 27 August 1936, Minnie Cox file, Sunflower County Library Vertical Files; Richardson quoted in Elmer Ramsey Dye, "Historical Research Assignment 13," Minnie Cox file, Sunflower County Library Vertical Files.

26. Letter from Woods C. Eastland to Phillip J. Briscoe Sr., 22 February 1938, Archives and Special Collections, University of Mississippi, James O. Eastland Collection, File Series 1, Subseries 2, Box 1, Folder 8.

27. The account of the chase is a synthesis of newspaper accounts in February 1904: *Daily Picayune*, *Memphis Commercial Appeal*, *Vicksburg Evening Post*, *Greenville Daily Democrat*, and *Greenwood Commonwealth*.

28. Finnegan, "Lynching and Political Power," 202.

29. The account of the lynching is a synthesis of newspaper accounts in February 1904: *Greenwood Commonwealth*, *Vicksburg Evening Post*, *Daily Picayune*, and *Commercial Appeal*.

30. *Memphis News* editorial, printed in the *Enterprise* (Greenwood), 13 February 1904.

31. *Voice of the Negro* 1, no. 3 (March 1904), 82.

32. *Birmingham News* editorial, quoted in *Vicksburg Evening Post*, 11 February 1904.

33. Economic function of lynching: Stewart Tolnay and E.M. Beck, *A Festival of Violence: An Analysis of Southern Lynching, 1882–1930* (Urbana: University of Illinois Press, 1995), 149, 158; lynching victims twice as likely to come from cotton areas: Tolnay and Beck, *Festival of Violence*, 119; lynching statistics: Charles S. Johnson, *Statistical Atlas of Southern Counties* (Chapel Hill: University of North Carolina Press, 1941), 172; for accounts of violence elsewhere, see Adam Hochschild, *King Leopold's Ghost: A*

Story of Greed, Terror, and Heroism in Colonial Africa (New York: Houghton Mifflin, 1998), and Hoganson, *Fighting for American Manhood*.

34. *Greenwood Commonwealth*, 17 September 1904.

35. The account of the indictment of Woods Eastland comes from newspaper accounts in September 1904: *The Enterprise* (Greenwood), *Greenwood Times*, *New York Times*, *Daily Picayune*, and *Jackson Evening News*.

2. PLANTER'S SON, SHARECROPPERS' DAUGHTER

1. Anne Eastland Howdershell, interview with author, 6 November 2001.

2. Lula Kemp et al., "Historial Research Project, Sunflower County, Assignment #20," in "Mississippi—Sunflower County, Doddsville," Sunflower County Library Vertical Files.

3. Geographic divisions: Albert D. Kirwan, *Revolt of the Rednecks: Mississippi Politics, 1876–1925* (New York: Harper & Row, 1952), 42; V.O. Key, *Southern Politics in State and Nation* (New York: Knopf, 1949), 229; Hills people are "different": Woods Eastland, interview with author, 16 October 2001; Delta aristocrats story: Edwin King, interview with author, 17 February 2006; W.F. Minor, interview with author, 17 February 2006.

4. Eastland roots and wealth in Scott County: Sanders and Harvey, *Scott County Mississippi*, 11; Eastland family history and Dr. Tischner story: Woods Eastland, interview with author, 16 February 2005.

5. Forrest's portrait: *Time*, 26 March 1956, 27; family background: Smith, "James O. Eastland," 6; toll of war: Woods Eastland, interview with author, 16 October 2001.

6. For more on the rise of the UDC and the "Lost Cause," see: Gaines Foster, *Ghosts of the Confederacy: Defeat, the Lost Cause, and the Emergence of the New South, 1865–1913*; (New York: Oxford University Press, 1988); Powdermaker, *After Freedom*, 39; Alma Eastland's UDC efforts: *Scott County Register*, 8 November 1911; Alma Eastland's stories of Reconstruction: Woods Eastland, interview with author, 16 October 2001; Sen. Eastland's views: letter from James O. Eastland to E.H. Anderson, 6 October 1941, University of Mississippi, Special Collections and Archives, James O. Eastland Collection, File Series 1, Subseries 7, Box 1, Folder 3.

7. Interview with Woods Eastland, 16 October 2001.

8. Eastland's train trips to the Delta: Smith, "James O. Eastland," 8; Eastland believed blacks were inferior: Anne Eastland Howdershell, interview with author, 7 November 2001.

9. "an uppity kid": *Time*, 26 March 1956, 27; Chester Eastland quoted in Smith, "James O. Eastland," 12; "my father controlled me": Smith, "James O. Eastland," 11. Although he never knew his grandfather, Eastland's son, Woods, acknowledged that he had heard his mother talk about how his grandfather Woods "dominated" Jim. Woods Eastland, interview with author, 16 October 2001.

10. Smith, "James O. Eastland," 11.

11. Woods Eastland and VMI story: Smith, "James O. Eastland," 12; Wisconsin professor quoted in David Sansing, *The University of Mississippi: A Sesquicentennial History* (Jackson: University Press of Mississippi, 1999), 213; Eastland's college activities: Ole Miss yearbook, 1923–25; background on Hermaean Society: Allan Cabaniss, *The University of Mississippi: Its First Hundred Years* (Hattiesburg: University and College Press of Mississippi, 1971), 18.

12. Lothrop Stoddard, *The Rising Tide of Color Against White World-Supremacy* (Westport, CT: Negro University Press, 1971, orig. 1920); Madison Grant, *The Passing of the Great Race* (New York: Ayer, 1970, orig. 1916).

13. *Time*, 26 March 1956, 27.

14. Father's help in first election: Clarence Pierce, interview with author, 28 September 2001; Bilbo's platform and influence: Chester Morgan, *Redneck Liberal: Theodore G. Bilbo and the New Deal* (Baton Rouge: Louisiana State University Press, 1985), 2–4; "mad Mussolini": *Indianola Enterprise*, 22 October 1931.

15. Eastland support for Long: Smith, "James O. Eastland," 24; Eastland's support for Bilbo: *Jackson Daily News*, 10 September 1979 and Clarence Pierce, interview with author, 28 September 2001; Bilbo's program: Roger D. Tate Jr., "Easing the Burden: The Era of Depression and the New Deal in Mississippi," PhD dissertation, University of Tennessee, 1978, 30–35; Sillers's relationship with Eastland: William Winter, interview with author, 22 March 2005.

16. Failure of Bilbo plan: Tate, "Easing the Burden," 38; William Winter, who later worked on Eastland's first campaign, remembered that Eastland "probably couldn't have won" if he had sought reelection in 1931: William Winter, interview with author, 22 March 2005; "I was a boy then": *Jackson Daily News*, 10 September 1979; "scratching a poor man's hip pocket": Smith, "James O. Eastland," 28; Eastland-Coleman courtship: Hemphill, *Fevers, Floods, and Faith*, 344; honeymoon: Smith, "James O. Eastland," 30–31.

17. "any fee from pigs to chickens . . .": "A Cotton Grower from the Mississippi Delta," biographical sketch, 1946, Archives and Special Collections, University of Mississippi, James O. Eastland Collection, File Series 1, Subseries 1, Box 1, Folder 3, 10; "many friends welcome them back": *Ruleville Record*, 30 November 1934; Eastland sets up practice: Smith, "James O. Eastland," 13–14, 20–21, 30–34; "listen to what his daddy say": Rosie Cole, interview with author, 25 September 2001; "my father is the boss": letter from James O. Eastland to Mrs. Lucille Eastland, 8 April 1940, Archives and Special Collections, University of Mississippi, James O. Eastland Collection, File Series 1, Subseries 2, Box 1, Folder 16.

18. "wonderful . . . childhood": Sue Eastland McRoberts, interview with author, 13 November 2001; "it was a fun place to be white . . .": Anne Eastland Howdershell, interview with author, 7 November 2001; "secure, small-town feeling": Sue Eastland McRoberts, interview with author, 13 November 2001.

19. Anne Eastland Howdershell, interview with author 7 November 2001; Woods

Eastland, interview with author, 16 October 2001. James Eastland never discussed the lynching while his children were growing up. In the 1970s, a college friend of Woods discovered evidence of the lynching and told Woods about it. When Woods confronted his father, the elder Eastland spoke briefly about the basic facts of the killing and said no more. Woods later informed his sisters. Woods Eastland, interview with author, 16 February 2005; Anne Eastland Howdershell, interview with author, 7 November 2001.

20. Anne Eastland Howdershell, interview with author, 7 November 2001; Sue Eastland McRoberts, interview with author, 13 November 2001; worker never had a conversation with Eastland: Willie Jackson, interview with author, 8 July 2000; "Were the Negroes oppressed in those days?": Wilson (Bill) Ferguson, *Mountain Moonshine to Delta Gumbo* (Stoneville, MS: Delta Press, 1990), 122.

21. Plantation manager murdered: *Ruleville Record*, 24 January 1935; most violence was black on black: Powdermaker, *After Freedom*, 395; "no killings on the place": letter from Robert Ormond to James O. Eastland, 14 July 1941, University of Mississippi, Special Collections and Archives, James O. Eastland Collection, File Series 1, Subseries 3, Box 1, Folder 31; "same visceral values": Anne Eastland Howdershell, interview with author, 7 November 2001.

22. Powdermaker, *After Freedom*, 51.

23. "For the sake of peace . . .": *Sunflower Tocsin*, 20 March 1916; "postulate of white domination": John Dollard, *Caste and Class in a Southern Town* (New York: Doubleday, 1957, orig. 1937), 207, 212; "no Negro man is safe": Powdermaker, *After Freedom*, 351.

24. Alfred Stone quoted in Charles Aiken, *The Cotton Plantation South Since the Civil War* (Baltimore: Johns Hopkins University Press, 1998), 60; "we must keep the darkies . . .": Powdermaker, *After Freedom*, 301; "dirt-cheap labor": Woods Eastland, interview with author, 16 October 2001.

25. Fannie Lou Hamer, "To Praise Our Bridges," in Dorothy Abbott, ed., *Mississippi Writers: Reflections of Childhood and Youth* (Jackson: University Press of Mississippi, 1986), 2:321; Fannie Lou Hamer interview with Robert Wright, 9 August 1968, Civil Rights Documentation Project, Moorland-Spingarn Research Center, Howard University, 1.

26. Liza Bramlett's rape: Chana Kai Lee, *For Freedom's Sake: The Life of Fannie Lou Hamer* (Urbana: University of Illinois Press, 1999), 9–10; Laura Ratliff quoted in Lee, 9; "We was used . . .": Fannie Lou Hamer, "The Special Plight and the Role of Black Woman," speech given at NAACP Legal Defense Fund Institute, 7 May 1971, in Gerda Lerner, ed., *Black Women in White America: A Documentary History* (New York: Pantheon Books, 1972), 611.

27. Hamer's family leaves Montgomery County: Jack O'Dell, "Life in Mississippi: An Interview with Fannie Lou Hamer," *Freedomways* 5, no. 2 (second quarter, 1965), 231; millions moved: Leon Litwack, *Trouble in Mind: Black Southerners in the Age of Jim Crow* (New York: Knopf, 1998), 487; for more on the Great Migration, see Alferdteen Harrison, ed., *Black Exodus* (Jackson: University Press of Mississippi, 1991), and

James Gregory, *The Southern Diaspora: How the Great Migrations of Black and White Southerners Transformed America* (Chapel Hill: University of North Carolina Press, 2005).

28. Farmers' anti-weevil methods: Hemphill, *Fevers, Floods and Faith*, 656–57; Plantation managers did not recognize the necessity of a centralized campaign and were not organized well enough to make a collective effort successful: Aiken, *Cotton Plantation*, 68–69, 77–78, 80–82.

29. Banning black publications: James Grossman, "Black Labor Is the Best Labor: Southern White Reactions to the Great Migration," in Harrison, ed., *Black Exodus*, 57; more than 100,000 Mississippians migrate: Cobb, *Most Southern Place on Earth*, 116.

30. "The higher cotton goes . . .": *Sunflower Tocsin*, 7 October 1915; sterner measures: Nan Elizabeth Woodruff, *American Congo: The African American Freedom Struggle in the Delta* (Cambridge, MA: Harvard University Press, 2003), 61.

31. $2 per hundred pounds picked: Grossman, "Black Labor is the Best Labor," 63; "cotton picking demands . . .": *Sunflower Tocsin*, 18 September 1919; "continually moving in from the hills," reporter quoted in Cobb, *Most Southern Place on Earth*, 116; Sunflower County population: U.S. Department of Commerce, Bureau of Census, *Fourteenth Census of the United States* (Washington: Government Printing Office, 1913), http://fisher.lib.virginia.edu/collections/stats/histcensus/php/county.php (found 14 February 2006); Ruleville population: Robertson and Conger, "Early History of the Town of Ruleville," 16; percentage of blacks in population: Mississippi Power and Light Company, "Mississippi Population 1800–1960," 68; "There are but few . . .": C.B. King, "Race Relations in Sunflower County," in Mississippi Welfare League, "The Negro Race in Sunflower County Mississippi" (1919), Archives and Special Collections, University of Mississippi, 18.

32. Revolution in black consciousness: David Levering Lewis, *When Harlem Was in Vogue* (New York: Penguin Books, 1997), 3–24; return to Reconstruction fears: *Sunflower Tocsin*, 29 May 1919.

33. Woodruff, *American Congo*, 74–109.

34. Young man hanged: *Ruleville Record*, 7 January 1921; "intelligent, industrious, . . .": Dick Bolling, "Sunflower County Mississippi: Where the Richness of the Soil Makes Living Easy and the Folks There Make Life Worthwhile" (Indianola, MS: 1924).

35. "Today a planter owns . . .": Dick Bolling, "Sunflower County Mississippi"; first appearance of tractors: Hemphill, *Fevers, Floods and Faith*, 656–57; Washington quoted in James Grossman, "Black Labor Is the Best Labor," 52.

36. Hamer moves to Brandon plantation: Fannie Lou Hamer, interview with Neil McMillen, 14 April 1972, University of Southern Mississippi Oral History Program, http://www.lib.usm.edu/~spcol/crda/oh/hamertrans.htm, 3; "The Richness of the Soil . . .": Dick Bolling, "Sunflower County Mississippi"; 96 percent of cotton picked by sharecroppers: Johnson, *Statistical Atlas of Southern Counties*, 272; Hamers supplemented income: Lee, *For Freedom's Sake*, 1; "scrapping cotton": Phyl Garland, "Builders

of a New South," *Ebony*, August 1966, 28; Hamer, "To Praise Our Bridges," 324; and Rev. Tommie Jean Lunsford, interview with Steve Estes and author, 12 July 2000; "life was worse than hard": Garland, "Builders of a New South," 28.

37. "By any modern standards . . .": Powdermaker, *After Freedom*, 83; Hamer's rough childhood: DeMuth, "Tired of Being Sick and Tired," 549; Hamer, "To Praise Our Bridges," 324; Lee, *For Freedom's Sake*, 2–3; and Susan Kling, *Fannie Lou Hamer: A Biography* (Chicago: Women for Racial and Economic Equality, 1979), 12; pellagra: Powdermaker, *After Freedom*, 80; nicknamed "Hip": Charles McLaurin, interview with author, 20 September 2001.

38. "She was one woman . . .": Garland, "Builders of a New South," 28, and Hamer interview with Robert Wright, 2; Lou Ella carried a gun: "Fannie Lou Hamer Speaks Out," *Essence* 2, no. 6 (October 1971), 54.

39. "It is a far different proposition . . .": *Sunflower Tocsin*, 22 January 1925; Hamer tricked into picking: O'Dell, "Life in Mississippi," 231–32.

40. "sunup to sundown": Earline Tillman, interview with author, 26 September 2001; preparing food: Rosie Cole, interview with author, 25 September 2001; "can to can't": Charles McLaurin, quoted in Tracy Sugarman, *Stranger at the Gates: A Summer in Mississippi* (New York: Hill and Wang, 1966); Charles S. Johnson, *Growing Up in the Black Belt* (Washington, DC: American Council on Education, 1941), 8; "We worked . . .": "Fannie Lou Hamer Speaks Out," 54.

41. Lee, *For Freedom's Sake*, 4.

42. DeMuth, "Tired of Being Sick and Tired," 549; "Marked for Murder—Mississippian Dares Death for Civil Rights," *Sepia*, April 1965, 33.

43. Hamer family's poverty: Hamer, "To Praise Our Bridges," 323; woefully inadequate schools: McMillen, *Dark Journey*, 72, see also Johnson, *Statistical Atlas of Southern Counties*, 272; school spending: Johnson, *Statistical Atlas of Southern Counties*, 172, and McMillen, *Dark Journey*, 73; the 1936–7 survey was quoted in Bureau of Educational Research, School of Education, University of Mississippi, "The Report of a Study of the Education of Negroes in Sunflower County, Mississippi," March 1950, 9.

44. "The elementary school course of study . . .": "What Do We Teach About the Negro?" *Journal of the National Education Association* 28, no. 1 (January 1939), 11–12; Epaminandus story: Lee, *For Freedom's Sake*, 4; "no matter how much education . . .": quoted in Powdermaker, *After Freedom*, 302.

45. "You didn't have absolutely nothing to do": Hamer interview with Robert Wright, 4; schools vs. churches: Dollard, *Caste and Class*, 248; Rosenwald schools: Dollard, *Caste and Class*, 45, and Powdermaker, *After Freedom*, 311; Delta Industrial Institute: "Professor W.F. Reden, Superintendent of the Delta Industrial Institute," in Mississippi Welfare League, "The Negro Race in Sunflower County Mississippi" (1919), 11–12; and Hazael Willis Barney, "Memories, Facts & Accomplishments of Delta Industrial Institute" (n.d.), chapter 1.

46. Hamer, "To Praise Our Bridges," 324; John Ware, interview with author, 21 February 2005; Hamers had no children of their own: Kay Mills, *This Little Light of*

Mine: The Life of Fannie Lou Hamer (New York: Plume, 1993), 21, and Lee, *For Freedom's Sake*, 21; Hamers bring Dorothy Jean in: DeMuth, "Tired of Being Sick and Tired," 549; Hamer as timekeeper: Garland, "Builders of a New South," 28–29; Ole Honey's toilet: Garland, "Builders of a New South," 29, and Raines, *My Soul Is Rested*, 255.

47. L.C. Dorsey, "Harder Times than These," in Dorothy Abbott, ed., *Mississippi Writers: Reflections of Youth and Childhood* (Jackson: University Press of Mississippi, 1986), 168; black informant quoted in Dollard, *Caste and Class*, 257–58; Raines, *My Soul Is Rested*, 255.

48. Hamer "gets back" at owner: interview with Aaron Henry, 1 March 1972, University of Southern Mississippi Oral History Program, http://anna.lib.usm.edu/ %7Espcol/crda/oh/ohhenryap.html; "only way I could rebel": Hamer interview with Robert Wright, 4–5.

49. Baptized at age twelve: John Egerton, *A Mind to Stay Here: Profiles from the South* (New York: Macmillan, 1970), 96; religion as alternative to white supremacy: Fredrick C. Harris, *Something Within: Religion in African-American Political Activism* (New York: Oxford University Press, 1999), 40.

50. "The Negro church could enjoy this freedom": E. Franklin Frazier, *The Negro Church in America* (New York: Schocken Books, 1963), 46; church as "antidote": Powdermaker, *After Freedom*, 285.

51. "If we hate whites" sermon quoted in Powdermaker, *After Freedom*, 247–48; "ain't no such of a thing . . .": Kling, *Fannie Lou Hamer*, 14; preacher quoted in Powdermaker, *After Freedom*, 270; "the theory was . . .": Aaron Henry with Constance Curry, *Aaron Henry: The Fire Ever Burning* (Jackson: University Press of Mississippi, 2000), 17.

52. "suppress discontent": Dollard, *Caste and Class*, 248–49; "the only thing we've had . . .": Hamer, "To Praise Our Bridges," 327; "the Negro church is the one institution . . .": Powdermaker, *After Freedom*, 223; sharecroppers command respect in church: Cheryl Townsend Gilkes, "The Politics of 'Silence': Dual-Sex Political Systems and Women's Traditions of Conflict in African-American Religion," in Paul E. Johnson, ed., *African American Christianity: Essays in History* (Berkeley: University of California Press, 1999), 92; "splendid opportunity . . .": Dollard, *Caste and Class*, 224; "the opportunity found . . .": Benjamin E. Mays and Joseph W. Nicholson, *The Negro's Church* (New York: Harper & Bros., 1933), 281.

53. Church "provides an avenue . . .": Powdermaker, *After Freedom*, 274; "leadership skills were honed and practiced": Clifton Taulbert, "As if we were there . . . Remembering Greenville," in *Separate but Equal: The Mississippi Photographs of Henry Clay Anderson* (New York: Public Affairs, 2002), 55; "it is largely the women": Powdermaker, *After Freedom*, 276; "church mothers": Gilkes, "The Politics of 'Silence,'" esp. 80–92; importance of singing: Lee, *For Freedom's Sake*, 14; "continuous surge of affirmation," Dollard, *Caste and Class*, 243.

54. Blacks reshape religion: Charles Marsh, *God's Long Summer: Stories of Faith and Civil Rights* (Princeton: Princeton University Press, 1997), 13; blacks "did not just become Christians . . .": Albert J. Raboteau, "African Americans, Exodus, and the American Israel," in Johnson, *African American Christianity*, 9; C. Eric Lincoln explains how fundamentalist black Christians like Hamer construed freedom: "The black church knew that its paramount mission was freedom . . . the freedom to belong to God, to worship God exclusively, and it is the freedom to participate in the divine agenda without selective hindrance from other human beings. . . . True freedom meant the absence of any inhibiting factors or conditions that could disrupt the divine agenda by arbitrarily conditioning the lives of selective human beings who are still held accountable to God and the community. Mankind was created with the powers of reason and creativity; hence, the absence of educational opportunity is a formidable assault on freedom. Hunger, improper health care, joblessness, drug addiction, debasement, and denigration all inhibit the full flowering of the human potential to belong wholly to God." In Andrew Billingsley, *Mighty Like a River: The Black Church and Social Reform* (New York: Oxford University Press, 1999), xxii–xxiii; sermon about economic equality: Powdermaker, *After Freedom*, 248.

3. "COTTON IS DYNAMITE": NEW DEALS IN SUNFLOWER COUNTY

1. "The best fertilizer is the owner's foot": Anne Eastland Howdershell, interview with author, 7 November 2001; Sue Eastland McRoberts, interview with author, 13 November 2001; "it is because of cotton": Powdermaker, *After Freedom*, 75.

2. "Cotton obsessed . . .": Vance, *Human Geography of the South*, 266; 90 percent of farmland was cotton: Johnson, *Statistical Atlas of Southern Counties*, 172. According to the 1930 census, this figure was second highest in the state; "a plantation center for trading . . .": Works Progress Administration, *Mississippi: The WPA Guide to the Magnolia State* (Jackson: University Press of Mississippi, 1988, orig. 1938), 409, and Mrs. P.C. Wilson, "Sunflower County—General Information," in "Mississippi—Sunflower County, History, WPA Source Material," Sunflower County Library Vertical Files; teacher quoted in Powdermaker, *After Freedom*, 7–9; planters kept workers year-round: Powdermaker, *After Freedom*, 77; Sunflower County population: U.S. Department of Commerce, Bureau of Census, *Fifteenth Census of the United States: Population, Volume III, Part 1* (Washington: GPO, 1931), 1286.

3. "a secular religion . . .": Cohn, *Mississippi Delta and the World*, 61; gas-powered chain saws: Mikko Saikku, *This Delta, This Land: An Environmental History of the Yazoo-Mississippi Floodplain* (Athens: University of Georgia Press, 2005), 108; Eastland's mother remembers fires: Anne Eastland Howdershell, interview with author, 7 November 2001; "just like a man": Hamer interview with Robert Wright, 3.

4. "hoeing the cotton": Hamer interview with Neil McMillen; 3; workers wore knee pads: Dollard, *Caste and Class*, 99.

5. As Alex Lichtenstein explains, rural laborers occupied different positions on a ladder. At the top of the ladder stood the rare "cash tenants," families that owned their own tools and animals, supplied their own seed, and managed their own work under the supervision of the landlord. Next came the majority of agricultural laborers, the "share tenants" and "sharecroppers." They generally did not own their own equipment and depended on the landlord to supply seed and fertilizer. In return, they paid one-fourth to one-half of their crop in rent. At the bottom were day laborers, who owned nothing and had no claim to the crop. Lichtenstein summarizes: "The further down the agricultural ladder one went, the more dependent one became upon the landlord for management, housing, tools, seed, fertilizer, mules, and everything else, and the more of the crop went to the landowner for both rent and to pay back the advances made at the beginning of the season." Alex Lichtenstein, "The Southern Tenant Farmers' Union: A Movement for Social Emancipation," introduction to Howard Kester's *Revolt Among the Sharecroppers* (Knoxville: University of Tennessee Press, 1997; orig., 1936), 26–28; "the belief is general among white people . . .": Powdermaker, *After Freedom*, 88; prices were higher at commissary stores: Dollard, *Caste and Class*, 109, and Powdermaker, *After Freedom*, 82; cropper gets remaining cash: Dollard, *Caste and Class*, 109–10.

6. "Do you mean to call me a liar?": Dollard, *Caste and Class*, 121; "that the debt may be fictitious . . .": Powdermaker, *After Freedom*, 88; "on Settlement Day . . .": Jordana Y. Shakoor, *Civil Rights Childhood* (Jackson: University Press of Mississippi, 1999), 9; "so many 'its' in cotton'": Hamer interview with Robert Wright, 17.

7. "nothing but a child . . .": Harris Dickson, *The Story of King Cotton* (Westport, CT: Negro Universities Press, 1970; orig. 1937), 173; "friend and protector": William Alexander Percy, *Lanterns on the Levee: Recollections of a Planter's Son* (Baton Rouge: Louisiana University Press, 1973; orig. 1941), 227; "profit-sharing . . .": Percy, 278; "to live among a people . . .": Percy, 298.

8. Dollard, *Caste and Class*, 121.

9. "mighty nice man": Mack Caples, interview with author, 8 July 2000; "workers didn't suffer for nothing": Willie Jackson, interview with author, 8 July 2000; "if they had been faithful . . .": Anne Eastland Howdershell, interview with author, 7 November 2001.

10. Mrs. Willie Jackson, interview with author, 8 July 2000; Rosie Cole, interview with author, 25 September 2001; Charles McLaurin, interview with author, 20 September 2001; Rev. Tommie Jean Lunsford, interview with Steve Estes and author, 12 July 2000; "We would never send a deputy . . .": Charlie Capps interview with Charles Bolton, 9 August 1999, Delta State Oral Histories, Capps Archives, Delta State University; "wouldn't let the polices come . . .": Rosie Cole, interview with author, 25 September 2001. Personal correspondence, particularly from Woods Eastland to local law officials, confirms this phenomenon. See, for example, letter from Woods C. Eastland to George T. Mitchell, 26 April 1940, Archives and Special Collections, University of Mississippi, James O. Eastland Collection, File Series 1, Subseries 2, Box 1, Folder 10;

Eastland gets sentence reduced: Mrs. Willie Jackson, interview with author, 8 July 2000, and Willie Jackson, interview with author, 8 July 2000; Eastlands appeal to law enforcement officials: letter from James O. Eastland to Paul B. Johnson, 7 May 1942, Archives and Special Collections, University of Mississippi, James O. Eastland Collection, File Series 1, Subseries 2, Box 1, Folder 12; letter from James O. Eastland to Allen Cox, 21 November 1946, University of Mississippi, Special Collections and Archives, James O. Eastland Collection, File Series 1, Subseries 3, Box 1, Folder 71; letter from Ed C. Brewer to James O. Eastland, 5 November, 1945, University of Mississippi, Special Collections and Archives, James O. Eastland Collection, File Series 1, Subseries 3, Box 1, Folder 58; "there are plenty of old Negroes": letter from Woods C. Eastland to Governor Paul B. Johnson, 13 May 1940, Archives and Special Collections, University of Mississippi, James O. Eastland Collection, File Series 1, Subseries 2, Box 1, Folder 10; Eastland acknowledged that his workers had many stills on the plantation, but insisted that his farm was no worse than any other: letter from James O. Eastland to Ed C. Brewer, 12 May 1945, University of Mississippi, Special Collections and Archives, James O. Eastland Collection, File Series 1, Subseries 3, Box 1, Folder 52; Cobb comment on Eastland workers quoted in Raines, *My Soul Is Rested*, 247; "that's those Eastland plantation folks": Rev. Tommie Jean Lunsford, interview with Steve Estes and author, 12 July 2000.

11. "The status of dependency . . .": Charles S. Johnson, Edwin R. Embree, and W.W. Alexander, *The Collapse of Cotton Tenancy* (Chapel Hill: University of North Carolina Press, 1935), 20–22.

12. "very intelligent Negro": quoted in Dollard, *Caste and Class*, 120; Johnson, Embree, and Alexander, *Collapse of Cotton Tenancy*, 20–22; "the Negroes are shiftless . . .": Dollard, *Caste and Class*, 104; "the ignorance and shiftlessness . . .": Dollard, *Caste and Class*, 113.

13. "world power": James A.B. Scherer, *Cotton as a World Power* (New York: Frederick Stokes, 1916), 358; "each of us a world citizen": Cohn, *Mississippi Delta and the World*, 93; "cotton is dynamite": folk saying quoted in Rupert B. Vance, *Human Geography of the South: A Study in Regional Resources and Human Adequacy* (New York: Russell & Russell, 1935, orig. 1932), 270.

14. Jacobson and Smith, *Cotton's Renaissance*, 41, 44–45.

15. Cotton boom: Brandfon, *Cotton Kingdom of the New South*, 115; centralized management: Aiken, *Cotton Plantation South*, 5–8, 55, and Jack Temple Kirby, *Rural Worlds Lost: The American South, 1920–1960* (Baton Rouge: Louisiana State University Press, 1987), 27; cotton statistics: Jacobson and Smith, *Cotton's Renaissance*, 59.

16. Interestingly, it was the American Civil War that had given the cotton-growing industry in foreign countries a jump-start. The shortage of raw cotton that resulted from the North's blockade of southern ports encouraged other nations to seek alternative sources of cotton for their textile mills. One historian calls the years of the U.S. Civil War an "important turning point" in the history of the Egyptian cotton industry. "In five years, the harvest had quadrupled, the area quintupled, and from then on cotton be-

came once and for all the crop which absorbed the major portion of Egyptian energies and produced an overwhelming share of its exports." E.R.J. Owen, *Cotton and the Egyptian Economy, 1820–1914* (Oxford: Clarendon Press, 1969), 89; Cyrill O'Donnell, *Recent Trends in the Demand for American Cotton* (Chicago: University of Chicago Press, 1945), 23; Jacobson and Smith, *Cotton's Renaissance*, 277; "English mills are now running . . .": "Cotton Facts," *Ruleville Record*, 10 February 1921, 1; Delta planters keep tabs: Walter Sillers article to local newspapers, 1931, Walter Sillers Papers, Capps Archives, Delta State University, Box 17:24.

17. British cotton executive quoted in Brandfon, *Cotton Kingdom of the New South*, 118–19.

18. Sven Beckert, "From Tuskegee to Togo: The Problem of Freedom in the Empire of Cotton," *Journal of American History* 92, no. 2 (September 2005), 498–526.

19. Zaire's cotton industry: Osumaka Likaka, *Rural Society and Cotton in Colonial Zaire* (Madison: University of Wisconsin Press, 1997), 5, 7–8, 14–15; Mozambique's cotton industry: Allen Isaacman, "Coercion, Paternalism and the Labour Process: The Mozambican Cotton Regime 1938–1961," *Journal of Southern African Studies* 18, no. 3 (September 1992), 487, 497.

20. "among the most erratic . . .": Johnson, Embree, and Alexander, *Collapse of Cotton Tenancy*, 38; "even in times of peace . . .": Scherer, *Cotton as a World Power*, 361; "every mite of data": Dickson, *Story of King Cotton*, 87.

21. Japan increased its number of cotton spindles from 3.8 million to 7.1 million; India from 6.5 million to 9 million; China from less than 4 million to more than 7 million; and Brazil from barely 1 million to nearly 3 million. W.J. Cash, *The Mind of the South* (New York: Knopf, 1941), 409; competition in other states: Johnson, Embree, and Alexander, *Collapse of Cotton Tenancy*, 36–39.

22. Salter quoted in David L. Cohn, *The Life and Times of King Cotton* (New York: Oxford University Press, 1966), 240; Brazil quadrupled production: I.W. Duggan and Paul W. Chapman, *'Round the World with Cotton* (Washington, DC: USDA, GPO, 1941), 81. As the American cotton industry lagged behind its foreign competitors, it lost its preeminence in the U.S. economy as well. Where in 1927 cotton had accounted for almost half of all American agricultural exports and 17 percent of total exports, ten years later it represented merely a third of agricultural exports and less than 10 percent of total exports. Duggan and Chapman, *'Round the World with Cotton*, 37, 134–35; Jacobson and Smith, *Cotton's Renaissance*, 59. Cyrill O'Donnell, *Recent Trends in the Demand for American Cotton* (Chicago: University of Chicago Press, 1945), Appendix.

23. "We had no rain . . .": Otha Shurden, *Cotton: Always "King" with Me* (W.O. Shurden, 1985), 12; cotton prices: U.S. Bureau of the Census, *Historical Statistics of the United States: Colonial Times to 1970* (Washington, DC: GPO, 1975), series K 554–56, 517; planters cut wages: *Indianola Enterprise*, 1 October 1931; "the most serious situation . . .": Walter Sillers article to local newspapers, 1933, Walter Sillers Papers, Capps Archives, Delta State University, Box 49:13.

24. Checks sent to planters, not sharecroppers: Louis Cantor, *A Prologue to the Protest Movement: The Missouri Sharecropper Roadside Demonstration of 1939* (Durham: Duke University Press, 1969), 19; planters often cheated tenants: Gavin Wright, *Old South, New South: Revolutions in the Southern Economy Since the Civil War* (Baton Rouge: Louisiana State University Press, 1986), 227–28, and Donald Holley, *The Second Great Emancipation: The Mechanical Cotton Picker, Black Migration, and How They Shaped the Modern South* (Fayetteville: University of Arkansas Press, 2000), 69; Percy quoted in Cobb, *Most Southern Place on Earth*, 190.

25. Roger D. Tate Jr., "Easing the Burden: The Era of Depression and the New Deal in Mississippi," PhD dissertation, University of Tennessee, 1978, 75–76.

26. Federal officials needed planter consent: Devra Weber, *Dark Sweat, White Gold: California Farm Workers, Cotton, and the New Deal* (Berkeley: University of California Press, 1994), 113; founding of Delta Council: Nan Woodruff, "Mississippi Delta Planters and Debates over Mechanization, Labor, and Civil Rights in the 1940s," *Journal of Southern History* 60 (May 1994), 264; "programs rescued and enriched . . .": Kirby, *Rural Worlds Lost*, 56.

27. Eastlands paid $26,000: Tate, "Easing the Burden," 81; payments for relief in Sunflower County: Johnson, Embree, and Alexander, *Collapse of Cotton Tenancy*, 62; Tate, "Easing the Burden," 85, 91; investigation of large payments: Lawrence J. Nelson, "Oscar Johnston, the New Deal, and the Cotton Subsidy Payments Controversy, 1936–1937," *Journal of Southern History* XL, no. 3 (August 1974), 399–416.

28. "planter's heaven . . .": Wright, *Old South, New South*, 236; Eastland plantation expansion: Sunflower County Chancery Clerk, Land Deed of Trust X7: 128, 214; C8: 15–16; F8: 208; Q8: 236; S8: 386; B9: 447; C9: 9; H9: 230; K9: 74, 233, 492; O9: 577, 596; W9: 458; C10: 486, 505–6, 557, 559; number of workers on Eastland farm: Woods Eastland, interview with author, 16 February 2005. This Woods Eastland is the grandson of the Woods Eastland who expanded the family farm in the 1930s. Staple Cotton Discount Corporation, Loan Budget Application, 8 February 1937, University of Mississippi, Special Collections and Archives, James O. Eastland Collection, File Series 1, Subseries 3, Box 1, Folder 14.

29. Holley, *Second Great Emancipation*, 2, 11; Cobb, *Most Southern Place on Earth*, 197; Wright, *Old South, New South*, 235; Warren Whatley, "Labor for the Picking: The New Deal in the South," *Journal of Economic History* 33, no. 4 (1983), 908.

30. "A successful cotton picker . . .": quoted in Wright, *Old South, New South*, 242; "the mechanical cotton picker . . .": *Sunflower Tocsin*, 24 February 1938.

31. Rust quoted in Holley, *Second Great Emancipation*, 61; heighten contradictions of capitalism: Sam H. Franklin Jr., "Early Years of the Delta Cooperative Farm and the Providence Cooperative Farm," 19–20, Jerry Dallas Delta Farm Cooperative Collection, Capps Archives, Delta State University, Box 1.

32. "There is impending . . .": Johnson, Embree, and Alexander, *Collapse of Cotton Tenancy*, 43–44; *Jackson Daily News* quoted in Holley, *Second Great Emancipation*,

77–78; renewed African colonization movement: Dollard, *Caste and Class*, 131; black farmer quoted in Holley, *Second Great Emancipation*, 65–66.

33. Among the products of this attention were Norman Thomas's *The Plight of the Sharecropper* (1935), Arthur Raper's *Preface to Peasantry* (1936), Henry I. Richards's *Cotton and the AAA* (1936), and James Agee's *Let Us Now Praise Famous Men* (1941); "Many parts of the south . . .": Reinhold Niebuhr, "Meditations from Mississippi," *Christian Century* 54 (10 February 1937), 184; "ought to give men plenty . . .": Jonathan Daniels, *A Southerner Discovers the South* (New York: Macmillan Company, 1938), 136.

34. Sixth World Congress declaration: Robin D.G. Kelley, *Hammer and Hoe: Alabama Communists in the Great Depression* (Chapel Hill: University of North Carolina Press, 1990), 13; Communist organizers in Delta: Woodruff, *American Congo*, 155; "a rebirth in the life . . .": "The Road to LIBERATION for the NEGRO PEOPLE," Workers Library Publishers, Inc., September 1937, in "South (Communism), 1949–1958," Subject Files, Records of the U.S. Senate, Senate Internal Security Subcommittee, Box 255.

35. Founding black member quoted in H.L. Mitchell, "The Founding and Early History of the Southern Tenant Farmers Union," *Arkansas Historical Quarterly* 32 (1973), 351; success of 1935 strike: Donald Grubbs, *Cry from the Cotton: The Southern Tenant Farmers' Union and the New Deal* (Chapel Hill: University of North Carolina Press, 1971), 84–86.

36. Reinhold Niebuhr, "Meditations from Mississippi," *Christian Century* 54 (10 February 1937), 184. Jerry Dallas Delta Farm Cooperative Collection, Capps Archives, Delta State University, Box 1, Folder 2; Sam H. Franklin Jr., "Early Years of the Delta Cooperative Farm and the Providence Cooperative Farm," Jerry Dallas Delta Farm Cooperative Collection, Capps Archives, Delta State University, Box 1, 12; see also Jerry W. Dallas, "The Delta and Providence Farms: A Mississippi Experiment in Cooperative Farming and Racial Cooperation, 1936–1956," *Mississippi Quarterly* 40 (summer 1987), 283–308; and H.L. Mitchell, *Mean Things Happening in This Land: The Life and Times of H.L. Mitchell, Co-Founder of the Southern Tenant Farmers' Union* (Montclair: Allanheld, Osmun, & Co., 1979), 133–34.

37. Rust's idea to create foundation: Sam H. Franklin Jr., "Early Years of the Delta Cooperative Farm and the Providence Cooperative Farm," Jerry Dallas Delta Farm Cooperative Collection, Capps Archives, Delta State University, Box 1, 19–20; Reinhold Niebuhr, "Meditations from Mississippi," *Christian Century* 54 (10 February 1937), 184.

38. Success of reform effort: Patricia Sullivan, *Days of Hope: Race and Democracy in the New Deal Era* (Chapel Hill: University of North Carolina Press, 1996), 94; "putting people on jobs": Hamer interview with Neil McMillen; "Say, my Lord knows . . .": Powdermaker, *After Freedom*, 138; "a good deal of resistance": Dollard, *Caste and Class*, 125.

39. Popularity of Communist Party in 1930s: John E. Haynes, *Red Scare or Red Menace? American Communism and Anticommunism in the Cold War Era* (Chicago: Ivan R. Dee, 1996), 11–16, and Ted Morgan, *Reds: McCarthyism in Twentieth-Century America* (New York: Random House, 2003), 166–69; "planters are having trouble": *Sunflower*

Tocsin, 25 February 1937; "every man and woman who can work . . . ": *Ruleville Record*, 21 June 1934.

40. Eastland's son notes that he initially had the outlook of a Hill farmer. Woods Eastland, interview with author, 16 October 2001.

41. Eastland originally declined job offer from Gov. Johnson: Erle Johnston, "Reminiscing: How a Senator Was Born," in Erle Johnston Papers, Box 3, Folder 8, McCain Library and Archives, University of Southern Mississippi; "the boy'll do it": Senator Joseph Biden recounted having heard this story from Senator Eastland. Nick Walters, "The Repairman Chairman: Senator James O. Eastland and His Influence on the U.S. Supreme Court," master's thesis, Mississippi College, 1992, 11–12. Judge Thomas Brady recalled having witnessed Gov. Johnson make the appointment, to the surprise of the younger Eastland. Interview with Thomas Brady, 17 May 1972, University of Southern Mississippi Oral History Program, http://anna.lib.usm.edu/%7Espcol/crda/oh/ohbradyt2p.html.

42. "a surprise almost amounting to a shock . . .": *Ruleville Record*, 3 July 1941.

43. On early American anti-Communism: Melvyn Leffler, *The Specter of Communism: The United States and the Origins of the Cold War 1917–1953* (New York: Hill and Wang, 1994), esp. chap. 2, and M.J. Heale, *McCarthy's Americans: Red Scare Politics in State and Nation, 1935–1965* (Athens: University of Georgia Press, 1998), xi–xvii; first "Red scare": Richard M. Fried, *Nightmare in Red: The McCarthy Era in Perspective* (New York: Oxford University Press, 1990), 47–49; "get rid of labor agitators and communists": *Sunflower Tocsin*, 21 January 1937; 25 February 1937 (quote); 20 May 1937.

44. "This is the big battle . . .": Letter from Walter Sillers to James Eastland, 27 August 1941, Walter Sillers Papers, Capps Archives, Delta State University, Box 98:3; Sillers background and nickname: Thomas R. Melton, "Mr. Speaker: A Biography of Walter Sillers," master's thesis, University of Mississippi, 1972, 1–14.

45. "Walter, I was amazed . . .": letter from James Eastland to Walter Sillers, Walter Sillers Papers, Capps Archives, Delta State University, Box 98:3; Hodding Carter quoted in Mary Rose Gladney, "I'll Take My Stand: The Southern Segregation Academy Movement," PhD dissertation, University of New Mexico, 1974, 31.

46. "If they must fight . . .": *Sunflower Tocsin*, 11 March 1937; "What has happened to the War?": *Delta Hub*, 26 September 1941.

47. "contemptible, malicious stab . . .": *Congressional Record* 87, 6983–4. As with the cotton industry as a whole, the cottonseed industry had faced upheaval during the Depression, with the net result that large producers began to consolidate their operations and made it more difficult for smaller operators to survive. Lynette Boney Wrenn, *Cinderella of the New South: A History of the Cottonseed Industry, 1855–1955* (Knoxville: University of Tennessee Press, 1995), 162–71.

48. Handwritten notes: Smith, "James O. Eastland," 48; "This attack on cotton . . .": James O. Eastland, "Brazilian Cotton, Henderson and Cottonseed Oil" (Washington, DC: GPO, 1941), 2.

49. "You have made many new friends . . .": letter from A.R. Beasley to James O.

Eastland, 13 September 1941, University of Mississippi, Special Collections and Archives, James O. Eastland Collection, File Series 1, Subseries 7, Box 1, Folder 3; cartoon: *Delta Hub*, 19 September 1941; "For God's sake . . .": letter from Woods C. Eastland to James O. Eastland, 11 August 1941, Archives and Special Collections, University of Mississippi, James O. Eastland Collection, File Series 1, Subseries 2, Box 1, Folder 11.

50. Eastland joins Bankhead on bill: *Delta Hub*, 24 October 1941; "The farmer of the South must work harder . . .": James Eastland, "World Cotton: The Farmer's Gateway Through the Tariff Wall—Bankhead-Eastland Cotton Bill" (Washington, DC: GPO, 1941), 7.

51. "hooked him": Anne Howdershell Eastland, interview with author, 6 November 2001, and William Winter, interview with author, 22 March 2005; "planter playboy": "Eastland's Value in Senate Doubted," letter to the editor, *Jackson Daily News*, 24 July 1942; roots in both regions as asset: Clarence Pierce, interview with author, 28 September 2001; "Jim Eastland and his father . . .": letter from Walter Sillers to M.S. Knowlton, 1 September 1942, Walter Sillers Papers, Capps Archives, Delta State University, Box 98:1; "poured into the campaign": Erle Johnston, *Politics: Mississippi Style* (Forest, MS: Lake Harbor Publishers, 1993), 64.

52. "surest safe-guard . . .": "Vote for Jim—You Can Depend on Him," campaign flyer, Mississippi Department of Archives and History, Subject Files, James O. Eastland file, 1941–42; Sillers is loyal supporter: letter from James O. Eastland to Alice Cumings Nagel, 20 January 1943, University of Mississippi, Special Collections and Archives, James O. Eastland Collection, File Series 1, Subseries 7, Box 1, Folder 5; "communism means social equality . . .": letter from Walter Sillers to James Eastland, Walter Sillers Papers, Capps Archives, Delta State University, Box 98:3.

53. Eastland campaigned circulated Doxey letters: William Winter, interview with author, 22 March 2005; "Traitors in Labor's robes . . .": James Eastland, untitled campaign speech, Paul B. Johnson Papers, Box 101, folder 20. McCain Library and Archives, University of Southern Mississippi.

54. "Better than any other candidate . . .": *Jackson Daily News*, 17 September 1942; "folks are tiring . . .": *Forest News Register*, 17 September 1942; "a man who is steeped . . .": *Tupelo Daily News*, 15 September 1942; "stand firm . . .": letter from Walter Sillers to James Eastland, 15 December 1942, Walter Sillers Papers, Capps Archives, Delta State University, Box 98:1; Johnston, *Politics*, 67.

4. "AN ENORMOUS TRAGEDY IN THE MAKING": REVOLUTIONS IN SUNFLOWER COUNTY AND ABROAD

1. "The white fields are alive . . .": Frank Smith, "Cotton's Kingdom," *South: The Magazine of Travel* 2, no. 7 (July 1946), 18; "The countryside was full of people": Woods

Eastland, interview with author, 16 October 2001; "The September visitor . . .": Smith, "Cotton's Kingdom," 9.

2. Letter from Oscar F. Bledsoe to James Eastland, 5 April 1943, Walter Sillers Papers, Capps Archives, Delta State University, Box 98:2.

3. Labor surplus: James H. Street, *The New Revolution in the Cotton Economy: Mechanization and Its Consequences* (Chapel Hill: University of North Carolina Press, 1957), 71–72; Cohn, *Life and Times of King Cotton*, 259; Warren Whatley, "Labor for the Picking," 905–29; Lillian Smith quoted in Cobb, *Most Southern Place on Earth*, 202; "The area no longer has any surplus . . .": "Annual Report of Delta Council, 1943–1944," 5, Delta Council Collection, Capps Archives, Delta State University, Box 1, Folder 3; Sunflower County lost 4,000 workers: *Ruleville Record*, 11 November 1943, 16 December 1943; "we have a much higher percentage . . .": *Ruleville Record*, 11 November 1943.

4. "I can't find a negro anywhere": undated letter, Elizabeth Eastland to James Eastland, Archives and Special Collections, University of Mississippi, James O. Eastland Collection, File Series 1, Subseries 2, Box 1, Folder 3; "dreadfully lonely": undated letter, Elizabeth Eastland to James Eastland; letter from Elizabeth Eastland to James Eastland, 1 March 1943; letter from Elizabeth Eastland to James Eastland, 15 May 1943, Archives and Special Collections, University of Mississippi, James O. Eastland Collection, File Series 1, Subseries 2, Box 1, Folder 3; Libby asks for apartment: letter from Elizabeth Eastland to James Eastland, 20 June 1943, Archives and Special Collections, University of Mississippi, James O. Eastland Collection, File Series 1, Subseries 2, Box 1, Folder 3; "lay off the liquor": letter from Woods C. Eastland to James O. Eastland, 26 August 1941, Archives and Special Collections, University of Mississippi, James O. Eastland Collection, File Series 1, Subseries 2, Box 1, Folder 11.

5. "unethical labor . . .": "Annual Report of Delta Council, 1943–1944," Delta Council Collection, Capps Archives, Delta State University, Box 1, Folder 3; wages jumped: Nan Woodruff, "Mississippi Delta Planters and Debates over Mechanization, Labor, and Civil Rights in the 1940s," *Journal of Southern History* 60 (May 1994), 266; "with those checks . . .": *Ruleville Record*, 11 January 1945.

6. Dorothy Lee Black of the Delta Council saw Eastland's role as essential in the passage of the ceiling: *Ruleville Record*, 13 September 1945, 20 September 1945; J. Lewis Henderson, "In the Cotton Delta," *Survey Graphic* 36, no. 1 (January 1948), 51.

7. POWs on Eastland farm: Eastland Plantation, Weekly Gin Report, 27 October 1945, University of Mississippi, Special Collections and Archives, James O. Eastland Collection, File Series 1, Subseries 3, Box 1, Folder 57; POWs paid $2 per hundred pounds: *Ruleville Record*, 30 September 1943; "trashy cotton": *Ruleville Record*, 1 February 1945; "Of course, they didn't know . . .": interview with Les Fletcher, 22 March 1989, Sunflower County Library Oral History Collection; "This labor, though unskilled . . .": "Annual Report of Delta Council, 1943–1944," Delta Council Collection,

Capps Archives, Delta State University, Box 1, Folder 3, 11; POWs stay on after war's end: "Delta Council Annual Report, 1945–1946," Delta Council Collection, Capps Archives, Delta State University, Box 1, Folder 3, 32.

8. Labor movement's wartime gains: John Jeffries, *Wartime America: The World War Two Home Front* (Chicago: Ivan R. Dee, 1996), chapter 3; "these labor gangsters": letter from Gherton E. Roberts to James O. Eastland, 5 January 1943, University of Mississippi, Special Collections and Archives, James O. Eastland Collection, File Series 1, Subseries 7, Box 1, Folder 5; "We are not only fighting . . .": letter from James O. Eastland to R. C. Weems, 15 January 1943, University of Mississippi, Special Collections and Archives, James O. Eastland Collection, File Series 1, Subseries 7, Box 1, Folder 5; CIO as "aliens": *Congressional Record* 90 (12 May 1944): 4402; Eastland proposed three bills: *Congressional Record Index*, vol. 89.

9. *Memphis Press Scimitar*, 12 November 1978; Anne Eastland Howdershell, interview with author, 7 November 2001.

10. The other members of the trip were: Senators Burnet Maybank (D-SC), Richard Russell (D-GA), Clyde Reed (R-KS), Stewart (D-TN), John McClellan (D-AR), Harry Byrd (D-VA), Chapman Revercomb (D-WV), and J. Chandler Gurney (R-SD). *Clarion-Ledger*, 14 June 1945; "nothing promising": *Clarion-Ledger*, 15 June 1945.

11. Interestingly, just as so many white southerners ignored black suffering during and after the Civil War, Eastland did not comment upon the suffering of Jews in Europe during World War II—he focused solely on white German suffering. "Shameful" era: *Congressional Record* 94 (9 February 1948), 1193. For a scholarly examination of the parallels between Reconstruction in the South and Germany, see Norbert Finzsch and Jurgen Martschukat, eds., *Different Restorations: Reconstruction and "Wiederaufbau" in Germany and the United States: 1865, 1945, and 1989* (Providence, RI: Berghahn Books, 1996); This extraordinarily powerful and enduring interpretation of American Reconstruction became an article of faith among white southerners well before the twentieth century. See Foner, *Reconstruction*, esp. xix–xxvii, 608–9; Howard Rabinowitz, "The Limits of Victory: Lessons from American Reconstruction for German Reconstruction and Reunification" in Finzsch and Martschukat, *Different Restorations*, 202–29; "The Republican Party attempted to destroy . . .": *Congressional Record* 94 (9 February 1948), 1193; Eastland family in Civil War: *Time*, 26 March 1956, 27; *Scott County Register*, 8 November 1911; "Germany has served . . .": *Congressional Record* 91 (4 December 1945), 11376.

12. Henry Morgenthau, *Germany Is Our Problem* (New York: Harper & Brothers, 1945), 16, 48. Warren F. Kimball, *Swords or Ploughshares? The Morgenthau Plan for Defeated Nazi Germany, 1943–1946* (Philadelphia: Lippincott, 1976), 3–5, 19–21; John Lewis Gaddis, *The United States and the Origins of the Cold War 1941–1947* (New York: Columbia University Press, 1972), 94–132; Jeffry M. Diefendorf, Axel Frohn, and Hermann-Josef Rupieper, eds., *American Policy and the Reconstruction of West Germany, 1945–1955* (Cambridge: Cambridge University Press, 1993), vii; John Gillingham, "From Morgenthau Plan to Schuman Plan: America and the Reorganization of Europe,"

in Diefendorf, Frohn, and Rupieper, *American Policy*, 111–18; on the post-Potsdam administration, see Gaddis, *United States and the Origins of the Cold War*, 94–132.

13. Rep. William Colmer, Senator Eastland's Mississippi colleague, issued a scathing indictment of U.S. policy based on observations made during a tour of Europe. Published on November 11, the Colmer report focused on the starvation rampant in Germany and urged immediate relief along with long-term economic rehabilitation. Two weeks later, Byron Price, the director of the Bureau of Censorship, seconded Colmer's recommendations in a separate report that emphasized the importance of developing German exports. The next day, General Dwight Eisenhower, military governor of the American zone in Germany, warned that population increases and a lack of adequate shelter in the U.S.-occupied territory could lead to disease and starvation. Wolfgang Schlauch, "Representative William Colmer and Senator James O. Eastland and the Reconstruction of Germany, 1945," *Journal of Mississippi History* 34 (August 1972), 200–201; "sadistic" policy: *Congressional Record* 91 (4 December 1945), 11375; "predatory, aggressor nation . . .": ibid., 11377.

14. *Congressional Record* 91 (4 December 1945), 11371–75.

15. State Department shifts policy: Schlauch, "Representative William Colmer and Senator James O. Eastland," 210–11; "This is the greatest crisis": *Congressional Record* 93 (11 April 1947), 3325.

16. Eastland had helped swing the Mississippi delegation to Truman during the 1944 Democratic National Convention: "A Cotton Grower from the Mississippi Delta," biographical sketch, 1946, Archives and Special Collections, University of Mississippi, James O. Eastland Collection, File Series 1, Subseries 1, Box 1, Folder 3. 7; Truman quoted in Mary Dudziak, *Cold War Civil Rights: Race and the Image of American Democracy* (Princeton: Princeton University Press, 2000), 27.

17. *Congressional Record* 93 (11 April 1947), 3324, 3328; *Jackson Daily News*, 11 April 1947.

18. *Congressional Record* 93 (11 April 1947), 3324–25; The American Forum of the Air, "Can America's Armies of Occupation Secure the Peace?" 30 April 1946 (Washington, DC: Ransdell Inc. 1946), University of Mississippi Special Collections and Archives, 3.

19. Cotton market in shambles after war: Delta Council, "A Prospectus of the Yazoo-Mississippi Delta" (Stoneville, MS: Delta Council, 1944), Delta Council Collection, Capps Archives, Delta State University, Box 1, 5–6; Wayne A. Grove, "Better Opportunities or Worse? The Demise of Cotton Harvest Labor, 1949–1964," *Journal of Economic History* 63, no. 2 (September 2003), 740; "If we don't get into the world market . . .": letter from Oscar F. Bledsoe to James Eastland, 5 April 1943, Walter Sillers Papers, Capps Archives, Delta State University, Box 98:2; "precarious future": Annual Report of Delta Council, 1943–1944," Delta Council Collection, Capps Archives, Delta State University, Box 1, Folder 3; "Let's Prevent Chaos in Cotton": *Jackson Daily News*, 10 June 1945.

20. Clayton's ideology: W.L. Clayton vs. Dr. Tait Butler, "Our National Cotton Policy"

(Clemson, SC: Clemson Agricultural College in cooperation with USDA, September 1934), 17; Clayton's ideas incorporated into Marshall Plan: Jacobson and Smith, *Cotton's Renaissance*, 282; success of Marshall Plan: Joseph A. Fry, *Dixie Looks Abroad: The South and U.S. Foreign Relations, 1789-1973* (Baton Rouge: Louisiana State University Press, 2002), 229; fears of "International New Deal": Michael J. Hogan, *Cross of Iron: Harry S Truman and the Creation of the National Security State, 1945-1954* (Cambridge: Cambridge University Press, 1998), 89-95. As Benjamin O. Fordham argues, even in times of heightened security, such as the early Cold War years of 1949-50, economic concerns play a prominent role in determining the foreign policy views of individual politicians. Benjamin O. Fordham, "Economic Interests, Party, and Ideology in Early Cold War Era U.S. Foreign Policy," *International Organization* 52, no. 2 (spring 1998), 359-96.

21. More than one-third of cotton exports to Western Europe: Read Dunn Jr., "Problems in Keeping Our Foreign Markets for Cotton," Report to the National Cotton Council, 1948, 4. In a 1948 report to the National Cotton Council, analyst Dunn argued that passing the Marshall Plan was the number one priority for cotton growers. Delta Council's support for Marshall Plan: "Delta Council in 1948-1949, Progress for Tomorrow," Delta Council Collection, Capps Archives, Delta State University, Box 1, Folder 3, 20; "historic markets": Fry, *Dixie Looks Abroad*, 229.

22. Mary Dudziak, "Desegregation as a Cold War Imperative," *Stanford Law Review* 41 (November 1988), 62, 73-76, 78-79, 98-102. See also Dudziak, *Cold War Civil Rights*, 3-46.

23. "interested in world markets . . .": *Ruleville Record*, 2 May 1946.

24. Bethune quoted in Sullivan, *Days of Hope*, 136. On FEPC, see also Andrew Edmund Kersten, *Race, Jobs, and the War: The FEPC in the Midwest, 1941-46* (Urbana: University of Illinois Press, 2000), 1-20; Louis Ruchames, *Race, Jobs, and Politics: The Story of FEPC* (New York: Columbia University Press, 1953), 3-45; Merl E. Reed, *Seedtime for the Modern Civil Rights Movement: The President's Committee on Fair Employment Practice, 1941-1946* (Baton Rouge: Louisiana State University Press, 1991), 11-20.

25. Paul Gordon Lauren, *Power and Prejudice: The Politics and Diplomacy of Racial Discrimination* (Boulder, CO: Westview Press, 1996), esp. chapters 4-5. See also Gerald Horne, *Black and Red: W.E.B. Du Bois and the Afro-American Response to the Cold War, 1944-1963* (Albany: State University of New York Press, 1986), 19-24, 277-78; Penny Von Eschen, *Race Against Empire: Black Americans and Anticolonialism, 1937-1957* (Ithaca: Cornell University Press, 1997), esp. chapters 1-2. Anthropologist Franz Boas and his students, including Margaret Mead and Ruth Benedict, conducted intensive fieldwork in various countries to show that, in Mead's words, "all human beings share in a basic humanity." John Dower, *War Without Mercy: Race and Power in the Pacific War* (New York: Pantheon, 1986), 119-20. On the impact of Myrdal, Paul Lauren argues that "no book, before or since, has ever had as much an impact upon how race in America is viewed." Paul Gordon Lauren, "Seen from the Outside: The International Per-

spective on America's Dilemma," in Brenda Gayle Plummer, ed., *Window on Freedom: Race, Civil Rights, and Foreign Affairs, 1945–1988* (Chapel Hill: University of North Carolina Press, 2003), 23; "America can demonstrate . . .": Gunnar Myrdal, *An American Dilemma: The Negro Problem and Modern Democracy* (New York: Harper & Brothers, 1944), 1021–22.

26. Randolph quoted in Timothy B. Tyson, *Radio Free Dixie: Robert F. Williams and the Roots of Black Power* (Chapel Hill: University of North Carolina Press, 1999), 29. Double V campaign: Brenda Gayle Plummer, *Rising Wind: Black Americans and Foreign Affairs, 1935–1960* (Chapel Hill: University of North Carolina Press, 1996), 85; Sullivan, *Days of Hope*, 106–8, 136–37; "an alarming tendency": *Current Biography 1949*, 185; race riots: Myrdal, *American Dilemma*, 567–68.

27. "not only un-American . . . ": *The Nation*, 16 June 1945, 663; FEPC bill: *New York Times*, 25 May 1945.

28. *Clarion-Ledger*, 30 June 1945; *Chicago Defender*, 7 July 1945; *New York Times*, 30 June 1945.

29. *Congressional Record* 91 (29 June 1945): 6992–95. American blacks were not the only despicable Negro soldiers, Eastland maintained. He accused French Senegalese troops of assaulting "several thousand Christian German girls from good families" while on duty—"white soldiers would not have been guilty of such a thing." *Congressional Record* 91 (29 June 1945), 6996.

30. *Congressional Record* 91 (29 June 1945), 6991.

31. *Congressional Record* 91 (29 June 1945), 6994–97; *Chicago Defender*, 28 July 1945, 14. A French army spokesman also said there was "no truth in the statement" Eastland made about French Senegalese troops. *Chicago Defender*, 7 July 1945.

32. "a fox had gotten loose": *Time*, 28 January 1946, 22; "two years if necessary,": ibid., 22; "senseless display . . .": *Washington Post*, 22 January 1946; other criticism: *New Republic*, 28 January 1946, 109.

33. *New York Times*, 19 January 1946; "as iniquitous as the Freedman's Bureau": *Congressional Record* 92 (5 February 1946), 883.

34. *Congressional Record* 92 (6 February 1946), 955, 884. Blacks were not the only other "race" that excited Eastland. Throughout his speeches during the filibuster, he specifically linked blacks and Jews together, but often he seemed to do so in a cynical manner that made him appear to be their staunch defender. For example, he emphasized the grave consequences minorities would face if the FEPC bill passed. He used the two groups interchangeably as he made rhetorical points. "If the Congress has the constitutional power to say that a person may not be discriminated against in employment because he happens to be a Negro, because he happens to be a Jew, or because he happens to be a member of some other minority race," Eastland warned, "then the Congress has the power to say that he may be discriminated against." The bill was being used as "vote bait in order to obtain some Negro or Jewish votes," he argued, and "the Jews of this country who think are the last ones who should support such a measure." Critics questioned Eastland's professed concern for blacks and Jews. In "Swastika over

the Senate," *Nation* columnist I.F. Stone attacked the southern senators, and Eastland in particular, for a filibuster "shot through with anti-Semitism." "If any such naked racism is displayed by a German political assembly," Stone charged, "we shall be forced to lengthen our term of occupation." *Congressional Record* 92 (9 February 1946), 1205; *Congressional Record* 92 (17 January 1946), 91; I.F. Stone, "Swastika over the Senate," *The Nation*, 9 February 1946, 158–59.

35. *Ruleville Record*, 2 August 1945.

36. Thomas Borstelmann, *The Cold War and the Color Line: American Race Relations in the Global Arena* (Cambridge, MA: Harvard University Press, 2001), 296.

37. Blacks push UN: Carol Anderson, "Symposium: African Americans and U.S. Foreign Relations," *Diplomatic History* 20, no. 4 (fall 1996), 541–42. See also Paul Gordon Lauren, "Seen from the Outside," in Plummer, *Window on Freedom*, 25; UN Commission on Human Rights: Dudziak, *Cold War Civil Rights*, 43; "It is not Russia . . .": Dubois quoted in Lauren, *Power and Prejudice*, 203.

38. Soviet counterpart quoted in Borstelmann, *Cold War and the Color Line*, 75; see also Dudziak, *Cold War Civil Rights*, 18–20; "The existence of discrimination . . .": "Foreign Policy and FEPC," *Crisis* 54, no. 5 (May 1947), 137.

39. "Our case for democracy . . .": Truman quoted in Borstelmann, *Cold War and the Color Line*, 59; *To Secure These Rights*: Von Eschen, *Rising Wind*, 183; Clifford quoted in Borstelmann, *Cold War and the Color Line*, 59.

40. *Congressional Record* 94 (9 February 1948), 1194.

41. Eastland influenced by Collins: Richard C. Ethridge, "Mississippi's Role in the Dixiecrat Movement," PhD dissertation, Mississippi State University, 1971, 26–27; "attempting to drive the South . . .": Charles Wallace Collins, *Whither Solid South? A Study in Politics and Race Relations* (New Orleans: Pelican, 1947), vii; Collins's electoral plan: Collins, *Whither Solid South?*, 258; "Battle of the South": *Ruleville Record*, 1 July 1948; Eastland's plan: Bill Minor, "States' Righters Make Progress Following Walkout at National Democratic Convention," *Times-Picayune*, 26 September 1948, in Bill Minor, *Eyes on Mississippi: A Fifty-Year Chronicle of Change* (Jackson, MS: J. Prichard Morris Books, 2001), 54–55.

42. Kari Frederickson, *The Dixiecrat Revolt and the End of the Solid South, 1932–1968* (Chapel Hill: University of North Carolina Press, 2001), 83–84.

43. "I think Truman's popularity . . .": A.S. Coody to James O. Eastland, 13 May 1948, Archibald S. Coody Papers, Mississippi Department of Archives and History, Box 5, Folder 81; "hopelessly defeated": *Ruleville Record*, 16 September 1948.

44. "States' Rights movement will never die": *Jackson Daily News*, 15 November 1948; "I think an organization . . .": James O. Eastland to A.S. Coody, 31 May 1948, Archibald S. Coody Papers, Mississippi Department of Archives and History, Box 5, Folder 81.

45. "Delta Council Annual Report, 1945–1946," Delta Council Collection, Capps Archives, Delta State University, Box 1, Folder 3, 5.

46. W.D. Marlow is listed as a supporter in "Keep Mississippi Seniority" pamphlet,

James O. Eastland file, McWherter Special Collections, University of Memphis; plantation living conditions: Charles Lapidary, "Ol' Massa Jim Eastland," *The Nation*, 9 February 1957, 121; Robert Sherrill, "James Eastland: Child of Scorn," *The Nation*, 4 October 1965, 192.

47. Hamers take in Dorothy Jean: DeMuth, "'Tired of Being Sick and Tired,'" 549; Hamers take care of Lou Ella: O'Dell, "Life in Mississippi," 232; 94 percent of blacks earn less than $2,000: "Wages Paid for Cotton Chopping in 15 Mississippi Counties," 1-10 June 1959, James Silver Papers, University of Mississippi Archives and Special Collections, Box 1, Folder 1; Eastland workers earn $40 a month: Charles Lapidary, "Ol' Massa Jim Eastland," 121. This on a plantation where, according to a Memphis newspaper, Senator Eastland collected nearly $150,000 in federal agricultural subsidies in 1959. *Memphis Press-Scimitar*, 5 May 1959.

48. Population statistics: Mississippi Power and Light Company, "Mississippi Population 1960-1800," 68; half of southern farm families leave: Pete Daniel, *Lost Revolutions: The South in the 1950s* (Chapel Hill: University of North Carolina Press, 2000), 60.

49. "The Delta cannot expect . . .": "Annual Report of Delta Council, 1943-1944," Delta Council Collection, Capps Archives, Delta State University, Box 1, Folder 3, 5; Hurst articles: *Ruleville Record*, 18 April 1945, 25 April 1945; Delta Branch Experiment Station studies: *Ruleville Record*, 5 September 1946; new breeds of cotton being developed: *Ruleville Record*, 19 June 1947.

50. Foreign growers triple production: Jacobson and Smith, *Cotton's Renaissance*, 116-17; Foreign cotton pickers earn 25-50¢ a day: Read Dunn, "Problems in Keeping Our Foreign Markets for Cotton," Cotton Collection, Archives and Special Collections, University of Mississippi, Folder 9; growth of mechanization: Street, *New Revolution in the Cotton Economy*, v. In the 1930s, Charles S. Johnson and his team of sociologists had recognized the growing threat of mechanized farming in the West to southern cotton industry. Johnson, Embree, Alexander, *Collapse of Cotton Tenancy*, 39.

51. Changing federal policies benefit large farmers: Daniel, *Lost Revolutions*, 9-60; price of mechanical picker: *Ruleville Record*, 21 July 1949; mechanical pickers on Eastland farm: Eastland Plantation, Weekly Gin Report, 11 February 1946, University of Mississippi, Special Collections and Archives, James O. Eastland Collection, File Series 1, Subseries 3, Box 1, Folder 62; letter from John Morrow to L.O. Crosby, 13 August 1946, University of Mississippi, Special Collections and Archives, James O. Eastland Collection, File Series 1, Subseries 3, Box 1, Folder 68; 14 percent of Delta cotton picked by machine: Daniel, *Lost Revolutions*, 35.

52. Delta Council, "A Prospectus of the Yazoo-Mississippi Delta" (Stoneville, MS: Delta Council, 1944), Delta Council Collection, Capps Archives, Delta State University, Box 1; Wayne A. Grove, "Better Opportunities or Worse? The Demise of Cotton Harvest Labor, 1949-1964," *Journal of Economic History* 63, no. 2 (September 2003), 740; Whatley, "Labor for the Picking," 928; sharecropping no longer a Census Bureau category: Holley, *Second Great Emancipation*, 158.

53. One of Eastland's daughters recalled her father seeing mechanization as a "relief" because he would no longer have to depend on black workers. Anne Howdershell Eastland, interview with author, 7 November 2001; Sue Eastland McRoberts, interview with author, 13 November 2001; "The farm tractor . . .": D.J. Pledger and D.J. Pledger Jr., *Cotton Culture on Hardscramble Plantation* (Shelby, MS: Hardscramble Plantation, 1951), 92–93, 101.

54. "an enormous tragedy in the making": Cohn, *Where I Was Born and Raised*, 329–30; "a reservoir of workers": Robert Baker Highsaw, *The Delta Looks Forward* (Stoneville, MS: Delta Council, 1949), 77; "economically, it is profitable": University of Mississippi School of Education, Bureau of Education Research, "The Report of a Study of the Education of Negroes in Sunflower County, Mississippi" March 1950, 6; "The education of the Negro . . .": "Annual Report of Delta Council, 1949–1950," Delta Council Collection, Capps Archives, Delta State University, Box 1, Folder 3, 8; "rural areas with a heavy concentration . . . ': "Annual Report of Delta Council, 1951–1952," Delta Council Collection, Capps Archives, Delta State University, Box 1, Folder 3, 20.

5. "FROM COTTON—TO COMMUNISM— TO SEGREGATION!": THE SENATOR'S RISE TO POWER

1. "the climate for a relatively liberal . . .": Frank Smith, *Congressman from Mississippi: An Autobiography of Frank E. Smith* (New York: Pantheon Books, 1964), 99; on postwar southern liberalism and racial gains, see Tony Badger, "'Closet Moderates': Why White Liberals Failed, 1940–1970," in Ted Ownby, ed., *The Role of Ideas in the Civil Rights Movement* (Jackson: University Press of Mississippi, 2002), 87–88; Egerton, *Speak Now Against the Day*, 513–32; Sherie Mershon and Steven Schlossman, *Foxholes and Color Lines: Desegregating the U.S. Armed Forces* (Baltimore: Johns Hopkins University Press, 1998) xii–xiii.

2. Egerton, *Speak Now Against the Day*, 517.

3. Hogan, *Cross of Iron*, 265–314; Fried, *Nightmare in Red*, 87.

4. *Jackson Daily News*, 8 November 1948; Numan Bartley, *A History of the New South* (Baton Rouge: Louisiana State University Press, 1967), 96; Sean J. Savage, "To Purge or Not to Purge: Hamlet Harry and the Dixiecrats, 1948–1952," *Presidential Studies Quarterly* 27 (fall 1997), 773–90; Suttle quoted in *Jackson Daily News*, 18 September 1949.

5. Communists did not appeal to NAACP rank and file: Woods, *Black Struggle, Red Scare*, 19–22; NAACP purge of Communists: *Carolina Times*, 1 July 1950; *Chicago Defender*, 1 July 1950; the effect of the Red scare and anti-Communism on grassroots civil rights efforts is explored in Robert Rogers Korstad, *Civil Rights Unionism: Tobacco Workers and the Struggle for Democracy in the Mid-Twentieth-Century South* (Chapel Hill: University of North Carolina Press, 2003), esp. 9–10, 413–19; Horne, *Black and Red*,

esp. Introduction. Some scholars have attacked the NAACP's decision to cut its ties to Communists. Carol Anderson argues, for example, that the organization had "draped itself in the flag" and "had allowed its Negro soul to be 'bleached . . . in a flood of white Americanism.'" Carol Anderson, "Bleached Souls and Red Negroes: The NAACP and Black Communists in the Early Cold War, 1948–1952," in Plummer, *Window on Freedom*, 107. This hyperbolic assessment ignores the practical and political dilemmas facing the organization's leaders and places an unfairly harsh judgment upon their decision.

6. "a carpetbag organization . . .": *Congressional Record* 92 (23 January 1946), 242; on Operation Dixie, see Barbara S. Griffith, *The Crisis of American Labor: Operation Dixie and the Defeat of the CIO* (Philadelphia: Temple University Press, 1988), esp. chapter 8; Korstad, *Civil Rights Unionism*, 290–300; for studies of the effect of anticommunism on labor activism, see Michael Honey, *Southern Labor and Black Civil Rights: Organizing Memphis Workers* (Urbana: University of Illinois Press, 1993), esp. chapter 9; Korstad, *Civil Rights Unionism*, 413–19.

7. David Caute, *The Great Fear: The Anti-Communist Purge Under Truman and Eisenhower* (New York: Simon & Schuster, 1978), 104; Ellen Schrecker, *Many Are the Crimes: McCarthyism in America* (Boston: Little, Brown, 1998), 215.

8. "Subversive Influence in the Dining Car and Railroad Food Workers Union," Hearings Before the Subcommittee to Investigate the Administration of the Internal Security Act and Other Internal Security Laws, 82nd Congress (Washington, DC: GPO, 1951), 37–45; "The Eagles in New York," *The Nation*, 13 April 1957, 306.

9. "Subversive Control of Distributive, Processing, and Office Workers of America," Hearings Before the Subcommittee to Investigate the Administration of the Internal Security Act and Other Internal Security Laws, 82nd Congress (Washington, DC: GPO, 1952), 40–43, 80.

10. "Subversive Control of Distributive, Processing, and Office Workers of America," 80–82, 146.

11. "Subversive Influence in the Dining Car and Railroad Food Workers Union," 75–76; "Subversive Control of Distributive, Processing, and Office Workers of America," 105; Victor Rabinowitz, *Unrepentant Leftist: A Lawyer's Memoir* (Urbana: University of Illinois Press, 1996), 108.

12. "Delta Council in 1948–1949, Progress for Tomorrow," Delta Council Collection, Capps Archives, Delta State University, Box 1, Folder 3, 21.

13. On Clinton Battle and the Indianola NAACP, see Joseph Todd Moye, *Let the People Decide: Black Freedom and White Resistance Movements in Sunflower County, Mississippi, 1945–1986* (Chapel Hill: University of North Carolina Press, 2004), 40–56; on other civil rights efforts in Mississippi, see John Dittmer, *Local People: The Struggle for Civil Rights in Mississippi* (Urbana: University of Illinois Press, 1994), 26, 32; Hamer recalled having attended some of the annual Mound Bayou Days that T.R.M. Howard sponsored, but her active involvement in civil rights activities did not begin until after SNCC arrived in 1962. Charles Payne, *I've Got the Light of Freedom: The Organizing*

Tradition and the Mississippi Freedom Struggle (Berkeley: University of California Press, 1995), 154–55; number of black voters tripled: Dittmer, *Local People*, 28; Bill Minor, "Negro Vote Shows Signs of Becoming a Factor," *Times-Picayune*, 24 May 1953, in Minor, *Eyes on Mississippi*, 66–68.

14. "It looks to me . . .": Letter from Walter Sillers to James Eastland, 3 October 1953, Walter Sillers Papers, Capps Archives, Delta State University, Box 105:13; amount of money spent per black pupil quintupled: Harry S. Ashmore, *The Negro and the Schools* (Chapel Hill: University of North Carolina Press, 1954), 153, 156.

15. Inter-Racial Committee chooses seven whites and three blacks: *Ruleville Record*, 24 March 1949; committee findings: University of Mississippi School of Education, "The Report of a Study of the Education of Negroes in Sunflower County, Mississippi," 59, 39.

16. "While the niggers do need . . .": Inez H. Fulwiler to Florence Sillers Ogden, 3 October 1951, Florence Sillers Ogden Papers, Capps Archives, Delta State University, Box 2, Folder 23; Eastland family school history: Anne Eastland Howdershell, interview with author, 7 November 2001.

17. O'Dell quoted in Griffin Fariello, *Red Scare: Memories of an American Inquisition: An Oral History* (New York: W.W. Norton, 1995), 501.

18. SCHW background: George B. Tindall, *The Emergence of the New South, 1913–1945* (Baton Rouge: Louisiana State University Press, 1967), 636–39; Eastland quoted in Dorothy Zellner, "Red Roadshow: Eastland in New Orleans, 1954," *Louisiana History* 33, no. 1 (1992), 33; *Congressional Record* 104 (14 May 1958), 8868; SCEF background: Egerton, *Speak Now Against the Day*, 355.

19. On the hearing: John A. Salmond, "'The Great Southern Commie Hunt': Aubrey Williams, the Southern Conference Educational Fund, and the Internal Security Subcommittee," *South Atlantic Quarterly* 77, no. 4 (August 1978), 433–52; Zellner, "Red Roadshow," 31–60; "Southern Conference Educational Fund, Inc.," Hearings Before the Subcommittee to Investigate the Administration of the Internal Security Act and Other Internal Security Laws, 83rd Congress (Washington, DC: GPO, 1955), vii; "peed on by a pole cat": Virginia Durr, interview with Stanley H. Smith, 1968, Civil Rights Documentation Project, Moorland-Spingarn Research Center, Howard University, 45–46. For more on the hearing and Durr's reaction, see also Egerton, *Speak Now Against the Day*, 570; Fariello, *Red Scare*, 489; on Paul Crouch: Sarah Hart Brown, *Standing Against Dragons: Three Southern Lawyers in an Era of Fear* (Baton Rouge: Louisiana State University Press, 1998), 121.

20. *Brown v. Board of Education of Topeka*, 347 U.S. 483 (1954). Though the Eisenhower administration was in office at the time of the decision, the Justice Department's *amicus curiae* briefs in favor of striking down public school segregation were filed during the Truman administration. On the reaction to *Brown*, see Neil McMillen, *The Citizens' Council: Organized Resistance to the Second Reconstruction, 1954–1964*, rev. ed. (Urbana: University of Illinois Press, 1994, orig. 1971), 5–11; Numan V. Bartley, *The Rise of Massive Resistance: Race and Politics in the South During the 1950s* rev. ed. (Baton Rouge: Louisiana State University Press, 1997), 67–81; Michael J. Klarman, "How

Brown Changed Race Relations: The Backlash Thesis," *Journal of American History* 81, no. 1 (June 1994), 81–118.

21. As Michael Klarman has shown, scholars have overemphasized the decision's effect on the movement itself; its long-term significance lay in its effect on white southerners such as Eastland. Klarman, "How *Brown* Changed Race Relations," 81–91.

22. Initial resignation: John Bartlow Martin, *The Deep South Says "Never"* (New York: Ballantine Books, 1957), 10–11; "seemingly followed the best course": Smith, *Congressman from Mississippi*, 260; "The South will not abide . . .": *Jackson Daily News*, 17 May 1954; Eastland calls for constitutional amendment: *Time*, 12 December 1955, 24; "It will justly cause evasion . . .": *Congressional Record* 100 (27 May 1954), 7251.

23. Eastland family school history: Anne Eastland Howdershell, interview with author, 7 November 2001; Warren quoted in Ed Cray, *Chief Justice: A Biography of Earl Warren* (New York: Simon & Schuster, 1997), 292.

24. Anne Eastland Howdershell, interview with author, 7 November 2001. "It was the authority of his presence" that set the tone of the household, she remembered.

25. Woods Eastland, interview with author, 16 October 2001; Anne Eastland Howdershell, interview with author, 7 November 2001; "I want for my children . . .": James Eastland, "To the Mothers and Fathers of Jackson," campaign letter, August 1954, Mississippi Department of Archives and History, Subject Files, James O. Eastland, 1954.

26. Bill Minor remembers that Eastland's stock was "quite low" and he was considered "beatable," *Scott County Times*, 26 February 1986; Eastland's sickness: *Jackson Daily News*, 28 February 1953. Some members of the Eastland family thought he might have had malaria; others thought it simply was stress. Anne Eastland Howdershell, interview with author, 7 November 2001; Gartin's challenge: *Jackson Daily News*, 20 June 1954; *Ruleville Record*, 26 August 1954; Frank Barber, the field man for the Eastland campaigned, recalled Gartin's candidacy as "very stiff" challenge, "the first time he'd really been seriously contested." Interview with Frank D. Barber, 30 May 1990, University of Southern Mississippi Oral History Program, McCain Library and Archives.

27. "Whether he needed it or not . . .": Erle Johnston, *Mississippi's Defiant Years, 1953–1973* (Forest, MS: Lake Harbor, 1990), 16; congratulatory letters pour in: *Sunflower Tocsin*, 10 June 1954.

28. "great crusade": *Jackson Daily News*, 28 June 1954; to see Eastland's speaking style, view Newsfile Collection, MP 80.01, Reel F–0425, Mississippi Department of Archives and History; "I had special pockets . . .": letter to Senator Green, NAACP Papers Part 21, "Civil Rights Legislation, Congressmen and Senators, Eastland, James O." Reel 7, 254–371; "They said I broke the law . . .": *Ruleville Record*, 12 August 1954; "an all-out fight . . .": Campaign brochure, Mississippi Department of Archives and History, Subject Files, James O. Eastland file, 1954; "100 percent anti-Negro campaign": statement of Roy Wilkins, 26 May 1955, NAACP Papers, Part 21, "James O. Eastland," 757; "Hell, no! . . .": Johnston, *Mississippi's Defiant Years*, 20; "Name the fight . . .": "Keep Mississippi Seniority" pamphlet, 1 September 1954, James O. Eastland files, McWherter Special Collections, University of Memphis; 114 black registered voters: McMillen, *Citizens' Council*, 320.

29. "The entire future of this country . . .": James Eastland, "We've Reached the Era of Judicial Tyranny," an address before the Statewide Convention of the Association of Citizens' Councils of Mississippi, Jackson, 1 December 1955 (Association of Citizens' Councils of Mississippi, Winona, 1955), 3; loss of middle ground: Walker Percy, "Mississippi: The Fallen Paradise," *Harper's Magazine*, April 1965, 167; "the two-fisted Mississippian": *South: The News Magazine of Dixie* 21, no. 7, (20 February 1956), 13.

30. "You and I know . . .": *Ruleville Record*, 27 May 1954; letter from Robert B. Patterson to James O. Eastland, 12 May 1954, University of Mississippi, Special Collections and Archives, James O. Eastland Collection, File Series 1, Subseries 19, Box 16, Folder 9; Moye, *Let the People Decide*, 68–69.

31. "we didn't want to lose complete control . . .": Willie M. Pitts, interview with author, 8 February 2005. Pitts argued that if the area had a black population of 20 percent or less, then he and other whites would not have felt threatened. Composition of Citizens' Council: *Time*, 12 December 1955, 25; Martin, *Deep South Says "Never,"* 12; "Its leadership is drawn . . .": Hodding Carter III, "Citadel of the Citizens Council," *New York Times Magazine*, 12 November 1961, 23; "This isn't the United States . . .": *Look* 20, no. 7 (3 April 1956), 27.

32. "courageous, intelligent, and forthright": James Eastland, "We've Reached the Era of Judicial Tyranny," 3. Eastland aide Frank Barber recalled that the senator had warned him not to become a member of the Citizens' Council because it might interfere with a federal appointment. Interview with Frank D. Barber, 30 May 1990, University of Southern Mississippi Oral History Program, McCain Library and Archives. "Organization": James Eastland, "We've Reached the Era of Judicial Tyranny," 7.

33. "Mississippi—Most Lied About State in the Nation": "First-hand Study," *South: The News Magazine of Dixie* 21, no. 39 (1 October 1956), 9; Sovereignty Commission efforts: Yasuhiro Katagiri, *The Mississippi State Sovereignty Commission: Civil Rights and States' Rights* (Jackson: University Press of Mississippi, 2001), 6–17; see also Joseph Crespino, *In Search of Another Country: Mississippi and the Conservative Counterrevolution* (Princeton: Princeton University Press, 2007), 26–30.

34. "tell the truth about the South": *Utica Advertiser*, 21 February 1958.

35. "The Communist conspiracy can never succed . . .": James Eastland, "We've Reached the Era of Judicial Tyranny," 10; "core of Americanism": "Longines Chronoscope [with] James O. Eastland," Longines Wittnauer Watch Company, Inc., Collection, ca. 1951–ca. 1955, Motion Picture Films of Television Interviews with Significant Newsmakers of the Early 1950s, Special Media Archives Services Division, National Archives at College Park.

36. "crusade to restore Americanism": Johnston, *Mississippi's Defiant Years*, 45; FCG activities: Bartley, *Rise of Massive Resistance*, 121–22; "the only thing that will save us . . .": *South: The News Magazine of Dixie* 21, no. 7 (20 February 1956), 4; "neutralize the smearing campaign . . .": A. Philip Randolph to Norman Thomas, 18 January 1956. "Civil Rights Legislation" file, Part 21, Papers of the National Association for the Advancement of Colored People.

37. "The most important speech . . .": Bartley, *Rise of Massive Resistance*, 119–20; "Who Is Obligated?": *Congressional Record* 101 (26 May 1955), 7124.

38. *Washington Post and Times Herald*, 7 January 1955; Sherrill, "James Eastland: Child of Scorn," 189–90; David Caute, *Great Fear*, 451–53; Fariello, *Red Scare*, 319.

39. "Mississippi McCarthy": I.F. Stone, quoted in Robert Sherrill, *Gothic Politics in the South: Stars of the New Confederacy* (New York: Grossman, 1968), 187; Eastland takes over Judiciary Committee: *New Republic*, 12 March 1956, 5; "A public official who . . .": The Dilemma of Senator Eastland," *America* 94 (21 January 1956), 447; "one seat of power . . .": Robert A. Caro, *Master of the Senate* (New York: Knopf, 2002), 783; "symbol of racism": press release, "Remarks of Senator Herbert H. Lehman on the Resolution Designating Senator Eastland as Chairman of the Judiciary Committee," NAACP Papers, part 21, "Civil Rights Legislation file"; Johnson helps Eastland win chairmanship: Senator James O. Eastland, interview with Dr. Joe B. Frantz, 19 February 1971, Lyndon B. Johnson Library Oral History Collection, University of Texas–Austin.

40. "Longines Chronoscope [with] James O. Eastland," Longines Wittnauer Watch Company, Inc., Collection, ca. 1951–ca. 1955, Motion Picture Films of Television Interviews with Significant Newsmakers of the Early 1950s, Special Media Archives Services Division, National Archives at College Park; "South's Mightiest Champion . . .": *Memphis Press-Scimitar*, 5 February 1956; "authentic voice": *Time*, 26 March 1956, 26; "frantic fringe": "A Slur on a Great American," *Collier's*, 31 August 1956, 78; "mad dog loose . . .": NAACP official Clarence Mitchell quoted in Sherrill, *Gothic Politics in the South*, 187.

41. "The Moscow Reds . . ." *News and Views*, no. 269 (April 1956), Race Relations Collection, Archives and Special Collections, University of Mississippi, Box 2, Folder 1; "fly in the ointment": *Enterprise Tocsin*, 8 March 1956; "Today you are . . ." Letter from Walter Sillers to James Eastland, 3 March 1956, Walter Sillers Papers, Capps Archives, Delta State University, Box 105:13.

42. "epitome of responsibility": *Time*, 26 March 1956, 26.

43. "I merely sit there": *Congressional Record* 103 (28 May 1957), 7825; Eastland institutes "blue slip" policy: Mitchel A. Sollenberger, "The Law: Must the Senate Take a Floor Vote on a Presidential Judicial Nominee?" *Presidential Studies Quarterly* 34, no. 2 (June 2004), 420–36; Eastland "goes out of his way . . .": Courtney Pace to A.S. Coody, 11 September 1959, Archibald S. Coody Papers, Mississippi Department of Archives and History, Box 5, Folder 83; "always courteous . . .": *Congressional Record* 103 (28 May 1957), 7824; only one bill made it out of committee: Johnston, *Mississippi's Defiant Years*, 18; "very seductive . . .": *Congressional Record* 103 (28 May 1957), 7829; writing in 1968, Robert Sherrill commented upon this apparent contradiction between Eastland's public image as a Bilboesque demagogue and his private geniality: "The private image of Eastland as a kindly paternal planter somehow keeps getting gobbled up by his carnivorous public image," Sherrill noted. "Despite the best efforts of his friends and family it remains true that none of America's anti-southern cults has more devotees

than the one that directs its hatred at Senator James Eastland. He, more than any other extant politician, seems to symbolize what intellectuals, seekers, mystics and mavericks are trying to remove from the world." Sherrill, *Gothic Politics in the South*, 187.

44. On race and international affairs: Borstelmann, *Cold War and the Color Line*, 93: *Brown* news translated into thirty-four languages: Taylor Branch, *Parting the Waters: America in the King Years, 1954–63* (New York: Touchstone Books, 1988), 113; National Security Council report quoted in Dudziak, *Cold War Civil Rights*, 109.

45. American Communist Party crushed in 1956: Morgan, *Reds*, 556.

46. For an excellent study of how foreign policy makers developed an "American nationalist ideology" centered on freedom of enterprise and freedom of religion, see John Fousek, *To Lead the Free World: American Nationalism and the Cultural Roots of the Cold War* (Chapel Hill: University of North Carolina Press, 2000), esp. 187–91. See also Borstelmann, *Cold War and the Color Line*, and Dudziak, *Cold War Civil Rights*; "There's no doubt that . . .": *Chicago Defender*, 5 August 1950; "We are happy . . .": "Freedom for Export Only," *The Nation*, 3 November 1956, 358; "It seems to be time . . .": "The Dilemma of Senator Eastland," *America* 94 (21 January 1956), 441.

47. "This is world Communism's finest hour . . .": press release, Office of Honorable Adam Clayton Powell Jr., 11 October 1955, in Christopher Metress, ed., *The Lynching of Emmett Till: A Documentary Narrative* (Charlottesville: University of Virginia Press, 2002), 135–36; "one of those iniquities": *L'Action* quoted in "Memo from the American Jewish Committee on European Reaction to the Till Case," 7 October 1955, in Metress, *The Lynching of Emmett Till*, 143.

48. King quoted in Borstelmann, *Cold War and the Color Line*, 97; "This is the last round up . . .": A.S. Coody to James O. Eastland, 29 August 1956, Archibald S. Coody Papers, Mississippi Department of Archives and History, Box 5, Folder 82.

49. The Fair Employment Practices Committee, as we saw in Chapter 3, had been created by executive order and had never been approved by Congress. Clarence Mitchell quoted in Caro, *Master of the Senate*, 842–43. NAACP attorney Thurgood Marshall claimed he would vote Republican because "I have terrible difficulty in separating Adlai Stevenson's Democratic Party from Senator Eastland's Democratic Party." *Time*, 12 March 1956, 26; Johnson's role in 1957 bill fight: James O. Eastland, interview with Joe B. Frantz, 19 February 1971, Lyndon Baines Johnson Library Oral History Collection, 6; "outrageous communist inspired . . .": Letter from Walter Sillers to James Eastland, 25 June 1957, Walter Sillers Papers, Capps Archives, Delta State University, Box 105:13; *Congressional Record* 103 (11 July 1957), 11349. In the 1950s, Eastland strongly supported Johnson, particularly after the majority leader had supported him for the Judiciary Committee chairmanship. Frank Barber, who worked on Eastland's staff for several years in the 1950s, remembered that Johnson was the only person "that I ever saw Senator Eastland have any great reservations about offending." Interview with Frank D. Barber. Eastland's attitude toward Johnson changed markedly after the latter became president; "almost a miracle": James O. Eastland to A.S. Coody, 12 August 1957, Archibald S. Coody Papers, Mississippi Department of Archives and History, Box 5, Folder 82.

50. Eastland speaks at Belzoni rally: Johnston, *Mississippi's Defiant Years*, 71; "peaceful assemblage . . ." and "The evil of *Brown* . . .": *Congressional Record* 104 (14 May 1958), 8666.

51. Dulles quoted in Dudziak, *Cold War Civil Rights*, 131.

52. Southerners had internationalist views, but southern blacks, by contrast, tended to be far more isolationist than their bosses, seeing international efforts as a distraction from more pressing domestic needs. Alfred O. Hero Jr. *The Southerner and World Affairs* (Baton Rouge: Louisiana State University Press, 1965), 6, 520; on the UN becoming more aggressive, see Lauren, *Power and Prejudice*, esp. chapter 7; Thomas Noer, "Segregationists and the World: The Foreign Policy of White Resistance," in Plummer, *Window on Freedom*, 147; "American Racial Integrity . . .": Russia, Communism and Race," State Sovereignty Commission pamphlet, Race Relations Collection, Archives and Special Collections, University of Mississippi, Box 3, Folder 9.

53. "Ethiopianization": G. Poper Atkins and Larman C. Wilson, *The Dominican Republic and the United States: From Imperialism to Transnationalism* (Athens: University of Georgia Press, 1998), 78–79; "one of the great men . . .": Sherrill, *Gothic Politics in the South*, 208; "create a vacuum": *Congressional Record* 106 (1 September 1960), 18993; Eastland twice was a guest of Trujillo: *Natchez Democrat*, 14 September 1977.

54. "The Communist objective . . .": *Congressional Record* 106 (24 August 1960), 17412; "If there is a rebellion . . . ': *Commercial Appeal*, 19 April 1962.

55. "in one manner . . .": *Congressional Record* 106 (23 February 1960), 3189.

6. "NO ONE CAN HONESTLY SAY NEGROES ARE SATISFIED": THE SHARECROPPER EMBRACES THE MOVEMENT

1. William Chapel is often called "Williams Chapel," by locals and outsiders alike. McLaurin is referring to the bank on top of which Eastland kept a small local office. Eastland did not own the bank. Sugarman, *Stranger at the Gates*, 117.

2. Carson, *In Struggle*, 11–30. Their dedication to nonviolent civil disobedience reflected the influence of foreign movements, particularly Mahatma Gandhi and his successful defeat of the British Empire in India; American activism, most notably the philosophy of Henry David Thoreau; and biblical injunctions against violence.

3. Editorial, "Rising Tide of Color," *Crisis* 67 (May 1960), 306–7.

4. Letter from Kitty Reynolds to James Eastland, 19 June 1960, State Sovereignty Commission Records, SCR ID #3–13A-0-117-1-1-1; letter from Walter Sillers to James Eastland, 14 June 1960, Walter Sillers Papers, Capps Archives, Delta State University, Box 105:13.

5. Hero, *Southerner and World Affairs*, 512; Raines, *My Soul Is Rested*, 249; Hamer, "To Praise Our Bridges," 324.

6. Though the white public schools in the Delta enjoyed more funding than their

black counterparts, they lagged far behind their national peers. When Senator Eastland went to Washington, he brought his children with him because the schools in the D.C. area were much better academically. Interview with Anne Howdershell Eastland, 7 November 2001; interview with Woods Eastland, 16 October 2001; Elizabeth Sutherland Martinez, *Letters from Mississippi*, rev. ed. (Brookline, MA: Zephyr Press, 2002), 105; Dittmer, *Local People*, 125; DeMuth, "'Tired of Being Sick and Tired,'" 550–51.

7. Bill Minor, "State's Black Voters Estimated at Near 25,000," *Times-Picayune*, 16 October 1960, in Minor, *Eyes on Mississippi*, 80–81; *Look* 28, no. 16 (8 September 1964), 24.

8. Letter from Cecil Campbell to James O. Eastland, 18 December 1947, University of Mississippi, Special Collections and Archives, James O. Eastland Collection, File Series 1, Subseries 19, Box 10, Folder 7; Dittmer, *Local People*, 53; Johnston, *Mississippi's Defiant Years*, 6; Jack Bass and Walter DeVries, *The Transformation of Southern Politics: Social Change and Political Consequences Since 1945* (New York: Basic Books, 1976), 195. Concerted voter registration efforts in the late 1950s helped the number of black voters on the state rolls grow to nearly 25,000. Minor, "State's Black Voters Estimated at Near 25,000"; *Congressional Record* 106 (29 January 1960), 1598.

9. Hamer interview with Neil McMillen; *Congressional Record* 106 (1 March 1960), 3982; *Congressional Record* 106 (15 March 1960), 5587.

10. James W. Silver, *Mississippi: The Closed Society* (New York: Harcourt, Brace & World, 1964); Marge Manderson, "A Solid South . . . or Else," *New South* 15 (April 1960), 3–11; Numan V. Bartley, *The Rise of Massive Resistance: Race and Politics in the South During the 1950s*, rev. ed. (Baton Rouge: Louisiana State University Press, 1997), 211; Sam H. Franklin Jr., "Early Years of the Delta Cooperative Farm and the Providence Cooperative Farm," Jerry Dallas Delta Farm Cooperative Collection, Capps Archives, Delta State University, Box 1, 86–90; Kenneth Toler, "Smoldering 'Suspicions' Flare over Farm Project Activities," Memphis *Commercial Appeal*, 1 October 1955; Jerry W. Dallas, "The Delta and Providence Farms: A Mississippi Experiment in Cooperative Farming and Racial Cooperation, 1936–1956," *Mississippi Quarterly* 40 (summer 1987), 283–308.

11. "eye to eye . . .": *Congressional Record* 107 (25 May 1961), 8958; Freedom Rides publicized worldwide: Mary L. Dudziak, *Cold War Civil Rights: Race and the Image of American Democracy* (Princeton: Princeton University Press, 2000), 159; Woods Eastland, interview with author, 16 October 2001.

12. Dittmer, *Local People*, 118–19. Charles Cobb emphasized the importance of setting up a project in Eastland's backyard. Raines, *My Soul Is Rested*, 245. Charles McLaurin agreed. Charles McLaurin, interview with author, 20 September 2001.

13. "The vote won't make . . .": Henry quoted in Charles McLaurin, interview with author, 20 September 2001; "make a Javits . . .": Henry quoted in Gayle Graham Yates, *Mississippi Mind: A Personal Cultural History of an American State* (Knoxville: University of Tennessee Press, 1990), 119. Henry's idea was that Eastland was primarily a politician who would respond to black political power. Nicholas Katzenbach, attorney

general in Lyndon Johnson's administration, also believed that Eastland was driven fundamentally by politics and money, not race. Jack Bass, *Unlikely Heroes: The Dramatic Story of the Southern Judges of the Fifth Circuit Who Translated the Supreme Court's* Brown *Decision into a Revolution for Equality* (New York: Simon & Schuster, 1981), 147. "The last thing . . .": interview with Charles Cobb, 21 October 1996, University of Southern Mississippi Oral History Program, http://www.lib.usm.edu/~spcol/ crda/oh/cobb.htm.

14. "until then I'd never heard . . .": Hamer, "To Praise Our Bridges," 324; Hamer interview with Neil McMillen; Tucker story quoted in Mills, *This Little Light of Mine*, 23–24.

15. Hamer later recalled that it was the first time she had heard such songs. Garland, "Builders of a New South," 29; Fannie Lou Hamer interview with Robert Wright, 9 August 1968, Civil Rights Documentation Project, Moorland-Spingarn Research Center, Howard University, 6–8; Hamer, "To Praise Our Bridges," 324; Fannie Lou Hamer interview with Raines, in *My Soul Is Rested*, 249.

16. Form letter from Fannie Lou Hamer, 30 September 1963, Southern Regional Council, Voter Education Project, Series VI: 205, reel 179; Charles McLaurin, "Voice of Calm," *Sojourners*, Reprint #102, December 1982.

17. Raines, *My Soul Is Rested*, 250–51; Garland, "Builders of a New South," 30.

18. Hamer interview with Neil McMillen; DeMuth, "'Tired of Being Sick and Tired,'" 550.

19. Raines, *My Soul Is Rested*, 246–47, 251; *Enterprise Tocsin*, 13 September 1962; Hamer, "To Praise Our Bridges," 325; "I walked through the shadows . . .": Hamer quoted in Harris, *Something Within*, 80.

20. Garland, "Builders of a New South," 30; *New York Times*, 16 March 1977.

21. It would be nearly two years before she could actually cast a ballot because she needed to have two years' worth of poll tax receipts As a result, Hamer recalled later, "I cast my first vote for myself." Fannie Lou Hamer, interview with Neil McMillen, 14 April 1972; Fisk conference: Lee, *For Freedom's Sake*, 37; "Mrs. Hamer returned": Pat Watters and Reese Cleghorn, *Climbing Jacob's Ladder: The Arrival of Negroes in Southern Politics* (New York: Harcourt, Brace & World, 1967), 147; sixth new voter: Moye, *Let the People Decide*, 108.

22. Raines, *My Soul Is Rested*, 252; Hamer interview with Neil McMillen; "One family's struggle for freedom," Operation Freedom pamphlet, SCR ID #99-114-0-12-4-1-1.

23. Sugarman, *Stranger at the Gates*, 117; Cheryl Townsend Gilkes, "The Politics of 'Silence': Dual-Sex Political Systems and Women's Traditions of Conflict in African-American Religion," in Johnson, *African American Christianity*, 93.

24. Form letter from Fannie Lou Hamer, 30 September 1963, Southern Regional Council, Voter Education Project, Series VI: 205, reel 179; Jack O'Dell, "Life in Mississippi," *Freedomways* 5, no. 2 (second quarter, 1965), 233; DeMuth, "'Tired of Being Sick and Tired,'" 549.

25. Charles McLaurin, interview with author, 20 September 2001; Pete Daniel,

Lost Revolutions: The South in the 1950s (Chapel Hill: University of North Carolina Press for Smithsonian Institution, 2000), 300.

26. *Chicago Sunday Tribune*, 26 August 1962; Marie Hemphill, "Eastland's Farm Manager Forecasts Bright Future," 11 May 1957, in "Mississippi—Sunflower County, Doddsville," Sunflower County Library Vertical Files; Hamer interview with Neil McMillen.

27. A.S. Coody to James O. Eastland, 5 January 1961, Archibald S. Coody Papers, Mississippi Department of Archives and History, Box 5, Folder 84.

28. Bass, *Unlikely Heroes*, 143; John Dittmer, "The Politics of Mississippi Movement," in Charles W. Eagles, ed., *The Civil Rights Movement in America* (Jackson: University Press of Mississippi, 1986), 76. Robert Kennedy remarked that Eastland's advice was "very, very helpful" and "I found it much more pleasant to deal with him than many of the so-called liberals in the House Judiciary Committee or in other parts of Congress or the Senate." Ibid., 164; Dittmer, *Local People*, 93–94.

29. Curt Gentry, *J. Edgar Hoover: The Man and His Secrets* (New York: Plume, 1991), 407; Kenneth O'Reilly, *"Racial Matters": The FBI's Secret File on Black America, 1960–1972* (New York: Free Press, 1989), 9–10, 349; Horace Harned Jr., interview with Yasuhiro Katagiri, 3 September 1993, University of Southern Mississippi Oral History Program, http://www.lib.usm.edu/%7Espcol/crda/oh/harned.htm.

30. Barnett ran against Carroll Gartin, who had opposed Eastland in 1954. There was no love lost between Eastland and Gartin. William Winter, interview with author, 22 March 2005; Memorandum, Jack J. Van Landingham to File, 18 February 1960, SCR ID #2-5-3-12-1-1-1; Erle Johnston, Jr., to James Eastland, 12 July 1963, SCR ID #2-34-0-22-1-1-1; *Clarion-Ledger*, 28 January 1990; Bill Minor, "Segregation Spy Agency Largely a Keystone Kops Affair," *Times-Picayune*, 19 March 1998, in Minor, *Eyes on Mississippi*, 274.

31. Johnston, *Mississippi's Defiant Years*, xxxi; Yasuhiro Katagiri, *The Mississippi State Sovereignty Commission: Civil Rights and States' Rights* (Jackson: University Press of Mississippi, 2001), 67–68.

32. "How long . . .": Eastland quoted in *Chicago Sunday Tribune*, 26 August 1962.

33. With the exception of Woodrow Wilson High School and its feeder schools in upper Northwest Washington, public schools in D.C. remained almost exclusively the terrain of minority students for the rest of the twentieth century. Interview with Frank D. Barber, 30 May 1990, University of Southern Mississippi Oral History Program, McCain Library and Archives; *Congressional Record* 106 (1 March 1960), 4023.

34. Walker Percy, "Mississippi: The Fallen Paradise," *Harper's Magazine*, April 1965, 167; Thomas J. Sugrue, *The Origins of the Urban Crisis: Race and Inequality in Postwar Detroit* (Princeton: Princeton University Press, 1996); Nicholas Lemann, *The Promised Land: The Great Black Migration and How It Changed America* (New York: Vintage, 1991); *Congressional Record* 106 (1 March 1960), 4022; *Congressional Record* 106 (23 February 1960), 3231.

35. "The Eagles in New York," *The Nation*, 13 April 1957, 306; letter from James Eastland to Walter Sillers, 1 September 1961, Walter Sillers Papers, Capps Archives, Delta State University, Box 105:13.

36. *Congressional Record* 106 (5 March 1960), 4580.

37. For an examination of southern black opponents of the movement, see Lauren F. Winner, "Doubtless Sincere: New Characters in the Civil Rights Cast," in Ted Ownby, ed., *The Role of Ideas in the Civil Rights South* (Jackson: University Press of Mississippi, 2002), 157–69. See also Jinx C. Broussard, "Saviors or Scalawags: The Mississippi Black Press's Contrasting Coverage of Civil Rights Workers and Freedom Summer, June-August 1964," *American Journalism* 19, no. 3 (summer 2002), 63–85; *Enterprise Tocsin*, 21 May 1964; Erle Johnston to J.H. White, 3 May 1963, SCR ID #2-45-1-73-1-1-1; interview with Percy Greene, 14 December 1972, University of Southern Mississippi Oral History Program, http://anna.lib.usm.edu/%7Espcol/crda/oh/ohgreenepp.html.

38. Interview with Frank D. Barber, 30 May 1990, University of Southern Mississippi Oral History Program, McCain Library and Archives; *Congressional Record* 107 (30 August 1961), 17490.

39. *Congressional Record* 107 (25 May 1961), 8956-57; *Congressional Record* 107 (30 August 1961), 17494.

40. Eastland's internal security subcommittee kept ample records of Communist support of black equality. See, for example, "The Road to LIBERATION for the NEGRO PEOPLE," Workers Library Publishers, Inc., September 1937, in "South (Communism), 1949–1958," Subject Files, Records of the U.S. Senate, Senate Internal Security Subcommittee, Box 255; and Doxey A. Wilkerson, "The People Versus Segregated Schools" (New York: New Century Publishers, February 1955), in "South (Communism), 1949–1958," Subject Files, Records of the U.S. Senate, Senate Internal Security Subcommittee, Box 255. Emphasis in original CPUSA resolution. "Resolution on the Negro Question," Proceedings of the 16th National Convention, Communist Party, U.S.A., 9–12 February 1957, in "South (Communism), 1949–1958," Subject Files, Records of the U.S. Senate, Senate Internal Security Subcommittee, Box 255: 294.

41. Clayborne Carson, *In Struggle: SNCC and the Black Awakening of the 1960s* (Cambridge, MA: Harvard University Press, 1995, orig. 1981), 105–6; Charles Cobb, interview with John Rachal, 21 October 1996, University of Southern Mississippi Oral History Program, http://www.lib.usm.edu/~spcol/crda/oh/cobb.htm. But that experience could cut both ways, particularly in the youthful SNCC. To Charles Cobb, who joined SNCC in 1962 and was assigned to Ruleville, the Communists in the organization had little influence because they "seemed stodgy and old-fashioned and fairly conservative." Charles Cobb, interview with John Rachal, 21 October 1996, University of Southern Mississippi Oral History Program, http://www.lib.usm.edu/~spcol/crda/oh/cobb.htm.

42. *New York Times*, 16 May 1967; *Clarion-Ledger*, 28 January 1990; *National*

Guardian, 11 March 1967; *People's World*, 16 March 1967; Arthur Kinoy, *Rights on Trial: The Odyssey of a People's Lawyer* (Cambridge, MA: Harvard University Press, 1983), 216–20; Robert G. Sherrill, "James Eastland: Child of Scorn," 189; "The Southern Conference Educational Fund, Inc.: Its Planned Activities and Financial Requirement, 1965," SCR ID #13-59-0-34-1-1-1.

43. P.D. East, editorial reprints from *The Petal Paper* (P.D. East, 1959). See, for example, his "letter to a friend," 16 February 1956; *Clarion-Ledger*, 23 June 1961; *Enterprise Tocsin*, 13 September 1962, 23 July 1964, 10 September 1964.

44. For more on the Oxford riot, see William Doyle, *An American Insurrection: James Meredith and the Battle of Oxford, Mississippi, 1962* (New York: Doubleday, 2001); Branch, *Parting the Waters*, 633–72; Dittmer, *Local People*, 138–42.

45. "The Winona Incident," Appendix I, in Watters and Cleghorn, *Climbing Jacob's Ladder*, 364–65; Raines, *My Soul Is Rested*, 253.

46. Payne, *I've Got the Light of Freedom*, 227; "Winona Incident," 366; Raines, *My Soul Is Rested*, 253.

47. "Winona Incident," 370–72.

48. Ibid., 374.

49. Henry, *Aaron Henry*, 160; Dittmer, *Local People*, 200–207; Payne, *I've Got the Light of Freedom*, 294–97.

50. "Winona Incident," 374.

7. 1964: CONFRONTATIONS

1. DeMuth, "'Tired of Being Sick and Tired,'" 548.

2. CBS Television Network, CBS News Special Report, "The Search in Mississippi," 25 June 1964, transcript in Civil Rights Documentation Project, Moorland-Spingarn Research Center, Howard University, 19.

3. Senator James O. Eastland, interview with Dr. Joe B. Frantz, 19 February 1971, Lyndon B. Johnson Library, Oral History Collection, University of Texas–Austin, 10; "No single event . . .": *Congressional Record* 109 (11 December 1963), 24127.

4. Senator James O. Eastland, interview with Dr. Joe B. Frantz, 16.

5. Kennedy not well-regarded by SNCC: Carson, *In Struggle*, 83; Fred Powledge, *Free at Last? The Civil Rights Movement and the People Who Made It* (New York: Harper-Perennial, 1991), 243–44; Baldwin quoted in Dittmer, *Local People*, 211.

6. Johnston, *Mississippi's Defiant Years*, 243.

7. Johnson quoted in Taylor Branch, *Pillar of Fire: America in the King Years, 1963–1965* (New York: Simon & Schuster, 1998), 92; King quoted in Nick Kotz, *Judgment Days: Lyndon Baines Johnson, Martin Luther King Jr., and the Laws That Changed America* (New York: Houghton Mifflin, 2005), 67.

8. Raines, *My Soul Is Rested*, 274.

9. Hamer quoted in Carson, *In Struggle*, 99. For more on the decision to include whites in the Mississippi Summer Project, see Henry Hampton and Steve Fayer, *Voices of Freedom: An Oral History of the Civil Rights Movement from the 1950s Through the 1980s* (New York: Bantam, 1990), 181–84; Carson, *In Struggle*, 96–105; Dittmer, *Local People*, 208–11; Raines, *My Soul Is Rested*, 273–74, 286–87.

10. Petition, Fannie Lou Hamer to Jamie L. Whitten, 3 December 1964, Walter Sillers Papers, Capps Archives, Delta State University, Box 19:9, 44; DeMuth, "'Tired of Being Sick and Tired,'" 549.

11. Hamer quoted in Sugarman, *Stranger at the Gates*, 117–19; DeMuth, "'Tired of Being Sick and Tired,'" 551.

12. Sam Kushner, "Interview with Fannie Lou Hamer," undated, Parallel Files, "Fannie Lou Hamer," Records of the U.S. Senate, Senate Internal Security Subcommittee.

13. SNCC worker quoted in Mills, *This Little Light of Mine*, 91; "Congressional Campaign Workers Harrassed in Ruleville, Mississippi," in Sunflower County Depositions, Council of Federated Organizations Papers, Mississippi Department of Archives and History, Box 3.

14. "proposing to swarm upon . . .": *Congressional Record* 110 (18 April 1964), 8355; CBS Television Network, "Search in Mississippi"; Johnston, *Mississippi's Defiant Years*, 254; Bill Minor, "Resurgence of Klan in Mississippi for First Time Since 1920," *Times-Picayune*, 24 May 1964, in Minor, *Eyes on Mississippi*, 222–23; rise of Klan and APWR: Crespino, *In Search of Another Country*, 110–15; "What are we going to do . . .": Wesley Pruden Jr., "'Never' Has Changed to 'Not Everything Now,'" *National Observer*, 14 September 1964.

15. For more on the passage of the civil rights bill, see Kotz, *Judgment Days*, esp. chapter 6, 112–55; CCFAF and its campaign: Crespino, *In Search of Another Country*, 92–100; "most monstrous . . .": *Congressional Record* 110 (18 April 1964), 8355; "The America that we have known . . .": *Congressional Record* 110 (17 June 1964), 14227.

16. "We didn't tell 'em no lies": Raines, *My Soul Is Rested*, 274n–275n; "publicity stunt": Michael R. Beschloss, ed., *Taking Charge: The Johnson White House Tapes, 1963–1964* (New York: Simon & Schuster, 1997), 432; *Congressional Record* 110 (22 July 1964), 16596; *Enterprise Tocsin*, 25 June 1964.

17. "quite unkempt": Hemphill, *Fevers, Floods, and Faith*, 750; "If our local colored citizens . . .": *Enterprise Tocsin*, 28 May 1964; "Report #1," in "Reports 1964," Jerry Tecklin Papers, Box 1, Folder 6, Wisconsin State Historical Society; "Violence hangs overhead . . .": Martinez, *Letters from Mississippi*, 171; "I don't think . . .": John Herbers, "Quiet Sunday in Ruleville, Miss., Ends as Rights Workers Arrive," *New York Times Magazine*, 29 June 1964.

18. "They didn't pay any attention": Margaret Kibbee, interview with Steve Estes, 20 July 2000; "If you was on the plantation . . .": Earline Tillman, interview with author, 26 September 2001. Fellow worker Mrs. Willie Jackson agreed that people on the plan-

tation weren't allowed to participate in demonstrations. Mrs. Willie Jackson, interview with author, 8 July 2000; "It was like being in the eye of the hurricane": Anne Eastland Howdershell, interview with author, 6 November 2001.

19. "nerve center": Sugarman, *Stranger at the Gates*, 114; "Christlike": Fannie Lou Hamer, "Foreword," in Sugarman, *Stranger at the Gates*, vii; "gag": Martinez, *Letters from Mississippi*, 18; "to watch her limp . . .": Martinez, *Letters from Mississippi*, 61; "The white man's afraid . . .": DeMuth, "'Tired of Being Sick and Tired,'" 550.

20. Fannie Lou Hamer, interview with Neil McMillen; Charles McLaurin, interview with author, 20 September 2001; *Congressional Record* 110 (22 July 1964), 16593.

21. "Report of the State Sovereignty Commission (1964–1967)," SCR ID #99-161-0-1-7-1-1: 7; *Congressional Record* 110 (22 July 1964), 16594; Larry Rubin, interview with John Rachal, 11 November 1995, Mississippi Oral History Program, University of Southern Mississippi.

22. Woods, *Black Struggle, Red Scare*, 210; *Congressional Record* 110 (22 July 1964), 16595–96; *Enterprise Tocsin*, 23 July 1964; *The Worker*, 4 August 1964.

23. Fannie Lou Hamer, interview with Anne and Howard Romaine, 1966, in *Mississippi Freedom Democratic Party; Interviews by Anne Romaine*, Mississippi Department of Archives and History, 1:5.

24. Carson, *In Struggle*, 123–25; Dittmer, *Local People*, 273; Henry, *Aaron Henry*, 175.

25. "If we mess with the group of Negroes that were elected to nothing," Johnson told Vice President Hubert Humphrey, "we will lose fifteen states without even campaigning." Beschloss, *Taking Charge*, 510–11, 515–16; Woods, *Black Struggle, Red Scare*, 215.

26. "Jesus and the moneychangers": Charles Marsh, *God's Long Summer: Stories of Faith and Civil Rights* (Princeton: Princeton University Press, 1997), 35; Hamer interview with Neil McMillen.

27. Fannie Lou Hamer interview with Robert Wright, 29; Martinez, *Letters from Mississippi*, 259. Despite her bitterness, she joined Henry in campaigning around Mississippi for the president's reelection.

28. John Herbers, "Communique from the Mississippi Front," *New York Times Magazine*, 8 November 1964, 34; Hamer interview with Neil McMillen; Hamer, "Foreword," vii; Hamer, "To Praise Our Bridges," 327.

29. Hamer, "To Praise Our Bridges," 329; Hamer interview with Neil McMillen.

30. O'Dell, "Life in Mississippi," 234; Carson, *In Struggle*, 134. As Charles McLaurin remembers, "The difference she saw was that in Africa people would take their freedom but in America we were given ours." Author interview with Charles McLaurin, 20 September 2001.

31. Fannie Lou Hamer, interview with Neil McMillen; Carson, *In Struggle*, 323.

32. O'Dell, "Life in Mississippi," 235.

33. Ibid., 241–42.

34. Lee, *For Freedom's Sake*, 108; Mills, *This Little Light of Mine*, 145–46.

35. Petition, Fannie Lou Hamer to Jamie L. Whitten, 3 December 1964, Walter Sillers Papers, Capps Archives, Delta State University, Box 19:9, 23; Dittmer, *Local People*, 323–24.

36. Kinoy, *Rights on Trial*, 267.

37. Mississippi Statistical Abstract 1970 (State College, MS: Mississippi State University, 1970), 516–18; Petition, Fannie Lou Hamer to Jamie L. Whitten, 3 December 1964, Walter Sillers Papers, Capps Archives, Delta State University, Box 19:9, 3–5; Response, Jamie L. Whitten to Fannie Lou Hamer, 3 December 1964, Walter Sillers Papers, Capps Archives, Delta State University, Box 19:9, 1–2.

38. *Washington Post*, 4 January 1965; William M. Kunstler with Sheila Isenberg, *My Life as a Radical Lawyer* (New York: Birch Lane Press, 1994), 144; Gray quoted in Kinoy, *Rights on Trial*, 274.

39. Fred Powledge, "Rights Leaders Split on Tactics," *New York Times*, 2 January 1965.

8. "THIS IS AMERICA'S SICKNESS"

1. Sugarman, *Stranger at the Gates*, 67.

2. David Chappell argues that the lack of faith in the "American creed" distinguished religious southern black activists such as Hamer, Fred Shuttlesworth, and Martin Luther King Jr. from secular northern white activists who followed the liberal traditions of Gunnar Myrdal and John Dewey. David L. Chappell, *Stone of Hope: Prophetic Religion and the Death of Jim Crow* (Chapel Hill: University of North Carolina Press, 2004), esp. 71–75; Hamer, "Foreword," ix.

3. O'Dell, "Life in Mississippi," 234–35; *New Republic*, 23 May 1966, 606.

4. Nick Kotz, "A Poor, Hard Life on Eastland Plantation," *Des Moines Register*, 26 February 1968. Many of Eastland's plantation workers had been registered during the summer of 1964. After Eastland complained to Nicholas Katzenbach at the Department of Justice about civil rights workers' threats to register the workers on his plantation, Katzenbach suggested that the senator avoid the potentially bad publicity that could arise from a confrontation by ensuring that his workers get registered. "They'll vote for you anyway," he argued. Eastland recognized the political advantage and agreed to do it. Bass, *Unlikely Heroes*, 146–47; Bill Minor, "Some Signs Racial Barriers Crumbling, and More Changes in Prospect," *Times-Picayune*, 3 January 1965, in Minor, *Eyes on Mississippi*, 225–27; *Commercial Appeal*, 4 April 1965; Charles Cobb, interview with John Rachal, 21 October 1996, University of Southern Mississippi Oral History Program, http://www.lib.usm.edu/~spcol/crda/oh/cobb.htm.

5. Sugarman, *Stranger at the Gates*, 197; "Now Is the Time," Mississippi Freedom Democratic Party flyer, fall 1964, SCR ID #10-77-0-9-1-1-1; Foster Davis, "The Delta: Rich Land and Poor People," *The Reporter*, 24 March 1966.

6. *Newsweek*, 7 March 1966, 28; Walter Rugaber, "The Delta: Poverty Is a Way of

Life," *New York Times*, 31 July 1967; Carl M. Cobb, "Starvation Leading Medical Problem in Bolivar County," *Boston Globe*, 16 July 1967.

7. Lee, *For Freedom's Sake*, 143; Fannie Lou Hamer, Ed King, Joe Harris, Lawrence Guyot, "Proposal for Six Month Project for Mississippi Freedom Democratic Party: Beginning July 1, 1967–December 31, 1967," undated, in "Mississippi Freedom Democratic Party," Subject Files, Records of the U.S. Senate, Senate Internal Security Subcommittee, Box 156.

8. The union also singled out the Eastland plantation for its "slave labor conditions," a charge the senator vehemently denied. *Memphis Press-Scimitar*, 16 July 1965; *Enterprise Tocsin*, 22 July 1965; Hamer interview with Neil McMillen; Kushner, "Interview with Fannie Lou Hamer"; *People's World*, 26 June 1965; *The Voice* 6, no. 3 (6 June 1965). Planter pressure in the 1930s had helped create a loophole for agricultural workers in the 1937 legislation establishing the minimum wage. "Campus Contact Newsletter," 20 May 1965, Student Nonviolent Coordinating Committee, in "Mississippi Freedom Democratic Party," Subject Files, Records of the U.S. Senate, Senate Internal Security Subcommittee, Box 156; *Commercial Appeal*, 18 April 1965; Claude Ramsey, "A Report on the Delta Farm Strike," 16 August 1965, James Silver Papers, University of Mississippi Archives and Special Collections, Box 1, Folder 1; Richard Armstrong, "Will SNICK Overcome?" *Saturday Evening Post*, 28 August 1965, 83.

9. *"greatly reducing the cost . . .":* Emphasis in original. James Eastland address to National Cotton Council, 30 January 1962, Walter Sillers Papers, Capps Archives, Delta State University, Box 33:15; *Commercial Appeal*, 18 April 1965.

10. See http://www.nass.usda.gov/ms/farmsize1950-2000.pdf; U.S. Department of Commerce, Bureau of Census, *County and City Data Book 1972* (Washington, DC: GPO, 1972), 280; B.F. Smith, "A Short History of Delta Cotton," *Delta Review* 1, no. 1 (winter 1963/64), 22; *Newsweek*, 7 March 1966, 28–29; Woods Eastland, interview with author, 16 February 2005; Nick Kotz, "Machine Shift Adds to Plight of Negroes," *Des Moines Register*, 27 February 1968; Andrew J. Glass, "Mississippi's Mighty Eastland Fears Lash of New Negro Votes," *New York Herald Tribune*, 17 April 1966.

11. Planter quoted in Sherrill, *Gothic Politics in the South*, 191; Martinez, *Letters from Mississippi*, 62; Sandra Nystrom and Eleanor Holmes Norton, "Times Changing in Sunflower," *New America*, 18 June 1967; *The Movement* 3, no. 10 (October 1967), 11.

12. Foster Davis, "The Delta: Rich Land and Poor People"; Paul Good, "The Thorntons of Mississippi," *The Atlantic*, September 1966, 98.

13. Nick Kotz, "Negroes' Plight on Eastland's Plantation," *Des Moines Register*, 25 February 1968; Woods Eastland, interview with author, 16 February 2005; Nick Kotz, "Machine Shift Adds to Plight of Negroes"; Walker Percy, "Mississippi: The Fallen Paradise," *Harper's Magazine* 230, April 1965, 169–70; Joanne Grant, "Mississippi and 'The Establishment,'" *Freedomways* 5, no. 2 (second quarter, 1965), 294–95.

14. Foster Davis, "Darkness on the Delta," *The Reporter*, 21 September 1967, 36; Nick Kotz, "Machine Shifts Adds to Plight of Negroes"; black woman quoted in Walter

Rugaber, "The Delta: Poverty Is a Way of Life"; Eastland quoted in Nick Kotz, "Machine Shifts Adds to Plight of Negroes."

15. Conditions on Eastland's farm, including the story of the Taylors and Charlie Edwards, were explored in an extraordinary series of articles by Nick Kotz that appeared in the *Des Moines Register* in February 1968: "Machine Shifts Adds to Plight of Negroes," "A Poor, Hard Life on Eastland Plantation," and "Clarify Data on Eastland"; Eastland was accused of charging interest of "two bits on the dollar" for loans, a charge he vehemently denied, saying that no one on his plantation had been charged interest after he won election to the Senate in 1942; "People need a place to live . . .": Glass, "Mississippi's Mighty Eastland Fears Lash of New Negro Votes"; W.F. Minor, "Eastland Facing First Test at Polls Since 1954," *Times-Picayune*, 17 July 1966.

16. Nick Kotz, "A Poor, Hard Life on Eastland Plantation" and "Delta Negroes Want Jobs, Not Handouts"; aged farmer quoted in Davis, "The Delta: Rich Land and Poor People."

17. O'Dell, "Life in Mississippi," 234; Hamer, "To Praise Our Bridges," 326; Carson, *In Struggle*, 209–10; Harry Bowie, interview with Jack Bass and Walter Devries, 31 March 1974, Southern Oral History Program #4007: A-98, 7. Akinyele K. Umoja argues that the disillusioning experiences of Freedom Summer triggered the abandonment of philosophical nonviolence in the civil rights movement. Akinyele K. Umoja, "1964: The Beginning of the End of Nonviolence in the Mississippi Freedom Movement," *Radical History Review* 85 (winter 2003), 202; Paule Marshall, "'Hunger Has No Colour Line," *Vogue*, June 1970, 192; Hamer, "To Praise Our Bridges," 324.

18. Hamer, "Foreword," vii; *The Movement* 3, no 10 (October 1967), 10; Andrew Kopkind, "The Future of 'Black Power,'" *New Republic*, 7 January 1967, 17; Carson, *In Struggle*, 240.

19. George C. Herring, *America's Longest War: The United States and Vietnam, 1950–1975* (New York: McGraw-Hill, 1996), 136–57.

20. Adam Fairclough, "Martin Luther King, Jr., and the War in Vietnam," *Phylon* 45 (1984), 25; Peter B. Levy, "Blacks and the Vietnam War," in D. Michael Shafer, ed., *The Legacy: The Vietnam War and the American Imagination* (Boston: Beacon Press, 1990), 220.

21. For a discussion of how blacks viewed the war, see Peter B. Levy, "Blacks and the Vietnam War," in Shafer, *The Legacy*, 209–32; O'Dell, "Life in Mississippi," 236; Taylor quoted in Nick Kotz, *Let Them Eat Promises: The Politics of Hunger in America* (New York: Anchor Books, 1971), 39–40; Bill Minor, "John Bell Williams Keeps All-White Draft Boards," *Times-Picayune*, 27 October 1968, in Minor, *Eyes on Mississippi*, 246–47.

22. *The Worker*, 13 July 1965, 3; *The Militant*, 17 January 1966; *Paterson* (NJ) *Morning News*, 20 October 1967; *The Worker*, 16 May 1967; *The Movement* 3, no. 10 (October 1967), 10.

23. William Leon Higgs, "Case of the Missing Registrars," *The Nation*, 13 Decem-

ber 1965; Johnson quoted in Michael H. Hunt, *Lyndon Johnson's War: America's Cold War Crusade in Vietnam, 1945–1968* (New York: Hill and Wang, 1996), 72.

24. Bass, *Unlikely Heroes*, 147–48; Hollis Watkins considered the charge of Communism as "simply a fear tactic to put into the minds of black people." Hollis Watkins, interview with John Rachal, 30 October 1995, http://www.lib.usm.edu/~spcol/crda/oh/watkins.htm; *Clarion-Ledger*, 8 August 1983.

25. *Congressional Record* 111 (3 February 1965), 1946; Brown, *Standing Against Dragons*, 21.

26. *Congressional Record* 111 (18 March 1965), 5450; (3 February 1965), 1944–7.

27. *Congressional Record* 111 (18 March 1965), 5452; James O. Eastland, "Report: The Black Revolution, A World Wide Conspiracy," reprint of *Congressional Record* distributed by Christian Nationalist Crusade, 1965, 10.

28. *Washington Post*, 18 March 1965; Dittmer, *Local People*, 341–43; Carson, *In Struggle*, 182.

29. Though most of the governmental investigations were conducted with at least a veneer of legality, the Supreme Court ruled in 1966 that Eastland had indeed violated the law by breaking into the SCEF offices in New Orleans. The Court's decision vindicated the SCEF's long-standing claims, but the lengthy legal process had sapped the organization of funds and energy. Morgan, *Reds*, 556, 567.

30. Morgan quoted in Gene Roberts, "From 'Freedom High' to 'Black Power,'" *New York Times Magazine*, 25 September 1966, 119; Woods, *Black Struggle, Red Scare*, 227–28.

31. 1966 civil rights bill: Kotz, *Judgment Days*, 367–68; and Dittmer, *Local People*, 391–92; Justice Department estimates: Glass, "Mississippi's Mighty Eastland Fears Lash of New Negro Votes"; sheriff and black voter quoted in *Delta Democrat Times*, 13 March 1967.

32. Glass, "Mississippi's Mighty Eastland Fears Lash of New Negro Votes"; "Let's Look at 'Big Jim's' Record," Race Relations Collection, Archives and Special Collections, University of Mississippi, Box 2, Folder 1; letter from Ann Sullivan to James O. Eastland, 18 September 1966, University of Mississippi, Special Collections and Archives, James O. Eastland Collection, File Series 1, Subseries 19, Box 27, Folder 5; letter from H.J. West to James O. Eastland, September 1966, University of Mississippi, Special Collections and Archives, James O. Eastland Collection, File Series 1, Subseries 19, Box 27, Folder 5; Whitley quoted in Dan Colburn, "James O. Eastland: Democratic Senator from Mississippi," Ralph Nader Congress Project, Citizens Look at Congress (Grossman Publishers, 1972), 19; Drew Pearson, "Eastland Runs for Political Life," *Washington Post*, 9 April 1966; A.L. Hopkins, "Observation of Election Results in Several Mississippi Counties Where a Larger Number of Negroes Are Registered to Vote than There Are White Citizens," 7, 8, 9, and 13 June 1966, SCR ID #2-109-0-47-1-1-1, 1–2.

33. *New Republic*, 23 May 1966, 606; Glass, "Mississippi's Mighty Eastland Fears Lash of New Negro Votes"; *Clarion-Ledger/Jackson Daily News*, 28 July 1966. Lapsan-

sky's public attack earned him and Tougaloo College, where he worked, a visit from State Sovereignty Commission investigators.

34. *Clarion-Ledger/Jackson Daily News*, 11 October 1966; "Who's Against Jim Eastland" pamphlet, MDAH, James O. Eastland Subject files, 1959–1967; *Clarion-Ledger/Jackson Daily News*, 21 October 1966; James Eastland, "Racial Battleground Is Shifting to North!" *Citizen*, vol. 11, no. 3 (December 1966), 4; Newsfile Collection, MP 80.01 reel, F-2274, Mississippi Department of Archives and History; "State of Southern States," *New South* 21 (Fall 1966), 103.

35. Eastland, "Racial Battleground Is Shifting to North!", 4–5; Newsfile Collection, MP 80.01 reel, F-2274, Mississippi Department of Archives and History.

36. Erle Johnston Jr. to James Coleman, 27 April 1967, SCR ID #3-18A-0-149-1-1-1; Erle Johnston Jr., to Courtney Pace, 31 March 1967, SCR ID #99-59-0-62-1-1-1.

37. James Eastland to Educator, 31 October 1966, Race Relations Collection, Archives and Special Collections, University of Mississippi, Box 2, Folder 1; *Clarion-Ledger/Jackson Daily News*, 28 June 1966; *Clarion-Ledger/Jackson Daily News*, 11 October 1966; Eastland, "Racial Battleground Is Shifting To North!" 7; *Clarion-Ledger/Jackson Daily News*, 30 October 1966.

38. *Mississippi Official and Statistical Register, 1968–1972* (Jackson, MS: 1968), 442.

39. For an in-depth look at an extraordinary man, see Scott Stossel, *Sarge: The Life and Times of Sargent Shriver* (Washington, DC: Smithsonian Books, 2004); Kotz, *Let Them Eat Promises*, 15.

40. Dittmer, *Local People*, 368–70; Peter Stewart, interview with Charles Bolton, 20 August 1997, University of Southern Mississippi Oral History Program, http://www.lib.usm.edu/%7Espcol/crda/oh/stewart.htm; For an insider's view of the CDGM, see Polly Greenberg, *The Devil Has Slippery Shoes: A Biased Biography of the Child Development Group of Mississippi* (Washington, DC: Youth Policy Institute, 1990, orig. 1969).

41. *Jackson Clarion-Ledger*, 4 May 1966; Report of the State Sovereignty Commission (1964–1967), SCR ID #99-161-0-1-1-1-1; Erle Johnston Jr. to Herman Glazer, 24 February 1966, SCR ID #6-45-3-34-1-1-1.

42. *Congressional Record* 112 (16 September 1966), 2279; Cobb, *Most Southern Place on Earth*, 259.

43. Christopher Jencks, "Accommodating Whites," *New Republic*, 16 April 1966, 21; "Memo for Discussion by CDGM Board," James F. McRee Papers, Mississippi Department of Archives and History, Box 1, Folder 10.

44. Nicholas Von Hoffman, "Manna from OEO Falls on Mississippi," *Washington Post*, 13 October 1966; Dittmer, *Local People*, 378.

45. Jencks, "Accommodating Whites," 19; Kotz, "Delta Negroes Want Jobs, Not Handouts"; Crespino, *In Search of Another Country*, 135–36.

46. Bass and Devries, *Transformation of Southern Politics*, 191; Kotz, "Machine Shift Adds to Plight of Negroes"; Dan Colburn, "James O. Eastland," 12; Victor Ullman, "In Darkest America," *The Nation*, 4 September 1967, 180; "Sunflower County Political

Handbook," Freedom Information Service, Fannie Lou Hamer Collection, University of Mississippi Special Collections and Archives, Box 2, Folder 1.

47. "Special Elections in the Towns of Sunflower and Moorhead to be Held May 2, 1967," Fannie Lou Hamer Papers, University of Mississippi, Archives and Special Collections, Box 2, Folder 3; *National Guardian*, 18 March 1967, 5.

48. Robert Analavage, "Mississippi Hopes Center in Sunflower," *Southern Patriot*, March 1967; *National Guardian*, 18 March 1967, 5; "Report of Visit to Mississippi Delta," statement by Percy Sutton, Charles Rangel, Paul Dwyer, Dorothy Jones, and Mary Hendrix, Fannie Lou Hamer Collection, University of Mississippi Special Collections and Archives, Box 2, Folder 1; *National Guardian*, 13 May 1967, 1.

49. Robert Analavage, "Mississippi Hopes Center in Sunflower"; Lee, *For Freedom's Sake*, 143; Mills, *This Little Light of Mine*, 191. It is unclear why Hamer did not take her daughter to the black-run hospital in Mound Bayou, less than twenty miles from Ruleville.

50. "Analysis and Statement on Behalf of the Negro Citizens of Sunflower County, Mississippi, to Ramsey Clark, Attorney General of the United States, Given April 26, 1967 by a Delegation Led by Representative William F. Ryan and Bayard Rustin," Fannie Lou Hamer Collection, University of Mississippi Special Collections and Archives, Box 2, Folder 1; statement of Otis Brown, 7 April 1967, Fannie Lou Hamer Collection, University of Mississippi Special Collections and Archives, Box 2, Folder 5; *New York Times*, 30 April 1967; *New York Post*, 3 May 1967; "Sunflower County and Its Activities," anonymous, Fannie Lou Hamer Collection, University of Mississippi Special Collections and Archives, Box 2, Folder 1.

51. Roger Rapoport, "Anatomy of a Mississippi Election," *Wall Street Journal*, 8 May 1967; *Southern Courier*, 6 May 1967.

52. Whites substituted John Sydney Parker, a known racist and brother of white alderman candidate Joel Parker, to serve as a poll watcher and assistant for black voters. Ullman, "In Darkest America"; "SNCC Campus Program: Survey for Summer Project in Mississippi," 7 May 1967, in "Mississippi Freedom Democratic Party," Subject Files, Records of the U.S. Senate, Senate Internal Security Subcommittee, Box 156, 4; Rapoport, "Anatomy of a Mississippi Election."

53. *Commercial Appeal*, 6 June 1965; Hamer, "To Praise Our Bridges," 327.

54. Fannie Lou Hamer interview with Robert Wright, 36; *The Movement* 3, no. 10 (October 1967), 11; Henry, *Fire Ever Burning*, 202.

55. *National Guardian*, 13 May 1967, 1; *The Movement* 3, no. 6, June 1967, 7; *National Guardian*, 13 May 1967, 9; *The Movement* 3, no. 10 (October 1967), 11.

9. "THE PENDULUM IS SWINGING BACK"

1. "Now the movement . . .": Egerton, *A Mind to Stay Here*, 94; "the cotton is gone": *The Movement* 3, no. 10 (October 1967), 11; "need to see something concrete . . .": Marshall, "'Hunger Has No Colour Line," 191.

2. "deeply entrenched habit . . .": Robert P. Moses and Charles E. Cobb Jr., *Radical Equations: Math Literacy and Civil Rights* (Boston: Beacon Press, 2001), 46; "trained from infancy": Silver quoted in CBS Television Network, "Search in Mississippi," 22; "So many of our people . . .": Hamer, "To Praise Our Bridges," 327.

3. "The black community must have . . .": Fannie Lou Hamer, "If the Name of the Game Is Survive, Survive," speech, 27 September 1971, Tougaloo College, Fannie Lou Hamer papers, Box 1, Folder 1, Sub-series A, emphasis in original; "For two years . . ." Egerton, *A Mind to Stay Here*, 105; Franklynn Peterson, "Sunflowers Don't Grow in Sunflower County," *Sepia*, February 1970, 17.

4. Seventy-one blacks own land: James M. Fallows, "Miss. Farmers Fight for Co-op," *Harvard Crimson*, 27 June 1969; "an oppressive pattern . . .": Paul Good, "The Thorntons of Mississippi," *The Atlantic* 218, September 1966, 97; "We must buy land . . .": Fannie Lou Hamer interview with Robert Wright, 3.

5. U.S. Department of Commerce, Bureau of Census, *County and City Data Book 1972* (Washington, DC: GPO, 1972), 270, 273; Dan Colburn, "James O. Eastland," 14; Wesley Pruden Jr., "'Never' Has Changed to 'Not Everything Now'"; *San Jose Mercury News*, 22 November 1964; Nick Kotz, "Negroes' Plight on Eastland's Plantation," *Des Moines Register*, 25 February 1968.

6. Hamer, "If the Name of the Game Is Survive, Survive"; other ideas included a "forty acres and a Cadillac" scheme, as well as an idea to promote catfish farming. Minutes of July 4, 1969, Meeting of the Fund for Education and Community Development, Fannie Lou Hamer Collection, University of Mississippi Special Collections and Archives, Box 1, Folder 5; gift from NCNW: *Daily World*, 10 December 1969; pig bank benefits hundreds of families: Lee, *For Freedom's Sake*, 148.

7. Hamer contacts Salamon: Egerton, *Mind to Stay Here*, 105; article to raise money: Fallows, "Miss. Farmers Fight for Co-op"; "not even the pooest . . .": Peterson, "Sunflowers Don't Grow in Sunflower County," 17; nineteen miles from Ruleville . . .: Egerton, *A Mind to Stay Here*, 94; land owned by Pratt and Silverblatt: Freedom Farm Corporation report, November 1971, Fannie Lou Hamer Collection, University of Mississippi Special Collections and Archives, Box 4, Folder 2; Townsend's legal work: Mills, *This Little Light of Mine*, 259; Freedom Farm donations: Fannie Lou Hamer to Harvey Siver, 28 September 1970, Fannie Lou Hamer Collection, University of Mississippi Special Collections and Archives, Box 4, Folder 2; Fannie Lou Hamer, interview with Neil McMillen.

8. One-third of all black-owned land: Lee, *For Freedom's Sake*, 148; "indispensable right-hand man": Marshall, "'Hunger Has No Colour Line," 191; thirty families paid dues: Moye, *Let the People Decide*, 156.

9. "houses, jobs, . . ." and Hamer's new home: Marshall, "'Hunger Has No Colour Line," 191–92; "We decided to organize . . ." and housing accomplishments: Hamer quoted in Mills, *This Little Light of Mine*, 262.

10. Plans for garment factory: letter from Joseph Harris to Dr. L.F. Packer, 12 January 1970, Fannie Lou Hamer Collection, University of Mississippi Special Collections

and Archives, Box 1, Folder 3; "Community living . . ." and "individual ownership of land . . .": Hamer, "If the Name of the Game Is Survive, Survive"; "black socialism": Peterson, "Sunflowers Don't Grow in Sunflower County," 17.

11. Dorsey quoted in Mills, *This Little Light of Mine*, 272.

12. Freedom Farm Corporation report, Board of Directors, Minutes of the Meeting, 2 March 1972, Fannie Lou Hamer Collection, University of Mississippi Special Collections and Archives, Box 4, Folder 3; Freedom Farm Corporation report, November 1971, Fannie Lou Hamer Collection, University of Mississippi Special Collections and Archives, Box 4, Folder 2; Freedom Farm Corporation, "Status Report and Request for Funds," July 1973, Fannie Lou Hamer Collection, University of Mississippi Special Collections and Archives, Box 4, Folder 4, 6; Freedom Farm Corporation, Proposal for Funding, 1975, Fannie Lou Hamer Collection, University of Mississippi Special Collections and Archives, Box 4, Folder 5; Danny J. Barfield to Board of Directors, 29 October 1976, Fannie Lou Hamer Collection, University of Mississippi Special Collections and Archives, Box 4, Folder 5.

13. U.S. Department of Commerce, Bureau of Census, *County and City Data Book 1972* (Washington, DC: 1972), 280; Lee, *For Freedom's Sake*, 162; Eastland was ranked the fourth-richest senator at the time. *Jackson Daily News/Clarion-Ledger*, 11 May 1969; Nick Kotz, "Delta Negroes Want Jobs, Not Handouts," *Des Moines Register*, 28 February 1968; "Activities of the Southern Christian Leadership Conference . . . ," undated report, p. 1, in University of Mississippi, Special Collections and Archives, James O. Eastland Collection, File Series 1, Subseries 7, Box 1, Folder 27; anonymous letter, 11 June 1969, SCR ID #9-31-9-7-1-1-1; *Washington Daily News*, 20 June 1969; Eastland claimed that the legal restructuring of his plantation was a result not of the 1970 law but rather of a clause in his father's will stating that Eastland's property should be split among his children after the youngest had reached age twenty-one. Eastland's youngest child, Woods, was twenty-six years old in 1971. Nick Kotz, "Rich Farmers Split Holdings to Save Subsidies," *Washington Post*, 5 July 1971; Colburn, "James O. Eastland," 12. Black farmers throughout Sunflower County typically did not have enough land to qualify for subsidies, loans, or credit. Valerie Grim, "The Impact of Mechanized Farming on Black Farm Families in the Rural South: A Study of Farm Life in the Brooks Farm Community, 1940–1970," *Agricultural History* 68, no. 2 (spring 1994), 172.

14. Thornton quoted in Mills, *This Little Light of Mine*, 271; C.J. Wilson, "Voices From Mississippi," *New South* 28 (spring 1973), 71.

15. Anthony Lake, *The "Tar Baby" Option: American Policy Toward Southern Rhodesia* (New York: Columbia University Press, 1976), 1–19; Borstelmann, *Cold War and the Color Line*, 146–47.

16. *Congressional Record* 112 (22 March 1966), 6500; Lake, *"Tar Baby" Option*, 103–10; Thomas Noer, "Segregationists and the World: The Foreign Policy of White Resistance," in Plummer, *Window on Freedom*, 145–46; *Congressional Record* 112 (2 March 1966), 4692.

17. *Congressional Record* 112 (2 March 1966), 4692; *Congressional Record* 112 (25 August 1966), 20541.

18. *Congressional Record* 112 (22 March 1966), 6501; *Congressional Record* 112 (25 August 1966), 20542.

19. *The Movement* 3, no. 10 (October 1967), 10.

20. *Clarion-Ledger*, 9 March 1969.

21. Ibid.

22. Ibid.

23. Clarence Pierce, interview with author, 28 September 2001. Eastland always had respected Robert Kennedy's fierce anti-Communism, which the Mississippian first had noticed when Kennedy worked on Joseph McCarthy's staff. The two had cultivated a strong working relationship during the Freedom Rides, a relationship that prompted criticism from conservatives within the state. "Let's Look at 'Big Jim's' Record," Race Relations Collection, Archives and Special Collections, University of Mississippi, Box 2, Folder 1. See also Bass, *Unlikely Heroes*, 145; James O. Eastland, interview with Dr. Joe B. Frantz, 19 February 1971, Lyndon Baines Johnson Library Oral History Collection, University of Texas, Austin, 15–16.

24. Eastland story quoted in Nick Walters, "The Repairman Chairman: Senator James O. Eastland and His Influence on the U.S. Supreme Court," master's thesis, Mississippi College, 1992, 66.

25. On racial issues, the Court consistently sided with white southerners against advocates of racial reform in cases ranging from the antebellum *Dred Scott* decision to the Reconstruction-era *Civil Rights Cases* to the infamous *Plessy* ruling in the late nineteenth century; even as the Court began to take slightly more liberal stances on race cases beginning in the 1920s, the justices rarely challenged national opinion. On economic matters, the post–Civil War Court regularly refused to hear worker complaints about unfair labor practices and, as in the 1905 case of *Lochner v. New York*, invalidated many of the social and economic reforms of the Progressive and New Deal eras. Michael J. Klarman, *From Jim Crow to Civil Rights: The Supreme Court and the Struggle for Racial Equality* (Oxford: Oxford University Press, 2004), 98–170, 443–68; Morton J. Horwitz, *The Warren Court and the Pursuit of Justice* (New York: Hill and Wang, 1998), 16–17, 76; Cray, *Chief Justice*, 1–10. By the late 1960s, the Warren Court's decisions on race were among its least controversial rulings. More exasperating to conservatives nationwide were court rulings that they believed etiolated the moral fiber and basic security of the country. The Court's 1962 ban on prayer in public schools in *Engel v. Vitale* sparked outrage among religious conservatives, while its *Miranda* ruling angered many citizens who feared that law enforcement officials would be crippled in their attempt to crack down on worsening violence. Henry J. Abraham, *Justices, Presidents, and Senators: A History of the U.S. Supreme Court Appointments from Washington to Clinton*, new and rev. ed. (Lanham, MD: Rowman & Littlefield, 1999), 196–97; Citizens Council Forum Collection, MP 86.01, reel 098, Mississippi Department of Archives and History.

26. Jack Bass and Walter DeVries, *The Transformation of Southern Politics: Social Change and Political Consequences Since 1945* (New York: Basic Books, 1976), 217; *Jackson Daily News*, 20 September 1978; Walters, "Repairman Chairman," 8–9; Senator John Tunney (D-CA), quoted in *Los Angeles Times*, 18 November 1977; Biloxi-Gulfport *Daily Herald*, 27 October 1977; *Clarion-Ledger/Jackson Daily News*, 1 October 1972.

27. The Constitution provides checks and balances to ensure that no one of the three branches of government can wield too much power. Though Supreme Court justices have lifetime tenure, the Court itself remains checked by the executive branch, which has the right to nominate replacement justices. The executive, too, is checked by the Senate, which must confirm any president's judicial nominees. The Senate confirmation process begins with the Judiciary Committee. Abraham, *Justices, Presidents, and Senators*, 19–23. Another widely repeated but unsubstantiated rumor was that the senator used Cox as leverage against President Kennedy in the latter's attempt to appoint Thurgood Marshall to a federal judgeship. Cox was appointed more than a year before Marshall, and his approval from the president resulted from a personal conversation between the two, during which Cox assured Kennedy that he would uphold the Constitution with respect to civil rights. As Kennedy and the rest of the nation soon realized, however, Cox had a different understanding of what it meant to "uphold the Constitution." Three-quarters of his civil rights decisions were overturned and, as political reporter Jack Bass noted, "for two decades Cox compiled an unmatched record of judicial conduct that not only obstructed civil rights progress in Mississippi but undermined respect for federal courts." Bass, *Unlikely Heroes*, 166–67. Clarence Pierce, interview with author, 28 September 2001; Walters, "The Repairman Chairman," 7.

28. Bill Minor, "Despite Republican in the White House, Eastland Still Pulls Patronage Strings," 2 November 1969, in Minor, *Eyes on Mississippi*, 80–81; Bass, *Unlikely Heroes*, 312.

29. Eastland also had supported Fortas to be attorney general, the original post Johnson had considered. Michael Beschloss, *Reaching for Glory: Lyndon Johnson's Secret White House Tapes, 1964–1965* (New York: Simon & Schuster, 2001), 167–68; *Clarion-Ledger*, 19 October 1966.

30. H. Rap Brown called Marshall a "tom" and told an approving audience that "anybody who sits before James O. Eastland—a camel-breath, peckerwood nasty honkey from Mississippi . . . [applause] . . . and lets James O. Eastland subject him to the type of questioning that he did, he's a strange breed of man." H. Rap Brown, Free Huey Rally, February 1968, The Pacifica Radio/UC Berkeley, Social Activism Sound Recording Project, http://www.lib.berkeley.edu/MRC/rapbrown.html; *Clarion-Ledger*, 20 July 1967; Juan Williams, *Thurgood Marshall: American Revolutionary* (New York: Random House, 1998), 332–33.

31. By Johnson's own admission and the admission of his staff, it was indeed an attempt to preserve the long-term liberal dominance of the Court. Joseph A. Califano Jr., *The Triumph and Tragedy of Lyndon Johnson: The White House Years* (College Station:

Texas A&M University Press, 2000), 307; *Newsweek*, 14 October 1968, 34; Lyndon B. Johnson, *The Vantage Point: Perspectives of the Presidency, 1963–1969* (New York: Holt, Rinehart, and Winston, 1971), 546; Walters, "Repairman Chairman," 32.

32. As the days passed, the hearings turned rancorous, with the abrasive Senator Thurmond hounding the demure justice about Court decisions he considered responsible for the increasing violence. When Fortas quietly but firmly rejected such a notion, the hearing audience burst into applause, prompting Chairman Eastland to threaten to clear the room. "Nominations of Abe Fortas and Homer Thornberry," Hearings Before the Committee on the Judiciary, United States Senate, 90th Congress (Washington, DC: GPO, 1968), 105, 180–219; John Holloman, quoted in Walters, "The Repairman Chairman," 32. President Johnson himself seemed to agree, noting in his memoirs that he first realized that Fortas would lose after meeting with Eastland. Johnson, *Vantage Point*, 546–47.

33. After earning his conservative credibility as a top aide to Barry Goldwater in 1964, Rehnquist practiced law in Arizona before joining the Nixon administration as an assistant attorney general. "Nominations of William H. Rehnquist and Lewis F. Powell," Hearings Before the Committee on the Judiciary, United States Senate, 92nd Congress (Washington, DC: GPO, 1971), 2–7. Eastland himself told the nominee Powell's confirmation was assured "because they think you're going to die." Bob Woodward and Scott Armstrong, *The Brethren: Inside the Supreme Court* (New York: Simon & Schuster, 1979), 162. Rep. John Conyers labeled him "out of tune." Andrew Biemiller of the AFL-CIO called him the "zealot." Professor Gary Orfield of Princeton gave the "lonely voice" comment. "Nominations of William H. Rehnquist and Lewis F. Powell," Hearings Before the Committee on the Judiciary, United States Senate, 92nd Congress (Washington, DC: GPO, 1971), 351, 400, 450–51; Walters, "Repairman Chairman," 71; Woodward and Armstrong, *The Brethren*, 162–63.

34. In the Sunflower County school district, only one black family exercised its "freedom of choice" and sent children to formerly all-white schools. Their ordeal is the subject of Constance Curry's *Silver Rights*. For harassment that blacks across the South faced for attending white schools, see U.S. Commission on Civil Rights, *Southern School Desegregation 1966–67* (Washington, DC: GPO, 1967). For more information on the academy movement, see Christopher Myers, "White Freedom Schools: Eastern North Carolina and the Segregation Academy Movement, 1954–1973," *North Carolina Historical Review* 81, no. 4 (October 2004), 393–425; and Michael W. Fuquay, "Civil Rights and the Private School Movement in Mississippi, 1964–1971," *History of Education Quarterly* 42, no. 2 (summer 2002), 159–80; Numan Bartley, *The New South, 1945–1980* (Baton Rouge: Louisiana State University Press, 1995), 373–74.

35. *Congressional Record* 116 (9 February 1970), 2883–84; Charles C. Bolton, *The Hardest Deal of All: The Battle over School Integration in Mississippi, 1870–1980* (Jackson: University Press of Mississippi, 2005), 169–73; Lee quoted in Moye, *Let the People Decide*, 179. In 2005, the public schools in Sunflower County had a student population that was more than 97 percent black; local private schools such as Indianola

Academy, North Sunflower Academy, and Mid-Delta Academy catered to a student population more than 95 percent white.

36. *Congressional Record* 116 (9 February 1970), 2884–86.

37. *Congressional Record* 115 (16 December 1969), 39355; Thomas J. Sugrue, *The Origins of the Urban Crisis: Race and Inequality in Postwar Detroit* (Princeton: Princeton University Press, 1996), 9–10, 43–44, 62–66; Ronald P. Formisano, *Boston Against Busing: Race, Class, and Ethnicity in the 1960s and 1970s* (Chapel Hill: University of North Carolina Press, 1991), 12–14; Kenneth T. Jackson, *Crabgrass Frontier: The Suburbanization of the United States* (New York: Oxford University Press, 1985), 289–90; *Congressional Record* 116 (9 February 1970), 2884–86.

38. On the Stennis amendment and Ribicoff, see Crespino, *In Search of Another Country*, 186–204; "Eastland outliberaling . . .": Jackson *Clarion-Ledger*, 23 January 1968. For a detailed account of the Swann case and desegregation in Charlotte, see Davison M. Douglas's *Reading, Writing, and Race: The Desegregation of the Charlotte Schools* (Chapel Hill: University of North Carolina Press, 1995); George Metcalf, *From Little Rock to Boston: The History of School Desegregation* (Greenwood, CT: Greenwood Press, 1983), esp. chapters 14, 16, and 19; J. Harvie Wilkinson III, *From Brown to Bakke: The Supreme Court and School Integration, 1954–1978* (New York: Oxford University Press, 1979), esp. chapters 6–8; Stewart Alsop, "The Myth and William Rehnquist," *Newsweek*, 6 December 1971, 124.

39. Mills, *This Little Light of Mine*, 242–46.

40. Wilson, "Voices from Mississippi," 65; William Simmons, interview with Jack Bass and Walter De Vries, 29 March 1974, Southern Oral History Program #4007: A-103.

41. *Jackson Daily News*, 24 May 1972.

42. *Commercial Appeal*, 28 December 1978; *Congressional Record* 116 (9 February 1970), 2884.

10. "RIGHT ON BACK TO THE PLANTATION"

1. Woods Eastland, interview with author, 16 February 2005.

2. Fannie Lou Hamer, interview with Neil McMillen; *Washington Post*, 17 March 1977; Lewis Perdue, "Giant Step to Moderation," *The Nation*, 1 January 1973, 19–20; Ted Ownby, *American Dreams in Mississippi: Consumers, Poverty, and Culture, 1830–1998* (Chapel Hill: University of North Carolina Press, 1999), 154–57.

3. *Congressional Record* 93 (11 April 1947): 3328. From 64.6 percent of U.S. mill fiber consumption in 1960, cotton fell to less than 40 percent in the early 1970s. U.S. Department of Agriculture, *Economic Research Service Statistics on Cotton and Related Data, 1920–1973* (Washington, DC: GPO, 1975), 15.

4. Wilson, "Voices from Mississippi," 63.

5. George Rogers, interview with Jack Bass and Walter Devries, 27 March 1974, Southern Oral History Program #4007: A-114, 8; Payne, *I've Got the Light of Freedom,*

363; Margaret Edds, "Another America," *Virginian Pilot/Ledger Star*, 1986, http://www.aliciapatterson.org/APF0901/Edds/Edds.html; W.F. Minor, interview with Jack Bass and Walter Devries, 25 March 1974, Southern Oral History Program #4007: A-110, 21; Aaron Henry, interview with Jack Bass and Walter Devries, 2 April 1974, Southern Oral History Program #4007: A-107, 10–29; Patt Derian, interview with Jack Bass and Walter Devries, 25 March 1974, Southern Oral History Program #4007: A-105, 28; Robert Clark, interview with Jack Bass and Walter Devries, 28 March 1974, Southern Oral History Program #4007: A-101, 9–18.

6. Frank Chapman, "Mississippi in the Mainstream," *Freedomways* 24, no. 2 (second quarter, 1984), 104; Howell Raines, "Revolution in South: Blacks at Polls and in Office," *New York Times*, 3 April 1978; Edds, "Another America."

7. Nick Kotz, "A Poor, Hard Life on Eastland Plantation," *Des Moines Register*, 26 February 1968; one black student at IA: Richard Schweid, *Catfish and the Delta: Confederate Fish Farming in the Mississippi Delta* (Berkeley: Ten Speed Press, 1992), 97; Willie M. Pitts, interview with author, 8 February 2005; Wilson, "Voices from Mississippi," 66; Bolton, *Hardest Deal of All*, esp. chapter 8, 193–216.

8. Woods Eastland, interview with author, 16 February 2005; E. Nolan Waller and Dani A. Smith, "Growth Profiles of Mississippi's Counties 1960–1980" (University, MS: Bureau of Business and Economic Research, 1985), 82.

9. Eastland's son, Woods, took over the family farm and moved to Indianola. His children dispersed across the South, living in Jackson, Memphis, and Dallas. Anne Eastland Howdershell, interview with author, 7 November 2001.

10. Woods Eastland, interview with author, 16 October 2001 and 16 February 2005; Earline Tillman, interview with author, 26 September 2001.

11. Fannie Lou Hamer, interview with Neil McMillen; Annie Mae King, interview with Robert Wright, 28 September 1968, Civil Rights Documentation Project, Moorland-Spingarn Research Center, Howard University, 20–21.

12. Tom Dent, "Annie Devine Remembers," *Freedomways* 22, no. 2 (second quarter, 1982), 84.

13. Lee, *For Freedom's Sake*, 171–74.

14. Program, Fannie Lou Hamer funeral, Fannie Lou Hamer Collection, University of Mississippi Special Collections and Archives, Box 1, Folder 1; *Clarion-Ledger*, 21 March 1977.

15. The president pro tempore followed the Speaker of the House as the next in line to the presidency after the vice president. In 1973, following Vice President Spiro Agnew's resignation, House Speaker Carl Albert was too ill to be considered next in line; had something happened to President Nixon, Eastland would have become president. Again, the following year, after Gerald Ford became president following Nixon's resignation, Eastland was next in line until Nelson Rockefeller was selected as vice president. *Jackson Daily News*, 28 December 1978.

16. *The Reporter*, 3 November 1977; Aaron Henry, interview with Jack Bass and Walter Devries, 2 April 1974, Southern Oral History Program #4007: A-107, 9–10.

17. William Winter, interview with author, 22 March 2005; *New York Times*, 3 April 1978; *Commercial Appeal*, 20 February 1986.

18. "Report of Aaron Henry before the Mississippi State Convention of the National Association for the Advancement of Colored People," 3 November 1977, Ed King Papers, University of Mississippi, Archives and Special Collections, Box 1, Folder 9; *Capital Reporter*, 20 October 1977; *Delta Democrat Times*, 22 March 1978.

19. Owen H. Brooks, form letter to Delta Ministry supporters, 26 January 1978, Ed King Papers, University of Mississippi, Archives and Special Collections, Box 1, Folder 9; Waller quoted in Jere Nash and Andy Taggart, *Mississippi Politics: The Struggle for Power, 1976–2006* (Jackson: University Press of Mississippi, 2006), 79; *Commercial Appeal*, 22 March 1978; *Delta Democrat Times*, 22 March 1978; *Delta Democrat Times*, 22 March 1978; on the campaign for Eastland's seat, see Nash and Taggart, *Mississippi Politics*, 79–83.

20. *Jackson Daily News*, 10 September 1979; *Delta Democrat Times*, 18 June 1978. Journalist Curtis Wilkie marveled at the relationship. "Nothing was stranger than the relationship between Aaron and Eastland," Wilkie wrote. Where Henry was "an exuberant, affectionate man who used the Latin abrazo when greeting friends," Eastland was "phlegmatic and rarely showed emotion." The senator once told aides in his Washington office to surround his desks with chairs to prevent Henry from touching him. Curtis Wilkie, *Dixie: A Personal Odyssey Through Events That Shaped the Modern South* (New York: Scribner, 2001), 251–53; *Commercial Appeal*, 21 February 1986.

21. *Jackson Daily News*, 10 September 1979; *Clarion-Ledger*, 5 September 1982; Sue Eastland McRoberts, interview with author, 13 November 2001; *Bolivar Commercial*, 24 July 1996; *Commercial Appeal*, 22 February 1986; *Bolivar Commercial*, 16 February 1986; *Commercial Appeal*, 20 February 1986.

22. *Clarion-Ledger*, 20 February 1986; *Jackson Daily News*, 10 September 1979. Born shortly after his namesake's election in 1912, Woodrow Wilson was in his mid-sixties at the time of the senator's death. Woodrow Wilson, interview with author, 8 July 2000. Willie Jackson and Rosa Lee Lackey shared the opinion that workers "didn't suffer for nothing" and life on the plantation "was nice." Willie Jackson, interview with author, 8 July 2000, Rosa Lee Lackey, interview with author, 8 July 2000. Mack Caples considered the senator a "mighty nice man." Mack Caples, interview with author, 8 July 2000.

23. *Washington Post*, 16 May 1979.

24. School statistics: Mississippi Assessment and Accountability Reporting System, http://orsap.mde.k12.ms.us:8080/MAARS/maarsMS_TestResultsProcessor.jsp?userSessionId=426&DistrictId=1223&TestPanel=1; Bill Minor interview with author, 17 February 2006; Carver Randle outlines exchange program: *Enterprise Tocsin*, 7 May 1998; Moye, *Let the People Decide*, 217–18. Other suggestions included having sports tournaments between Indianola's public schools and the private schools, though Indianola Academy only wanted to compete in the traditionally white-dominated sports of golf, tennis, and baseball.

25. Gary Orfield, Susan E. Eaton, and the Harvard Project on School Desegregation, *Dismantling Desegregation: The Quiet Reversal of* Brown v. Board of Education (New York: The New Press, 1996).

26. Edwards quoted in Cathy Hayden, "Delta Schools Search for Answers," *Clarion-Ledger*, 21 December 1999; Mississippi Department of Education, Mississippi Report Card 99; ACT scores: Mississippi Assessment and Accountability Reporting System, http://orsap.mde.k12.ms.us:8080/MAARS/maarsMS_TestResultsProcessor.jsp? userSessionId=426&DistrictId=1223&TestPanel=1; ten worst schools: *Clarion-Ledger*, 5 September 2003.

27. The preceding paragraph, along with other unattributed observations in preceding and subsequent paragraphs, derive from the author's personal experience as an educator and resident of Sunflower County for more than eight years between 1994 and 2006.

Index

Acheson, Dean, 112, 121

Africa: and Cold War, 160, 264; and colonialism, 77, 264–65; global cotton and American plantation model, 76–77, 311n16; impact of *Brown* decision, 159, 164; independence movements, 169–70; SNCC Guinea trip (1964), 214–16, 338n30; white-ruled Rhodesia, 262–66

Agricultural Adjustment Administration (AAA), 79–83

agricultural mechanization, 74, 82–84, 127–31, 226–27, 256, 266; and John Rust, 83–84; effect of World War II on, 127–31; and civil rights movement, 226–27

Alexander v. Holmes County, Mississippi, Board of Education, 274, 277

Alsop, Stewart, 276–77

America magazine, 156, 161

American Bar Association (ABA), 269, 272–73

American Civil Liberties Union (ACLU), 237

American Communist Party, 85–86, 121, 160. *See also* Communism/anti-Communism

American Federation of Labor (AFL), 136

American Freedom from Hunger Foundation, 258

Americans for Democratic Action, 156

Americans for the Preservation of the White Race, 206

Anderson, Jack, 269

Ashmore, Harry, 133

Austin, Richmond, 36

Baker, Ella, 169

Baldanzi, George, 136

Baldwin, James, 200

Bankhead, John, 95

Barber, Frank, 186, 330n49

Barnett, Ross, 183, 184, 192–93

Battle, Clinton C., 141

Belafonte, Harry, 214, 248, 258

Belgian colonialism, 77, 264–65

Bethune, Mary McLeod, 114

Bevel, James, 176

Beveridge, Albert, 18

Bilbo, Theodore, 40–41, 96, 116

Birmingham News, 30

Black, Hugo, 145

black church, 59–64, 309n54

black lodges, 25

Black Panther Party, 230, 239

black power, 230, 237, 239–40

Bolivar County, 14, 71, 87, 225

Bolshevik revolution, 91

Boynton v. Virginia, 174

Bramlett, Liza, 47–48

Brandon, E.W., 52, 73

Brazilian cotton, 79, 94

Bromson, Theodore, 140

Brooks, Lela Mae, 252

Brooks, Owen, 288

Brooks, Preston, 94

Brotherhood of Sleeping Car Porters, 114

Brown, H. Rap, 348n30

Brown, Otis, 249

Brown v. Board of Education of Topeka,
133, 144, 145–50; Eastland's reaction,
147–49, 150–55, 163, 166; global
impact/international reaction, 159,
164; post-*Brown* desegregation
mandates, 273–74, 278. *See also*
school desegregation

Bruce, Blanche K., 36

Bryant, Roy, 167

Bunche, Ralph, 138

Burger, Warren, 273

Burns, Vida, 39

Byrnes, James, 115, 121

Calhoun, John C., 118

Campbell, Cecil, 172

Caperton, Betty, 36

Caperton, Woods, 24

Caples, Mack, 71

Caples, Wiley, 290

Carmichael, Stokely, 230, 249

Carr, Albert, 7–9, 23–24

Carter, Hodding, 92, 133

Carter, Hodding, III, 246, 280

Carter, Jimmy, 287

Caste and Class in a Southern Town
(Dollard), 46

Castro, Fidel, 165–66, 237

CBS News Special Report (1964),
198–99

Central Delta Academy, 283

Chaney, James, 207

Chappell, David, 339n2

Chavez, Dennis, 118

Chicago, Illinois, 49, 240, 267

Chicago Defender, 49, 118, 160

Child Development Group of Mississippi
(CDGM), 243–46

China, 134, 281

Choctaw Indians, 10–11

Churchill, Winston, 108

Citizens' Council, 4, 151, 154, 162, 163,
223, 241

Civil Rights Act (1957), 162–63, 166,
201

Civil Rights Act (1964), 206–7, 223, 273

civil rights bill, failed (1966), 240, 242

Claiborne, William C.C., 17

Clarion-Ledger, 38, 90, 192, 265

Clark, Charles, 269–70

Clark, Robert, 282

Clark, Septima, 193

Clayton, Will, 111

Clifford, Clark, 122

Clinton, Bill, 291

Cobb, Charles, 72, 175–76, 178, 223,
335n41

Cochran, Thad, 289

Cohn, David, 9, 12, 67, 74, 130

Cold War, 134–40, 189, 215–16; and
American cotton industry, 110–12;
and American foreign policy, 104–12,
159–61, 165–66, 264; and racial
equality, 120; and Truman's domestic
policies, 134–35. *See also* Communism/
anti-Communism

Cole, Rosie, 42, 54

Coleman, Elizabeth, 41. *See also* Eastland, Libby

Coleman, James, 152, 184

Collier's magazine, 156

Collins, Charles, W., *Whither Solid South?*, 123

Commodity Credit Corporation (CCC), 80–81

Communism/anti-Communism: American parties, 85–86, 121, 160, 190, 236–37; and *Brown* decision, 153–55; in the Caribbean, 165–66; and civil rights militancy, 237, 239–40; and civil rights movement, 135–36, 144–45, 161, 170, 182–84, 189–92, 209–10, 233–37, 239–40, 244–45, 335n41; early radicals and anti-racism, 85–86, 88, 121; Eastland and FEPC debates/filibusters, 117, 119, 321n34; Eastland and internationalism, 164–66; Eastland and late 1930s, 91–93, 97; Eastland and postwar American foreign policy, 107–10, 113, 164–66; Eastland and SCEF hearings, 144–45; Eastland and SISS hearings, 137–40, 155–56; Eastland's postwar domestic crusade, 113, 117, 119–21, 134–35, 137–40, 143–45, 155–56, 161; and labor organizing, 86, 88; and Marxist ideology, 237; Palmer raids/Red Scare, 91; and plantation system, 91, 92–93

Communist Part USA (CPUSA), 190, 236–37

Congo, 170, 264–65

Congress of Industrial Organizations (CIO), 91, 103, 104, 136, 190

Congress of Racial Equality (CORE), 174, 190, 217

Coody, Archibald, 125, 158, 162

Coordinating Committee for Fundamental American Freedoms (CCFAF), 206

cotton economy and Sunflower County, 11–12, 16–17, 66; and agricultural revolution, 127–31; boll weevil, 48–49; and child labor, 53–54; and cotton gin, 12; and the cotton year, 68; cultivation and domestication, 11; and economic justice, 225–30; federal farm bill (1965), 227–28; and global cotton/foreign competition, 19–21, 73–79, 128–29, 281, 311n16, 312n22; and Indian culture, 11; labor shortages, 48–49, 101–4, 127, 129–31, 140; and the land/soil, 12; mechanization and labor issues, 82–84, 100, 125, 127–31, 226–27, 260; "plantation mentality," 66, 72–73; POW labor, 103; and railroad boom, 16–17; sharecropping credit system, 68–70; switch to wage labor, 82–83; and tariffs, 78–79, 95, 111; wages, 50, 79, 82–83, 102; post–Civil War, 16–18, 75; World War I–era, 49–50; post–World War I, 48–54; (1930s), 43–46, 66–89; and New Deal, 42, 79–83, 84–85, 88–89; post–World War II, 93, 99–104, 127–31, 140; (1970s), 281. *See also* sharecropping

Coughlin, Charles, 85

Council of Federated Organizations (COFO), 174, 178, 196, 202–3, 217, 236

Courts, Gus, 171

Cox, Harold, 269, 348n27

Cox, Minnie, 22

Crisis (NAACP magazine), 49, 170

Crockett, George, 210

Cronkite, Walter, 156, 198

Crouch, Paul, 145

Cuba, 165–66

Daniels, Jonathan, 85

Dantin, Maurice, 289

Darwin, Charles, 18

Davis, Sidney Fant, 8

DCRFWU (Dining Car and Railroad Food Workers Union), 137, 140

Delta Chamber of Commerce, 81. *See also* Delta Council

Delta Cooperative Farm, 87, 173

Delta Council: Cold War–era, 110, 111–12; creation, 81; mechanization and agricultural revolution, 125, 127, 129, 130–31, 140; World War II–era, 101, 102, 103, 127

Delta Democrat Times, 289

Delta Hub, 93, 94

Delta Industrial Institute, 57

Democratic National Convention in Atlantic City (1964), 3–4, 210–14, 215

Democratic National Convention in Chicago (1968), 267

Democratic National Convention in Philadelphia (1948), 123–24

Dennis, Dave, 202

Depression era, 43–45, 82. *See also* New Deal

desegregation. *See* school desegregation

Devine, Annie, 217–20, 285

Dies, Martin, 91

Dixiecrat revolt, 123–25, 135

Doar, John, 200

Dodd, Jim and Sid, 6

Doddsville: Holbert incident and mob lynchings, 7–9, 23–32, 33–34; today, 33, 65, 67, 291

Dollard, John, 46, 57, 58, 60, 61–62, 69, 71, 73, 84, 89

Dombrowski, Jim, 144

Dominican Republic, 165–66

Dorsey, L.C., 58, 259

"Double V" campaign, 115

Doxey, Wall, 96, 97–98

DPOWA (Distributive, Processing, and Office Workers of America), 137–39

Draper, Wickliffe Preston, 206

Du Bois, W.E.B., 50, 120, 121, 135, 154

Dulles, John Foster, 164

Dunbar, Paul Lawrence, 59

Dunn, Read, 128

Durr, Clifford, 144–45

Durr, Virginia Foster, 144–45

Durrough, Charles, 204

Eastland, Alma Austin, 34, 36–37, 67

Eastland, Anne, 43, 44, 45, 71, 143, 147, 148, 208

Eastland, Chester, 38

Eastland, Hiram (uncle), 33

Eastland, Hiriam (great-grandfather), 17, 36

Eastland, James: early life, 34–40; education, 38–40; and black migration, 256; and black voters, 171–73; Dixiecrat revolt, 123–25; early career, 40–43; economic agenda, 91–98, 100–104; economic philosophy, 41, 89, 97; family life, 41–47, 147–48; father's influence, 34, 38, 41, 42, 90, 94–95, 101–2; FEPC debates and filibusters, 116–19, 321n34; freedom concept, 95–96, 205, 241–42; and Freedom Summer, 205–6, 208–10; Hills and Delta roots, 35–36, 96; and Johnson's civil rights agenda, 201, 206–7, 330n49; Judiciary Committee chairmanship, 155–59, 166, 183, 253, 267–73, 286–87; and Pres. Kennedy, 182–83, 199–200; and Robert Kennedy, 183, 267, 334n28, 347n23; and labor unions, 97–98, 104; in late 1930s, 90–98, 100–102; in the 1960s, 238, 267; in the 1970s, 281, 286–90; and northern whites, 185–87, 241; and postwar American foreign policy, 104–12, 113, 164–66; and Roosevelt administration, 94, 95, 106–8; and school desegregation, 147–49, 150–55, 163, 166, 192–93, 274–78; and Supreme Court, 268, 270–73; and Truman's civil rights agenda, 115–16, 122–23; and white-ruled Rhodesia, 262–66; as president pro tempore, 287, 351n15; changing views of black

community, 287–88, 289; retirement, 289; death and funeral, 289–90; how he is remembered today, 291–92. *See also* Communism/anti-Communism; Senate Judiciary Committee
Eastland, James (uncle), 4–5, 7–9
Eastland, Libby, 41–42, 100, 101, 147, 199, 289
Eastland, Nell, 43
Eastland, Oliver, 6, 17, 19–20, 36
Eastland, Sue, 43, 44, 289
Eastland, Woods Caperton (father): birth, 36; early law practice, 37–38; early political ambitions, 37; and Eastland plantation, 17, 42; Holbert manhunt and lynching, 4, 23–32, 304–5n19; influence on son, 34, 38, 41, 42, 90, 94–95, 101–2; prosecution and trial, 31–32, 34
Eastland, Woods (son), 37, 43, 44, 46–47, 100, 304–5n19; and the Eastland plantation, 71–72, 279, 283; on his father, 148; and Pap Hamer, 284
Eastland plantation: and the Depression, 82; and federal farm payments, 227–28, 260; and Holbert incident (1904), 7–9, 23–32; the home, 13; James Eastland assuming control of (1930s), 42–45; laborers, 103, 182, 226, 229–30, 283; living conditions, 126, 341n15; mechanization, 129, 226; POW labor, 103; property taxes, 247; by 1960s, 182, 229–30; by 1970s, 283; sharecroppers' opinions of the senator, 71; today, 279; voter registration on, 208, 223, 339n4; and Woods Eastland (son), 71–72, 279, 283
Edwards, Charlie, 229, 232, 283
Edwards, Thomas, 295
Egerton, John, 254
Egypt, 160, 311n16
Eisenhower, Dwight, 147, 162–64, 268, 319n13

Elementary and Secondary Education Act, 274
Ellender, Allen, 119
Emergency Farm Labor Supply Program, 102–3
Enterprise Tocsin (Indianola), 192, 293
Ervin, Sam, 270
European reconstruction, 106–8, 319n13
Evans, Rowland, 236
Evers, Charles, 288, 289
Evers, Medgar, 195

"Fair Deal," 134
Fair Employment Practices Committee (FEPC), 114, 115–19, 196, 330n49
Fair Labor Standards Act, 88
Fallows, James, 257
Fannie Lou Hamer Recreational Complex, 167, 290
Faulkner, William, 133
Federal Bureau of Investigation (FBI), 137, 183–84, 191
federal farm bill (1965), 227–28, 260–61
Federation for Constitutional Government (FCG), 153–54
Fifteenth Amendment, 15
Folsom, "Big Jim," 133
Forest, Mississippi, 7, 17, 25, 35, 38–39, 42, 89, 98, 149, 291
Forest News Register, 98
Forman, James, 176
Forrest, Nathan Bedford, 15, 36, 157
Fortas, Abe, 270, 271–72, 349n32
Fourteenth Amendment, 15
Frazier, E. Franklin, 155
Freedman's Bureau, 114, 118
Freedom Farm, 88, 254–62, 279
Freedom Farm Corporation (FFC), 257–58, 259
Freedom Rides, 174, 183, 189–90, 192
Freedom Schools, 174, 217, 283
"Freedom Summer," 198, 202–3, 205–14

"Freedom Vote," 196–97, 217–18

Freedomways magazine, 223, 228

Gaines v. Oklahoma, 141

Galbraith, John Kenneth, 248

Gartin, Carroll, 149, 150, 327n26, 334n30

Garvey, Marcus, 50–51

Georgia Pacific Railroad, 16

Germany, 76–77, 106–8, 319n13

Ghana, 160, 169–70

Goldberg, Arthur, 270

Goldwater, Barry, 211, 218, 223

Goodman, Andrew, 207

Grant, Madison, *The Passing of the Great Race*, 40

Gray, Victoria, 217–20

Great Britain: global cotton, 74, 75–76; and Rhodesia, 262–63, 264

Great Migration, First, 48–50

Great Migration, Second, 127

Great Society programs, 223, 233, 237–38, 243

Green v. County School Board of Kent County, Virginia, 273–74

Greene, George, 204–5

Greene, Percy, 189

Greensboro sit-in, 169, 200

Greenville Daily Democrat, 24–25

Greenwood Commonwealth, 24, 31

Guinea, 160, 170, 214–16

Guyot, Lawrence, 249

Hale, Dennis, 184–85

Hamer, Dorothy Jean, 58, 171, 224, 248–49

Hamer, Fannie Lou: birth, 47; early life, 47–50, 52–57; parents, 47–48, 52–53; education, 55–57; family life, 57–59, 125–26; Africa trip (1964), 214–16, 338n30; campaigns for state office, 203–4, 282; and Communism, 234; Democratic National Convention testimony, 3–4, 210–14; on economic freedom and racial equality, 224–25, 252, 255–56; freedom concept, 63, 179–80, 205, 214–15, 224, 254–55, 281, 309n54; and Freedom Farm, 254–62; and Freedom Summer, 203, 205, 208–10; health problems, 260, 282, 284, 285–86; on James Eastland, 229; and MFDP, 3–4, 210–14, 216–20; and middle-class blacks, 246, 250–52, 296–97; on "plantation mentality," 255, 284–85; public call for revolution, 230–33; religious faith, 47, 59–64, 179–80, 208–9, 230–31, 291; on Roosevelt's federal relief efforts, 88; and school desegregation, 277; share-cropping and plantation work, 52–55, 57–59, 66, 67–68, 125–27; skepticism regarding America's racial hypocrisy, 222–25; Vietnam War critique, 231–33; voter rights work, 176–79, 182, 203–4, 224, 248; Winona beating, 193–95; in the 1970s, 280–82, 284–86; death and funeral, 286; how she is remembered today, 167, 279–80, 290–92

Hamer, Lou Ella, 53, 126

Hamer, Pap, 57–58, 125–26, 176, 178, 204, 249, 284

Hamer, Vergie, 58, 146, 171, 204, 277

Hamer et al. v. Sunflower County, 277

Hamer v. Campbell, 248

Harlem riots (1964), 230

Harlem's *Crusader*, 51

Harris, Joseph, 258, 260

Harrison, Pat, 89–90

Hawley-Smoot tariff, 78–79

Haywood, James, 292

Head Start, 237–38, 243, 245

Hederman family, 37–38, 90

Henderson, Leon, 93–94

Henry, Aaron, 151, 250, 251; and the black church, 61; and early NAACP chapter in the Delta, 141;

and Eastland's 1972 reelection bid, 287–88; and MAP, 246; and MFDP, 211, 213, 217; relationship with Eastland, 287–88, 289, 352n20; and voting rights campaigns, 175, 196

Hicks, Ruby Sheppard, 11

Highlander Folk School, 144

Hiss, Alger, 137

Holbert, Luther, 7–9, 23–32; lynching, 26–32; manhunt, 24–26

Holbert, Mary, 24, 25, 28, 31

Hoover, J. Edgar, 137, 183–84, 237

Horton, Myles, 144–45

House Un-American Activities Committee, 91, 137, 144, 235

Howard, T.R.M., 141

Humphrey, Hubert, 212–13

Hurst, Fred, 127

India, 159, 160

Indian tribes in Delta region, 10–11

Indianola, Mississippi: and cotton, 67; mandated school desegregation, 274; and Minnie Cox, 22–23; NAACP chapter, 141; school board boycott (1986), 292

Indianola Academy, 2, 273, 283, 293

Indianola Enterprise, 40–41

Industrial Revolution, 74

International Harvester, 83, 84, 129

International Labor Defense (ILD), 86

Inter-Racial Committee (Sunflower County), 142

Jackson, Andrew, 10

Jackson, Willie, 44, 71, 352n22

Jackson Advocate, 189

Jackson Daily News, 84, 96, 239

Jencks, Christopher, 246

Jews, 318n11, 321n34

Jiang Jeshi, 134

Job Corps, 223, 238, 243

John Deere, 83

Johnson, Charles S., 72, 73, 84, 87

Johnson, June, 194

Johnson, Lyndon: and American policy in Rhodesia, 264–65; civil rights agenda, 200–201, 206–7, 237–38, 240, 242, 330n49; Great Society programs, 223, 233, 237–38, 243; Marshall nomination to Supreme Court, 270; and MFDP delegation to Democratic Convention (1964), 211–12; as Senator, 156, 162–63; and Vietnam War, 231–33; War on Poverty, 243–47

Johnson, Manning, 138

Johnson, Paul, 37, 72, 89–90

Johnston, Erle, 149, 185, 201, 241, 246

Johnston, Oscar, 80, 81, 111

Jones, James, 175

Jones, Sam, 142

Judiciary Committee. See Senate Judiciary Committee

Katzenbach, Nicholas, 339n4

Keady, William, 269–70, 274, 277

Kennedy, Edward, 268, 287

Kennedy, John F.: and anti-Communism, 182–83, 189; civil rights agenda, 195–96, 200, 201–2, 206; death, 199–200, 202; and Freedom Riders, 183

Kennedy, Robert, 183, 193, 200, 238; death, 267; and Eastland, 183, 267, 334n28, 347n23

Khrushchev, Nikita, 160, 189

Kilgore, Harvey, 155

King, Annie Mae, 285

King, Ed, 213

King, Martin Luther, Jr., 60, 196, 239, 240, 248; and Communism, 190; death, 267; and Johnson, 202, 206; and Montgomery bus boycott, 162

Kinoy, Arthur, 218, 235

Kirksey, Henry, 289

Korean War, 134, 136, 159, 160

Ku Klux Klan, 15, 36, 39, 50, 151, 205–6

Kunstler, William, 218, 219

labor organizing: black unions and SISS hearings, 137–40; and Communism/anti-Communism, 86, 88, 136, 137–40; Eastland's attacks on, 97–98, 104; MFLU, 225; sharecroppers, 86, 88

Lackey, Rosa Lee, 352n22

Lapsansky, Phil, 239

Lashley, Lee, 138–39

Lavender, V.H., 26

Lee, Rev. George, 171

Lee, Isabel, 274

Leflore County, 11, 70

Lehman, Herbert, 156

Levingstone, Sydney, 204

Lewis, John, 236

Lewis, John L., 98

Lichtenstein, Alex, 310n5

Lincoln, C. Eric, 309n54

literacy tests for voting, 15–16, 45, 172

Little Rock Central High School (1957), 163–64

Long, Huey, 41, 85

lynching, 8; critics, 28–31; economic aspects, 29–32; post–World War I, 46, 51; press on, 27–30; Reconstruction era, 21–22; Woods Eastland and 1904 Holbert lynching, 7–9, 27–32, 33–34, 304–5n19

Mansfield, Mike, 269

Mao Zedong, 134, 237

Marble, Arthur, 292

March on Washington for Jobs and Freedom, 196

Marlow, W.D., 58, 73, 125, 177–78

Marshall, George C., 111–12

Marshall, Thurgood, 270, 330n49, 348n27, 348n30

Marshall Plan, 111–12, 164

Marx, Karl, 237

Mays, Benjamin, 62

McCarthy, Joseph, 134, 137, 159–60

McLaurin, Anselm J., 31–32

McLaurin, Charles, 168, 175, 177, 181, 281, 338n30

McLaurin v. Oklahoma, 141

McMath, Sid, 133

McMullan family, 38

McNair, Landy, 175

Measure for Measure, 257

mechanical cotton picker, 83–84, 127–30

Memphis *Commercial Appeal*, 24

Memphis News, 29

Memphis Press-Scimitar, 156

Meredith, James, 192–93

Merritt, Robert, 292

migration, black: first Great Migration, 48–50; Second Great Migration, 127; (1970s), 256–57

militancy and civil rights movement, 230, 237, 239–42

Milliken v. Bradley, 278

minimum wage bill (1966), 228

Minor, W.F. (Bill), 185, 229, 288, 289, 293

Mississippi Action for Progress (MAP), 246–47

Mississippi Freedom Democratic Party (MFDP): and Communism, 240; delegation to Democratic Convention (1964), 3–4, 210–14; and divisions in civil rights community, 219–20; and Hamer, 3–4, 210–14, 216–20; and Mississippi congressional delegation, 216–20; and new elections in Sunflower County (1967), 248–52; and black candidates, 238–39, 247

Mississippi Freedom Labor Union (MFLU), 225–26

Mississippi Progressive Voters League, 141

Mississippi State University, 280

Mississippi Summer Project ("Freedom Summer"), 198, 202–3, 205–14; and MFDP delegation to Democratic Convention, 210–14; violence against, 202, 207–8; whites' involvement, 202–3

Mitchell, Clarence, 162

Mondale, Walter, 287

Montgomery Advertiser, 145

Montgomery bus boycott, 162

Moore, Amzie, 179

Morgan, Charles, 237

Morgenthau, Henry, 94, 106

Morgenthau plan, 106–7

Moses, Bob, 175, 176, 178, 179, 203, 213, 215, 255

Mound Bayou, Mississippi, 14, 141

Movement magazine, 231

Mozambique, 77

Murray, Philip, 136

Myrdal, Gunnar, 114–15, 154, 320n25

The Nation, 187, 280

National Association for the Advancement of Colored People (NAACP): and *Brown* decision, 145–46, 270; and Cold War, 160–61; and Communism/anti-Communism, 135–36, 190, 209, 236, 324–25n5; early law-based strategy, 168–69; and Eastland's 1954 reelection bid, 149; and Eastland's 1972 reelection bid, 288; and opposition to Eastland as Judiciary chair, 156; postwar era, 133; Sunflower County chapters (early 1950s), 140–41; Truman address, 121

National Committee for Free Elections in Sunflower, 248

National Cotton Council, 111, 128, 226

National Council of Negro Women, 257

National Labor Relations Board, 88

National Lawyers Guild (NLG), 210, 234–35

National Origins Act (1924), 39–40

National Recovery Act, Section 7a, 85

National Security Act, 109

National Urban League, 174

nativism, 39–40

New Deal, 42, 79–83, 84–85, 88–89; Agricultural Adjustment Administration (AAA), 79–83; Commodity Credit Corporation (CCC), 80–81; and Communism, 137; consequences for cotton industry, 82–83; and planters, 80–82; Second New Deal, 88–89

"New Negro," 50–51

New Orleans' *Daily Picayune*, 31

New Republic, 156, 246

New York Times, 155, 220

Newsweek, 271

Nicholson, Joseph, 62

Niebuhr, Reinhold, 85, 87

Nixon, Richard, 163, 269–70, 272, 278, 281

nonviolent direct action, 169, 230, 331n2

North Sunflower Academy, 273, 283

Norton, Eleanor Holmes, 226–27

Novak, Robert, 236

Nystrom, Sandra, 226–27

O'Dell, Jack, 143

Office of Economic Opportunity (OEO), 243, 246

Office of Price Administration (OPA), 93, 102–3

Omerberg, Maynard, 210

O'Neal, E.L., 26

Operation Dixie, 136

Operation Freedom, 179

Pace, Courtney, 158

Palmer, Mitchell, 91

Parker, John Sydney, 2

Parks, Rosa, 162

paternalism, 70–71, 73, 255, 266

Patterson, Robert, 117, 151

Patterson, W.L., 249

Peace Corps, 216, 232

Percy, LeRoy, 246

Percy, Walker, 228

Percy, William Alexander, 10, 70, 80, 228

Pestana, Frank, 210

Pittsburgh Courier, 115

"plantation mentality," 66, 72–73, 255, 284–85, 296, 298

poll tax, 45, 97, 172, 333n21

Pond, Chester, 20–21

Ponder, Annelle, 193, 194

Portuguese colonialism, 77

Potsdam agreement, 106–7

POW camps (Sunflower County), 103

Powdermaker, Hortense, 8, 37, 45, 46, 52–53, 60–63, 66, 67, 69, 88

Powell, Adam Clayton, Jr., 161

Powell, Lewis, 272, 349n33

Powledge, Fred, 220

Pratt, C.B., 257–58

Progressive Farmers and Household Union of America, 51

Providence Farm, 87, 173

Rabinowitz, Victor, 139, 140, 234

race riots (1919), 51

railroad boom (late nineteenth-century), 16–17

Randle, Carver, 277, 293

Randolph, A. Philip, 114, 115, 154

Ratliff, Laura, 47

Reconstruction: and black land owner-ship, 14; and black voting rights/ political empowerment, 13–14, 15–16; Eastland's fears of specter of, 118–19, 240; lynching/mob violence, 21–22; Sunflower County, 13–16, 21–22, 36–37; white resistance to, 14–15, 21–23, 36–37

Red Scare, 91

Regional Council of Negro Leadership (RCNL), 141

Rehnquist, William, 272–73, 278, 349n33

Rhodesia, 262–66

Ribicoff, Abraham, 276, 278

Richardson, J.A., 22, 24, 27

Ricks, Willy, 230

Robeson, Paul, 135

Robinson, Alonzo, 188

Robinson, Reggie, 176

Roosevelt, Franklin D.: Eastland's attacks on administration policies, 94, 95, 106–8; and New Deal, 79, 85, 88; and postwar American foreign policy, 106–8; and Supreme Court, 268

Roosevelt, Theodore, 22

Rosenwald, Julius, 57

Rosenwald Schools, 57

Rubin, Larry, 209–10

Ruleville, Mississippi: World War I–era population, 50; (1964), 198; today, 132, 167, 221, 279–80, 290

Ruleville Middle School, 132–33, 146, 166

Ruleville Record, 51, 75, 89, 127, 150–51

Rust, John, 83–84, 87

Rust, Mack, 87

Ryan, William Fitts, 219

Salamon, Lester, 257

Salter, Sir Arthur, 78

Salter, John, 184

Samstein, Mendy, 204–5

Satterfield, John, 206

Scherer, James, 77–78

school desegregation: pre-*Brown* deci-sions, 141–42; *Brown* decision, 133, 144, 145–50; busing, 276–78; and Clark nomination, 269–70; and Eastland, 147–49, 150–55, 163, 166, 192–93, 274–78; Little Rock, 163–64; organized white resistance, 146–47, 150–55; post-*Brown* federal mandates, 273–74, 278; and resegregation, 283,

293–96, 349n35; Sunflower County, 146, 273, 283, 293; and Warren Court, 273

schools, segregated: black supporters, 188–89; mid-century, 55–57, 142–43, 166, 331–32n6; northern, 186; pre-*Brown* decisions, 141–42; post-*Brown* resegregation, 283, 293–96, 349n35; of the 1970s, 283; and school expenditures, 131, 142–43; "segregation academies," 273, 283, 293; Sunflower County, 55–57, 131, 142–43, 166, 170–71, 188–89, 273, 283, 293

Schwerner, Michael, 207

"scientific racism," 18–19

Scott County, 35–36, 37–38

Scottsboro trial (1931), 86, 121, 135

"segregation academies," 273, 283, 293. *See also* schools, segregated

Self-Preservation Loyalty League, 50

Selma campaign, 223, 234

Senate Internal Security Subcommittee (SISS), 137–40, 143, 155, 184, 192, 209

Senate Judiciary Committee: Eastland's chairmanship, 155–59, 166, 183, 253, 267–73, 278, 286–87; and federal appointments, 269–70; Subcommittee on Civil Rights, 135, 149; and Supreme Court nomination process, 268, 270–73, 278, 348n27, 349n32

Share Croppers Union (SCU), 86

sharecropping, 19–21, 48–50, 66, 68–73, 82–83; credit system, 68–70; Hamer's plantation work, 52–55, 57–59, 66, 67–68, 125–27; labor organizing, 85, 86–87; lien law, 20; living and working conditions, 52–55, 84–85, 310n5; and paternalism, 70–71, 73, 255, 266; Pond's industrial experiment, 20–21; and switch to wage labor, 82–83; and workers' resistance, 58–64. *See also* cotton economy and Sunflower County

Sherrill, Robert, 329n43

Shriver, Sargent, 243

Sillers, Florence Ogden, 143

Sillers, Walter, 41, 79, 89, 91–92, 96, 98, 141–42, 152, 156, 163, 170, 187

Silver, James, 173, 255

Silverbatt, Paul, 258

Simmons, William, 277

sit-ins, 169, 200

slavery, 12–13, 47–48, 60

Smith, B.F., 226

Smith, Benjamin, 235

Smith, Frank, 99–100, 130, 133, 146

Smith, Ian, 262–64

Smith, Lamar, 171

Smith, Lillian, 101, 133

Smith v. Allwright, 115

social Darwinism, 18–19

South (periodical), 150, 154, 156

Southern Christian Leadership Conference (SCLC), 169, 178, 193

Southern Conference Educational Foundation (SCEF), 144–45, 191, 210

Southern Conference for Human Welfare (SCHW), 144

Southern Manifesto (1956), 201

Southern Regional Council, 195

Southern Tenant Farmers Union, 86–87, 103

Soviet Union, 88, 104–5, 108–12, 121, 189

Spanish Civil War, 91

Speakes, Larry, 290

Stalin, Joseph, 108, 159

State Sovereignty Commission (SSC), 152, 184–85, 191, 205, 206, 209, 210, 241, 244, 246–47

Stavis, Morton, 235

Stembridge, Jane, 181

Stennis, John, 124, 135, 244, 274

Stephensville, 14

Stoddard, Lothrop, *The Rising Tide of Color Against World White Supremacy*, 40

Stone, Alfred, 46

Stone, I.F., 155, 321–22n34

Stranger's Home Baptist Church,
60, 62

Student Nonviolent Coordinating Committee (SNCC): Africa trip (1964),
214–16; and Communism, 190–91,
209, 235, 236, 335n41; creation, 169;
"Freedom Vote," 196, 217; Hamer's
early organizing work, 178–82; Mississippi movement, 168, 173–81, 196,
202–14, 217; Mississippi Summer
Project, 198, 202–3, 205–14; separatism, 231; and Vietnam War, 233

Sugarman, Tracy, 180

Sullivan, Ann, 238

Sumner, Charles, 94

Sunflower County: earliest white settlers,
6–7, 10–13; early twentieth-century,
6–32; Civil War era, 11, 13; Reconstruction era, 13–16, 21–22, 36–37;
Depression era, 43–45, 82; post–World
War I, 48–52; (1930s), 42–47, 55–57,
61–63, 66–73, 79–83, 88–89; post–
World War II, 93, 99–104, 127–31,
140; (1960s), 247–52, 254; (1970s),
256, 280–86; today, 1–5, 33, 65, 99,
132, 167, 221, 279–80, 290–98;
Holbert lynchings, 7–9, 23–32; the
land/soil, 12, 253; name, 11; nature/
geographic setting, 9–12. See also
cotton economy and Sunflower County;
sharecropping

Sunflower County Inter-Racial Committee, 171

Sunflower County Voters League, 282

Sunflower, Mississippi (town), 1–3,
248–52, 301; racial incident involving
author in, 1–3; elections in, 248–52

Sunflower Tocsin, 22, 24, 27, 45, 49–50,
53, 83, 88, 91, 93

Supreme Court, 268–73; pre-Brown
decisions regarding school segregation,

141–42; Brown decision, 145–50; and
Eastland-led Judiciary Committee, 268,
270–73, 278; post-Brown desegregation mandates, 273–74, 278; Warren
Court, 268, 270–71, 273, 347n25

Suttle, Howard, 135

Swann v. Charlotte-Mecklenburg Board of
Education, 276

Sweatt v. Painter, 141

Taft-Hartley bill, 134

tariffs: Cold War and European reconstruction, 111; Eastland's view, 78,
95, 111; post–Civil War, 78–79, 95;
Roosevelt administration, 95

Taulbert, Clifton, 62

Taylor, Atley, 229

Taylor, Irene, 229

Tecklin, Jerry, 210

Thomas, Sara, 292

Thompson, Bennie, 292

Thornton, Ron, 261

Thurmond, Strom, 123, 270, 287,
349n32

Till, Emmett, 161, 167, 204

Tillman, Earlene, 208, 284

Time magazine, 156

To Secure These Rights (report of Truman's
Committee on Civil Rights), 121–22,
134

Togoland, 76–77

Touré, Sekou, 160, 215

Townsend, Francis, 85

Townsend, James Lee, 47, 48

Townsend, Lou Ella Bramlett, 47, 48

Townsend, Pascol, Jr., 258

Trujillo, Rafael, 165, 166

Truman, Harry: civil rights agenda,
115–16, 120, 121–24, 134; Cold War
and domestic policies, 134–35; and
postwar American foreign policy,
108–12

Truman Doctrine, 108–9, 164

Tucker, Mary, 176
Tuskegee Institute, 76–77

UN Commission on Human Rights,
120–21
United Daughters of the Confederacy
(UDC), 37
United Mine Workers of America, 98
United Nations, 120–21, 164, 166, 262
United Negro Improvement Association
(UNIA), 50–51
United States Information Agency
(USIA), 215
University of Alabama, 40
University of Mississippi, 39, 142,
192–93
University of Mississippi Foundation,
291
urban crime, 186–87

Van Landingham, Jack, 184
Vance, Rupert, 66
Vanderbilt University, 40
Vardaman, James, 22, 27, 31, 57, 97
Vicksburg *Evening Post*, 28
Vietnam War, 231–33, 262–63, 264,
281
violence against civil rights workers, 178,
193–95, 204–5; Freedom Summer,
202, 207–8; Hamer's beating, 193–95;
lessening of, 223–24; voter registration
activities, 171, 193, 202, 217–18
The Voice of the Negro, 29–30
voting rights: Freedom Summer, 202–3,
205–10; Freedom Vote, 196–97,
217–18; institutional/psychological
barriers, 171–73; literacy tests, 15–16,
45, 172; Mississippi campaigns,
171–72, 175–78, 196–97, 202–4,
205–10, 216–17; poll tax, 45, 97, 172,
333n21; Reconstruction period, 13–14,
15–16; and violence, 171, 193, 202,
217–18

Voting Rights Act (1965), 223, 231,
240

Wagner Act, 88
Walker, Prentiss, 238, 240
Wall Street crash (1929), 78
Wallace, George, 287
Wallace, Henry, 124
Waller, William, 280, 288
Walls, Johnnie E., Jr., 282
War Manpower Commission, 102
War on Poverty, 243–47
Warren, Earl, 141–42, 147, 268, 271
Washington, Booker T., 22, 28–29, 52, 76
Washington County, 70
Washington Post, 118, 155, 236
West, H.J., 238
White, J.H., 188
White, Walter, 135–36
Whitley, Clifton, 238
Whitten, Jamie, 203, 217, 218, 219
Whitten, Les, 269
Wilkie, Curtis, 352n20
Wilkins, Roy, 236
William Chapel (Ruleville), 167–68, 176,
280; firebombing (1964), 207–8;
Hamer's funeral, 286
Williams, Aubrey, 144
Williams, Hosea, 282
Wilson, Woodrow, 91
Wilson, Woodrow (plantation laborer),
229, 290, 352n22
Winter, William, 287, 295
Wofford, Harris, 200
Works Progress Administration (WPA),
67, 88
World War I and postwar period:
American politics and intellectual
life, 39–40; lynching, 46, 51; racial
rhetoric/white supremacy, 39–40;
Sunflower County cotton economy,
48–54; war effort and Great
Migration, 49

World War II and postwar period: European reconstruction, 106–8, 319n13; freedom rhetoric and racial progress, 114–16, 133–34; Sunflower County, 93, 99–104, 127–31, 140

Wright, Fielding, 123

Yazoo-Mississippi Delta, 9–10

"Year of Africa" (1960), 169

Young, Andrew, 195, 286

Zaire, 77

Zambia, 262

Zinn, Howard, 248